Explaining Foreign Policy

Explaining Foreign Policy

U.S. Decision-Making and the Persian Gulf War

Steve A. Yetiv

The Johns Hopkins University Press
Baltimore and London

The Johns Hopkins University Press
2715 North Charles Street
Baltimore, Maryland 21218-4363
www.press.jhu.edu

Library of Congress Cataloging-in-Publication Data
Yetiv, Steven A.
    Explaining foreign policy : U.S. decision-making and the Persian
Gulf War / Steve A. Yetiv.
      p.   cm.
Includes bibliographical references and index.
    ISBN 0-8018-7810-1 (hardcover : alk. paper)
    ISBN 0-8018-7811-X (pbk. : alk. paper)
      1. Persian Gulf War, 1991 — Causes. 2. Persian Gulf War, 1991 —
Diplomatic history. 3. United States — Foreign relations — 1989–1993.
I. Title.
DS79.72.Y475 2004
956.7044'22 — dc21

                                                        2003010643

A catalog record for this book is available from the British Library.

Contents

Acknowledgments

This book benefited greatly from the many people who gave graciously of their time. I especially would like to thank the individuals in the United States and Middle East who granted interviews in the past five years. I would especially like to thank the members of President Bush's inner circle and their deputies for their extensive input and time, without which this book could not have been possible.

In addition, I would like to thank Debbie Carter at the George Bush Presidential Library in College Station, Texas, for support in tracking down key documents, and to Colin Powell for allowing me to study his papers. I would also like to thank the following individuals for reading or commenting on parts or all of the manuscript: Nurettin Altundeger, James Bill, Anouar Boukhars, Clark McCauley, Michael Dziubinski, Engin Erdem, Kurt Taylor Gaubatz, Age Gavrilis, Jon Hermann, Wayne Holcomb, Wanda Kaplan, David Lesch, Melanie Meerschwam, Jeff McNeil, Stephen Medvic, Eric Miller, Gregory Moorhead, John Owen, Frederic Ruiz-Ramon, Philip Tetlock, Saadia Touval, Philip Zelikow, and a number of referees from the *British Journal of Political Science*, *Security Studies*, and the Johns Hopkins University Press.

I would also like to thank Martin Schneider for meticulous copyediting and the staff at the Johns Hopkins University Press, especially Henry Tom for his able hand as editor.

Explaining Foreign Policy

Introduction

Why did Germany invade the Soviet Union in World War II? Why did Pakistan support the U.S.-led war on terrorism following the devastating September 11, 2001, terrorist attacks on the World Trade Center and the Pentagon? How did the United States make the decision to impose tariffs on imported steel in 2002? Such questions are vital to explore because the behavior of governments shapes not only our lives but also the course of states and of history.

In this book, I develop and apply an integrated approach that generates and integrates insights from multiple perspectives for explaining government behavior. I then use this approach to explore a major foreign policy event: how did the United States make the decisions that took it to war in the Persian Gulf in 1991, and why did it choose war?

To what extent were the decisions made through careful cost/benefit analysis of the options available? Did analogies to World War II and the Vietnam War play a key role? In what measure did domestic politics shape the decisions that led to war? How can an understanding of the dynamics in the president's inner circle illuminate us? To what extent were bureaucratic politics and rivalry important? The integrated approach considers and explores such questions, using five perspectives that can be applied to myriad foreign policy cases. In so doing, the approach outlined in this book can help us understand the Persian Gulf War case better and advance the study of government behavior in general.

The Persian Gulf crisis of 1990–91 was triggered by Iraq's stunning invasion of next-door Kuwait on August 2, 1990. It proved to be one of the defining events of the 1990s, an anachronism that clashed with visions of a more peaceful post–Cold War era. Iraq's president, Saddam Hussein, was infamous for using force abroad and killing enemies both real and perceived at home, but few leaders fathomed that he would launch such an ambitious attack, leaving Kuwait at his mercy and a region with over two-thirds of the world's oil reserves in turmoil.[1]

Like many other countries, at the time the United States was focusing on the unification of Germany, the domino-like fall of communist dictators in Eastern Europe, and the end of the Cold War, all three developments a partial product of the economic and political reforms of Soviet leader Mikhail Gorbachev. In the view of U.S. Secretary of State James Baker, "We were living in a revolutionary time. What I had known all my life had changed. We weren't thinking about balance of power in the Middle East because power was changing all over the world."[2] After the invasion, the focus rapidly shifted from how to end the Cold War to how to contain Iraq.

By invading Kuwait, Iraq placed itself on a warpath with the soon-to-be-formed, U.S.-led coalition composed of twenty-eight countries. On August 6, Iraq annexed Kuwait as its nineteenth province, seeking to erase it from the global map altogether and raising fears that it might invade oil-rich Saudi Arabia as well. Ultimately, Iraq refused to withdraw from Kuwait after more than five months of occupation, despite numerous attempts to come to terms peacefully and various threatening U.N. resolutions, including a U.S.-led ultimatum that Iraq would face war if it were not to withdraw unconditionally. The war to expel Iraq from Kuwait was launched on January 16, 1991. Iraq's military capability was trimmed substantially, it was forced to sign a cease-fire on February 27, 1991, and Saddam faced the most serious challenge to his rule he had ever faced. However, as is well known, he survived the war, despite being targeted by U.S. aircraft and despite postwar uprisings by anti-regime Shia Muslims in the south of Iraq and Iraqi Kurds in the north.[3] His survival generated concern, especially among Kuwaitis, that he might decide to invade Kuwait again one day.[4] After the September 11 terrorist attacks, the question arose of whether or not the United States should force him from power in the broader war on terrorism.

The Integrated Approach

The integrated approach is not complex. It consists of presenting different perspectives on government behavior, testing them against the record, integrating the resulting insights into better explanations of government behavior, and bridging areas of theory that tend to be treated as separate. I argue that this approach enhances the study of government behavior in several ways.

Existing approaches often advance just one perspective or model preferred by the analyst.[5] While the model will vary with the analyst, most of us tend to use one model consciously or subconsciously when trying to explain government behavior. We assume that states carefully weigh the costs and benefits of various options for dealing with the issue at hand, and then choose, or try to choose, the best option for advancing national interests.[6] We then describe their behavior as if they had acted as unitary, coordinated units rather than as amalgamations of competing groups, bureaucracies, organizations, committees, and individuals, all with their own interests, preferences, and modes of behavior. To use a common metaphor, we portray states as akin to billiard balls, bouncing off each other on the "table" of world affairs, and pursuing national interests *rationally* when faced with a strategic problem. This conception of government behavior is captured explicitly in the state-centric version of the rational actor model (RAM).

To be sure, mono-theoretical explanations, such as those derived from the RAM, can certainly help us understand aspects of government behavior. Often, they are crucial building blocks to more complex explanations. And, in some cases, they may capture enough of what is vital to be satisfactory on their own. But they are just as often misleading or incomplete because each seeks to force a complex reality into a single, preexisting box.[7]

In sharp contrast, the multiple perspectives used in this book cover different, key elements of government behavior, and thus offer alternative and sometimes competing explanations.[8] It is through this explanatory tension that we can gain leverage on government behavior and understand the perspectives better as well. In this book, I apply the RAM as a baseline explanation for U.S. government behavior. It then becomes possible to compare explanations derived from the other perspectives used in the book against aspects of the RAM explanation, and to use the RAM to explore explanations derived from the other perspectives. This fills an important gap in the literature. Indeed, critics of the RAM have been taken to task for not comparing it to other plausible explanations.[9] Criticism of the RAM has also been overwhelmingly theoretical, rather than empirical.[10] This book offers a case study and general analysis of the model. Beyond exploring government behavior from multiple perspectives, the integrated approach calls for testing them against the record. Many scholars have called for such tests, but, thus far, largely in vain.[11] By testing multiple perspectives side by side, we can see which ones are the most telling in a given case and interrogate the perspectives in general as well. We also gain the ability to integrate the insights that they yield, which is important. For instance, as Valerie Hudson points out in her exhaustive review of the literature, "Integrative studies are few and far between . . . and scholars working at a particular level of analysis should consider how to incorporate findings from other levels."[12] As former International Studies Association President Michael Brecher puts it, failure to do so has "long bedeviled International Studies."[13]

The integrated approach requires that we use multiple perspectives, but it does not presume *a priori* which one is best overall or which should be used as a first or predominant cut on reality. Nor does it preclude the use of perspectives other than those used in this book. Rather, it requires only that the chosen perspectives cover basic aspects of government behavior, as Table 1 in the next section of the introduction illustrates.[14] This does not mean that all of the perspectives will be telling in each case, much less equally telling. Rather, it means that we should explore all of them as part of a systematic process that decreases the common risk of ignoring, overlooking, or exaggerating any one of them.

Integrating insights into one account can yield better explanations of events, but the approach also allows for theory development, a process that is demonstrated towards the end of the book, and for another type of integration, which is an area of growing interest: integrating areas of theoretical study that are commonly treated as separate and distinct. For now, I will simply describe these areas as domestic and international relations theory. The use of multiple perspectives allows us to draw varied insights, which can bridge these areas. In chapter 10, I will elaborate on such integration, after the groundwork for doing so is in place and the reader is better able to absorb the effort.

The Perspectives of the Book in Brief

Before laying out the central arguments of the book, it makes sense to provide at least a thumbnail sketch of the five perspectives that it uses, four of which are existing perspectives and one of which, the domestic politics model, is developed by the author in its present version. I will elaborate on each of them in chapters 2 through 6, respectively, but they are described below in a simple overview so as to give the reader a reference point. The perspectives are chosen because they are based, as Table 1 suggests, on different assumptions about what level of analysis is most crucial (*Level of Analysis*), what the direct or indirect goals or results of the behavior of the central actor posited in the perspective are (*Goal or Result*), and how that actor makes decisions consciously or subconsciously (*Decision-making Mode*). For its part, the RAM, as we have already noted, explains government behavior by focusing on the state in a broader strategic setting whose goal it is to maximize perceived national interests. That is accomplished largely through undertaking a cost/benefit analysis for various options. The cognitive approach offers a different explanation, or part of an explanation, for government behavior by focusing on the minds of decision makers. It assumes that they consciously or subconsciously use mental shortcuts, such as analogies to past events, to simplify

Table 1. Five Perspectives: An Overview

	Level of Analysis	Goal or Result	Decision-making Mode
RAM	Unitary actor/ strategic context	Maximize perceived national interests	Cost/benefit analysis
Cognitive	Human mind/ information processing	Simplify reality and decision making process	Schema/analogies/ biases
Domestic Politics	Politicians/domestic politics	Meet domestic objectives/distract public attention from domestic problems	Constrained by domestic concerns
Groupthink	Group of like-minded decision makers	Defective decision making likely	Group dynamics
Government Politics Model	Individual in Committee Setting	Push agency interests/generate collage	Bargaining/conflict

reality in order to facilitate decision-making. The domestic politics model, a version of which I have developed, focuses not on how the minds of leaders work, but rather on how government behavior is shaped by leaders who wish to meet their own domestic-level goals at least as much as, if not more than, national objectives. Unlike the other models, it sees leaders as concerned with their position, influence, and reputation in the domestic realm, and as seeking to use the media to construct the adversary as a major threat.

By contrast, the theory of groupthink, which has spawned a growing litera-ture, mainly outside the field of political science, focuses on the impact of group dynamics on decision-making. For its part, the government politics model, which remains important in political science and informs other disciplines, such as business management, centers chiefly on individuals within a committee set-ting who bargain with others and take positions driven by the interests and politics of their respective bureaucracies.[15]

These perspectives help explain government behavior, which in this book means two things: how decisions are made (decision-making) and why govern-ments do what they do. Decision-making explores process and choice. It examines the factors that shape how decisions are made as well as the way actors choose among different options. By contrast, asking why governments do what they do addresses the reasons for their actions. All of the perspectives of this book can offer insight into these two dimensions of government behavior. For instance, the RAM suggests that the United States made its decisions through rational choice, and that the chief reasons that it went to war are located in the broader strategic context. These two dimensions are related, because the manner by which decisions are made can sometimes explain the reasons for actions as well. Thus, for instance, this book will show how the theory of groupthink provides insight into how group dynamics shaped decisions, but those group dynamics also explain why brakes were not put on the move toward war. Group dynamics created conditions wherein the president's move toward war was not challenged or even questioned within his inner circle.

Another distinction is important. All five perspectives explain aspects of government behavior, but this book characterizes perspectives two through five as domestic theory explanations for government behavior and the RAM as an international relations theory explanation. There has been much useful debate about how to categorize different perspectives, and this discussion has involved many important issues.[16] For our purposes, a domestic theory explanation for government behavior will have the following characteristics: It will refer fundamentally to one or more domestic actors and make predictions about an individual state's behavior (Level of Analysis). At a minimum, it will allow for, and possibly emphasize, motivations that do not aim at protecting and advancing national interests (Goal or Result). And it will stress decision-making that is either nonrational or that predicts suboptimal foreign policy choices for the nation as a whole (Decision-making). By contrast, an international relations theory explanation of government behavior will have these characteristics: It will treat states as unitary actors that interact with other states in a broader strategic or international setting (Level of Analysis). It will presume that the motivation for behavior is to protect or advance national interests (Goal or Result). And it will assume that the manner by which decisions are made is rational (Decision-making).

As a last point here, some thinkers might prefer to call the perspectives of this book "models," "frameworks," "theories," or even "paradigms." I prefer the word "perspective" simply because it applies to all of them. They are all lenses through which we can explain government behavior. They focus attention on some causal factors and divert our attention from others, thus simplifying the complex thicket of reality that daily bombards us. As a result, in using them side by side in one book, we are forced to ask new questions about a case or explore old questions that had seemed to be answered, and to consider insights that we may have discounted, ignored, or overlooked.[17]

The Central Arguments of the Book

The integrated approach is intended for application to the study of government behavior in general. In this study, however, it yields three main arguments, which are described below in simpler form so as to orient the reader.

The RAM and Its Discontents

The RAM yields useful insights into why the United States went to war. Most importantly, it highlights the broader strategic environment, one in which Iraq's invasion of Kuwait threatened significant U.S. regional and global interests. The threat Iraq posed made it quite tempting not only to reverse the invasion but also to eviscerate its military capability. The RAM also illuminates the unstable nature of Iraq's strategic interaction with the United States. On that score, this book argues that, with some important exceptions, Iraq became increasingly pliant as the crisis proceeded, and the United States became increasingly implacable. As a result, the window of opportunity for their preferences to meet in favor of non-war was either short or did not open at all. Iraq's minimal demands for withdrawal probably at no time met Washington's maximum concessions, making the United States more inclined to go to war. This can help explain why a farrago of private and public diplomatic efforts, chiefly by France, Russia, Jordan, and Egypt, never managed to bear much fruit.

But while the RAM illuminates the broader context of the crisis and of U.S.-Iraqi strategic interaction, it only partly informs us — when not actively misleading us — about how decisions were made. Using the RAM, we would presume that the United States carefully weighed the costs and benefits of options for dealing with Iraq. In fact, the reality is far more complex and deserves to be understood better. Nonrational behavior was prominent, as we shall see when we open up the black box of decision-making, where the wheels of government turn. The other perspectives allow us to do so and create the potential to complement and challenge the RAM's emphasis on rational decision-making. They assume that domestic actors can be driven by fundamentally different dynamics and interests than a unitary actor would be, and that the independent or combined interaction of these dynamics and interests may yield a potentially nonrational outcome.

The RAM, for instance, cannot explain why President Bush sometimes responded impetuously to Saddam's challenge, or why some officials, such as National Security Advisor Brent Scowcroft, had to caution him about using emotional rhetoric against Saddam.[18] The cognitive approach, which emphasizes Bush as someone significantly affected by past events, does address this, so it can help explain why negotiations failed as well. The RAM, because it "black boxes" decision-making and because it assumes that the decisions we observe result from a calculated form of cost/benefit analysis, cannot by its nature account for some of the important decisions in the Persian Gulf War case that were made without carefully considering alternative options. The other perspectives offer the potential for doing so.

As we shall see as the story unfolds, all this is not to say that U.S. decision-making was without rhyme and reason. Rather, it is to say that we would frequently be misled if we assumed that it did result from rational processes, as defined academically, no matter how useful the rationality assumption may be for theory-building. This finding introduces a puzzle. As Mark Schafer and Scott Crichlow point out, scholars from "business schools, public policy programs, social psychology departments, and political science departments have taught for many years the very general proposition" that the quality of the decision-making process is "important for achieving better outcomes."[19] Yet I argue that in the Persian Gulf War case we have a counterintuitive outcome: nonrational behaviors were prominent in decision-making, but the outcome was at least nonnegative. Why was there no apparent correlation between the quality of decision-making and the outcome? I address that question in chapter 9.

The non-RAM perspectives provide the possibility of opening up the black box of decision-making and yield insight into why the United States went to war. For instance, the cognitive approach tells us that Bush personalized the conflict and was less likely to negotiate with Iraq. The theory of groupthink helps explain why no real brakes were placed on the road to war.

The Individual as a Force

The second argument is that, by applying and evaluating the five perspectives, we find that while some are revealing in their own right, their successes and failures as explanations highlight the importance of the individual, specifically of President Bush. The RAM, that is, cannot account for how Bush shifted the course of the crisis at critical junctures. The cognitive perspective highlights how analogies influenced his perception and behavior. The domestic politics model suggests, though not convincingly in the present case, that Bush's behavior could be related to individual, party, and institutional interests. The theory of group-think strongly highlights Bush's leadership role in shaping and decreasing challenges to group consensus, although not strongly enough, as we shall see. The government politics model, meanwhile, fails in the Persian Gulf War case, partly because Bush helped preempt the petty politics of bureaucratic competition. He operated within a context of personal, domestic, global, and historical constraints — which the multiple perspectives highlight — but he was a decisive actor in direct and subtle ways. It is too simple to say that he wanted war with Iraq. His behavior was conflicted on that score at times, and he did at least emphasize sporadically in private correspondence, and with foreign leaders such as Mikhail Gorbachev, that he would "have been satisfied with the political settlement," meaning Iraq's unconditional withdrawal from Kuwait.[20]

However, this book argues that by late October 1990, the president and key members of his inner circle strongly tended toward war as a desirable option. Bush not only moved the United States to a war footing, as is well known, but in many ways sought to create and foster conditions that would allow the coalition to cut Iraq down to size in war. Over time, his inclination toward war carried the day. This was despite strong domestic and international pressures to give economic sanctions against Iraq a chance to work. Such pressure came especially from France, which had longstanding political and economic ties to Baghdad and had been Iraq's number two arms supplier, and from the Soviet Union, which also had had a highly developed strategic relationship with Baghdad, and was Iraq's top arms supplier.[21] But these pressures did little to deter President Bush.

We should expect the president to play a key role in crises, but that expectation does not tell us much about how far that role extends, how the role is executed, when the president is crucial, and how the president behaves in a broader decision-making setting involving a plethora of domestic and international actors. Indeed, since presidents have played quite different roles in crises, we know that crises alone can tell us only part of what shapes the role and behavior each adopts in each case. The argument presented here — that the president, and in turn the United States, viewed war as a desirable option by October — is certainly not one that we could assume would apply to any president in this situation.

Bush was crucial for several key reasons. His foreign policy experience ranked among the highest for American presidents. He was driven by the Munich analogy and his own personal experience in World War II to act determinedly against Saddam Hussein. Partly as a result of this, he drove group dynamics in ways that generated some key elements of groupthink, and he also preempted petty bureaucratic politics. But Bush also had good luck. He benefited from trusted and pliable colleagues. He confronted Iraq at the end of the Cold War, which allowed for U.S.-Soviet cooperation and for the freeing of U.S. forces in Europe for the Persian Gulf crisis. And he also benefited greatly from a decade-long buildup of U.S. rapid deployment capability and of regional military bases, both of which were essential to the U.S.-led efforts against Iraq.

This study demonstrates that while some of the complex perspectives were revealing in their own right, we must not forget the impact of individuals in history as a separate explanation. None of the perspectives feature the individual centrally as driving history, although they do offer some of their own insights into that question. The state-centric RAM ignores the individual as a unique and vital actor. As Daniel Byman and Kenneth Pollack have shown, political scientists tend to ignore the role of individuals in international relations altogether, placing a preference on impersonal forces in history.[22] Meanwhile, the other perspectives do feature the individual prominently but posit or emphasize a particular set of assumptions that sets them apart from a core argument that individuals matter in driving history. The cognitive perspective, for instance, does inform us about how decision makers process information, but it does not tell us that they are vital actors in driving history. Their mental processes could, in fact, make them inconsequential by rendering them indecisive.

This book argues that individuals *can* count in the broader scheme of things, and that they *can* drive historical events in fundamental ways. And it largely rejects the determinism promulgated by thinkers across disciplines such as Leo Tolstoy, the nineteenth-century Russian novelist who believed that prior history determines everything that follows, and that no particular individual can alter history much, if at all.[23] This book emphasizes the need to balance the parsimony and structure that each of the perspectives bring to our analysis with the unique, capricious role of the individual, a role that is not easily captured or structured by any perspective or model. It forces us to understand the myriad influences that shape us as human beings and sometimes allow us, by design or serendipity, to change history in ways that are hard to predict and systematize.

The Domestic and International Determinants of Government Behavior

The third argument is a reflection of the first two, but ties into a central theoretical debate. It argues that the best explanations for government behavior ultimately integrate empirical insights yielded from the use of both international and domestic theory. Scholars often view these theories as analytically separate — indeed, entire sub-disciplines focus on one or the other — but this dichotomy, while useful for theory-building by isolating causal variables, is problematic for explanation.[24]

The RAM, which has international relations theory dimensions, offers a compelling portrait if we want to explain how and why the United States went to war in terms of international determinants such as U.S.-Iraqi dynamics, power politics among nations under conditions of global anarchy (there is no highly effective government and policing force above them), and the Iraqi threat to perceived U.S. national interests. But that only solves part of the puzzle, partly because the RAM purposefully ignores domestic-level factors. To achieve parsimony, which is central to theory-building, it assumes that states are broadly similar in terms of their decision-making approaches, preferences, and interests. They all seek in rational ways to protect and enhance their security. They are socialized by anarchy to do so. For RAM analysts, what varies significantly, rather, lies at the international level, which is privileged as an explanation for government behavior.

The propensity to privilege international over domestic explanations is not limited to the RAM. It is also true of the more modern and/or parsimonious international relations theories of neorealism developed by Kenneth Waltz, the neo-institutionalism most often associated with Robert Keohane (sometimes also referred to as neoliberal institutionalism), and game theory approaches.[25] Waltz, for instance, prefers to study state behavior using an "outside-in" approach that focuses on the structure of the broader system, rather than an "inside-out" approach that explains state behavior by referring to domestic factors.[26] The outside-in approach emphasizes that good or bad states would suffer a similar fate because of the difficult situation in which they must operate. Neorealism explains state behavior by focusing only on the systemic level of world affairs. It assumes that anarchy pushes states to behave in similar ways. For example, nearly all states in the world have an army and spend significant amounts of money on weapons and defense. Neorealism has a matter-of-fact explanation for this: failure to conform to the pressures imposed on states by a system in which anarchy is the distinguishing feature will be punished. Under anarchy, military forces are crucial to ensuring self-help, because states in world affairs cannot count on a government or policing force above them for protection. Anarchy thus socializes them. For Waltz, the intentions and preferences of actors do not matter because outcomes in international relations can seldom be explained by them and because we cannot derive useful theoretical generalizations from them.[27] Rather, outcomes can be explained by understanding the impact of anarchy and the distribution of capability. As Bruce Bueno de Mesquita and David Lalman describe it, from the neorealist viewpoint "foreign policy leaders live in a rarefied world of high politics that is responsive to external pulls and tugs but is relatively inattentive to and unconstrained by the low politics of domestic affairs."[28]

In fact, many leading theoreticians in the field of political science exhibit such a penchant.[29] As Andrew Moravcsik points out, most international relations theorists recommend that the analyst give priority to international explanations and use other theories, such as those of domestic politics, only to explain anomalies.[30] They believe that we need not examine domestic factors much in order to understand government behavior and outcomes in world affairs and that we can explain them adequately with parsimonious models cast at higher levels.[31] In this sense, the nature of and variations in domestic factors, including the decision-making process itself, are unlikely to matter much. Commenting on this state of affairs, Helen Milner points out that to "understand the major issues of international politics, such as the likelihood of peace, the sources of conflict, and the possibility of cooperation among states, international relations theorists must bring a systematic analysis" of domestic-level variables into the field.[32]

This book is designed to do so. While the RAM black boxes what occurs inside states by treating them as actors that speak with one voice, the other four perspectives help us look inside the black box. They explore such things as the roles, peculiarities, dynamics, and psychological dimensions of individuals acting alone and in interaction with others, the impact of domestic politics, and decision-making in groups and bureaucratic settings. This fills a vital void. Systemic pressures and incentives can shape the broad contours of government behavior, but they are too broad to explain why states in a similar structural position sometimes do not act alike, to explain specific actions, or to explain a range of behaviors that appear irrational or are motivated by non-national interests like individual, group, or institutional goals. Similarly, domestic theories can illuminate the domestic context, but do not account for international factors and the complex strategic interactions between states that shape government behavior. They also cannot explain why states that have similar domestic contexts behave differently or why a state in fact may pursue its perceived national interest, despite a plethora of domestic actors with non-national interests to protect or advance.

To be sure, some scholars increasingly recognize the need to draw on domestic theories, concepts, and variables to inform international relations theories and analyses.[33] However, the integrated approach seeks to move us in that direction more systematically by applying, juxtaposing, and evaluating international and domestic theory within one broader approach for explaining government behavior.

The Key Decision Makers, Groups, and Decisions of the Crisis

While this book considers the interplay of global and domestic factors, it focuses attention on three decision-making groups in the United States responsible for many of the key decisions: the group of four, the group of eight (also referred to as the "gang of eight" by some of its members), and, to a smaller extent, the deputies committee, which has been ignored in books on the crisis and which I will discuss later in the book. While President Bush sometimes made decisions alone or in one-on-one interactions, the group of four was the smallest decision-making group. It included President Bush, Vice President Dan Quayle, National Security Advisor Brent Scowcroft and Chief of Staff John Sununu. After Scowcroft and Sununu received a CIA briefing early in the morning, they met with Bush virtually every day, in staff meetings from 8 a.m. until as late as 10 a.m., often with Quayle present as well. While Scowcroft would broach security questions, Sununu would focus on political ones, especially in the domestic arena, such as those relating to Congress. These meetings would in part help prepare the agenda for the group of eight meetings.[34]

The group of eight met less frequently than the group of four. It consisted of the group of four, plus Secretary of State James Baker, Secretary of Defense Richard Cheney, Chairman of the Joint Chiefs of Staff Colin Powell, and Deputy National Security Advisor Robert Gates; the latter acted as a link to the deputies committee. White House Press Secretary Marlin Fitzwater also joined the group and participated in its deliberations, particularly on questions of public relations. However, according to Fitzwater, he was not officially appointed because making the press secretary a member of the exclusive group of eight would have generated jealousies outside the White House. Given Washington's politics, high-ranking officials in various bureaucracies would have argued that they also should be included in the group of eight. An informal role for Fitzwater avoided that problem.[35]

The Persian Gulf War case was a crisis because of the speed of the invasion, the urgency of the response, the perceived threat to national interests and values, and the potential for major conflict. Because they involve high stakes, crises are of special interest.[36] Yet the Persian Gulf War case also included noncrisis elements. The buildup to war took months, which meant that many decisions could be made slowly, without the time pressure that we associate with crises. In this sense, the case can offer insight into both crisis and noncrisis situations.

While the crisis was *sui generis*, it also brought to light many questions that affect the current foreign policy debate. To what extent could great powers cooperate? Was the concept of a "new world order" a chimera? Did collective security function or was the United Nations simply political cover for U.S. unilateralism? Why did diplomacy fail? To what extent could Western forces operate within an Islamic context without causing a political backlash?

The crisis was composed of innumerable different phenomena; this book does not ignore those phenomena, but rather focuses on the following decisions, associated approximately with the following meetings and dates:

— the decision to deploy forces to the Persian Gulf (August 3 National Security Council (NSC) meeting).
— the decision to reject the option of protecting Saudi Arabia in favor of reversing the invasion of Kuwait (partly the August 3 NSC meeting but especially the August 5 statement by Bush that the invasion would not stand).
— the decision to move away from the use of economic sanctions toward a proclivity to use force (October 11 NSC meeting).
— the decision to double the size of U.S. forces deployed to the Persian Gulf (October 31 NSC meeting).
— the decision to cast Saddam Hussein in Hitler-like terms. This was not so much a clear-cut decision as a sporadic response to the crisis by President Bush outside the group setting, but it had weighty implications.
— the decision to issue Iraq an ultimatum (November 1 to 8).

Each of these decisions is analyzed, as are many others that are related to them, including how to deal with the U.S. Congress, states around the world, and the United Nations. However, the decision to go to war is also treated as an aggregate of all of these decisions, because they all contributed to it. Disaggregating the decisions is useful for understanding each one, and for evaluating the usefulness of the perspectives at different junctures, but putting these decisions back together in the broader process is of obvious importance.

Breaking Some New Ground

The contributions of the book are suggested in the foregoing discussion, but two additional points are worth mentioning. The journalist Bob Woodward offers an interesting account of decision-making in Bush's inner circle in his book *The Commanders*, which has been heavily cited by scholars. Outside of the work by Michael Gordon and Bernard Trainor, which focuses on the military dimension of the crisis, Woodward's is the only account of the crisis so far that draws on a wide set of interviews with the key decision makers.[37] However, beyond the obvious fact that Woodward was unconcerned with the academic issues and approaches pursued in this book, which involve their own arguments and debates, he chose not to cite interviewees, making it hard to judge his sources and re-creation of events. He also did not explore the dynamics in the deputies group, which played an important role in the crisis. Much information, furthermore, has come out since his book was published in 1991, including thousands of pages of memoirs, documents at the George Bush Presidential Library, secondary sources, and subsequent author interviews with many of the key players. This book draws on those sources, as well as on the widest set of cited interviews with the key players until now, including those in President Bush's inner circle and the deputies committee that reported to the inner circle.

The second point is about the use of multiple perspectives. This book draws inspiration from the classic work by Graham Allison on the 1962 Cuban missile crisis — *Essence of Decision*. Although Allison recently revised this book with historian Philip Zelikow to good effect, little work has examined world events since the Cuban missile crisis using developed multiple perspectives.[38] And yet the world has changed significantly, making it interesting to do so in a more modern case that takes into consideration the ending of the Cold War and other global changes.

The integrated approach of this book, however, extends well beyond *Essence of Decision*. That book, while pathbreaking in its original formulation, uses models as frames of reference. Allison's goal was to generate important insights from these models, not to integrate them into one tale of the Cuban missile crisis, to test the models against the evidence, or to bridge areas of study that are often treated as separate. Nor did he seek to develop theory about the models, as I do in chapter 9 regarding the theory of groupthink and the government politics model. Moreover, while the revised edition of *Essence of Decision* discusses cognitive models and the theory of groupthink, it does not actually use them as perspectives, nor does it include a domestic politics model.[39] This book does so. It uses three perspectives not used in *Essence of Decision*: cognitive, domestic politics, and groupthink. The RAM, cognitive, groupthink, and government politics perspectives are existing perspectives, while the book develops its own version of the domestic politics model, as will become clear in chapter 4. As a final point, while this book focuses on U.S. decision-making, it treats the crisis in no small part as a strategic interaction between the United States and Iraq, and makes arguments about U.S. decision-making and the road to war within that context.

The Overview of the Book

The book is divided into four parts. The first section is the introduction and chapter 1, in which I place the U.S. regional role in historical and general perspective, as well as U.S.-Iraqi relations in particular. This provides background for a better understanding of the Persian Gulf War case as well as contemporary affairs in the region.

The balance of the book is organized simply. It executes the integrated approach. The next major section of the book explores, from different perspectives, how the United States made decisions and why war was chosen over other options. Each chapter lays out the relevant perspective. It then puts forth the best, reasonable explanation from that perspective without distorting the facts of the case.

The setup of the book allows scholars from different theoretical camps, purveyors of the crisis, and students grappling with theory and/or with the crisis to engage in sensible debate without necessarily agreeing with any one perspective. The book is also designed so that the reader can cycle back through the evidence and decide on his or her own which perspectives are most telling, if any. While we have excellent case studies of government behavior, we do not often see case studies and perspectives side by side in one book. Doing so, while it might be slightly repetitive, can improve understanding of the salient case and theory for students, decision makers, and scholars of world affairs.

While chapter 2 lays out the RAM perspective, chapter 3 offers another cut on the case. Drawing on one key strand of the cognitive perspective, it argues that historical analogies played a key role in affecting the way that key U.S. decision makers viewed Iraq's invasion, Saddam's ambitions, the issue of U.S. credibility, and the best way to resolve the crisis. In chapter 4, I develop and present a version of what I call "the domestic politics model" and then lay out an explanation of U.S. decision-making and why war was chosen based on that perspective. Chapters 5 and 6 take us into Bush's inner circle and into the workings of the deputies committee, focusing on the groupthink and government politics model, respectively. For some important reasons discussed in chapter 6, the approach in that chapter differs from that of the previous chapters, while still following closely in line with the integrated approach.

Following the integrated approach, chapter 7 cycles back on the evidence to test the perspectives, and chapter 8 draws on the resulting insights to tell a more complete tale of the crisis. Using these approaches leads us, in important ways, towards an understanding of how and why President Bush, as an individual, was important in driving the crisis.

The end of the book is more theory-oriented. Chapter 9 explains in theoretical terms the puzzle of how important elements of groupthink can exist, as in the Persian Gulf War case, and yet not produce a fiasco, which is what the theory predicts. It develops a theory to explain when government politics is unlikely to take place, and also shows how this theory can help us understand the Persian Gulf War and the Cuban missile crisis cases better. And it explains more broadly why nonrational behaviors did not produce a negative outcome. Chapter 10 picks up on the theme of multiple perspectives and integration, and shows how we can integrate insights from international and domestic theory. The concluding chapter elaborates on how the integrated approach can be used in other cases, and offers a brief example with respect to the war on terrorism.

Appendix 1 follows the concluding chapter and explores the end of the Persian Gulf War and the question of how to judge the success of the war. This is important because our view of the extent to which it succeeded depends fundamentally on our definition of success. While this book has treated it as a military victory, I offer a competing interpretation of success as well. Following this discussion, it is sensible to offer the postscript to the book. This section explores the period preceding the 2003 Iraq War and that war itself. It then applies a scaled-down version of the integrated approach in a preliminary manner to the task of thinking about this war.

CHAPTER ONE

The United States, Iraq, and the Crisis

Some Background

The goal of this chapter is to offer a brief sketch, rather than a deep historical analysis, of how and why the Persian Gulf became important to the United States. It also seeks to explain the backdrop to Iraq's invasion of Kuwait, and to argue that numerous outcomes other than war were possible. That sets up the central questions of this book: how did the United States make the decisions that took it to war and how did war result as an outcome? Following this chapter, we will then begin to explore the crisis by use of multiple perspectives, beginning with the rational actor model.

U.S. National Interests: How the Persian Gulf Entered the American Consciousness

The Persian Gulf, a region that includes Iran, Iraq, Saudi Arabia, Kuwait, Oman, Qatar, Bahrain, and the United Arab Emirates, is now emblazoned on the American psyche. But it entered the American consciousness slowly. Washington began to appreciate the vital role of Saudi oil as an economic source at least as early as the 1930s. It made informal commitments to Saudi security in the early 1940s, and, depending on one's interpretation, formally committed itself as early as 1947, when President Harry S. Truman and King Abdul Aziz bin Saud, the founder of the modern Saudi kingdom, made a pact. Described in a State Department cable, the United States pledged that if Saudi Arabia were attacked by another power or were under threat of attack such as the one that Iraq would pose in 1990, Washington would take "energetic measures under the auspices of the United Nations to confront such aggression."[1]

However, while the United States did make certain commitments to the Saudis from 1945 to 1971, Britain was largely responsible for regional security, with Uncle Sam playing a distant second in the region. In 1968, Britain announced that it would withdraw "East of Suez," and did so by 1971, thus leaving principal responsibility for regional stability to the United States.

The Arab-Israeli War and the Arab oil embargo, both of 1973, linked the Arab-Israeli and Persian Gulf arenas and underscored the vital importance of Persian Gulf oil to world stability. While that raised consciousness in Washington about events in and around the Persian Gulf, the United States still preferred not to assume the responsibility of protecting Persian Gulf stability directly. Rather, Iran and to a much lesser extent Saudi Arabia formed the pillars of the Nixon Doctrine or "twin pillar" strategy. Under this approach, Washington would rely primarily on Iran, and secondarily on Saudi Arabia, to safeguard regional security and safe access to oil at reasonable prices in exchange for American arms and technical support. That would obviate the need for the United States to intervene directly in the region, or even to build a major capability to do so, in the post-Vietnam period when the U.S. public was wary of such commitments.

Little did the United States know that its reliance on regional actors would leave it highly vulnerable. In the late 1970s, the region became such a hotbed of activity that the United States had to take notice. During the Iranian revolution, the Shah of Iran fled his country on January 16, 1979; American hostages were seized by Iranian militants in November. Meanwhile, the Soviets invaded Afghanistan on December 24, 1979. These events forced Washington to become committed to Persian Gulf security in a direct role, which increased throughout the 1980s. On January 23, 1980, President Carter issued the Carter Doctrine, one of the most forceful statements of his presidency; it indicated a major change from the noninterventionist U.S. role of previous decades. In response largely to the Soviet invasion, the Carter Doctrine committed the United States to deter or respond to "outside," as opposed to internal, threats to Persian Gulf security.[2]

Concerned with global and regional threats to Persian Gulf security, Washington was determined not only to improve its capability to deter "outside" pressure on the Persian Gulf, but also to deal with pressures arising within the Persian Gulf. In that spirit, President Ronald Reagan stated in October 1981 that there was "no way" the United States could "stand by" and see Saudi Arabia threatened to the point that the flow of oil could be shut down.[3] This statement and others of a similar kind later became known as the Reagan Doctrine, which represented a U.S. commitment to protect Saudi Arabia against not only external but also internal threats within the Persian Gulf region and in terms of domestic threats to the regime. The United States had made a tacit agreement to protect the Saudis in the 1940s, the Carter Doctrine had asserted a U.S. commitment to protect the free flow of oil from threats outside the region, and now Reagan was elevating the U.S. commitment one more notch. Saudi Arabia would become the linchpin of U.S. security in the Persian Gulf region.

The events of 1979 also awakened the U.S. public, at least temporarily, to the region's vital importance. But Americans remained oblivious to the rise of a dictator who, a decade later, would transform the Persian Gulf from an area of rising importance to a *bona fide* American priority. News of Saddam's rise to power in July 1979 received little attention in the newspapers.

The Saddam Factor: Two Invasions in Ten Years

When we think of modern conflict, few leaders come to mind more prominently than Iraq's president, Saddam Hussein. He assumed the position of second-in-command in Iraq in 1968 when the ideological, secular Baath political party in which he was active seized power in a bloodless coup. In July 1979, after a decade as the *de facto* dictator of Iraq under then–President Bakr, Saddam officially became president. Less than one year later, he invaded next-door Iran, confronting the Ayatollah Khomeini's Islamic revolution and triggering one of the century's bloodiest wars, with more than one million casualties. That war ended in a cease-fire in 1988, but Saddam was not done. Just two years later Iraq would invade Kuwait.

It is useful here to offer a brief sketch of why Iraq invaded Kuwait.[4] In September 1980, Iraq, a state slightly larger than California, launched a major war against Iran. In many ways, the bloody and lengthy Iran-Iraq War (1980–1988) set the stage for Iraq's invasion of Kuwait in 1990. The first war devastated Iraq's economy and left it heavily in debt to Kuwait and Saudi Arabia. They had loaned Saddam considerable amounts for the war against revolutionary Iran, which at the time they feared more than Iraq. Estimates suggest that Iraq began that war with $35 billion in reserve and ended the war $80–$100 billion in debt. Interestingly, Iraqi Foreign Minister Tariq Aziz claimed shortly after the invasion of Kuwait in 1990 that Baghdad was forced to "resort to this method" of invasion because its economic situation had deteriorated to the point that it had no alternative.[5] Kuwait was quite a tempting economic prize.

Iraq also emerged from the first war a much stronger military power than Iran. That Iraq no longer had to contend with a powerful Iran on its border presumably made an invasion of Kuwait more possible.[6] Moreover, Iraq's huge standing army, expanded during the Iran-Iraq War, could not be effectively reintegrated into the shaky Iraqi economy after the war. Like Napoleon, Saddam may have understood that an idle, restless army could pose a much greater threat to his regime than one kept busy in war. In addition, the war taught Iraq that its short coastline was a major vulnerability. Iran cut Iraq off from the Persian Gulf when it took the Faw peninsula in a major military victory in February 1986. Occupying Kuwait would give Iraq much greater access to the Persian Gulf.

The invasion also appealed to Iraqis who viewed Kuwait as part of historic Iraq.[7] Since Iraq's rise as an independent state in 1932, it consistently challenged Kuwait's right to exist. In the 1930s, the Iraqi King Ghazi openly demanded the incorporation of all of Kuwait into Iraq, a demand reiterated by Abd al-Karim Qassim, the Iraqi ruler who overthrew the monarchy in July 1958. In 1961 Iraq actually invaded Kuwaiti border posts, only to retreat under severe British political and military pressure. Again, in 1973, Iraqi forces occupied Kuwaiti territory along a narrow border strip on the pretense of protecting the Iraqi coastline against an alleged impending attack by Iran. These forces remained there for a decade, against Kuwaiti wishes.

The merger of Iraq and Kuwait after the 1990 invasion wed the two countries, and from Iraq's perspective, corrected a historical wrong.[8] Under Ottoman rule, Iraq was not a unified or independent state. Rather, it consisted of three disparate provinces — Mosul, Baghdad, and Basra. From Iraq's perspective, Kuwait was always part of Basra under the Ottoman Empire. Kuwait, however, viewed such Iraqi claims as a smoke screen for aggression. After all, the royal family had established an autonomous sheikdom in Kuwait in 1756, and Iraq, for that matter, was artificial as well, having been carved out of the Ottoman Empire in an *ad hoc* manner.

Iraq's Baathist Party ideology also may have played a role. It sought to sweep away artificial borders, and Saddam wanted to unite the Arab world behind Baghdad. He would even assert that it was during war that the Iraqi army "rose to the level of the [Islamic] mission," trying, in a Herculean feat, to pass off Baath party ideology as holy.[9]

We can surmise that Saddam's personal ambitions, up and beyond state or institutional interests, further pushed Iraq to invade Kuwait. A few months before the outbreak of the war, he spoke in typical terms of Iraq achieving great "glory," calling on the faithful to play a role in this unfolding of history.[10] It is not too much to assume that Saddam's visions and, some might say, delusions of grandeur were at play, among the many other motivations for invading Kuwait.

However, while these motivations may very well have been key underlying causes for the invasion, the more immediate cause was Iraq's growing tensions with Kuwait. At the Arab League summit meeting in May 1990, Saddam attacked the other Persian Gulf states, particularly Kuwait, for ignoring oil production quotas, keeping oil prices down, refusing to forgive Iraq's war debts from the Iran-Iraq War, and failing to provide war reconstruction credits.[11] Despite the fact that Iraq had attacked Iran in September 1980, Baghdad repeatedly argued that it had sacrificed treasure and blood to check Iran's fundamentalist Islamic threat to all Arab states, especially the Persian Gulf monarchies that Iran's Ayatollah Khomeini wanted to overthrow through political means. Thus, from Iraq's perspective at least, Iraq deserved Arab allegiance and economic support, and Kuwait could not expect to get a free ride on Iraq's military back.[12]

Because the Kuwaitis and Saudis were not particularly forthcoming with postwar economic support and because Iraq's economy was devastated, Saddam sought to raise money for economic recovery by limiting OPEC production, thus increasing the price of oil. By agreeing to production quotas, the many members of OPEC, which included the Persian Gulf states, could control the price of oil. The less oil they pumped, the more expensive oil would be on the market. States that sought a short-term fix were more interested in pumping much oil, while those with a long-term view were less interested in doing so.

Moreover, Kuwait indirectly lowered oil prices by pumping too much oil, some from the Rumaila oil field, over which Iraq laid joint claim. Iraq also accused Kuwait of slant-drilling into this oil field. By starting oil wells on their side of the Iraqi-Kuwaiti border, and angling their oil equipment under the border, the Kuwaitis could draw on oil from Iraqi sources. In January 2001, Aziz would reflect back and assert that Kuwait "got what it deserved" in 1990 because it had undermined Iraq's oil prices and undertaken slant-drilling.[13]

Despite his status as a dictator, Saddam also justified the invasion by citing the Emir of Kuwait's dissolution of the 1986 Kuwaiti National Assembly, Kuwait's lack of elections, and its status as a rentier state that in effect was a royal family exploiting its control of an oil state—in effect, he pointed to the regime's illegitimacy. As reflected in initial communiqués from Baghdad, Iraq asserted that it would support a popular revolution against the illegitimate Kuwaiti monarchy, organize elections, and then withdraw.[14] Kuwait was reluctant to bend to Saddam's brinkmanship, perhaps not recognizing his seriousness.

By July 30, Iraq had eight divisions, 100,000 well-trained troops, and 350 tanks poised on the Kuwaiti border, in formation for extensive operations. The CIA, however, was not predicting an invasion, nor were Arab leaders, who told Washington that Saddam was just bluffing. On July 25, U.S. Ambassador to Iraq

April Glaspie had met with Saddam Hussein. In responding to Saddam's queries about U.S. intentions, she made the now-infamous statement that the United States had "no opinion on the Arab-Arab conflicts, like your border disagreement with Kuwait."[15] While Saddam asserted in an interview in 1992 that he saw her statement as providing a green light to invade Kuwait, it is unclear to what extent we should view his statement at face value, given the gravity of his invasion and the fact that conspiracy theory was very prevalent in Baghdad. Why should we assume that Saddam saw a "green light" when he was just as likely to see a trap at play?[16]

What is clearer is that Glaspie's remarks, as well as subsequent ones by State Department spokeswoman Margaret Tutwiler and Assistant Secretary of State for Near East and South Asian Affairs John Kelly before the House Foreign Affairs Committee two days before the invasion, did in fact reflect broader administration policy. That policy, within the context of U.S. accommodationist policies of the 1980s, which are discussed in the next section of this chapter, may very well have contributed to Saddam's belief that even if he had not been given a green light *per se*, at least his invasion would not lead to a dramatic response by Washington over Kuwait, much less to war.[17] In this sense, we may surmise that Saddam was not so naive as to see a "green light," but at the same time he did not expect a massive U.S.-led response.

On August 2, into Kuwait roared 140,000 Iraqi troops and 1,800 tanks, spearheaded by two Republican Guard divisions, the Hammurabi and the Medina. What had been viewed as mere brinkmanship in late July in the effort to scare the Kuwaitis into making some key economic and territorial concessions, was suddenly a full-blown invasion using Iraq's best forces. The United States responded a few days later with Operation Desert Shield, which was intended to protect Saudi Arabia from any further military action by Iraq.

The Guard was conceived as the dictator's personal military force, equipped with the best weapon systems. It was very loyal to Saddam and politically committed to the ruling Baath Party. It is no surprise that Saddam spared these forces from the wrath of the U.S.-led alliance, which attacked Iraq in order to evict Iraqi forces from Kuwait in Operation Desert Storm on January 16, 1991. He pulled these forces back to Baghdad at the end of the war and kept some Guard divisions out of the conflict altogether. They not only fought for Iraq, but much more importantly, they protected Saddam himself. And for any dictator, that is the key goal. The lightning-fast attack on Kuwait was conducted professionally and successfully. While a limited number of Kuwaiti A-4 aircraft, armored vehicles,

Chieftain tanks, and elements of the navy fought for about three days, Iraq's blitzkrieg was overwhelming. Kuwaitis awakened at 2 a.m. on the morning of August 2 to the piercing noise of machine-gun fire and artillery shells, only to see Kuwait City ringed with Iraqi tanks and Saddam's jets and gunships buzzing the city, sporadically firing rockets at key sites such as the Dasman palace of the Emir of Kuwait.

From Strange Bedfellows to War

Another dimension of the pre-crisis international relations of the Persian Gulf is also important to consider. Understanding Western policy toward Iraq not only sheds some light on Iraq's invasion, but more importantly it helps us understand the ensuing crisis, the U.S. role in it, and U.S.-Iraqi relations. The United States, as well as European states and the Soviet Union, was criticized for supporting Iraq, especially after the eight-year Iran-Iraq War ended in 1988. The need to balance against revolutionary Iran had decreased substantially, but Saddam was still acting aggressively. Even after the war, the United States continued to pursue a policy of "constructive engagement." That approach was not without reason, although hindsight revealed its folly. Constructive engagement was motivated by the fact that Iraq, as one official put it, emerged from the war as the "most powerful country in a key part of the world to us," and so the "feeling at the time" was that the United States needed to "develop a workable relationship with Saddam Hussein."[18]

However, Saddam became increasingly aggressive from 1988 to 1990. In several speeches, beginning with a famous one on February 24, 1990, Saddam spearheaded a new offensive against the United States. He may have considered the fact that most Arab leaders and elites viewed the decline of the Soviet Union as heralding a new era of American hegemony at the global level, and therefore of Israel's potential hegemony in the region, and that the time was ripe to capitalize on these perceived concerns about American and Israeli power by challenging the United States. So he called on Arab states to offset U.S. power and on the United States to withdraw from the region and eschew involvement in Arab affairs.[19]

In addition, Iraq did not noticeably demobilize its army after the war, and used chemical weapons and torture on its own people in an effort to depopulate Iraqi Kurdistan.[20] On April 2, 1990, Saddam announced that Iraqi scientists had developed advanced chemical weapons, which could "eat up half of Israel, if it tries to do anything against Iraq."[21] The State Department, fairly quiet until now, called the statement "inflammatory, outrageous and irresponsible."[22] In May, Saddam assailed the other Persian Gulf states, particularly Kuwait, for waging economic war against Iraq.[23] From February through late August, he issued various threats backed by military maneuvers that implied potential military action against Kuwait. At one point, he even asserted, in conjunction with a diatribe against perceived Kuwaiti efforts to "sabotage" Iraq's economic interests, that it is "more painful to have one's head cut off than one's sustenance."[24] In retrospect, it appears that he was suggesting that Kuwait could merely hurt Iraq economically, whereas Iraq could eliminate Kuwait as a state altogether.

U.S. officials clearly recognized that Iraq, in addition to being the strongest Persian Gulf state, was now also the chief threat in the aftermath of the Iran-Iraq War. As Powell later recalled: "Iran represented less of a problem to our interests than Iraq in 1988."[25] In the fall of 1989, the administration conducted a study on Saddam, which concluded that he was a "very bad man, this is an aggressor, this is a man who has weapons of mass destruction . . . and the question is whether by offering some inducements . . . we might be able to bring him inside the tent."[26]

Yet, as Secretary of States James Baker noted, while the United States did get somewhat "tougher" with Saddam from February to August 1990, Washington still did not take a very tough line against Baghdad, in part because Arab allies were not behind it.[27] Throughout much of 1988 to 1990, U.S. behavior toward Iraq remained conciliatory. At a September 1989 NSC meeting, National Security Advisor Brent Scowcroft summed up the administration consensus that little would be lost by building ties to Iraq. This view was reflected in National Security Directive 26, signed by President Bush on October 1989.[28] As Scowcroft put it: "We wanted to see if we could transform Iraq into a moderately responsible leader in world politics. We knew Iraq was rich and that it would initiate a massive reconstruction program and we saw no reason why U.S. business shouldn't be there."[29] The administration was still reluctant to check Iraq more strongly, despite recognizing Iraq's military strength and despite the fact that "no one was under the illusion that Saddam was other than bad news."[30] The view was that pressuring a strong Iraq would be counterproductive; instead, the United States continued to pursue "constructive engagement" as a means of influencing Saddam's behavior.[31]

By October 1989, the administration was reconsidering its approach and had become more "pragmatic and cautious."[32] The last approval of commodity credits to Iraq came in November, although further credit extensions were discussed but not pursued.[33] Yet even as late as May 1990, Assistant Secretary of State for Near East and South Asian Affairs John Kelly argued against taking a tougher line against Baghdad.[34] While the conciliatory approach was failing, it was unclear what might replace it. Using Iran to check Iraq's ambitions was a nonstarter, given U.S.-Iranian tensions. But this left in place residual elements of the conciliatory approach and the difficulty of altering an entrenched policy, which had been developed across the bureaucratic and governmental spectrum.

In retrospect, the U.S. approach of constructive engagement proved neither constructive nor very engaging. While the United States was slowly moving away from its Iraq policy, Iraq's invasion of Kuwait on August 2, 1990, changed everything. We can surmise that the invasion, by suggesting the folly of U.S. efforts to appease Iraq in the late 1980s, made the United States more likely to take a strong stand against Iraq, not only to compensate for its past mistakes, but also because Iraq revealed itself as surprisingly incorrigible, in embarrassing contrast to prior U.S. appraisals.

Alternative Pasts and Futures

In hindsight, it appears that the U.S.-led attack on Iraq was a natural, logical extension of Iraq's invasion of Kuwait and subsequent developments. The very fact that the United States had important interests in the region suggests that it would defend them vigorously. Yet there is very good reason to believe that numerous outcomes could have occurred other than war, or at least the war that did commence on January 16, 1991, which makes it interesting to ask why and how the U.S.-led coalition went to war. As Philip Tetlock and Aaron Belkin point out, research shows that once people learn the outcome of an event, "they not only perceive that outcome as more likely ex post than they did ex ante . . . , they often fail to remember their ex ante assessment of what was and was not likely to happen."[35]

In the Persian Gulf War case, it is quite possible to fathom other trajectories in the historical process. Saddam could have been offered a clandestine or public carrot to withdraw from Kuwait, or U.N. economic sanctions against Iraq could have been put in place much longer before moving to war, as Baker and Powell, among others, preferred. Or the United States could have practiced punitive containment or sporadic bombing campaigns short of war. Saddam, for his part, could have withdrawn partly from Kuwait, thus undermining U.S.-led efforts to use force against him.[36] Such outcomes are not hard to imagine.

While few people argued that Iraq should be allowed to occupy Kuwait altogether, the notion of appeasing Saddam was advanced by some Arab leaders, to the point that Bush feared such action, noting that there was an "historical Arab propensity" to strike such deals.[37] Later, as Powell recalls, some Saudi, Egyptian, and other leaders argued that if the United States bombed Iraqi forces a little bit, "they'll quit."[38] As discussed later in the book, France and Russia also sought to advance proposals that fell short of Washington's demand that Iraq withdraw unconditionally from Kuwait, and even in the United States and in Bush's inner circle serious doubts arose about how strongly Washington should respond to the invasion.[39]

Despite Washington's repeated demand that Iraq withdraw unconditionally, polls suggested that the public was willing to negotiate with Iraq. For instance, in a November poll, people were presented with the choice of compromise with Saddam or war, and 58 percent chose compromise.[40] On November 15, even Bush acknowledged "a certain frustration" among the American public regarding the move toward war. Other polls showed that only one in four Americans wanted to go to war and that most wanted to stick with economic sanctions even if they failed to get Iraq out of Kuwait by January or February 1991.[41] While public support for the move toward war increased as the conflict neared, it was soft at crucial times when key decisions were made.

Even with the president's credibility on the line, and despite a U.N. resolution authorizing the coalition to use force if Saddam did not withdraw by January 15, 1991, the U.S. Senate barely passed a similar resolution by a vote of 52–47 on January 12. An opposing resolution sponsored by Senators Sam Nunn and George Mitchell called for the continued use of economic sanctions in lieu of force. It would have carried the day had it not been for a few swing votes. It lost by 53 to 46 in the Senate. The House, like the Senate, had to have overnight sessions on Friday before the vote in order to accommodate the emotional speeches on the floor. It voted 250 to 183 against an anti-war resolution and in favor of a congressional resolution sponsored by Stephen Solarz and Robert Mitchel supporting the president in his use of force, so long as he had exhausted all diplomatic means. But, as Solarz noted, for some time support in Congress was quite dubious and the president was on "thin political ice."[42]

The 52–47 vote in the Senate no doubt reflected not only partisan politics but also deep concern, as shown in a letter on November 28 from Senator-elect Paul Wellstone of Minnesota to the president: "There is still time to stop the momentum towards war. We can suspend the current troop build up and return to a policy based on stringent economic sanctions coupled with vigorous and creative diplomatic initiatives."[43] Indeed, as the vote neared, the administration could only count on the certain support of thirty to thirty-five senators. Before the vote, key administration officials and their aides made many calls and visits to Congress to lobby for support, in a well-orchestrated strategy that stressed Iraq's intransigence, threat, and the damage that the conflict could have on the U.S. and global economy.[44] John Sununu and Robert Gates in particular had to pound the pavement to land the last key votes.[45]

Even after the Persian Gulf War started, the United States still had some options short of a major ground war, which would later commence on February 24, 1991. Forty-two percent of the public still thought it should start talks with Iraq on January 20.[46] It might have sought some settlement prior to the ground war, seeing that Saddam's forces were battered and that he appeared increasingly compliant. Instead, Bush confounded even some in his own administration by pushing for an all-out ground war.[47] One of Baker's close aides perhaps best underscored the potential for many different outcomes. Baker, he said, "very quickly saw this could go very wrong. He saw it could lead to many getting killed. He saw we were vulnerable if it starts too soon. He saw the possibility the Europeans could retreat. He saw the prospect the Soviets could block the United Nations resolutions. He saw the things that could isolate us. He saw that you could have the president become 'Carterized.' "[48] While Baker was right, these and other outcomes did not result, which raises a question: if other outcomes could have occurred, then why did the decisions and outcomes that we observed occur?

Conclusion

If we took a snapshot of history on August 2, 1990, we would find Saddam confident and energized; the United States equivocating; Saudi Arabia unsure about allowing U.S. forces into the kingdom; China, the U.S.S.R. and France not resolved to do more than condemn the invasion; and the U.S. public appalled by the invasion, but, perhaps remembering the Vietnam debacle, reluctant to send U.S. troops into danger abroad. That was not a recipe for reversing Iraq's invasion.

The following chapters offer different perspectives on aspects of how the United States made the decisions that took it to war, and why war was not avoided as an outcome. In the decisions of the crisis, which these perspectives try to capture, we can see a little of what we all may experience individually — group and committee dynamics; the politics of bureaucracies; human emotions and biases amid efforts to make rational, calculated decisions; struggles to control and set agendas; reluctance to question authority and assert our views even when we have serious doubts; and politicians who may be affected at varying levels of intensity by domestic politics. In this sense, the Persian Gulf crisis, while unique in its own right, is also a microcosm for broader phenomena, for phenomena that are germane to how we all think and make decisions.

CHAPTER TWO

The Rational Actor Model

The version of the rational actor model presented in this book is based on several key assumptions. As noted in the introduction, it is a faceless model, one that black boxes what occurs inside states and treats them as unitary actors that make decisions in terms of rational choice. The rational choice approach is labeled and often treated differently across and within disciplines, but, in general, we can say that rational choice is assumed to involve identifying objectives, options, expected consequences, and then making a rational choice.[1] Rational choice assumptions are applied to different actors, including individuals, in what are sometimes referred to as "rationalist" arguments. In this book, it is applied to the unitary state.

We can briefly look at objectives, options, expected consequences, and choice. In the present version of the RAM, the strategic objectives of a state are derived from its perceived national interests. The model assumes that a range of plausible options, rather than just one or two, are typically generated and considered in the effort to meet these objectives. Such consideration requires that the consequences of each option be assessed. These consequences involve benefits and costs. That is, each option is expected to produce a set of benefits and costs, which can be evaluated in terms of meeting these objectives.

The aspect of choice refers to value-maximizing behavior. While exploring this notion can take us into complex discussions, suffice it to say that the rational agent selects (or *seeks* to select, as assumed herein) the option that ranks highest in terms of its goals and objectives, based on how it perceives them. And that in estimating the effects of options, the rational agent does not consider just a single moment, but rather recognizes that the costs and benefits of a single decision may be spread over time.[2] We expect an actor to behave differently as the strategic context in which it must make decisions itself changes. If this changing context increases the perceived costs and decreases the perceived benefits of a certain alternative compared to others, that alternative will be less likely to be pursued.

There are many ways to enrich the RAM and make it more complex. We can do so by drawing on the broader literatures of rational choice, traditional state-centric views of international relations associated with classical realism, and neo-realism (otherwise referred to as structural realism for its theoretical emphasis on the systemic-level features of global anarchy and the balance of power).[3] All these literatures, to some extent, share key assumptions about international relations, primarily that states can be viewed as rational and crucial actors in world affairs.

However, while there are many ways that we can enrich the model, there is one dimension that is crucial to add to our discussion here. As Jonathan Bendor and Thomas Hammond point out, a developed RAM of international relations should have two essential components: decision- and game-theoretic components.[4] So far, we have focused mostly on its decision-theoretic component, which characterized the RAM in the original *Essence of Decision*. It refers to how one actor selects among various alternatives by weighing their costs and benefits and by trying to choose the alternative that maximizes expected utility or, in simple terms, best serves its interests. Under this aspect of the model, the actor seeks to do so without concern for what others are expected to do. The game-theoretic aspect assumes this same basic logic, with the added presumption that the best alternative depends on what other actors do. We can refer to this dependency and linked fates as strategic interaction, which may be inferred from the assumptions of the RAM posited above or added to the model to expand its reach.

Strategic interaction assumes that because moves by one actor carry implications for the other, each actor will select a course of action that incorporates the probable choices of others. It will try to assess how its actions and the reactions of others will yield outcomes, and will try to choose that course of action that leads to the outcome that maximizes utility. Utility is the value that any actor places on a given outcome. More specifically, such interaction assumes that actors possess preferences, defined simply as how they rank the possible outcomes of strategic interaction. In their preference ordering, they rank the outcomes from best to worst, and do so in a transitive manner. By "transitive," we mean that if the actor prefers A to B and B to C, then it will prefer A to C.[5]

Game theorists try to capture strategic interaction mathematically. They show how expectations of outcomes can cause outcomes, and how the strategic choices of rational actors play themselves out under different conditions. The rational agent is one that multiplies each outcome's utility either by the probability that his action will bring it about or by its probability, given the agent's action.[6] It then either chooses (in strict formulations), or seeks to choose (in less stringent ones, such as that laid out here) the maximizing option.

For our purposes here, we can provide a skeletal summation of the RAM model: it assumes that the actor identifies various options for problem-solving, weighs their costs and benefits in terms of perceived national objectives, and, while taking into consideration possible responses to its actions by other actors, *seeks* to choose the option whose consequences rank highest in meeting those objectives. Thinkers who subscribe knowingly or unknowingly to the RAM's assumptions will try to explain government behavior by asking these questions: What were the objective facts of the situation? What perceived national interests did behavior serve? How did the actor seek to maximize benefits over costs compared to other alternative approaches? What was the nature and effect of strategic interaction? They will recreate how the decision was made through an assumption that the state went through a reasoned, calculated process of comparing options.

Two qualifications are worth making regarding this version of the RAM. First, I employ a modified rationality, as suggested earlier. I relax the assumption of more stringent models that the actor considers all alternatives, weighs all costs and benefits in light of perfect information about the other players and the nature of the game, and chooses the best alternative to be considered rational. The word "seeks," in fact, suggests that actors are rational so long as they seriously attempt to maximize utility under conditions of incomplete information, in which at least one player usually does not know something about the game or the other players, and in which the key actor under consideration faces uncertainty deriving from such things as unpredictable acts of nature and doubts about an adversary's motives.[7] While the assumption of strict rationality plays an important role for economists and political scientists who engage in game theory and mathematical modeling, a relaxed rationality is more sensible for actually using perspectives.[8]

Second, the present version of the RAM does not consider a plethora of dimensions including risk propensity, misperception, and uncertainty.[9] To what extent and how they should be included remains subject to debate, as does the broader question of the extent of care that states must exercise in comparing options if we are to judge them as acting in line with what the RAM posits.[10] However, most versions of rationality, whether applied to states or individuals, view the failure to compare options as compromising rational behavior. This book focuses attention on that yardstick as a way to judge rationality.

The Argument of the Chapter

This chapter explains how and why the United States went to war from the RAM perspective. The argument is that the United States perceived itself as having vital national interests at stake in the Persian Gulf. In order to protect them, it tried to consider and exhaust diplomatic and economic alternatives to war. It faced an intransigent Iraqi regime, and over time believed that the costs of waiting for sanctions to work increasingly exceeded the benefits. Therefore, taking into consideration Iraq's behavior in the crisis, and its continuing threat even if it had withdrawn from Kuwait, Washington increasingly saw war as sensible. While Iraq may or may not have reached a similar conclusion, it was also the case that the two sides could not locate or agree upon a negotiated settlement, because their bargaining positions did not overlap much, if at all. This further inclined the United States towards war. Furthermore, the structural condition of anarchy in international relations reinforced this logic. In their strategic interaction, the United States could not trust Iraq to withdraw from Kuwait and not to reinvade at a later time, and Iraq could not trust the United States not to attack or harass it, if it agreed to withdraw.

The Oil Factor

In the RAM perspective, states are assumed to respond to perceived threats to national interests. Thus, any RAM explanation must search for such interests. Chapter 1 laid out the evolution of the U.S. national commitment to ensuring the unimpeded flow of oil, protecting Saudi stability, and limiting anti-American influences. While we might question the nature and relative priority of U.S. national interests, we do know that these three interests were stated repeatedly by American officials.[11]

Iraq, for its part, had already established a brutal track record, which added to the perception that it was capable of high-risk, dangerous actions.[12] With Kuwait under its belt, Iraq now controlled 19 percent of the world's oil reserves. A potential invasion of Saudi Arabia would have raised that to approximately 44 percent. If left unopposed, Iraq might have gained enough capability to shift seriously the regional balance of power, to blackmail other Arab states into supporting its inflated foreign policy agenda, and to threaten Israel, to whose interests the United States was committed. Down the road, it might also have taken actions to raise global oil prices, which would have facilitated Iraq's efforts to build weapons of mass destruction and which could have driven the global economy into recession, a problem that the United States was already facing. Thus, while the United States received only 8.7 percent of its oil from Iraq and Kuwait combined, Iraq's invasion still posed a serious threat, in a world of global interdependence.

After some discussions with Washington, Riyadh also accepted the U.S. view of the potential Iraqi threat. As General Khaled bin Sultan, the commander of Saudi forces, put it, Saudi Arabia may have been a target but even if it wasn't, Iraq would be in a position on "all important matters — particularly oil policy and foreign affairs," to "dictate terms."[13] While Iraq strongly denied any designs on Saudi Arabia, citing its nonaggression pact with the Saudi kingdom of March 1989 and excellent bilateral relations, the United States and Saudi Arabia were doubtful.[14] They even doubted statements made by Iraq to Palestinian Liberation Organization (PLO) leader Yasser Arafat and King Hussein of Jordan that it had no designs on Saudi Arabia, a message that they relayed to King Fahd.[15]

While the crisis was primarily between Iraq and the United States, in truth, many Arab leaders also wanted Saddam cut down to size, especially the Persian Gulf states that most directly faced the Iraqi threat.[16] That helps explain why so few Arab leaders supported Iraq, and why states such as Syria and Egypt joined the U.S.-led coalition. However, despite the recognized threat that Iraq posed, Washington still had to convince Saudi Arabia to accept U.S. forces. King Fahd, the eleventh of forty-three sons of Abdul Aziz bin Saud, faced a predicament that his father never had to worry about. Fahd was concerned that by allowing Western soldiers onto sacred soil, he would anger the powerful religious right in a kingdom that prided itself on protecting the two holy shrines of Islam at Mecca and Medina. This in part explains his initial hesitancy in accepting an F-15 squadron that Bush offered him on August 2, 1990, and his repeated assertions that the U.S.-led forces were "temporary in nature" and would leave "Saudi territory immediately at the request of the Kingdom."[17]

King Fahd, who ascended the throne in 1982 in the midst of the Iran-Iraq War, liked to practice compromise. If he could make a threat go away with monetary inducements, he would try. Washington had solid intelligence that the Saudis were considering such pocket-book diplomacy with Iraq.[18] That Fahd doubted U.S. resolve made such compromise more attractive.

On August 3, Prince Bandar of Saudi Arabia was invited to the White House. When Bandar, who became ambassador to the United States in 1983, was informed that the U.S. strategy would involve an initial 100,000 troops, he was pleasantly surprised.[19] This is because the Saudis remembered that when they called on U.S. military support in 1979 to signal post-revolutionary Iran of Washington's commitment to their security, Washington proved ineffective. It flew high-performance aircraft to the Persian Gulf in an apparent show of force, but Washington announced that they were unarmed while the aircraft were in midair.[20] That produced serious doubts about U.S. resolve, a resolve which would now be crucial in persuading Saudi Arabia to resist rather than appease Iraq. It was apparent that the Saudis were concerned about "casting their lot" with the United States, and in fact all the leaders of the region, as John Kelly pointed out, wondered if Washington would "stay the course."[21]

After the White House meeting, Bandar called King Fahd and expressed his belief in the need to take a stand against Iraq. The King, however, needed some more time, responding evasively to repeated pressure from Washington, and instead focusing on the upcoming August 6 trip of high-level U.S. officials to the kingdom.[22] That led Bush to wonder about Saudi will and the possibility that they might "bug out."[23] In one of Bush's repeated calls to Fahd, he noted that the United States could provide the Saudis with Muslim cover by inviting Arab countries to join the coalition. That appeared to make a difference in the King's view, although he remained reluctant to make a clear, blatant, and public break with Saudi tradition by allowing Western forces into the sacred kingdom.[24]

Meanwhile, the United States was anxious to deter a possible invasion of Saudi Arabia, and was deciding which forces to send there.[25] But just as Saudi Arabia was trying to assess if it could trust Washington, the United States needed to know that it could rely on the Saudis. U.S. pressure and the Iraqi threat had already inclined Saudi Arabia to give the go-ahead for U.S. forces.[26] King Fahd did not want to wait for an "unambiguous" threat from Iraq, as some of his advisers counseled, noting that the Kuwaitis had done just that.[27] CIA photographs revealed to him that Iraq's forces were less than 250 miles from Saudi oil fields, within striking range of Riyadh. Fahd did discuss the crisis in general with members of the royal family during the previous weekend, but made the final decision, virtually alone for the first time in his fifty years in public life, to allow U.S. forces mass entry into his kingdom.[28]

President Bush was convinced that Iraq had Saudi Arabia in his sights, which added energy to his counteroffensive.[29] As early as August 2 in a meeting in Aspen, Colorado, Bush and Thatcher contemplated which countries would be with them if Saudi Arabia were invaded.[30] The president would assert a few days later that while he believed that economic sanctions "in this instance, if fully enforced, can be very, very effective," no single thing tipped Washington's hand in sending troops to Saudi Arabia, except perhaps that the Iraqis were heading south toward Saudi Arabia when "they said they were withdrawing."[31] In an August 9 letter to Congress, Bush observed that Iraq was "capable of initiating further hostilities with little or no additional preparation . . . and pose a direct threat to neighboring countries."[32]

While Iraq's intentions were not clear, its behavior raised suspicions. If Iraq only wanted to annex Kuwait, why did Iraqi units have the weapons, supply, and positioning for a forward thrust into the Saudi kingdom? Why did U.S. satellite images reveal that at least six divisions of Iraqi forces were moving toward the Saudi-Kuwaiti border? Why did Iraqi forces enter Saudi territory on three occasions beginning on August 3, prompting the Saudis to activate a "hot line" to Iraq's army?[33] Iraq explained the incursions as mistakes, but in the first three weeks of the crisis U.S. forces could have been overrun by the Iraqi military on the way to Riyadh. Such a prospect weighed heavily on the minds of U.S. officials. Even if Iraq had no intention of invading Saudi Arabia, the United States had to act under conditions of incomplete information and uncertainty regarding its motives. That meant that it had to consider and prepare for the scenario of an Iraqi invasion of Saudi Arabia. That the United States had to act under global conditions of anarchy where self-help was a *sine qua non* for protecting vital interests further added to its propensity to assume that Iraq had ambitions beyond Kuwait. It could not count on international institutions, policing forces, or laws to stop Iraq.

After obtaining Saudi agreement for U.S. access, President Bush began to inform the public of the U.S. approach. In an August 8 national address, the president asserted that U.S. goals included the unconditional withdrawal of all Iraqi forces from Kuwait, the removal of a puppet regime put in place by Iraq and the restoration of Kuwait's legitimate government, the longstanding and historical role of ensuring regional stability, and the protection of the lives of Americans abroad.[34] Throughout the crisis, the dominant U.S. national concern would be the threat that the invasion posed to global, and in turn, U.S. economic interests through the "potential domination of the energy resources that are crucial to the entire world."[35] This U.S. concern was reflected in the motivations of Bush as well as other key officials. For Scowcroft, two fundamental things motivated U.S. behavior: "our key interests in the Persian Gulf which required that under no circumstances could Saddam get control of oil, and on top of that the horror of what Saddam was doing in Kuwait."[36]

In retrospect, the less hawkish Secretary Baker agreed, arguing that the fundamental reason that the United States fought the war was that secure access to Persian Gulf oil had been a national interest of the United States "all the way back to Roosevelt."[37] Baker, indeed, argued at the United Nations on November 29 in the effort to secure U.N. support for the U.S.-led use of force, that "Saddam's actions, the vast arms he possesses, the weapons of mass destruction he seeks, indicate clearly that Kuwait was not only not the first but probably not the last target on his list."[38]

Fashioning a New Era

Within the context of a RAM explanation, the United States was most concerned about domination of global energy supplies, but, even in terms of strategic and international-level motivations, the crisis was about more than oil. The ending of the Cold War made it possible to talk of a new world order—a cerebral and vague notion that developed in bits and pieces. Although it was never clearly enunciated, and while it certainly served political goals, it essentially referred to an era in which the aggressive use of force was unacceptable, in which it would be rejected through collective security, and in which great power cooperation was possible and necessary.[39]

While Moscow had longstanding relations with Iraq, and was very reluctant to see it attacked by the United States and its allies, it was more interested in good relations with the United States than in playing its Baghdad card.[40] It needed Western technology and economic support to transform its economy away from communism and toward hybrid capitalism, and it needed U.S. political support to integrate itself into the western-dominated world economy. This consideration, and Iraq's blatant aggression against Kuwait, helped Washington gain the support it needed from the U.S.S.R. in the U.N. Security Council, where it had veto power, and hence could have, along with France and China, more strongly pushed a resolution seeking compromise with Iraq and undermining U.S. interests. Had Iraq invaded Kuwait during the Cold War when it was one of the U.S.S.R.'s regional allies, and when the superpowers were stuck in global rivalry, the costs to the United States of taking a strong stance against Iraq would have been far higher. The U.S.S.R. could not have turned its back on a country with which it signed a Treaty of Friendship and Cooperation in 1972, thus the act would have pitted the superpowers against each other. Even under the positive circumstances that developed with the end of the Cold War, the United States still repeatedly had to use the strategy of first bringing in France and Britain on U.N. resolutions against Iraq, and then slowly bringing Russia in, and then finally China, which would not want to be the sole detractor.[41]

While expectations of a better world arose before the Persian Gulf crisis, the crisis allowed the new world order concept to be developed and executed. Prior to it, the notion of a new era was in the air, but it was ambiguous, nascent, and divorced from a broader vision of a new world order.[42] Moreover, in 1989, Bush spoke positively about Moscow's "new thinking," but his main concern was that it now had "an obligation and an opportunity" to demonstrate it.[43] While the superpowers had already begun to engage in productive dialogue on a series of issues ranging from resolving regional conflicts to economic reform, the Persian Gulf crisis offered Moscow the opportunity to demonstrate that it could cooperate with the United States on a crucial global question, against a former ally and still-important state.[44]

Prior to the crisis, moreover, the United States had not assumed a *bona fide* leadership role in attempting to fashion elements of a new world order. It understood and asserted that American leadership in the world had become crucial, but such assertions had a rhetorical ring, partly because America was widely viewed as in decline at the time, and many observers, in fact, were calling for a U.S. policy of isolationism. The Persian Gulf crisis allowed Washington to transform feelings about a new era into a more palpable vision and approach, while simultaneously advancing its national interests and asserting its global primacy at a time that it was viewed, in some quarters, as in decline, as a country that might be eclipsed by a rising Germany and Japan.

The concept of a new world order began a slow evolution during the Persian Gulf crisis and was tested in the Persian Gulf War. Bush first broached it in an August 8 address to the nation in which he spoke of a "new era" that would be full of promise if aggression could be successfully checked. Thereafter, he invoked it at several critical junctures, after discussing it more fully for the first time with Brent Scowcroft in late August. For instance, on September 9, Bush told Gorbachev in Finland that he thought there was "an opportunity to have develop out of this tragedy a new world order. But the bottom line . . . must be that Saddam Hussein cannot be allowed to profit from his aggression."[45] Balancing vitriol against Iraq with hopeful visions of a future world, Bush officially asserted later on September 11, 1990, that the United States had a "fifth objective" in the Persian Gulf crisis, that of producing a new world order that "one hundred generations have searched for" in vain but have not achieved.[46]

The United States was concerned that Iraq's invasion, if successful, would set "all the wrong standards for the post–Cold War world by suggesting to regional dictators that naked aggression pays and by hurting U.S. credibility at a critical juncture in history, if it did not take strong action."[47] Other dictators would get the idea that it was open season. That would wreak havoc on the global political and economic system that the United States was seeking to stabilize, and place stress on U.S. leadership at a vulnerable transition to the post–Cold War era.[48] Thus, Iraq had to be controlled and punished.

While the United States was serious about the new world order concept, some in the media interpreted it to mean that Washington would turn over influence to the United Nations.[49] In fact, it is fair to say that the United States preferred to realize its national interests fully, even if that meant dispensing with a larger U.N. and multilateral role, but preferred the latter route if it could meet U.S. interests. It is unclear how much U.S. sovereignty Washington was willing to forego to achieve a collective approach to the invasion, but it managed to avoid a serious tradeoff between the two.

Giving Iraq Chances: Slow Escalation

While a RAM-oriented perspective emphasizes perceived national interests as central motivating factors, it also emphasizes that the actor will carefully consider alternatives prior to choosing among them. We can note that the United States did not bomb Iraq until five months after the invasion. In the meantime, numerous approaches appeared to be attempted to end the crisis without war, albeit within a charged atmosphere of U.S.-Iraqi recriminations, whose impact on decisions and the broader crisis deserves further consideration in later chapters. However, the fact that the United States waited many months to go to war and appeared to try different avenues to avoid it suggests that we could explain its overall approach as one that at least at some level was reasoned and measured.

The Arab Formula

In the wake of Iraq's invasion, Arab leaders, shuttling back and forth between capitals, attempted to resolve the crisis.[50] On August 2, Jordan's King Hussein flew to Egypt to meet President Mubarak. Together, they sought to produce a formula that would allow Iraq a dignified withdrawal, to pressure Bush into giving an Arab solution time to work, and to arrange for a mini–Arab summit at Jeddah, Saudi Arabia, which Saddam could attend. Although Iraq accepted the invitation in theory, it rejected Egypt's precondition that Iraq must first withdraw and restore Kuwait's royal family. On August 8, 1990, while Iraq was in the process of annexing Kuwait officially and making it the nineteenth province of Iraq, President Bush talked tough to the nation about a mad dictator in the Persian Gulf. Meanwhile, the Arab plan ran into problems — as well as Iraq's intransigence.

The Arab League was divided over the invasion. Led by Egypt, it met in an emergency summit in Cairo on August 10. It condemned the invasion, and twelve of the twenty-one states attending the Cairo summit voted in favor of a joint Egyptian-Gulf Cooperation Council resolution.[51] Resolution 195 condemned the invasion and endorsed U.N. Security Council Resolutions 660, 661, and 662, which called for the immediate and unconditional Iraqi withdrawal from Kuwait, for the imposition of economic sanctions on Iraq, and for the annexation of Kuwait to be considered null and void, respectively.[52] Iraq, Libya, and the PLO opposed the resolution, Algeria and Yemen abstained, and Jordan, Mauritania, and Sudan expressed reservations. While the vote was not exactly overwhelming, it did provide some support and legitimacy to the Saudis' decision to invite U.S.-led forces onto their soil, and allowed for individual Arab states to join Desert Storm. In response to the Cairo summit and to the U.N. Security Council resolutions, Iraq offered on August 12 to link its withdrawal from Kuwait to Syria's withdrawal from Lebanon and to Israel's immediate and unconditional withdrawal from the occupied territories of the West Bank, the Gaza Strip, East Jerusalem and the Golan Heights. Israel had captured the territories in the 1967 Six Day War, when, in an act that the United Nations considered to be self-defense, it launched a preemptive military strike against Syria, Egypt, and Jordan, which declined Israeli requests to stay out of the war.[53] Iraq attached so many conditions to its withdrawal proposal that it led many Arab leaders to believe that it wanted to occupy Kuwait permanently.[54]

In a surprising move, Iraq agreed to make peace with Iran on Iran's terms by pulling out of occupied Iranian territory, returning Iranian prisoners of war, and accepting the midpoint of the Shatt al-Arab waterway as the border between Iran and Iraq. By September 9, Iran and Iraq had agreed to resume diplomatic relations, opening up the potential for some cooperation on issues related to the Persian Gulf crisis. Some Iranian officials even argued to join Iraq against the "Western imperial onslaught" or at least to fight U.S. hegemony, while others saw Iran as "one of the targets of U.S. expedition [*sic*] in the Persian Gulf."[55] Yet while Iran was clearly uncomfortable with the U.S. regional role, it recognized the illegitimacy of Iraq's invasion, supported the U.N. Security Council resolutions against it, and tended to view Iraq as a more serious threat than the United States. At the same time, it repeated its concern that if "infidel forces" were to stay in Islamic territories, they may one day have to be expelled.[56]

In weighing its concerns about U.S. forces in the region, Iran ultimately decided to remain neutral, while tilting slightly in favor of the coalition. Teheran's generally nonhostile position further decreased the potential costs to the United States of taking a strong, and ultimately, military stand against Iraq. Thus, while Iran did express concern that a big victory in what would later be called the Persian Gulf War would make the United States an arrogant regional powerhouse, and while Iran did try to broker a peace deal to avoid war, Washington did not have to be as concerned that Iran would use the crisis to try to undermine U.S. interests and to pave the way for Teheran's resurgence as a major regional power.[57] In fact, by late August, Iran appeared to give Washington implicit approval to strike Iraq, provided that U.S. forces leave the region quickly thereafter — a recurring theme in Iran's foreign policy, one tied to Iran's post-revolutionary position that regional security should be left to regional states and not to "arrogant" hegemons.[58]

While Iraq was increasingly facing international and regional isolation, it did have some regional supporters that the United States had to consider. Over time, King Hussein, the diplomatic interlocutor, as well as Yemen, Libya, and the Palestinians, among others, would side with Saddam politically, while trying not to disrupt relations with key members of the U.S.-led coalition and while seeking a peaceful conclusion to the crisis.[59] As late as September 1990, Jordan suggested, despite Bush's adamant opposition, that Saddam withdraw in exchange for a promise that all outstanding territorial and other disputes with Kuwait would be discussed thereafter, to Saddam's satisfaction.[60]

Jordan was a quite different case than Syria and Egypt. As a perceived defender of Palestinian rights in some quarters, Saddam was very popular in Jordan, with its predominant Palestinian population. Jordan, moreover, needed Iraq's cheap oil and could not ignore the fact that next-door Iraq could always pose a threat if angered, and yet could also play the role of bulwark against Israel if placated.[61] Jordan could not take for granted the notion that Iraq would never attack it or seek to undermine its security. Leaning toward Iraq, however, did not come without costs. King Hussein alienated the wealthy Persian Gulf Arabs and his longtime friend George Bush, who viewed his actions as surprising and painful.[62]

Taking into consideration the failed Arab diplomatic effort, the United States had further reason to believe that it needed to take a stronger position against Iraq. Moreover, the fact that Iraq had at best weak allies further raised the expected utility of going to war. The United States did not have to consider the possibility of third parties intervening on Iraq's behalf.

Global Diplomatic and Economic Pressure

In an effort to explore various options for pressuring Iraq, Washington also exerted diplomatic pressure through U.N. resolutions and by building a broad coalition. U.S. action at the United Nations was a significant element of its global strategy. Resolution 660 was the first resolution to address the situation, and, with the exception of a Yemeni abstention, unanimously condemned Iraq's invasion and demanded that Iraq "withdraw immediately and unconditionally all of its forces to the position in which they were located on August 1, 1990." Thereafter, economic sanctions were imposed on Iraq (except for humanitarian or medical purposes) under U.N. Resolution 661, adopted on August 6. Meanwhile, the United States was busy creating the anti-Iraq coalition and lobbying for additional U.N. resolutions.

The U.S.-led operation proved to be the best case in the history of U.N. collective security in which many nations joined under U.N. auspices and in line with international law against an aggressor, but it was hardly a pure case. Contrary to popular conceptions, the overall political approach was a classic case of coercive diplomacy. Washington led and said, "Do you want to be with us?"[63] Thus, prior to the vote on November 29, Secretary Baker went to many states to argue the U.S. position as well as to coerce cooperation, and he also engaged in such diplomacy at the United Nations.[64]

The coalition was made up of strange bedfellows across the political spectrum. But it was not, as Baker pointed out from perhaps the most authoritative position, "multilateralism as widely believed," but rather a U.S. operation that received financial support from states as powerful as Japan and Germany and as small and unlikely as Malaysia.[65] Nonetheless, other allies such as Britain did play vital military roles, and on the political side, the United States did want the appearance of multilateralism. Such an approach had the benefit of placating European states that might otherwise view the international effort as a "lone ranger operation," and, by including Arab states such as Syria, also of providing political cover in the Arab world.[66]

The United States and the Saudis put much effort into securing and maintaining Syria's participation, as well as that of Egypt.[67] As a state on the U.S. list of countries engaged in state-sponsored terrorism, and as an Arab world leader and stalwart against Israel in every major war, Syria boasted superb anti-Western credentials. It added Arab legitimacy to the coalition. While Syria refused to participate in the war itself, joining the U.S.-led coalition could bring it economic benefits from the GCC states and better standing with the West, help it undermine its longtime Iraqi rival, and generate Arab support from Riyadh and Cairo to press Israel to return the Golan Heights.[68] With eyes fixed on Iraq, with Iraq not focused on Lebanon, and with the West in need of Syria's support, it also used the opportunity to invade the Christian enclave in Lebanon, thus consolidating its power there.

Egypt, like Syria, preferred an Arab solution to the problem, including possible concessions to Iraq, but unlike Syria it was far more inclined to support force as a last-resort option.[69] Iraq had promised Egypt that it would not invade Kuwait.[70] Thus, the invasion contained a particular threat, leading Egypt to assert that Iraq could also strike Saudi Arabia and must be stopped lest it gain the power to "impose its will" on the region.[71] That Egypt benefited from massive U.S. assistance added to its interest in playing a key role, as did its ambitions in the broader Middle East and a proclivity, like that of Syria, to want to balance Iraqi power. Indirect support from long-term and temporary allies increased the U.S. inclination to stand steadfast against Iraq, and ultimately, enhanced the expected utility of going to war.

Drawing the Line in the Sand

On August 2 Iraq installed a provisional government of nine handpicked military officers whose origin was unclear, to replace the ruling royal family. Although Iraq failed to seize the emir and other members of the royal family who had fled to Saudi Arabia, it nonetheless was quickly trying to make its invasion a *fait accompli*. The United States refused to tolerate this political maneuver. Upon his return on August 5 from a decision-making meeting at Camp David over the weekend, Bush learned that Arab diplomacy was failing in getting Iraq out of Kuwait and that Iraq was bolstering its position. Turning to reporters near his helicopter, a visibly angered Bush stated in no uncertain terms that Iraq's aggression "will not stand." The president's "line in the sand" statement was critical because it sent a strong message of U.S. resolve and asserted that in addition to protecting Saudi Arabia, the United States would seek to evict Iraq from Kuwait, despite the fact that the administration had not yet even secured Saudi Arabia's acceptance to allow U.S. troops to enter the kingdom. The president's line could be explained in different ways, but under the RAM perspective it could reasonably be viewed as a deliberate attempt by the United States to signal a U.S. commitment to reverse the invasion, to convince the Saudis and others of U.S. resolve, and to deter others from floating proposals to appease Iraq. Bush's statement clearly elevated the longstanding, evolving U.S. commitment to Persian Gulf stability. Washington would commit force not just to deter outside threats to the Persian Gulf as outlined in the Carter Doctrine or to protect Saudi Arabia as laid out in the Reagan Doctrine, but also to reverse regional aggression.

After King Fahd gave the nod and Bush asserted that the invasion would not stand, the 82nd Airborne Division was on its way, along with the first fighter squadrons. Desert Shield would become one of history's largest military deployments. The U.S.-led alliance of twenty-eight members grew to thirty-seven by war's end and included more than half a million soldiers with a 10,000-soldier brigade from the Arab Persian Gulf states, 7,000 Kuwaiti soldiers, and 15,000 Syrian troops who only fought on Kuwaiti soil. On the European side, the British sent 43,000 troops and significant military equipment, while France sent 16,000 soldiers. Japan, Kuwait, Saudi Arabia, and Germany helped foot the bill for the war, while the United States bore most of the burden in actual fighting. By late October, U.S. forces numbered more than 240,000 army personnel and about 1,600 sophisticated combat aircraft. By January 1991, an incredible half of all U.S. combat forces worldwide would be deployed to the Persian Gulf.

Time Running Out: Rethinking Economic Sanctions

The United States appeared content for at least six weeks with squeezing Iraq economically and isolating it politically. But that began to change in mid-September. The U.S. position was that if sanctions could work, it would be in an "unacceptable time frame."[72] In explaining the American position on January 21, Bush asserted that sanctions, "though having some effect, showed no signs of accomplishing their objective . . . and we and our allies concluded that sanctions alone would not force Saddam from Kuwait."[73] Several factors, discussed in the following sections of this chapter, underscored these time constraints, and added to the perceived costs of allowing diplomatic and economic sanctions to run longer. Under a RAM explanation, we would expect that if changes in the context of decision increase the perceived costs of a certain alternative and decrease its perceived benefits compared to others, the actor will be less likely to pursue that alternative.

A Disappearing Kuwait and a Vulnerable Coalition

From the U.S. perspective, there was a race between the sanctions and the dismantling of Kuwait. While recognizing that sanctions do need time to work, the "systematic destruction" of Kuwait was shortening the time that the United States could wait.[74] That issue started to become especially prominent in mid-October, and certainly by November, the president viewed it as quite serious.[75] Kuwaiti lobbying in Washington was aimed at heightening such concerns and making them a national priority.[76]

Beyond the issue of Kuwait's plight, the United States as well as the Saudis were concerned throughout the crisis that the U.S.-led coalition could unravel, which meant that Washington could not "dilly-dally."[77] Iraq, for its part, did all it could to split the Arab members from the coalition. Iraq invoked Islam, employed Islamic themes, and drew on popularized battles and figures in the history of Islam to try to generate support in the Muslim world against the West.[78] Throughout the war, Iraq referred to the conflict as a jihad, or holy war, to emphasize Islamic themes — a clear manipulation of Islam.[79]

Moreover, Iraq sought to create the perception of secret U.S.-Israeli military cooperation in the Persian Gulf crisis, repeatedly floating stories of Israeli drone airplanes and spies at work.[80] More importantly, Iraq attacked Israel with Scud missiles, with the presumed intention of drawing it into the war and placing Arab states in the U.S.-led coalition in the awkward position of fighting, at least in theory, on Israel's side. However, Israel refused to take that bait and pursued a strategy of restraint, partly as the result of U.S. pressure.[81] Iraq's best chance to play the Israeli card would come on October 8. Facing an uprising in which Arabs were throwing stones at Jewish worshippers praying at the Western Wall just below the Temple Mount in Jerusalem, Israeli security forces, in the ensuing conflict, killed twenty-two Palestinians.[82] Iraq immediately sought to whip up anti-American sentiment, to incite "the Arab Street," and in turn to put pressure on Arab governments in the U.S.-led coalition, all of which factored such opinion in their foreign policy decisions.[83] The incident elevated concern about the coalition's fragility and contributed to the U.S. interest in giving Iraq an ultimatum to withdraw or face war.[84]

Iraq also tried to enlist the support of the Soviet Union and France, which at times championed a face-saving withdrawal for Baghdad. While Iraq appeared to be surprised that Moscow would cooperate with Washington against Baghdad and that it did not take a more pro-Iraqi role, the potential always existed during the crisis that pressures from various quarters could mount on Washington to give Saddam an incentive or two, or risk losing members of the coalition.[85] In fact, from start to finish, the Soviet Union and France, as British Prime Minister Margaret Thatcher put it, tended to be "suspicious of American-led ventures," and vice versa.[86] While they opposed the invasion, they were far more inclined than Washington to compromise and to believe that war could be avoided. As mentioned earlier in the book, they had developed ties to Iraq as its two best arms suppliers. France and the U.S.S.R. tried to win Saddam a face-saving withdrawal from Kuwait virtually until the bombs started falling on Baghdad. That would have given them influence and avoided a war that would undermine Iraq's ability to pay them billions of dollars for arms. Only Britain, in fact, was as hawkish and steadfast on securing Iraq's total and unconditional withdrawal from Kuwait as was the United States. Many members of the coalition were concerned about "incurring significant costs by adhering to sanctions and many may be inclined to ease" their stance, "especially if it appeared that the coalition was beginning to fray."[87]

Another major U.S. concern was that Iraq would engage in a partial withdrawal, remain in control of key sites in Kuwait such as the Rumaila oil field, split the coalition (which would no longer agree on going to war), and return at a later date to reconquer Kuwait.[88] This was such a serious concern that the president instructed decision makers to prepare contingency plans. The analysis revealed that the amount of U.S. force that would have had to stay in the Persian Gulf to deter Iraq would have been "enormous" and very costly.[89] Such analysis of the potential countermoves by Iraq and their implications for the United States further raised the positive expected utility of war.[90]

Nuclear, Biological, and Chemical Weapons

Time constraints were also reflected in another manner. At the White House, a flurry of cables and reports on Iraq's nuclear potential were passed around, starting with about five from September 17 to 28.[91] In mid-September, in the first public statement of its kind, CIA Director William Webster asserted, in a little-noticed speech, that Iraq had "a sizable stockpile of chemical and biological weapons."[92] Congressman Les Aspin later publicized Iraq's capability more openly, triggering a media frenzy on the subject. The nuclear threat, although exaggerated, could not be underestimated, especially given that hundreds of thousands of

American troops were in the area, and that the United States lacked an "intrusive enough process" to check and stop Iraq's weapons program.[93] The American position was essentially that "each day that passes brings Saddam Hussein further on the path to developing biological and nuclear weapons, and the missiles to deliver them. If Saddam corners the world energy market, he can then finance further aggression, terror and blackmail."[94]

While an unfettered Iraq could grow much more threatening, it would have been quite difficult for any actor to corner the world energy market. That was especially true given that Saudi Arabia had shown a proclivity to put more oil on the market to replace that lost from Iraq. Nonetheless, as a rational actor, the United States had to consider the future costs and benefits of its behavior, and allowing an oil-rich, nuclear-armed Iraq to develop posed a major potential future cost of not seeking to cut Iraq down to size.

Fledgling Democracies

In the process of threatening U.S. and global oil interests, the Iraqi invasion was also perceived as affecting basic American interests, such as the stability of democracies and developing nations. This theme was repeated numerous times officially. Global interdependence meant that higher oil prices and recession in major countries would hurt smaller ones as well. Events and issue areas that in earlier periods could be separated were now much more connected. By threatening the jugular vein of the world economy, Iraq produced far-ranging consequences that it could not have anticipated and far-ranging effects that motivated a sharp response to the invasion. Had the invasion taken place in earlier centuries, the global consensus may well have been far less pronounced and significant.

Ramadan and Strategic Planning

The United States, furthermore, weighed time dimensions. In October 1990, U.S. Ambassador to Saudi Arabia Chas Freeman sent Scowcroft, Cheney, and Baker a series of telegrams arguing that the United States had to make a decision on Desert Storm because "we were running up against the Islamic Holy month of Ramadan and increasingly bad weather."[95] During Ramadan, Muslims abstain from food, drink, sex, and lustful thoughts from sunrise to sunset, and instead celebrate through various social and spiritual activities. The holiday comes in the ninth month of the Islamic calendar.

The first problematic date fell on the 27th of Rajab, which corresponded with the beginning of February. This date celebrated the raising of the prophet Muhammad to heaven. Another sensitive date came one month later, when Muslims engaged in atonement and forgiveness. March, for sure, would be fully encumbered by Ramadan. On the whole, from the U.S. perspective, that made an attack on Iraq difficult as March approached. While the Arab allies, perhaps remembering the 1973 Yom Kippur War, said that the coalition could fight during Ramadan, Washington preferred to avoid any religious or political problems that might arise.[96] At a minimum, those in the Muslim world who did not appreciate the Western presence in the region would have had even more ammunition for generating anti-American sentiment.

Wishful Sanctions and an Unyielding Iraq

To be sure, Iraq's dependence on oil, and international unity against Baghdad, increased the possibility that sanctions could work and that Iraq could be cut off economically. However, at the same time, Iraq achieved a bumper agricultural harvest in 1990, four times as large as its 1989 harvest, and was expected to have similar success in 1991, and Iraq's austerity measures reduced consumption. Meanwhile, it asserted in October and sporadically thereafter that it had enough oil to meet its requirements, despite the embargo, and was engaging in other efforts to break the blockade, which it expected to be unsuccessful.[97] In fact, Washington was concerned about too much "leakage" across borders with Jordan, Turkey, and even Iran.[98]

Over time, the United States doubted that sanctions could work at all.[99] The historical success of sanctions in meeting critical political objectives was, at best, mixed. Totalitarian states, moreover, could husband resources to protect the government, and while sanctions might degrade Iraq's air force, Saddam never relied on it much against Iran anyway.[100] Webster reflected the broader U.S. position on January 10 in a letter to Les Aspin. As he put it, even if sanctions could be enforced for six to twelve more months, "economic hardship alone is unlikely to compel Saddam to retreat from Kuwait or cause regime-threatening popular discontent in Iraq." Rather, Saddam probably "continues to believe that Iraq can endure sanctions longer than the international coalition will hold and hopes that avoiding war will buy him time to negotiate a settlement more favorable to him."[101] In a January 16 letter to Congress, the day Desert Storm was launched, the president summed up the U.S. stand on prospects for generating

Iraq's peaceful withdrawal from Kuwait. The United States had used all appropriate diplomatic and other peaceful means and these efforts "have not been and would not be successful in obtaining such compliance."[102] We could say from the RAM perspective that with the chief instrument of economic sanctions in doubt, the costs of waiting for sanctions to work increased significantly.

Raising the Stakes

By November, time was running out and Iraq was not budging an inch, at least not on U.S. terms. Thus, Washington decided to take the next step. Desert Shield was not enough to give U.S.-led forces an offensive option against Iraqi forces in Kuwait. On November 8, the United States announced plans to deploy up to 200,000 additional troops to the Persian Gulf.

The United States tried diplomacy, albeit with a heavy and resolute hand, as did its allies. It also tried coalition building, economic sanctions, and threats of force. But Iraq remained in Kuwait. The Arab League, the Islamic Conference Organization, the United Nations, the French, the Soviets, and individual Arab states all made major efforts to persuade Iraq to withdraw from Kuwait — to no avail. That not only hardened American resolve but also that of Arab states such as Saudi Arabia.[103] In one last effort in which Iraq acquiesced, the two sides did meet in Geneva, Switzerland, on January 9, 1991.

In Geneva, the United States argued that Iraq would have to withdraw unconditionally to avoid war. In a letter sent to Congress on January 8, 1991, seeking support for a war resolution, the president said that peace on Iraq's terms would only feed Saddam's "appetite for conquest" and would be "paid many times over in greater sacrifice and suffering."[104] While Washington insisted on unconditional Iraqi withdrawal, Iraq presented a list of demands, including Israel's withdrawal from territories captured in the 1967 Six Day War and Syria's withdrawal from Lebanon, that were viewed as unacceptable by the United States. As Baker recalls, Gorbachev believed that he had worked something out with Saddam for his withdrawal, but we kept saying "No, you are continually suggesting approaches which do not require an unconditional withdrawal."[105] In fact, Baker worked under the assumption that Washington's hands were tied: "We could not — having gone into the Security Council and obtained Security Council resolutions — then ourselves negotiate down from those resolutions. That was just never a possibility."[106] Once the resolutions requiring unconditional withdrawal were in place, the crisis trajectory appeared, pending withdrawal by Iraq.

The Geneva meeting ultimately proved fruitless. In a *Voice of America* broadcast to the Iraqi people, the president would later say that the "Iraqi position was one of complete intransigence and miscalculation of world opinion and determination."[107] While the U.S. position was at least equally intransigent, Iraq was its own worst enemy. It painted itself as a long-range, unmitigated threat whose potential to cause harm would only increase. That enticed the United States to go to war while all the ducks were lined up — the coalition, Congress, the United Nations, world opinion, U.S. firepower, and the Saudis. Moreover, even though at times Iraq appeared more pliable, it had failed to be more compliant earlier in the crisis. On August 6, a few days after the invasion, Saddam met with U.S. chargé d'affaires Joseph Wilson in Baghdad. Wearing his gun and holster, Saddam sought to intimidate Wilson and to make him as "uneasy as possible."[108] In a long lecture, he asserted that Iraq would never capitulate, despite his recognition that the United States was a superpower that would hurt Iraq, and that the Al Sabah royal family of Kuwait was history.[109]

The failure of diplomacy in Geneva did help convince many skeptics in the United States and around the world that war was either necessary or inevitable. Three days after the Geneva meeting, the U.S. Senate authorized the president to wage war against Iraq, and the president asserted, as he had before, that the administration had been slow to "raise our hand in anger and eager to explore every peaceful means of settling our disputes. But when we have exhausted every alternative, when conflict is thrust upon us, there is no nation on Earth with greater resolve or stronger steadiness of purpose."[110]

Trying to Weigh Costs and Benefits

As the story line so far may suggest, the RAM perspective places great emphasis on careful, calculated decisions based on the exploration of alternative courses of action. At a broad level, we would explain, without opening the black box of decision-making much, that the administration made key decisions after attempting to weigh the costs and benefits of different options, under conditions of imperfect information, uncertainty about Iraq's motives and the broader strategic setting, and consideration of the future implications of its behavior. By October, the United States believed that Iraq could pose a far greater threat years down the road, if it were allowed to become much stronger.[111] While the costs of not going to war were viewed as high, a perception also developed that the costs of war would be low.

On January 16, the president explained to the nation why the United States had resorted to war. He noted that waiting for Iraq to withdraw was costly to the coalition, to burgeoning democracies, and to the Kuwaiti people, who were being pillaged unspeakably.[112] Added to these costs, the United States, as noted earlier, considered the great expense and problems inherent in keeping such a large army in the Persian Gulf. Moreover, it considered the costs to future leaders and peoples, if Iraq were not checked.

The United States was concerned about potential American casualties, but over time it became more convinced that the military mismatch would result in a short war with few casualties.[113] Washington also knew that it had a mandate from the United Nations and the U.S. Congress to use force, as well as support from a large coalition. While it planned to attack Iraq even without a majority vote in the Congress, and believed that it had the right to do so even without a final U.N. vote, the operation would have been more complicated and costly without such support.[114] Support from the Soviet Union, which even included information about its military cooperation with Iraq, also removed a large stumbling block and meant that regional conflict would be, for the first time in decades, decoupled from global rivalry.[115] That further decreased the perceived third-party costs attendant in using force against Iraq, thus enhancing the positive expected utility of war as compared to other options.[116]

An Unstable Strategic Interaction

We can now see that the United States had significant interests at stake, which it perceived as being threatened, and also had an increasingly positive expected utility for war. That is really no more than saying that the expected benefits less the costs were greater than the expected utility of nonwar. But that still raises two key, related questions about the crisis, even from within the RAM perspective. We can only answer these questions effectively if we move from the decision-theoretic aspect of the RAM model that focuses on a single actor's decision-making process to the game-theoretic aspect of the model. This aspect underscores strategic interaction between two actors whose fates were linked.

The first question is why Iraq did not back down, thus depriving the United States of the chance to cut it down to size. A number of explanations can be offered, but the most simple RAM explanation is that Iraq also had a positive expected utility for war.[117] If we set aside the characteristics of its leader, we can still reconstruct a three-tiered RAM explanation for such an argument.

The first explanation is that Iraq feared that if it withdrew, the United States would still threaten its interests. It could harass it with a policy of containment and periodic attacks, or outright decide to create a pretext for marching on Baghdad and destroying the regime. Some strong evidence, presented later in the book, certainly supports this interpretation.

Second, while Iraq was concerned that it would be vulnerable if the United States launched Operation Desert Storm, it could not be sure that the United States would actually attack if Iraq stood its ground in defensive positions in Kuwait. Iraq could not have picked its best strategy, if we assume that its behavior was rational, without assessing what the United States was likely to do. Iraq had to assess which type of behavior would lead to a maximizing outcome. If we assume that Iraq attempted to maximize, it must have considered what the United States would do if Iraq were to withdraw. And since Iraq could not have known U.S. intentions, it presumed the United States might attack, even if Iraq withdrew unconditionally, and wanted to avoid being the actor who cooperated, while the other side cheated on any agreement governing its withdrawal from Kuwait.

Third, we could argue that Iraq determined that even if it presumed incorrectly, the United States might back down once Iraq imposed severe casualties on U.S. troops. It could emerge from the war scathed but politically victorious. Iraq, in fact, did portray itself as able to take massive casualties, but was hamstrung by incomplete information about the U.S. proclivity to fight, and simply guessed wrong about U.S. intentions, thus precipitating war.[118]

These three explanations fit with the RAM perspective, but we still need to address the second question: why did Iraq and the United States not prefer an alternative other than war? Indeed, as James Fearon notes, a "coherent rationalist explanation for war must do more than give reasons why armed conflict might appear an attractive option to a rational leader under some circumstances — it must show why states are unable to locate an alternative outcome that both would prefer to a fight."[119] Positive expected utility by itself does not supply a sufficiently coherent or compelling explanation for war.[120] While we can reconstruct the reasons that Iraq and the United States had for going to war, the question of why they could not strike a negotiated deal of sorts that they preferred to war remains. Rationalist accounts would assume that Iraq and the United States would have preferred a negotiated outcome that achieves the same outcome as war without the human and other costs.

In fact, a central thrust of this chapter is that the United States increasingly preferred war, while Iraq became increasingly amenable to a negotiated outcome, albeit not amenable enough from Washington's perspective. The trajectories of their preferences never crossed; in fact they tended to move in opposite directions. If there was ever any chance that both parties would at the same time have preferred a negotiated settlement to the vagaries of war, it either was evanescent or nonexistent. In this sense, they did not have a bargaining problem *per se*, where two or more parties prefer outcomes or agreements to nonagreement, but disagree on which agreement is best.[121] Rather, in theoretical terms, we could say that the *de facto* bargaining range within which agreement could arise between the actors was too limited, if it existed at all, to avoid war.[122] The "win set" — in other words, the number of options acceptable to both sides short of war — was very narrow. If anything, it became even more so over time, thus making agreement highly improbable and war quite likely.

As the book proceeds, we will also explain why this *de facto* bargaining range was so limited, eventually closing down altogether, by importing explanations from the other perspectives. But it is worth offering one key RAM-oriented explanation here. As the two actors examined their options, they had to determine not only if any agreement was possible, but also whether, if any agreement were struck, it would be honored and enforced. Under conditions of quasi-anarchy, and in the absence of trust among the actors, that was very difficult to expect. Both sides expected that the other side would defect from any agreement, which made both less likely to take actions to locate, identify, and bargain over such an agreement in the first place — much less agree to it.

We can draw on a basic game in game theory — the Prisoner's Dilemma (PD) — to explain why states may be unable to settle on an efficient bargained outcome. In a simple version of this game, two prisoners are suspected of a significant crime. The police, however, have enough evidence to convict on only a minor charge. If neither prisoner squeals on the other, both will draw a light sentence on the minor charge. If one prisoner squeals but the other does not, the squealer will go free and the "sucker" will draw a heavy sentence. If both squeal, they will both draw a moderate sentence in between these extremes. The best for each individual is to squeal on the other and to obtain freedom. The second-best outcome is for both to stay silent and spend minimal time in jail. A worse outcome is for both to squeal, landing them both in prison for a longer time. Worse yet, is to stay silent while the other squeals.

While the best outcome for both actors taken together is to cooperate and not to squeal, the best independent strategy is to cheat. The temptation to cheat and the fear of being the sucker drive both actors to a strategy of cheating, thus leaving them both worse off than if they had cooperated. In this strategic interaction, the crux of the game is that if both actors independently seek their best outcome, they both get a poor outcome. This holds especially if the prisoners expect to play the game just once and do not have to factor the future into their expectations. We can see such a dynamic at play in many different areas of world affairs where actors may make agreements, which they can then honor or violate.

In the Persian Gulf War case, we can say that Iraq feared being the sucker by agreeing to withdraw from Kuwait, in conjunction with an agreement to end the crisis, only to be attacked or continually harassed for its trouble. From Iraq's perspective, being the sucker could have meant elimination (of the regime), thus making strategies of cooperation infeasible. Fear of such an outcome made it less willing, though not entirely unwilling, to try to generate a negotiated outcome. Under this argument, we can say that states are less likely to expend significant energies to generate an outcome that they may prefer if that outcome is highly unlikely to transpire or poses risks than they are to generate an outcome that they may prefer if doing so poses less risk and has a greater probability of success.

In the U.S. case, being the sucker meant agreeing to allow Iraq to withdraw, in order to bring the crisis to an end, only to see Iraq invade Kuwait again some time down the road, after the bulk of U.S. troops were withdrawn from the region. The high risk of that potential outcome made Washington far more inclined to push a very tough bargain on Iraq, which narrowed the *de facto* bargaining range in the first place. The fact that no superior authority could enforce a potential agreement in a world of quasi-anarchy further heightened the expectations of both actors that the other might be left the unenviable fate of being cheated on as the sucker, for it did not have to factor into its calculations the probability that a higher authority would impose serious costs for defection, and that the other side, knowing that, might be deterred.[123] Under these conditions, anarchy mattered because mistrust made it hard to reach agreement in the first place, but also because both actors must have anticipated that the other would have reasons to renege on any agreement.

The PD can take on many variants. Cooperation can be increased if the PD game is played repeatedly or is expected by the players to display such an iterated characteristic — referred to as iterated PD. But neither Iraq nor the United States could have expected an iterative form of interaction, under the plausible scenarios that they must have considered. Quite the contrary, they faced either a major war if Iraq did not withdraw or serious ongoing tensions in the event that it did so, notwithstanding the fall of Iraq's regime (thus changing the game anyhow). Indeed, the shadow of the future was quite short for both states in that they did not see interaction extending into the future. Thus, they could not have expected present cooperation to be reciprocated with future cooperation by the adversary or present defection to be reciprocated with future defection by the adversary. Since they could largely discount any future benefits from cooperation or future costs from defection, given that their interaction was not iterated, the perceived payoffs of defection increased. And, moreover, we could surmise that they both recognized that the other side faced a similar dynamic, thus further making cooperation harder to achieve. If the other side was inclined to cheat, that raised the probability of being the sucker — an outcome that any rational actor would view most unfavorably and try to avoid.

In essence, then, expectations of being in a PD dynamic made Iraq and the United States less likely even to consider a bargain or an effort to generate an agreement that would avoid war. While that argument is empirical, it also offers a different angle on theory. More specifically, James Fearon rightly claims that we need to distinguish the stage of bargaining among actors from that where PD dynamics may be at play.[124] Bargaining, he asserts, determines whether an agreement will be reached in the first place. PD can then inform us about whether or not actors are likely to defect from it. Yet the present argument makes a different case. It argues, and seeks to demonstrate in the case of U.S.-Iraqi dynamics, that the proclivity of actors to bargain in the first place will be affected significantly by their expectations of whether they will be in a noniterated PD situation. If they expect defection from an agreement, they will be less inclined to strike a bargain or agreement. In this sense, PD can also help us understand why actors do not reach a bargaining problem in the first place.[125]

Overall, we can say that as the crisis proceeded, the United States considered different outcomes that were likely to result given its actions and Iraq's likely countermoves. In multiplying each outcome's utility by its probability given Iraq's action, by October it saw a hardheaded approach towards Iraq that would generate an outcome of war as the best course of action. Strategic interaction influenced the utility calculations of the United States, underscoring the link between the decision- and game-theoretic components of the RAM. Expectations of Iraq's behavior in strategic interaction with the United States affected the expected utility of war for the United States.

Conclusion

Iraq's invasion of Kuwait was viewed with trepidation not just in the United States, but around the oil-dependent world as well. The invasion threatened longstanding U.S. interests in the Persian Gulf at a time of global change when U.S. leadership was in question. Desert Shield was motivated initially to protect Saudi Arabia from further potential aggression by Iraq, a country that controlled 25% of the world's oil and that Washington was informally committed to protect. Allowing Iraq to gain control or influence over that oil not only raised the specter of global economic instability, but of a more influential Iraq.

While oil concerns drove Operation Desert Shield, an array of additional concerns can help explain why and when the United States went to war. Over time, Washington became concerned that Kuwait was disappearing as a country, that the U.S.-led coalition would unravel, that troop morale would dip, and that the Islamic holy month of Ramadan would decrease the window of opportunity for war. More importantly, it also believed that economic sanctions would fail, and that time would allow Iraq to develop nuclear capability, which would have transformed the entire crisis. The fact that reversing Iraq's aggression would also set a positive precedent for a new world order was added incentive for checking Iraq, although this notion was formally broached in late August and early September, and thus could not explain some of the early decisions that put the United States on the path to war.

The decisions to go to war were made slowly, apparently after alternative options were considered. Washington first tried diplomacy, as did the Arab League. Then, continuing those efforts, it tried economic sanctions and the threat of force. Ultimately, war was perceived to be the best option. The increasing positive expected utility of war, a narrow or nonexistent *de facto* bargaining range, and the overlay of the structural realities of anarchy made it hard to identify an alternative to war that both sides could pursue.

As we can see, the RAM perspective allows us to reconstruct events on the road to war quite convincingly. But it yields little insight into how, to what extent, and in what manner decision makers interpreted the situations that they faced during the crisis, identified the various options discussed in this chapter for dealing with the crisis, and engaged in information search and assessment. It yields insights into how decisions could have been made once alternatives were generated, but it depends on a reconstruction of events rather than a direct foray into the processes by which decisions were actually made. In that sense, for instance, it can only go so far in explaining why the *de facto* bargaining range, as we may call it, either was not open long or never did open. As we open up the black box of decision-making, we will gain greater insight into decision-making.

The RAM also focused our attention on strategic and international motivations, but not on those that we will derive from the other perspectives.

CHAPTER THREE

A Cognitive Compass

Analogies at Work

The rational actor model offers a seductive and useful explanation for how the United States made the decisions that took it to war and why war was not avoided — seductive enough that other explanations may seem unnecessary. Yet, upon closer inspection, we will see how the RAM misses important parts of the picture. For instance, some close friends and advisers described a president that sometimes responded impetuously to Saddam's challenge, thus affecting the trajectory of U.S. behavior and the Persian Gulf crisis.[1] Even Scowcroft at one point had to caution Bush that his emotional rhetoric against Saddam was not helping.[2] What could explain Bush's emotional response within the broader context of decision-making? How can we account for Bush's emphatic rejection of any form of compromise with Saddam, when others pushed it? Why is it that Bush at times was inclined to go to war, ahead of his advisers? A cognitive approach can yield insights that the other perspectives cannot.

Cognitive Approaches to Decision-Making

While the RAM and cognitive perspectives are not mutually exclusive, they do differ in key ways, thus offering a different lens through which to view events.[3] The RAM treats governments as unitary actors in the broader strategic environment. By contrast, the cognitive approach, which consists of myriad sub-theories and hypotheses, opens up the black box of decision-making and tries to get into the minds of the decision makers.[4] In that sense, it focuses much more attention on the individual, albeit in a narrow sense of how cognition affects individual behavior. The two perspectives also differ on rationality. They tend to distinguish between individual and government rationality. The RAM refers to the latter, to the behavior of a state as a whole, rather than to the behavior of particular individuals, or of groups and bureaucracies, for that matter. The cognitive approach focuses on the individual.

Cognitive approaches often assume that decision makers are overtaxed, subject to onerous information-processing demands, faced with unreliable information and uncertainty, and under time pressure. As a result of these constraints, they become cognitive misers.[5] Rather than weighing the costs and benefits of different options, they may consciously or subconsciously use mental shortcuts for quick, easy decisions in which they can feel confident.[6] They seek ways to simplify reality and make it more manageable in their own minds.

Cognitive approaches sometimes posit as a central proposition that individuals — and, by implication, other types of actors — are nonrational. Cognitive shortcuts and heuristics, while different in how they influence decision-making, can include various cognitive limitations or abilities to deal with assessing reality. They can also include motivated biases, which are deviations from rationality that stem not from purely cognitive limitations, but rather from psychological pressures and needs. In addition, they may include such things as personal or organizational biases, subconscious preferences and priorities, *a priori* assumptions and beliefs about how the world works, and systematic or one-time misperceptions. Some of these cognitive shortcuts overlap and reinforce each other in their effects. Many cognitivists believe that drawing on such phenomena explains how the actual process of decision occurs, something the RAM cannot achieve.[7]

Historical Analogies

This chapter focuses on the impact of analogies on decision-making — something which, as Yuen Foong Khong notes, is rarely demonstrated — and on the war outcome in the Persian Gulf crisis.[8] Exploring analogies is a good way to draw on the cognitive approach. Indeed, much of cognitive psychology revolves around schemas, scripts, and analogies, which are different to some extent but are largely treated as similar.[9] It focuses on how decision makers create their own images of reality and simplify decision-making through the use of analogies, a process that we all undertake at one time or another.[10] Indeed, all of us draw lessons from the past to deal with current issues. Sometimes we do it consciously, and at other times we may not even be aware of it, which can make us more confident than we should be about our decisions.[11]

Knowledge structures such as analogies can help human beings process and evaluate information, in part by assisting them in matching new pieces of information against their stored memories.[12] How decision makers frame and understand problems, in turn, is crucial to the decisions they make.[13] As Khong lays it out, analogical reasoning takes this form: event A resembles event B in having characteristic X; A also has characteristic Y; therefore it is inferred that B also has characteristic Y.[14]

The way that analogies work is complex, and there is no broad scholarly agreement on their impact, especially with respect to rationality. Allison and Zelikow treat the schools of cognitive and rational thought within the same family of perspectives. But the literature appears split on this issue. Rational choice theorists often question the value of cognitive approaches, while it is "almost fashionable in cognitive psychology to engage in rational choice bashing."[15] Some rational choice theorists and cognitivists, however, see the two approaches as somewhat complementary and seek to bridge them.[16] Thus, some rational choice theorists have been trying to account for cognitive, constructivist, ideational, and other variables within rational choice models.[17] Meanwhile, some cognitivists prefer to view rational choice and cognitive approaches as fuzzy-set categories that often blur into each other, but which are also distinct in certain ways. For them, rational choice can co-opt cognitive predictions by making assumptions about such things as how decision makers search for information and analyze costs and benefits.[18]

The cognitive/rational debate is an important one, rich in nuance; in the context of that debate, I present the RAM and cognitive approaches as different, but still related and not necessarily at odds.[19] They differ insofar as the RAM includes assumptions, such as the unitary actor and the emphasis on national goals in a strategic environment, that cognitive approaches do not, but also in terms of their proclivities towards rationality. Distinguishing them helps illuminate more clearly how cognitive factors such as biases or emotive responses challenged rational behavior in the Persian Gulf, while not precluding an effort to show how they can also complement each other as explanations of government behavior. I also distinguish the RAM more definitively from other perspectives, such as the cognitive approach, which some observers have criticized Allison and Zelikow for not doing.[20] Naturally, the choice of how to classify models, theories, and perspectives is largely subjective. But the manner by which rationality is defined has profound implications for what we consider rational, as well as for how we categorize and explain decision-making behavior.

Overall, analogies can complement or undermine rational approaches. As Philip Tetlock and Charles McGuire argue, "Reliance on prior beliefs and expectations is not irrational *per se* (one would expect it from a'good Bayesian'; it becomes irrational only when perseverance and denial dominate openness and flexibility)."[21] Analogical thinking can complement rational approaches by help-ing to define the nature of the situation, assess the stakes, provide prescriptions, and evaluate the moral rightness and potential dangers associated with various options.[22] However, such thinking can undermine rational processes if it intro-duces significant biases, excludes or restricts the search for novel information, or pushes actors to ignore the facts and options that clash with the message encoded in the analogy.[23] That can make them less likely and able to consider alternatives.

The Argument of the Chapter

Decision makers were clearly affected by the Munich and Vietnam analogies. For Bush, compromising with Saddam, as many wanted at home and abroad, would have made him a modern-day Neville Chamberlain. As Britain's Prime Minister, he yielded Germany the Sudetenland of Czechoslovakia at the 1938 Munich conference, a borderland area of German speakers that Hitler wanted to reintegrate into Germany. Chamberlain, duped by Hitler, believed that his action at Munich, which followed repeated efforts by Britain to appease Nazi Germany, would bring what he called "peace in our time." In fact, Hitler proceeded to seize Czechoslovakia and to invade Poland, forcing a change in British policy and creating the Munich analogy, which referred to the failure of appeasement in the face of brutal aggression. Through the Munich lens, Bush tended to see Saddam as a Hitler-like dictator who could not be accommodated or even offered a minor, veiled carrot. Many other leaders understood the analogy and shared it as a refer-ence point with Bush. While it affected them independently, Bush also impressed it upon them more deeply, and communicated its implications to the nation and the world through innumerable comparisons to the World War II period.

Under the cognitive perspective, Bush was genuinely affected by the Munich analogy, contrary to what skeptics of the importance of analogies might say.[24] The analogy made Bush more likely to personalize the conflict with Saddam, to undermine others' efforts at compromise with Saddam, and to prefer war to the continued use of economic sanctions. While the Munich analogy shaped U.S. decision-making on the road to war, the Vietnam analogy affected how decision makers prepared for and fought the war. The two analogies worked separately and jointly, in several ways, to shape the U.S. decisions that took the country to war. The Vietnam analogy may have also affected Saddam's perceptions that Washington would shy away from war. In this sense, war was more likely than a negotiated outcome because of inconsistent expectations between the United States and Iraq.

The Ubiquitous Ghosts of Munich: An Analogy with Pedigree

The Munich analogy itself has achieved special status in the pantheon of historical analogies. In order to avoid the horrors of World War I, British and French leaders adopted a more conciliatory policy towards Hitler throughout the 1930s. World War I was viewed as resulting in part from overreaction and rigid diplomacy. The United States, for its part, wanted to avoid any more great wars, as many Americans believed it had been duped into World War I. The result was a series of four neutrality acts from 1935 to 1939 enacted by Congress. Yet, this benign neglect on the part of European and American leaders helped produce one of the most significant historical analogies: Munich. Appeasing Hitler at Munich created an intense memory and cognitive map as to what happens if power goes unchecked. In explaining to Congress why he decided to send troops to Korea, President Truman spoke of the "fateful events of the nineteen-thirties, when aggression unopposed bred more aggression and eventually war," an analogy which played a key role in the U.S. entrance into that conflict, even though it was not invoked as effectively as it could have been.[25] John F. Kennedy, for his part, interpreted the world in terms of the "Munich Syndrome."[26] And for President Lyndon Johnson, "surrender in Vietnam [would not] bring peace, because we learned from Hitler at Munich that success only feeds the appetite of aggression."[27]

The Psychological-Historical Dimension: Being There Counts

For Bush, however, the analogy was especially strong, largely because he experienced World War II firsthand, even though he fought in the Pacific and not in Europe. Indeed, it may have affected him more than he himself knew. As Robert Jervis notes, analogies sometimes "shape our thought in ways which we ourselves do not understand."[28] Marlin Fitzwater, who spent a great deal of time with Bush and who did not particularly like his references to Hitler and World War II, put it this way: "The war experience was alive in him and was a major factor in his mind which he talked about a lot. It made the question of appeasement and evil dictators vivid, thus altering how he saw the crisis and his approach."[29]

As a 19-year-old Navy lieutenant pilot, Bush saw a fellow flyer ripped in two when his plane missed its landing on an aircraft carrier, a story that he would retell during the Persian Gulf crisis. Later, he himself would be shot down after flying fifty-eight missions as the youngest pilot in the Navy. In a letter the twenty-year-old Bush wrote his parents on September 3, 1944, one day after he was rescued by the *U.S.S. Finback* at sea: "Yesterday was a day which will long stand in my memory. . . . the fact remains that we got hit."[30] Rattled by the death of his copilots, Bush did not know just how right he would be.

Listening to Bush during the crisis, Cheney recalled, "triggered for me the memory that he was a guy whose formative years had been spent in World War II as a Navy pilot in the Pacific . . . and all of that had a big impact on his thinking."[31] William Webster, who also fought in World War II, not only confirmed the impact on Bush but also noted that it affected his own thinking in the Persian Gulf crisis as well.[32]

Even in his private discussions, Bush invoked Munich when it was not intended for public consumption. That is telling. For instance, aboard a helicopter with General Norman Schwarzkopf, the in-theater commander of the U.S.-led coalition, Sununu handed Bush his daily news digest. Bush quickly pointed to interviews conducted by British and American television correspondents with Saddam, and asserted: "Look at this. Can you imagine anyone interviewing Hitler in World War II the way they do Saddam?" He then compared Iraq's invasion to the Nazi invasion of Czechoslovakia. Bush and Sununu were quite bothered that the press, especially reporter Peter Arnett of CNN, treated the Iraqis with kid gloves, which made it harder to check Saddam. They were annoyed enough that public relations occupied 15–20% of their daily discussions on the crisis.[33] Earlier in the crisis, when it appeared that Saddam might invade Saudi Arabia and when Bush was still forming his crucial first impressions, he explained to aides what it felt like to stand on the deck of an aircraft carrier during World War II and watch a crashing airplane kill a friend.[34] That was one of his central images.

That Munich was personal to Bush was important. While the cognitive approach would stress the information-processing impact of analogies, the historical-psychological approach stresses the degree to which direct experience is important. It is important to distinguish the two approaches, but they are also quite related. We know that events from which people learn the most are those that they experience firsthand.[35] The psychological-historical impact of Bush's experience, one can argue, magnified and meshed with the cognitive impact of the Munich analogy in terms of how Bush processed the Persian Gulf case. That cannot be said of all presidents. As one of his key advisers put it, Bush may "very well have been one of the last of the meteors, of those who had experience in World War II."[36] He repeatedly invoked Munich at critical moments, and that had some meaning. From Gates's perspective, "Bush was the last President who was a World War II veteran and it was a critical factor in his mind. He believed Saddam must be punished because he was an aspiring aggressor who would not stop."[37]

Communicating by Metaphor: An Analogy on the Loose

Before delivering his August 8 speech to the nation, Bush checked to see if his hand was shaking, recognizing that he was not "nearly as good as Ronald Reagan in these situations," and proceeded to tighten up the language to strengthen the similarity he saw to the "Rhineland in the 1930s, when Hitler simply defied the Treaty of Versailles and marched in," and to emphasize that he wanted "no appeasement."[38] Was this show and tell? It does not seem so. Although Bush's hands were not shaking on television, as he feared they might, his voice quivered a bit and he appeared out of sorts, as he twisted history into modernity, meshing a national metaphor into the public mind, as he would many times thereafter.

Bush's use of the analogy generated a veritable echo chamber of similar comparisons, which further affected the atmosphere in which the crisis was framed. That was possible because the Munich analogy was the intellectual basis for the domino theory. As one scholar aptly noted, Chamberlain's policy of appeasement did not merely describe reality, it reiterated "an entire moral play: a preconfigured script in which negotiation and compromise invariably produced humiliation and defeat."[39]

Iraq's perceived level of threat to national interests, something that a RAM explanation would seek to point out, did not matter so much. It did not matter that he governed a third-world country with a relatively small population. This was also about perception, subjective interpretations driven by analogy, and human emotion. By the end of August, Bush had already made over fifteen direct references to Munich, and many indirect ones.

The Effect of the Munich Analogy

How influential was the Munich analogy on decision-making? We know that Bush lived through Munich and that the analogy was quite bandied about during the crisis. However, one may counterargue that World War II took place in another era, that it involved different interests, personalities, and stakes, and that analogies can help sort things out, but do not define decisions. This counterargument, however, would not hold up well in the Persian Gulf War case, as we shall see.

Thatcher, Munich, and an Arab Solution

Sandwiched in between two critical NSC meetings on August 2 and 3, Bush went to Aspen, where he met Margaret Thatcher for two hours. In Aspen, an energized Bush called King Fahd at the height of concern about whether Saddam might invade Saudi Arabia. An agitated Fahd asserted that Saddam "seems to think only of himself. He is following Hitler in creating world problems — with a difference: one was conceited and one is both conceited and crazy. I believe nothing will work with Saddam but the use of force."[40] Some in the Saudi press echoed that sentiment, comparing Saddam to Hitler.[41] That Fahd appeared to view the invasion in Hitlerian terms was important, given that he was initially reluctant to allow U.S. forces into the kingdom to contain and later fight Iraqi forces. It suggested that he felt that Saddam, like Hitler, would not stop after one major aggression, but would proceed until stopped.[42] Thatcher, an unabashed admirer of Winston Churchill, had reached a similar conclusion. Her steely personality and Britain's historical role in Kuwait and the broader Persian Gulf probably added to her intensity, as did her own recollections of World War II. On a long walk in the Aspen mountains, it became perfectly clear to her that "aggression must be stopped." That, after all, "is the lesson of this century. And if an aggressor gets away with it, others will want to get away with it too, so he must be stopped, and turned back. You cannot gain from your aggression." And so she told that to President Bush, when he asked her for advice on Saddam. In her view, World War II "had been caused because we didn't deal firmly enough with Hitler in the early stages."[43]

In fact, Thatcher did serve to "reinforce" Bush's convictions, as he would later recall, and did impress upon him the hazards of an Arab-brokered compromise.[44] But she noted that Bush was resolved against Saddam even before they talked in Aspen, as did her foreign policy adviser Charles Powell, who asserted that it was "just wrong" that Thatcher stiffened Bush's backbone, a charge that has gained some currency in the literature.[45] Indeed, Bush had already called both King Hussein and Hosni Mubarak aboard Air Force One on the way to Aspen. He was becoming increasingly "wary" that they might give Saddam a compromise that the United States could not reject and from which Saddam could declare victory.[46]

Bush would invoke Munich prominently for the first time on August 3 in a phone conversation with Prime Minister Turgut Ozal of Turkey. Noting that the Saudis might strike a deal with Saddam, he asserted that "if the solution is that Iraq pulls back and Kuwait pays, that is not a solution but another Munich," to which Ozal responded that they should "not repeat the mistakes made at the beginning of World War II."[47] And so the analogy made the global rounds.

Rejecting and Undermining Compromise

Perhaps because he recognized that he had misread U.S. resolve, Saddam floated some ideas for negotiation. It is not clear to what extent he was serious. He may have been trying to split the coalition, test U.S. resolve, and buy time to complete his domination of Kuwait. But, while doing so, he also may have been trying to escape an unpredicted mess, especially if he could finesse a face-saving withdrawal from Kuwait and show his army and people that he had gained something. The Munich analogy, however, was a factor in rejecting Saddam's sporadic overtures, and, more importantly, those from other sources. The analogy tended to put Bush in a particular role. As Hirschbein suggests, in some ways and in certain cases, "crises throw actors into situations in which they feel compelled somehow to live up to mythic, larger-than-life narratives militated by the remembered past."[48] Bush would not be a negotiator, as many would find out, including his own presiding Episcopal bishop, the Reverend Edmond Browning, who visited Bush in December 1990. An unrelenting pacifist, Browning told him directly that the use of force was simply immoral. Bush responded with a penetrating query: "If we had saved 2 million Jews from their fate in the gas chambers by using force — would it have been moral, or would it have been immoral?"[49]

While Saddam turned up the rhetoric, he also broached an initiative as early as August 7 in a letter to President Bush, in which he offered to withdraw from Kuwait and cooperate on oil pricing if the United States recognized Iraq's sacrifice in the Iran-Iraq War in indirectly protecting U.S. interests by checking revolutionary Iran. As a *quid pro quo*, Saddam purportedly requested that (1.) Iraq be allowed to retain Bubiyan and Warba islands (offshore islands that would allow Iraq desperately needed access to Persian Gulf waters) and an area of northern Kuwait bordering Iraq, (2.) the United States attempt to ensure that Iraq's wartime debts to both Western and Arab states would be eliminated, and (3.) suitable funds be provided for Iraq's postwar rehabilitation. Bush promptly rejected the offer.[50] In fact, as Saddam was putting forth proposals, a skeptical Bush was indefatigably working the phone to build the coalition, and Baker was on the road twisting arms.

Some evidence also suggests that a more compromising proposal, shorn of requirements (2) and (3), appeared to be floated by Iraq via secret channels in late August and mid-October, although its seriousness was never clear.[51] In any event, other ideas for negotiation that immediately followed were viewed as less compromising. On August 12, Saddam proposed to link Iraq's withdrawal from Kuwait to Israel's withdrawal from the "occupied territories of Palestine, Syria and Lebanon" and Syria's withdrawal from Lebanon.[52] While the proposal was not viewed as serious by most Arab leaders or U.S. decision makers, it may have represented a move forward on Saddam's part, or at least from his perspective. Saddam asserted that the proposal was viewed as "positive" by Gorbachev but rejected by Bush "only two hours after we broadcast it on the air without bothering to ask for an official copy of the initiative."[53] What is not well known is that Saddam also appeared to couple his public initiative with "certain clandestine moves," as Dilip Hiro has put it, whereby Iraq would make some more compromising steps towards the United States through third parties, which it could deny in public if necessary.[54]

After seeing Saddam on August 13, King Hussein urgently wanted an audience with Bush. Despite the King's voluble and public opposition to "foreign" forces on Arab soil, Bush invited him to his vacation home in Kennebunkport, Maine, on August 16. Bush noted in his diary that the King pressed for some "middle ground that could solve the problem, but I kept on saying that there isn't any—it's got to be withdrawal and restoration of the Kuwaiti regime. There cannot be any middle ground, because tomorrow, it will be somebody else's aggression."[55] From Jordan's perspective, the United States prevented "any meaningful dialogue" with Iraq, partly due to the personalization of the conflict, although by September Saddam also ignored a letter from King Hussein calling for a more moderate approach.[56]

Iraq again called for negotiations to end the crisis around August 21, but Washington's quick response was that it first must withdraw its forces from Kuwait, which Iraq rejected. Iraq's evolving proposals remained too demanding for the United States, which repeatedly asserted that Saddam would have to follow international law to a T, with no conditions attached, if he wanted to end the crisis.[57] Saddam, one might imagine, probably preferred to take his chances than to do that, especially because Bush was humiliating him with heavy rhetoric. Saddam had already cited Bush's rhetoric as increasing his belief "in the correct stand of every eager Arab and Muslim who chooses the path of holy war against the invading forces."[58] And Iraq was clearly sensitive to how the United States treated it in diplomatic interaction, even demanding respect and commenting on its condescending diplomatic approach, and questioning its presumption that it can speak "on behalf of the international community," as it repeatedly attempted to do.[59]

Bush downplayed and ignored Iraq's efforts at negotiation, possibly because they clashed with his own preexisting beliefs and positions on Saddam Hussein — a form of cognitive dissonance. When Bush was asked in late August about whether he would accept Saddam's proposal to debate him and Thatcher, he said with disdain that you could "put an empty chair there as far as I'm concerned."[60] Clearly, he would not sit down with Saddam, much less pay him any respect. Yet Bush realized that Congress questioned sending Americans to die for undemocratic Kuwait. As Bush put it, some are arguing that "we have no real national interest in restoring Kuwait's rulers," and that since they are "not democratic," the United States should not push to restore them but rather to call for U.N.-sponsored elections in Kuwait.[61]

On September 9, at a meeting with Bush in Finland, Gorbachev introduced a peace proposal. In it, Saddam would withdraw and restore the Kuwaiti government in exchange for a reduction of U.S. forces and an agreement to follow up by holding an international conference on peace in the Middle East. Such a conference might have appealed to Saddam, who could portray himself as the champion of the Palestinian cause, as the man who would liberate Jerusalem and divert attention from his invasion of Kuwait. If Saddam could portray himself in that light, regardless of its truth, he might gain popularity among the Muslim masses that sympathized with the Palestinians, place indirect pressure on Washington's Arab allies, and possibly undermine the coalition. Almost exactly eleven years later, Osama bin Laden would try to do the same in order to rally Muslims against the United States.

But Bush and other observers saw Saddam's ploy as linking the Arab-Israeli and Persian Gulf crisis cases, which were in many ways quite separate from each other. Bush responded that any "agreement on a plan which left the Kuwait issue open would be a major defeat for the collective action which has gotten us so far," and allow Saddam "to return to aggression as soon as the U.S. leaves."[62] In an intense interaction with Gorbachev, Bush argued that if "we had offered Hitler some way out, would it have succeeded?" Gorbachev, who may well have been pushing compromise in order to placate his own pro-Arab diplomats, responded tersely that this was not "the same situation."[63] Eduard Shevardnadze, foreign minister until January 1991, represented one group as the sole spokesperson for closer U.S. cooperation, while Soviet Foreign Minister Yevgeny Primakov sought a more competitive stance, with Gorbachev moving back and forth between the two. Primakov, considered a friend of Saddam's with access to him during the crisis, had known Saddam since the mid-1960s, when he had acted as an intermediary between the rebel Kurds in northern Iraq and the Iraqi government, and as a diplomat in Moscow's equivalent of the U.S. State Department.[64]

While Bush and Margaret Thatcher pushed Gorbachev repeatedly in closed quarters to be unyielding and steadfast, this internal power struggle remained intense.[65] As one high-level Soviet insider noted, "I was not sure the Americans were fully aware of the mounting criticism of our cooperation with them in the Gulf crisis [and] whether they really understood how much heat Shevardnadze and Gorbachev were taking from the military and the Arabists was not clear to me."[66]

For his part, Saddam continued to show some mixed signs of softening his position, while periodically being bombastic as well. On September 30, in response to French diplomacy, he backed away for the first time from asserting that the invasion was irreversible, although Iraq still tied its withdrawal from Kuwait to Israel's and Syria's withdrawals from occupied lands, and although Saddam appeared to become less flexible in mid-October about withdrawing from Kuwait.[67] Nonetheless, on October 16, King Hussein, buoyed by some comments out of Baghdad, said that he thought that Saddam was willing to leave most of Kuwait if some of his requirements were met, a notion viewed with optimism in Paris and Moscow but skepticism in Washington.[68] Aziz described the Franco-Soviet summit on October 29 as having gone well. Meanwhile, Iraqi First Deputy Prime Minister Taha Yasin Ramadan asserted that Iraq was "interested" in it, because it recognized a link among the region's issues and a need to have comprehensive solutions, and he noted that the position of France, the Soviet Union, and China differed from that of Britain and the United States, both of which had "imperialist objectives in the region."[69]

The key point is that each time talk of concessions or compromise emerged in the first few months, Bush shot it down. From Iraq's perspective, the administration was "closing all doors for dialogue and peaceful efforts and obstructing initiatives in order to wage a war to realize its ambitions and impose its hegemony on the region."[70] Baghdad proposed that U.S. actions were aimed not at resolving the crisis, but at humiliating and eventually dominating Iraq.[71]

On October 19, Bush reasserted his position that Saddam should not be rewarded with any compromise; one day later, he sent a private letter to King

Hussein reprimanding him for supporting Iraq and ignoring Saddam's treachery in Kuwait, pointing out that Saddam's behavior was "indeed reminiscent of how Hitler behaved in Poland before the rest of the world came to its senses and stood up against him."[72] That the correspondence was not written for public consumption suggested that the Munich analogy was genuinely at play. On October 23, Bush again compared Saddam to Hitler and said that there could never be any compromise with him on Kuwait. Interestingly, Saddam had recently released fourteen sick and elderly Americans who had been held hostage, an act that led some to think that he once again might be probing for a compromise. And on October 31, two days after the Franco-Soviet summit, the group of eight decided to double U.S. force levels in the Persian Gulf.

When Bush discussed the Kuwaiti Emir's visit with Thatcher, her adviser noted that he had "rarely seen a man so moved to suppressed fury and disgust by what he had heard, and I think it became a very important part of his overall approach to resolving this problem."[73] Scowcroft and Quayle described Bush as profoundly affected and genuinely horrified.[74] Bush even sent the Amnesty International paper on Iraqi atrocities to all key members of Congress, and sent the Emir of Kuwait a letter on October 17, 1990, in which he reiterated that Iraq would "fail in its ultimate goal of dominion" over Kuwait and that Kuwait would "endure as a free and sovereign state."[75] To emphasize his determination, Bush made some strong remarks on October 23: "I'm reading a book, and it's a book of history — great, big, thick history about World War II. And there's a parallel between what Hitler did to Poland and what Saddam Hussein has done to Kuwait. Hitler rolled his tanks and troops into Poland. . . . And do you know what followed the troops? It was the Death's Head regiment. They were the ones that went in and lined up the kids that were passing out leaflets. . . . Do you know what happened in Kuwait the other day? Two young kids, mid-teens, passing out leaflets — Iraqi soldiers came, got their parents out and watched as they killed them."[76]

This statement came at a propitious time. In late October, Primakov again suggested the pursuit of what Bush perceived to be a face-saving way out for Saddam who, from the standpoint of some Russian and other diplomats around the world, was being demonized in the United States.[77] Primakov had been cautiously optimistic, because Saddam had indicated that he might settle for the islands of Warba and Bubiyan and the southern section of the Rumaila oil field, over which Iraq and Kuwait had had a dispute preceding the invasion.[78] Primakov had room to maneuver in large part because Gorbachev and Shevardnadze were at odds. The latter wanted to be unequivocal and forceful against Iraq, in line with the American approach, while Gorbachev also had a political eye on appeasing domestic opponents who supported Primakov and his approach towards Iraq.[79] Primakov was widely perceived in Washington as trying to save Saddam, but the U.S. goal, as Assistant Secretary of State Lawrence Eagleburger saw it, was to convince Gorbachev that he was being "had by one of his own."[80]

When Gorbachev sent Primakov to Washington to brief Bush on his talks with Saddam, Bush again rejected any face-saving approach in strong terms.[81] More importantly, Bush made the Hitler comparison on the same day that the Saudi Defense Minister, Prince Sultan, reflecting some broader sentiment among Saudi strategists and military officials, floated the idea of giving Saddam a carrot to resolve the crisis, including possible territorial concessions.[82] Prince Sultan had on September 22 actually stated in front of twenty-six Arab and foreign correspondents that he saw no problem with one Arab country giving another "any land or money or outlet to the sea."[83] Some Saudi leaders, wary of their powerful Iraqi neighbor and their own internal instability, wanted to hedge their bets, but Bush did not want such overtures to mislead Saddam or to complicate the strong-handed U.S. approach. Sentiment on appeasing Saddam at Kuwait's expense, in fact, left Kuwaiti leaders livid, and clearly made Washington nervous because it threatened to make it even harder to create and maintain an anti-Iraq coalition and because it recalled images from the 1930s.[84] On Wednesday, October 24, three hours after his usual morning breakfast meeting with Scowcroft and Baker, Cheney was called back to the White House. For several reasons, Bush was giving renewed attention to doubling U.S. forces in the Persian Gulf, one of which was that he was disturbed by Prince Sultan's idea of potential compromise with Iraq. On October 23, Bush told a political rally in New Hampshire that he was "more determined than ever to see that this invading dictator get out of Kuwait with no compromise of any kind whatsoever."[85] Interestingly, on October 31, Saddam Hussein made one of his few direct remarks about being compared to Hitler, when asked about it by a CNN reporter: "Do you not think he [Bush] is closing the door to dialogue and peace with that head of state [i.e., himself] by making such descriptions at this phase [of the crisis]?"[86]

By early December, pressures for negotiation were mounting again. France pushed the idea of linking Iraq's withdrawal to a Middle East peace conference. On December 4, possibly in response to the U.S. effort to seek a meeting with Iraq to see if it would back down, Saddam allegedly implied at a mini-summit in Baghdad with King Hussein, Yasser Arafat, and President Saleh of Yemen, that the French formula might work, if Kuwait also made the types of economic concessions that Saddam had sought prior to the invasion.[87] Moreover, several days after Thatcher and Bush had asserted in late November that no great Arab leader would ever hide behind women and children, Saddam slowly began to release foreign hostages, announcing on December 6 that even the Americans would be freed. That came at a time when Bush faced a public controversy in Congress and around the nation over his decision to double U.S. forces in the Persian Gulf.

Bush remained steadfast. Asked about giving Saddam a face-saving way out of Kuwait, he said: "I don't care about face. He doesn't need any face," prompting one Arab ambassador to observe that Saddam would "opt for war rather than humiliation."[88] In fact, on September 20, in a common and ironic refrain for an unabashed invader, Saddam asserted that Iraqis are "not a people to grovel before someone who threatens us."[89] Later, on September 23, one day after Saudi Prince Sultan hinted that Saddam be given some land in exchange for withdrawal from Kuwait, Saddam asserted, in not atypical fashion, that if the Arabs and Iraqis were to be "afraid of war and thereby lose these values [i.e., honor, sovereignty, and peace] . . . they will lose their very existence."[90]

Bush's steadfastness and provocation had something to do with the Munich analogy, as even Schwarzkopf recognized. When he first heard the analogy in one of Bush's speeches at the Pentagon on August 14, he looked at Powell and thought that this "did not sound like a leader bent on compromise."[91] Schwarzkopf noticed that Saddam, through a spokesman on Iraqi television, was replying to the president's speech with a "rhetorical blast" of his own: "You, the President of the United States . . . have lied to your people. . . . You are going to be defeated."[92]

As soon as the Baker-Aziz meeting in Geneva was announced for January 9, the question arose as to whether Baker might go to Baghdad if invited, to which Bush said tersely before boarding a helicopter, "No."[93] Bush had already offered to send Baker on fifteen different dates, and by January 3, after being rebuffed, decided to retract his offer. He was not only holding his ground, he was being provocative and it caught on. As early as November 29, even the formerly dovish Baker urged all at the United Nations to "remember the lesson of the 1930s" in his effort to obtain a U.N. endorsement for war.[94]

In retrospect, it appears that Saddam did not understand that the United States could not have massively attacked Iraq had he withdrawn fully from Kuwait. Unaware of world affairs, raised in an environment of extraordinary suspicion, and aware of the gravity of his invasion, he had no reason to trust Washington. Yet he was far closer than he may have believed to complicating U.S. efforts. Simply agreeing to French, Russian, or even U.N. proposals to withdraw in exchange for a peace conference on the Middle East would have done so. Such proposals threatened to erode the U.S. demands for unconditional withdrawal. Indeed, to Baker's chagrin, the French broached and backed such a proposal as late as January 7 to 10, while Baker was at Geneva trying to reject such a prospect.

On January 11, while France was playing diplomatic Houdini, U.N. Secretary-General Javier Perez de Cuellar visited Baghdad. As Iraqi transcripts of the meeting reveal, de Cuellar flattered Saddam by telling him that he had placed the Palestinian cause on the world agenda, suggesting that President Bush eagerly sought a solution, and even indicating that Saddam's peace plan of August 12 could serve as a basis for resolving the crisis, despite the fact that Washington had rejected it outright.[95] Saddam, however, was quite defiant. He preferred to talk about Zionist-American conspiracies, to blame others for the crisis, and to reiterate doubts about Kuwait's sovereign status. Moreover, in one revealing comment, he stated that "to utter the word withdrawal while there is still a chance of war means that we would be creating the psychological conditions for enemy victory over us."[96] This comment suggests that Saddam did not want to move down the road of unconditional withdrawal unless he had a comfortable level of certainty that it would avoid war.

While de Cuellar was trying diplomacy in Baghdad, Gorbachev called Bush to urge once again a postponement of the attack and to broach some compromise with Iraq. Bush, however, was not budging. He was willing to accommodate Moscow only insofar as Washington would temporarily overlook the Soviet crackdown in the Baltics.[97] On January 14, France again pushed the compromise notion of Iraqi withdrawal. Iraq was promised that the coalition would not attack and that a peace conference would follow Iraq's withdrawal. France sought to advance that compromise as a potential U.N. resolution, which Britain and the United States opposed in closed U.N. sessions. Saddam, perhaps because he knew of U.S. opposition and of Bush's strong and emotive stand, and because he had already resigned himself to war, showed no interest at all.[98]

In general, Bush valued Baker's diplomatic initiatives with Iraq as necessary steps prior to war, but Baker appeared to try to provide Iraq a face-saving withdrawal even after the war started. On January 29, while preparing his State of the Union address, Bush was hit by news that made him "furious." Baker and Russian Foreign Minister Aleksandr Bessmertnykh had issued a joint statement. Bessmertnykh had replaced Eduard Shevardnadze, who had struck a close relationship with Baker and helped bring Gorbachev along during the crisis but had resigned on December 20. The statement indicated that the coalition would link a cease-fire to negotiations on the Palestinian question. In Bush's view, that statement challenged his position that withdrawal must be unconditional and must not benefit Saddam.[99] He knew that Baker did not intend to "blindside" him, although others around Bush — for example, Fitzwater — believed that Baker had the potential to do exactly that to Bush.[100] Baker's behavior, however, may simply have reflected the fact that he had virtually "preoccupied himself with diplomacy and negotiations from the outset to the end."[101]

Personalizing a Conflict: Backing Saddam into a Corner

Bush's dislike for Saddam, a man who had even degraded Bush in an open letter to the American people, grew to such a point that his rhetoric made his own advisers uncomfortable. Powell even suggested to Cheney and Scowcroft to try to get the president to "cool the rhetoric" because he believed it was "unwise to elevate public expectations by making the man out to be the devil incarnate and then leaving him in place."[102] Conservative commentator George Will, shocked by the casual comparisons to Hitler, quoted two anonymous administrators who questioned whether decisions were being made based on Bush's "moods" rather than on a game plan.[103] Even Scowcroft, Bush's trusted friend and confidant, had developed serious doubts: "Reading historian Martin Gilbert's book on World War II and seeing Kuwaiti atrocities made Bush emotional. He tended to personalize it too much. We started to travel with him, Bob Gates and I, to cool him down. He was turning people off. It was counterproductive."[104] While Bush backed off for political reasons, he returned to using the analogy which, as Fitzwater notes, was not "prepared in our public relations campaign but rather was his own personal feelings."[105] Later, Fitzwater would state that it "never pays to reference Hitler," whether it be President Clinton referring to Slobodan Milosevic of Yugoslavia, or Bush during the Persian Gulf crisis.[106] Bush obviously saw it differently.

At a minimum, while we cannot forget that Saddam triggered the crisis by treacherously invading Kuwait, it is fair to say that Bush's rhetoric and strong stance made it hard for Saddam to step down. Negotiation became a chimera and war presumably a more attractive option for both sides. Saddam appeared to respond to Bush's rhetoric with his own extreme acts. For instance, the day after Bush's August 7 press announcement that he had committed troops to Saudi

Arabia — in which he compared Saddam to Hitler — Iraq proclaimed the outright annexation of Kuwait "as a return to the mother homeland" in an "eternal merger" of the two countries.[107] One day after Baker's October 29 speech, which was widely disseminated in the Middle East and which signaled America's waning patience and willingness to use force if necessary, Saddam put Iraq's forces on "extreme alert."[108] Bush followed on November 1 with even stronger messages, which continued thereafter. Later, Saddam responded with strong rhetoric in a message to the Iraqi National Assembly about standing firm against "the infidels, profligates, and traitors," meaning the U.S.-led coalition.[109]

Saddam provoked Bush; Bush antagonized Saddam; Saddam became further entrenched, which only solidified Bush's convictions that Saddam was intransigent and that war was becoming more certain. This cycle may well have contributed to war in a manner that Bush may or may not have anticipated or recognized, depending on one's interpretation of the evidence. For Saddam, dignity counted, despite his own boorish behavior. It was particularly important in military matters. Saddam had never been a military officer and he had the slenderest of military credentials, thus making bravado in security matters essential. Major humiliation for him, which would accompany an unconditional withdrawal, would have been worse than a major military defeat, which he could at least pass off as a political victory. Even his ambassador to the United Nations, Abdul Amir Al-Anbari, talked about how it was necessary to "endure hardship" and not to submit to the U.N. embargo and Western pressure; to do otherwise would be to be "humiliated forever."[110]

Cutting Hitler Down to Size

While the key lesson of Munich was not to appease aggressors, the analogy had wings of its own. It made economic sanctions look less sensible and war preferable, and it seemed to bolster Bush's preexisting beliefs and preferences, a common effect of analogies.[111] Ideas that seemed to clash with the lesson of the analogy were discounted. After all, would economic sanctions have gotten Hitler out of Poland in 1939? France in 1940? The U.S.S.R. in 1941? A person contemplating Munich would be likely to wonder why anyone would argue for economic sanctions as a long-term strategy. By the logic of the Munich analogy, such an action, as many asserted in Congress on January 12 (much to Bush's delight), would only whet a dictator's appetite.[112] Of the fifty-two senators who supported the January 9 Dole-Warner resolution authorizing the president to use force in order to bring about Iraq's withdrawal, thirty-four believed that force was the only way to stop aggression; many of them cited the lessons of the 1930s.[113]

The analogy also helped avoid the inherent complexity and uncertainty of decision-making. Regional stability required that Iraq not only be controlled but cut down to size. After all, would it be possible to imagine a secure Europe if Hitler had withdrawn from Poland only to prepare for another attack? On January 25, Bush explained the war decision by saying that he was "absolutely convinced that to head off what very well could have been an unleashing of a new Hitler, we have done the right, moral thing."[114]

Saddam Inadvertently Plays into the Analogy

Leaders are rarely insightful enough to see how they themselves sow the seeds of their own destruction. Call it hubris. Call it narrowmindedness. Call it over-confidence. But when Saddam invaded Kuwait, he probably had no idea that he had created the basis for such a powerful analogy. After his meeting with April Glaspie, he probably thought that he could get away with the invasion without provoking a major war. A few days after that meeting, Iraq's ambassador to Washington, Muhammad al-Mashat, reported that "few risks" existed of an American reaction in the event of an attack on Kuwait.[115] That helps explain Iraq's obsession with conspiracy prior to and during the crisis, and also why it was hard for Saddam to stand down.[116] Indeed, Iraq's ambassador to the United Nations, Abdul Amir Al-Anbari, asserted on August 12 that Washington must have been "looking for fig leaves to commit an aggression against my country."[117] Iraq's ambassador to the United States asserted one week later that "there was a preconceived plan to destroy Iraq and occupy the oil fields of all the Gulf. This is the crux of the situation."[118] If that mindset prevailed, then Iraq must have been concerned that Washington would attack even if it did withdraw from Kuwait.

That Saddam, like Hitler, displayed the characteristics of a tyrant did not help him much. On July 24, he told Egypt's Mubarak, whom the Arab League had chosen as a mediator between Iraq and Kuwait, that he would not use force if diplomacy had any chance. Duped by this Machiavellian ploy, Mubarak passed the message on to the Kuwaitis and Americans. Mubarak would later express deep resentment and uncharacteristic anger at Saddam's lie, one that, in his words, had "paralyzed" his thoughts.[119]

Invading Kuwait outright and annexing it did not help Saddam either. The word "annexation" smacked of the 1930s, because Hitler had annexed Austria in 1938. To add to matters, Saddam had invited King Fahd to Baghdad after the

Iran-Iraq War ended in 1988 to sign a nonaggression pact, which Fahd found strange since he saw their relations as stronger than that.[120] This made it appear that Saddam was trying to ensure Fahd's support in the event that Iraq were to attack Kuwait. To Americans and Europeans, this accord evoked the 1939 Nazi-Soviet pact, which ensured that Hitler could attack France and Poland without having to worry about the U.S.S.R. Iraq also tried to shore up its relations with Iran prior to the invasion, another act that concerned President Bush.[121]

The Vietnam Analogy and Generation

The Munich analogy was not the only historical referent point in play. Vietnam also played a role.[122] While World War II shaped Bush's view, as it did for others of his generation, the Vietnam War had a much broader impact on the younger generation of decision makers and on the public and Congress. The word "Vietnam" appeared 7,229 times in the central news coverage of the crisis from August 1, 1990, to February 28, 1991.[123] Moreover, one hundred members of Congress during the crisis had served in Vietnam — twenty-four senators and seventy-six representatives. The use of the Vietnam analogy can't be accounted for by the RAM, which ignores such mental processes. But that is not to say that it did not feed into rational behavior at the individual level. The Vietnam experience was perceived as teaching at least four general lessons, which helped leaders assess the costs and benefits of different options and decisions.

The first was to keep the public well informed. Bush told Fitzwater at several points that he "wouldn't make the mistakes of Vietnam," which included second-guessing and hamstringing the military, and failing to communicate the stakes to the public.[124] Rather, he would mount a public relations campaign of grand proportions. The second was that soldiers, not politicians, should run a war.[125] The third lesson had to do with military force. The Vietnam analogy was repeatedly invoked by Bush in his private and public discourse as an example of how not to conduct a war. Powell told Prince Bandar of Saudi Arabia in a meeting at the Pentagon on November 9 that the president had ordered that the Persian Gulf War not turn into another Vietnam, where the United States escalated slowly and ineffectively. Powell took that seriously.[126] This meant a massive, decisive attack, later to be dubbed the Powell Doctrine. As Baker recalls, "Vietnam was very much in our minds throughout, both diplomatically and militarily. The President was determined to let the military run the war . . . to give the military everything they needed and everything they wanted."[127] To ensure that the force would be massive and decisive, in November the president doubled U.S. military power in the Persian Gulf.

A fourth lesson that some skeptics drew from the Vietnam debacle was that the United States lacked resolve. Saddam at times asserted that the Iraqis could impose another Vietnam-like debacle again on U.S. troops in the region, and he told Ambassador Glaspie that Americans, unlike Iraqis, would not be able to "accept 10,000 dead in one battle."[128] Later, Saddam and the Iraqi media returned repeatedly to the Vietnam issue as a way of assailing American credibility. In one interview, he asserted that as the "war is prolonged the international position of the United States will alter. When war begins and continues for some time, America cannot maintain its level of supremacy."[129] Insofar as the Vietnam analogy was invoked, it was not illogical. The only other times since World War II that the United States had sent more than half a million troops halfway across the globe was to stop the spread of communism during the Cold War (Korea and Vietnam), and it had preferred to protect the Persian Gulf only at arm's length. While America learned from Vietnam to use massive force partly as a way of avoiding casualties, Saddam may very well have learned from Vietnam that imposing casualties in a bloody ground war might work.

It is possible that Saddam preferred to take his chances and to test post-Vietnam America, especially if he could not be assured of a face-saving withdrawal from Kuwait and of not being attacked thereafter. Leaders such as Yasser Arafat who had access to Saddam, in fact, were making speeches in Baghdad and telling private audiences in the United States that Washington would not go to war, and that if it did, it would get bogged down in the Persian Gulf or lose outright.[130] For his part, Tariq Aziz repeatedly made similar comments when he met Secretary Baker during their meeting in Geneva prior to the war.[131] And Soviet generals, even two weeks into the war, were predicting publicly that the war would end in a major U.S. defeat akin to Vietnam.[132] For his part, Saddam referred to Vietnam from the beginning of the crisis, noting that Iraq had the determination to "face the invaders," as the Vietnamese did, and that the "outcome" of Vietnam is well known to all.[133]

While the use of analogies can undermine rational behavior, the supposed conflict between Bush's use of the Munich analogy and Saddam's potential use of the Vietnam analogy does not necessarily prove that either party was behaving irrationally. In other words, we could say that war and not a negotiated outcome happened because of inconsistent expectations between Bush and Saddam, or even just because of miscalculation on Saddam's part about U.S. willingness to fight, which we could ascribe to analogical reasoning.[134] That could combine a cognitive explanation to support a nonetheless rationalist account. Indeed, if bargaining and persuasion are dependent on a shared conceptual framework that generates similar interpretations of and solutions to a problem, we can see that inconsistent expectations could make it harder for both actors, even if viewed as quite rational, to find an alternative other than war or to dissuade them from trying.

Iraq may have thought not only of Vietnam, but also of another analogy. Saddam and his advisers may have thought back to Egypt's President Gamal Nasser in the Suez War of 1956, a leader whom so many in Saddam's generation had grown up emulating. The Persian Gulf crisis from this perspective was one in which Saddam could stand up to the great powers and snatch political victory from military defeat. Aziz even told Baker in Geneva to remember what had happened to Nasser when he was defeated in 1967. He resigned, and then "the people, the masses returned him to power."[135] Bush did tend to interpret Saddam's behavior in that light. As Bush speculated, Saddam "didn't think we would use force . . . and for some odd reason felt that, if we use force, he could emerge victorious even if it was through some kind of stalemate of a long standoff in the desert."[136]

The latter two lessons of Vietnam discussed above worked separately and in tandem to make war more, rather than less, likely. The massive U.S.-led buildup might have compelled another aggressor to stand down, but in Saddam's case, it seems to have had the opposite effect. It communicated that the United States was preparing to challenge Iraq at some time, regardless of whether he withdrew. Historically speaking, such military buildups usually result in war between armies in close proximity.

With the prospect of an enduring American challenge appearing inevitable, Saddam may have concluded that Iraq should fight on the ground to impose casualties on U.S. troops and force a Vietnam-like withdrawal. Such analogical reasoning could only have been reinforced by the Nasser analogy, wherein the mere act of fighting could mean victory, no matter how disastrous the military outcome.

To be sure, the approach by the Vietnam generation differed from that of those shaped by World War II. The Vietnam veterans such as Powell and Schwarzkopf were quite uneasy about the notion of war, while the World War II generation was more in favor of it. That is not very surprising. The Vietnam War was the nadir of the American experience, whereas World War II was an apex.

Given their experience and successes, the older generation tended to believe that war was necessary, while the younger generation believed that it should be avoided, and if fought, conducted in a manner quite unlike Vietnam.

Over time, however, each generation, driven by different motivations and assumptions, tended to accept the other generation's experience as a guide, and the analogies by chance reinforced each other on the road to war. The very fact that the United States had created such a massive and decisive capability, in line with the Vietnam analogy, made going to war against an aggressor, in line with the World War II analogy, an easier undertaking.

Kicking Vietnam: Another Legacy in the Bag

The Vietnam War also served as an added impetus for a strong-armed approach to Saddam in another way. The Persian Gulf War allowed Bush to try to reverse one of the worst legacies in all of American history. The Vietnam debacle, to be sure, was caused by much more than a failure to unleash the U.S. military. Weak South Vietnamese support, for one, was at play, in addition to the sheer difficulty of translating military capability into political results against a hardened and determined enemy. But at the core, the problem was one of U.S. credibility, about how the United States perceived itself and its role on the world scene, and about a lack of vision. President Bush was discerning in invoking Vietnam, perhaps unlike his more emotive use of Munich. When he wanted to show the public that the Persian Gulf War was not going to be a Vietnam, he attacked the analogy, in effect showing how powerful it was as a motivating force: "We are not looking at another Vietnam. The analogy is totally different in who is supporting you, what the topography is, what the force is, what the determination of the military is — the whole array — the coalition. All of these things come together and argue very forcefully this is not another Vietnam."[137]

In February, during the ground war, Bush asserted that it was his hope that "when this is over we will have kicked, once and for all, the so-called Vietnam syndrome."[138] At the end of the war, he would revisit this notion again and again, for instance with regard to his satisfied assertion on March 1 that the United States had "kicked the Vietnam syndrome once and for all."[139]

Conclusion

Crises and the threats that they generate are interpreted by impressionable human beings with myriad biases who face significant pressures when they make decisions. Analogies are one way that individuals try to interpret and frame events. While some might want to downplay the Munich analogy by noting that many presidents have invoked it, the intensity, frequency, and extent of its use in the Persian Gulf crisis is perhaps unparalleled.

Munich was one of several analogies that played a role in the crisis. As Scowcroft pointed out, "Korea suggested not to change objectives once you are doing well and Vietnam taught to be clear about what you are doing and how you can accomplish it."[140] But the Munich analogy played a particularly important role. Drawing on the cognitive perspective, it ruled out negotiation with Saddam or the offer of any face-saving formula for his withdrawal from Kuwait. Moreover, it motivated the United States to try to undermine the myriad efforts to compromise with Saddam, short of his unconditional withdrawal, and it helped frame Saddam as a significant threat against which a strong stand was necessary. It also made economic sanctions appear less sensible as an option, and helped make war preferable to Saddam's withdrawal, notwithstanding the partial element of pretense behind "going the last mile" for peace in Geneva. It is no surprise that Bush, who experienced and drew on Munich, took a far stronger stand than so many others did, and that options short of war were not given serious or even perhaps careful consideration. Events experienced firsthand tend to have a more powerful psychological impact.

CHAPTER FOUR

Constructing the Threat

Saddam the Global Menace

Through the lens of the rational actor perspective, we see Iraq as a major threat to U.S. and global interests and the United States as an actor that considered alternatives carefully and, given its preferences and strategic interaction with Iraq, ultimately tried to choose the best alternative. As we switch lenses, the cognitive perspective draws our attention to another set of motivating factors, emphasizing the genuine impact of analogies and the possibility that nonrational behavior was more prominent than the RAM perspective would suggest. But while these perspectives are useful, they cannot address the possibility that President Bush was dramatizing the Iraqi threat for political effect, or to meet personal goals or goals having to do with domestic policy. They also cannot tell us about the implications of such dramatization for U.S. decision-making and U.S.-Iraqi interaction on the road to war. The domestic politics perspective can.

The Domestic Politics Perspective (DPM)

In its entirety, the DPM does not correspond well to existing theories, though it is informed by them. In this sense, it is developed here as a new perspective that builds on some existing work. We can summarize the DPM and then develop it below. The perspective illuminates government behavior in four key ways: (1) it explains how domestic political concerns can affect the plausibility of decision alternatives as those alternatives are being generated, or at any later date, (2) it underscores the political motivations for some of the government behaviors that we observe, (3) it highlights the potential for nonconsideration of alternatives at any point in the decision-making process, and (4) it emphasizes that prior decisions and actions have lagged effects that influence the way that future decisions are made.

The first assumption of the DPM, as I conceive of it in this chapter, is that decision makers place a high premium on domestic-level goals, and in particular on two types of goals. Type 1 goals refer to personal goals such as image enhancement and electability; to institutional goals involving, for instance, party politics or benefits related to the military-industrial complex; and to advancing the perception of dealing effectively with domestic problems, chiefly economic.[1] Type 2 goals are promotional. They revolve around preparing for or promoting a potentially favored alternative or one already chosen. Thus, for instance, selling the war option, once chosen, to the public is a Type 2 goal.

Second, decision makers see the construction of international issues as useful in achieving Type 1 and 2 goals. They consciously try to construct the reality they would like others to see.[2] In part they do so, as diversionary theories tell us, because they believe that hostile foreign policies adopted by their own country will create the perception of a foreign enemy, and that this will foster internal cohesion, reduce internal political conflict, and bolster support for the ruling elite. Force may be used in the belief that it will divert attention from such things as a sagging economy, rising unemployment, or public disapproval.[3] While quantitative analyses are split on the viability of diversionary theories, and while different versions of the theory exist, at the center of the theory is the idea that, as Karl DeRouen puts it, leaders "want attention away from domestic problems, and they want to boost their image by creating a vivid image of forceful leadership."[4] The DPM adjusts the theory. It assumes that the display, threat and/or use of force may be used for diversionary purposes, rather than just the use of force. The DPM could conceivably also allow for diversion through diplomatic and economic statecraft.

The third assumption of the DPM, which is absent in other domestic politics perspectives, is that efforts to construct an event to meet either Type 1 or 2 goals will produce lagged effects.[5] These efforts can (1) purposefully or inadvertently signal a leader's commitment to a certain alternative or to the avoidance of others, (2) alter how advisers view the leader's position, thus making them less likely to express reservations and present alternatives, (3) foster an action-reaction cycle of construction that polarizes the atmosphere of interaction among nations, and (4) make the adversary less likely to meet expressed demands for a peaceable outcome.

The foregoing assumptions are important, but they do not tell us how decisions are actually made. The fourth assumption is that domestic considerations may influence how decisions are made at any time. They may even produce what Nehemia Geva and Alex Mintz refer to as noncompensatory decision-making. This is the notion that foreign policy decisions are "often grounded in the rejection or adoption of alternatives on the basis of one or a few dimensions."[6] If a certain alternative is unacceptable to the decision maker because it fails to meet one goal (e.g., at the domestic level), then it will be eliminated, even if it meets a range of other goals (e.g., strategic). A high score on meeting other goals cannot save that alternative or compensate for its failure to meet the domestic level consideration.[7]

The DPM allows for noncompensatory decision-making to occur at any time due to domestic considerations. But it also theorizes that efforts to construct adversaries produce lagged effects. Thus, Bush could seek to construct Saddam as Hitler at point X and Y, and yet only feel the impact of such construction at point Z. These lagged effects feed back into the decision-making process. And their effects can be quite important.

The lagged effects of various forms of construction can trap a leader or decrease choices. They send a variety of signals to the domestic audience, which affect expectations. In the Persian Gulf case, they generated expectations that Bush would be unyielding, even aggressive. Thus, picking an alternative that clashed with such signals and expectations could hurt his ability to meet Type 1 and 2 goals.[8] He could lose credibility, damage his image, hamper his effort to sell an alternative (e.g., war) domestically, and undermine his ability to use the event to divert attention from domestic problems and so forth. The lagged effects, in other words, make domestic politics even more important and noncompensatory decision-making even more likely. They make it more important for leaders to do what the domestic audience expects.

As a vehicle for explanation, the DPM is flexible. While it includes construction and feedback effects, it can also explain events where construction is not so prominent. In such a case, decision-making can still be influenced by domestic considerations, but the feedback effect aspect will fall out of the perspective.

While the DPM need not conflict with rationalist explanations, it certainly does offer that potential. First, a focus on domestic-level concerns may make it quite hard to list all sensible options, evaluate their costs and benefits, and attempt to choose the one that maximizes utility. Second, the actor may not be able to adjust to shifting circumstances because it is trapped by the effects of its own acts of construction. That can make it harder to consider or reconsider alternatives at a later stage, or may even lead to noncompensatory decision-making.[9]

Third, the DPM allows for the potential that different decision-making strategies, analytic and noncompensatory for instance, can be used in one case, rather than a single decision rule.[10] The use of different strategies violates a hallmark of rationality.

Fourth, more technically, we can say that the impact of feedback effects violates the invariance assumption of rationalist perspectives. That assumption asserts that irrespective of the order in which alternatives appear and dimensions are considered, the outcomes should remain the same. With the DPM, however, the political dimension is given a premium in decision-making calculations and the problem may be framed early on with that dimension as prominent, and/or because construction and its effects reemphasize that alternative. That can bias a consideration of alternatives either at that stage or later, when feedback effects kick in. The decision maker may or may not be aware of that bias. Indeed, such framing effects are, as Rose McDermott puts it, often "embedded in decision problems in such a way that few decision makers realize the disproportionate impact that these framing effects have on them."[11]

The Argument of the Chapter

While the cognitive approach of this book focuses on how an analogy can genuinely affect decision-making, the DPM takes us well beyond that. Constructing Saddam as Hitler, Iraq as a major threat, and the crisis in global terms served several Type 1 and 2 objectives. It offered the military-industrial complex and the Department of Defense a demon to replace the Soviet menace in the post–Cold War period, and it served the Republicans at the domestic level, especially in the 1990 midterm elections. Reversing Iraq's aggression and promoting a new world order could also help President Bush address two major criticisms that dogged his presidency: the notion that he lacked vision and suffered from the "wimp factor."[12] Taking a strong stand against Iraq could also help Bush shore up his own legacy.[13] In addition, it would be useful in preparing the public for possible war and in selling the war option to the public. Furthermore, it could help undermine some efforts at negotiation with Saddam, which Bush may have wanted to fail at various junctures in the crisis. These domestic-level interests made the nonwar alternatives less appealing. While such concerns may or may not have generated noncompensatory behavior *per se* in the Persian Gulf case, Bush would proceed to construct Saddam repeatedly.

In constructing Saddam, Bush also sent a signal of presidential commitment to avoiding certain alternatives. That signal was sent, both tacitly and explicitly, to both his domestic and international audiences. In this sense, Bush's construction of Saddam altered the decision-making environment, thus delimiting what alternatives others were likely to entertain, including Saddam Hussein, but more importantly, what alternatives Bush and the group of eight could consider as the crisis progressed. If Saddam was constructed as Hitler-like and Iraq as a great threat, then Bush had no choice but to be tough. That meant that some alternatives would not be given full consideration and that war at some point would become preferable.

The Construction Effort

The presidency is the perfect pulpit from which to construct reality because the president has great influence over the media, the public agenda, and the symbols of rhetoric.[14] In the Persian Gulf case, Bush and his handlers had far more influence over global communications than Saddam did, and they had a huge domestic and global audience. The crisis riveted the attention of Americans. For over five months, leaders and citizens debated whether the U.S.-led coalition and Iraq's highly touted "million-man army" would go to war in what Saddam would later call the "Mother of All Battles" in a speech to his nation on January 20, 1991.[15] As a sign of the importance of the Persian Gulf crisis, the *New York Times* and the *Washington Post* published a combined total of 4,214 stories, editorials, and columns on the crisis between August 2, when Iraq invaded Kuwait, and November 8, 1990.[16] No less than 1,400 journalists were in the Persian Gulf when Operation Desert Storm was launched on January 16, 1991, the start of history's most intense aerial bombardment; it was also history's most widely and instantaneously covered war.[17] "Real-time" images, half a world away, were daily displayed in the living rooms of America.

Against this background of interest, Bush and his advisers worked hard to construct certain aspects of the crisis. Harsh critics of the war even argued that the war had been planned in Washington long before the first Iraqi soldier entered Kuwait.[18] There is no evidence to support that view, but it does hold sway in some Middle Eastern quarters, and it was also trumpeted by Iraqi officials in the days following Iraq's invasion of Kuwait.[19]

From Iraq's perspective, events must have looked suspicious. The July 25 meeting between Saddam and U.S. Ambassador to Iraq April Glaspie may have further raised such suspicions, as could have his meeting with U.S. chargé d'affaires Joseph Wilson on August 6. Many U.S. diplomatic exchanges as well as the Iraqi transcript of the Wilson meeting confirm that, while Saddam warned Washington not to intervene in the crisis, he also claimed that he would assure a "reasonable price" of $25 per barrel, if Washington would accept the annexation of Kuwait and his position as a senior U.S. ally in the Persian Gulf.[20] From Iraq's perspective, it may have appeared from the outset that Washington wanted to exaggerate its threat or even to go to war. Thus, on August 6, Saddam Hussein asserted: "We don't understand the meaning of your [Bush's] declarations that you are afraid of Iraq's intentions with respect to Saudi Arabia and that after Kuwait will come Saudi Arabia. . . . We are ready to give them [our Saudi brothers] any guarantees they want, to remove that worry."[21] From Washington's angle, the crisis was portrayed as good versus evil. When war erupted, Bush went into full swing. While the Munich analogy was genuine in some ways, as chapter 3 showed, it was also useful for construction and manipulation. Indeed, at the August 3 NSC meeting, Bush questioned Cheney's skepticism about world resolve against Saddam, noting that "lots of people," were calling him Hitler.[22]

The administration's public relations machine also was fully activated. Every morning, White House, Pentagon, State Department and CIA representatives gathered to plan the public relations for the day. Talking points were faxed virtually every day to those friendly to the administration. And at the end of most of the group of eight meetings, the discussion of the day would turn to the public relations angle of explaining or promoting the decisions made that day.[23]

The Bush administration had a lot of help constructing the crisis. Kuwait hired no less than seven firms to work on its behalf, among them Hill and Knowlton, one of the largest public relations firms in the country. The war was on even before the first smart bomb was dropped — the propaganda war, that is. The Kuwaitis did not "leave one stone unturned" in trying to influence U.S. public opinion, in part by contributing to a stream of media reports about Iraq's inhumane behavior.[24] In one case, a Kuwaiti woman identifying herself only as Nayirah testified at a hearing of the Congressional Human Rights Caucus; she gave a tear-jerking, firsthand account of Iraqi soldiers taking babies out of incubators and absconding with the incubators. Before long, the largely fabricated story, which Bush repeated several times, dominated the news. Later, it was learned that Nayirah was the daughter of the Kuwaiti ambassador to the United States, and that Hill & Knowlton had helped her prepare and rehearse the testimony in front of video cameras at the company's Washington offices.[25]

While Kuwait was described as weak and defenseless, Iraq's invasion by Bush was described as a "throwback to another era, a dark relic from a dark time."[26] The Persian Gulf crisis, Bush would say, "threatens to turn the dream of a new international order into a grim nightmare of anarchy in which the law of the jungle supplants the law of nations."[27] Saddam was presented repeatedly as nothing less than evil incarnate. While he was no doubt a threat and while it would be folly to say that U.S.-led forces had an easy job of dealing with him, the threat to U.S. and global oil supplies was repeatedly presented in almost cosmic terms. The Iraqi threat to Saudi Arabia, for instance, could not be ignored, but it may very well have been played up to get Saudi support.[28] In November, Admiral William Crowe, a former chairman of the Joint Chiefs of Staff, would testify in front of Congress that it had been "graphically demonstrated that the West can live rather well without Iraqi and Kuwaiti oil after we had survived the initial shock."[29]

In fact, Iraq posed a serious threat if left unchallenged, but Saddam was totally outclassed when it came to war. General Sultan, the key Saudi military leader on the ground claimed that both he and "most knowledgeable Arabs" understood that Iraq had a "vast military machine" but that it was "not nearly as strong as the Americans chose to bill it."[30] Among other things, Iraq lacked allies, aircraft carriers, and Tomahawk missiles, and Saddam was likely receiving poor advice from those close to him.[31] He had no international organizations supporting him and faced hostile neighbors on all sides — Iran, Turkey, Syria, and Israel. He had a single-product economy, and an army in the desert whose weapons were deteriorating from lack of spare parts. The picture, to put it bluntly, was quite bleak for the "gangster" from Takrit, as some Kuwaitis would later call him.[32] Indeed, 100,000 Iraqi troops would desert during the conflict. The crisis itself was a major event, but it was not nearly the big war that it was played up to be. Throughout the crisis, the media often benefited U.S. efforts to construct Iraq by perhaps unwittingly using words and phrases that depicted the United States, its allies and Kuwait as good, and Iraq as evil.[33]

Using the RAM, it would be hard to explain the behavior of the United States without assuming that it viewed Iraq as a major threat at the strategic level that could not be addressed ultimately without war. Using the cognitive perspective, we would assume that the Munich analogy drove important elements of government behavior in a genuine way. Using the DPM perspective, we would reconstruct such behavior in a quite different way.

Construction and Domestic-Level Politics

Under the DPM, the construction of Iraq as a massive threat and Saddam as Hitler served several Type 1 and 2 goals, each one of which can directly or indirectly help explain how and why the United States went to war, while also addressing some of the broader aspects of the crisis.

A New Demon: Construction and Institutional Goals (Type 1)

During the Cold War, the United States focused on the cosmic clash between two opposing schools of thought. There was nothing like an enemy to unite people and excite them toward greater heights. None other than Michel 'Aflaq, an originator of the Baathist ideology to which Saddam subscribed, asserted that the "existence of a real, live enemy imparts vitality to our doctrine and makes our blood circulate."[34]

After the Cold War ended and the Soviet Union fell apart, there was a need to identify a new threat. Enter Saddam Hussein. The armed forces could see him as confirming their importance. The military-industrial complex could view him as a ticket for producing and selling more and better weapons. And the much-maligned CIA could obtain a mission in the post–Cold War era. Political pundits, for their part, had much to talk about on television shows, comics had unending material from this tough-guy dictator who thumbed his nose at the world, politicians could define their patriotism and assert their machismo, moviemakers could abandon using Soviets as a catch-all enemy in favor of turbaned fanatics from the Middle East.

Construction: Serving Personal Goals (Type 1)

We could view the importance of image and legacy as heightened by the fact that Bush had widely been derided as a "wimp" in previous years. He even refused to utter the word "wimp" himself when asked about it at press conferences; that "awful, ugly word" at which he so "chafed," as Scowcroft put it.[35] In October 1987, *Newsweek* ran a big story entitled, "Bush Battles the Wimp Factor," and speculated about the then Vice President's supposedly most persistent political liability. The article questioned whether he could overcome an "epithet that had made its way from the high school locker room into everyday jargon and stuck like graffiti on Bush."[36] Bush was even asked about the wimp factor during the CBS television program *60 Minutes* on March 15, 1987; the subject visibly caused Bush to bristle, and he responded by recalling his tough times in World War II and as CIA director.[37] The joke making the rounds in 1988 went that Bush should choose Jeane Kirkpatrick as a running mate to add some machismo to the ticket. Cartoons, anecdotes, and late-night humor skits painted Bush into the wimp candidate, in contrast to the cowboy-like Ronald Reagan. Bush was widely perceived as soft, Reagan as tough. That Bush chose Dan Quayle as a running mate did not help matters, because Quayle was not viewed as particularly powerful, given his youth and privileged background. Influential conservative columnist George Will preferred to call Bush a "lapdog" for Reagan, a notion that caught on.[38]

In 1988, Bush's unforgettable, tough campaign pledge of "read my lips, no new taxes" helped him temporarily break the wimp image. But he would break that pledge during the 1990 budget negotiations when the government felt it necessary to send a signal to the financial markets that it was taking deficit reduction seriously. He was savaged for doing so in October, reviving talk that he was, beneath it all, still a big wimp who could not hold his own in budget negotiations.[39] While Bush did project a stronger image than Dukakis in the 1988 campaign, the wimp image still dogged him.

The media had constructed Bush as an indecisive wimp, and, as conceived in the DPM perspective, he would reconstruct himself as a no-nonsense global cop. This was his time to shine after a lifetime of loyal work with no glory and some ridicule. He would deal with those polls showing doubts about his credibility. Bush was going to become the epitome of toughness against Saddam, and the Persian Gulf War could help him erase the so-called "wimp factor."[40] He would tell the world that "this aggression will not stand," and then proceed to prove just that, in a manner that some White House aides believed was aimed in part to make up for the credibility gap caused by reneging on his tax pledge.[41]

In the first weeks of the crisis, Bush seemed "invigorated," according to a close adviser, as if "this was the test he had been waiting for all along."[42] After flipping on taxes and flopping on the deficit, ripping on Saddam sent his "spirits soaring," another aide asserted, as if he thought "he could turn this thing around now."[43] After Desert Storm was launched, the same press outlets that had ridiculed Bush sang his praises. One commentator said that Bush's performance "may have allowed him to recover, at least for the time being, from reaction against his broken pledge not to raise taxes."[44] Others argued that the Persian Gulf crisis was helping Bush shed images accrued over years in which he had been Mr. Reagan's silent shadow and loyal No. 2: "wimpy," "excessively cautious," "inarticulate," "lacking in vision." Even *Newsweek*, which had speculated about "the wimp factor," was now calling Bush the "WASP warrior."[45]

Bush had succeeded in altering his image, with a little help from the media.[46] As portrayed by his friends, Bush took on the qualities of a latter-day Winston

Churchill, spinning "a fable" that he was checking the Hitler-like Saddam.[47] Bush must have viewed with tremendous satisfaction a *New York Times* column in mid-September that speculated about whether, given Congress's dubious efforts in reducing the budget deficit and Bush's bravado against Iraq, the "wimp mantle has been passed from George Bush to Capitol Hill."[48] Later, when Bush decided to double U.S. forces in the Persian Gulf and many Democrats balked, the *New Republic* ran a piece entitled, "The Wimp Factor: the Democrats and the Gulf."[49] Senator Sam Nunn — some would soon jokingly call him "Neville," as Bush noted in his diary — proceeded to hold public hearings from late November through January, meetings at which a parade of former high-ranking intelligence, defense, and foreign policy officials and experts from both parties counseled a more patient course.[50]

The Vision Thing (Type 1)

If the wimp factor was not motivation enough, Bush also had to contend with the stinging criticism that he was someone who lacked vision, and failed to show independence from Reagan. His one major attempt at vision was widely ridiculed. As a presidential candidate in 1988, he tried to repackage his Republican brand of politics under the motto of "A Thousand Points of Light." After Bush attained the presidency, he continued trying to create some vision at the domestic level, but the world was in transformation. The Berlin Wall had fallen, thus offering a metaphor for what would soon be the end of the Cold War. Democracy was on the move. And global cooperation was a buzzword. But Bush was not given much credit for this transformation — nor did he seek it, despite Bush's experience in world affairs and his central role in the Reagan administration. Quite the contrary, insofar as the credit went to any leader, much of it went to Reagan — the ideologue who told Gorbachev to "tear down that wall." His anti-communist rhetoric electrified the Republican right. His military build up and strong-arm tactics were perceived in some quarters as putting pressure on the economy of the U.S.S.R., which perhaps contributed to its demise. If Bush could not get any credit for that effort and if he still suffered from a reputation for lacking vision, the DPM perspective would highlight his expectation of a great deal of credit if he were to reverse Iraq's invasion by force and, in the process, create prospects for a new world order. That would help offset criticisms that the United States had no strategy in the Persian Gulf, no broader vision.[51] Indeed, in Scowcroft's words: "We tried to behave in the Gulf crisis in ways that would be a model for dealing with future crisis in the post–Cold War world. That's how the new world order came up. We wanted to establish a model for dealing with aggressors. The United States should behave in a way that others can trust and get UN support."[52]

However, while the new world order was an important U.S. motivation, as explained in chapter 2, it was also somewhat of an ambiguous and hyped afterthought. The concept, after all, was hatched in earnest well after Iraq invaded Kuwait and after Washington had laid out its goals, and did not appear prominently in official speeches until well into September. As Robert Gates would jokingly say to Scowcroft, such concepts come about when "you send Brent and Bush fishing with time on their hands."[53] According to Gates, the concept "didn't come up" in the group of eight meetings.[54]

Yet President Bush may have overstated the importance to the United States of a new world order, possibly because it served domestic interests. Several days after launching Desert Storm, Bush invoked Thomas Paine, the eighteenth-century American writer, in a major address to the nation. Paine, he said, wrote many years ago: "These are the times that try men's souls."[55] Thereafter, Bush was fully aware that he himself was in the process of making history, and that, as Secretary of State Lawrence Eagleburger put it, "the United States was at a turning point in history."[56] The individual who so many thought would just be a caretaker president, continuing the legacy of Ronald Reagan — except in a "kinder, gentler" way — had his own seeds to sow. The "visionless wimp" would become the erstwhile visionary, an assertive, no-nonsense war leader.

Talk of the new world order could serve two additional goals as well. Bush would erase doubts about U.S. power at a time when it was viewed as in decline in comparison to Japan and a newly united Germany, and he could address the criticism that the warpath lacked virtue.[57]

For Posterity: Bush's White House Ghosts (Type 1)

In addition to being a vision corrective, we may infer from Bush's behavior, within the context of the DPM, that he was aware of his own legacy. The Middle East in particular holds sway in presidential legacies. Some presidents have forged their legacies there, others lost them. Truman recognized Israel in the face of advice from nearly his entire staff of advisers. Eisenhower got stuck in Lebanon. Nixon, with a little help from Kissinger, escaped the dangers of the 1973 Yom Kippur War, in which the superpowers came dangerously close to a nuclear showdown. Carter helped Egypt and Israel make peace at Camp David — a rare crowning achievement of a riddled presidency — but was humiliated by the

Iranian hostage crisis. Reagan was bedeviled by the death of 243 Marines in a terrorist attack in Lebanon in 1983 and by the Iran-Contra scandal in the mid-1980s. Bush and Clinton faced Saddam, and then President George W. Bush was beset by the September 11 attacks, although he achieved partial redemption by eliminating Saddam Hussein in 2003.

We can surmise that Bush liked his White House ghosts. Lincoln and Eisenhower were favorites, and Teddy Roosevelt too. Bush drew parallels between himself and Teddy. Both experienced difficult wars when they were young, and both were reared in a family accustomed to wealth and power. Both sought to prove themselves, Roosevelt in the American West and, later, by intervening militarily in what is now Panama, and Bush in the Texas oil industry and then in modern world affairs. "Who knows," Bush commented in March 1989, "maybe I'll turn out to be a Teddy Roosevelt."[58] Bush placed a portrait of the rough rider in the Cabinet Room and a sculpture of Roosevelt in the Oval Office.[59]

Beside his bedroom, he would stop to show guests a painting of Abraham Lincoln conferring with his generals during the Civil War, noting that "he was tested by fire and showed his greatness." To one friend, Bush would ask how he too might be tested and whether he would be one of a handful of presidents destined to alter the course of history.[60] He referred to this notion repeatedly. In an interview with David Frost, Bush appeared enamored of Abraham Lincoln, whom he once again described as having an administration "tested by fire." Did Bush himself relish the opportunity, in the midst of the Persian Gulf crisis, to be "tested by fire"? In another national broadcast, Bush gave Diane Sawyer a televised tour of the White House, during which he looked at a portrait of George Washington with great admiration. Unlike Washington, Bush noted that his administration — his aides interpreted this to mean Bush himself — had not yet been "tested by fire." One of Bush's campaign slogans had been, "Ready to be a Great President from Day 1." In addition to emphasizing his impressive resume, this slogan underscored that he had greatness on his mind.

All presidents and many average citizens want a legacy, but not all of them talk about being "tested by fire"; not all of them have been ridiculed nationally for being a "wimp" and for lacking vision; not all of them have had to play second fiddle to an extraordinarily well-liked and charismatic leader. No, there were unique elements at play that could push Bush to seek a legacy. And that would hardly be strange or abnormal, particularly given that national goals could be served by clipping Saddam's wings. On November 22, while visiting U.S. troops in the desert for Thanksgiving, Bush repeatedly told the Emir of Kuwait that

Saddam had made the conflict a "question of him or me," adding, "The future of my presidency and my place in history depends on the outcome."[61] Public opinion polls would reveal the war's positive impact on Bush's popularity. Numerous polls showed that Bush's approval ratings were moderate in October 1990, at about 55 percent. They began to increase as U.S. forces amassed in the Middle East and as the United States launched air attacks on January 16. By the end of the war, they had risen to 90 percent.[62]

Diverting Attention from Domestic Problems (Type 1)

Initially, the administration's public relations efforts were aimed at preparing the public for a war, should Saddam invade Saudi Arabia. At the end of the Bush-Thatcher meeting in Aspen on August 2, after Bush decided that Saddam had to be stopped, he turned to Fitzwater and said that they needed "to think about how to get the U.S. public ready for this . . . for possible war."[63] On August 18 in Kennebunkport, he once again told Fitzwater that "war could happen at any minute" if Iraqi ships were to try to challenge the U.S.-led blockade or in the event that "American hostages are killed, forcing our retaliation."[64]

However, after these initial days, the public relations efforts could have served other goals not directly related to the crisis. The administration faced a time-consuming and politically damaging budget impasse with Congress. On October 5, after months of negotiations between the White House and Congress, the House rejected a bipartisan agreement to trim the massive budget deficit over a five-year period. While the two sides sought a compromise, nonessential national services were shut down and Congress was forced to pass a temporary spending bill to keep the federal government operating. The fallout from this much-publicized failure hurt the president.

The budget impasse ended on October 24 in a compromise, after Bush reneged on his "no new taxes" pledge in a responsible effort to avoid increasing the national deficit. However, in doing so, he angered the Republican right and many taxpayers. Cheney felt that the White House's poor handling of the budget talks not only hurt Bush in the polls, but also cast a pall over the entire administration and raised key questions about its competence.[65] The budget debacle and the Persian Gulf crisis, however, were somewhat related. Earlier, on September 7, Bush expressed hope that "Iraq and the country's unity can now be parlayed into support for the budget agreement" and that the crisis "will be the fulcrum that we need to lever a deal through Congress."[66] While it is not clear if that occurred at the time, a strong stand on the Persian Gulf crisis could not hurt in reversing the negative fallout from budget negotiations.

It may not be a coincidence that the height of Bush's rhetoric on Munich, Hitler, and the use of force preceded or coincided with critical domestic developments such as the budget negotiations, political fundraisers, and Senate elections. Citing atrocities in Kuwait including the shooting of children and zoo animals, Bush and Baker were explicit about the threat to use force on October 29, as well as on November 1, when Bush said that he had "had it" with the treatment of the hostages. It could not have been lost on Bush's handlers that such saber rattling almost always translates into short-term increases in popularity.[67] Bush, we should remember, also faced a slate of serious domestic problems that made a focus on Iraq enticing. The threat of recession in particular was a real public concern. This is underscored by one government report that noted that the country had entered 1991 in the midst of its ninth recession since World War II.[68] The impact on the nation had become clear months before. Two polls showed that the war did cause a significant surge in consumer confidence, but, depending on the poll, that rise was enough only to bring consumer confidence back to where it had been before the crisis, and perhaps not even that far. By either poll, however, confidence declined by the fall of 1991 to a level where it had been in October 1990 — the lows of the Bush administration.[69]

The recession would have been exacerbated by rising oil prices. In describing the economy in late November, Federal Reserve Board Chairman Alan Greenspan noted that the economy had gone into a "meaningful downturn" as a result of the tightening of credit standards by the banks and rising oil prices caused by uncertainty about how the Persian Gulf crisis would be resolved.[70] Bush recognized that a "continuation in the Gulf of this kind of standoff" would adversely affect the U.S. and global economy.[71]

The recession also would have hurt Republicans in the critical midterm elections, in which White House incumbent parties have historically lost support. In addition to elections for all seats in the House of Representatives, one third of the Senate seats would be up for election. Of course, Bush would also stand for election in 1992. The Bush administration, we may recall, was attacked by Democrats for backing Saddam in the years preceding his invasion of Kuwait. Democrats reminded the White House that even as late as July 31, 1990, Assistant Secretary of State John Kelly told the House Foreign Relations Committee that "the US had no defense treaty with Kuwait and no obligation to come to its aid if attacked by Iraq."[72] The second factor was that Bush was weathering enormous criticism for abandoning his pledge not to raise taxes.

On November 1, Bush was asked why he was addressing the Kuwait issue with such intensity and "urgency." He responded that "the sand is running through the glass." The reporter, however, was suggesting that his action was motivated by his domestic problems, including the budget battle.[73] Was there some truth in the insinuation? It is interesting that Fitzwater, when asked about the administration's strategy, quipped that in many ways it was "too bad that we had that dip in attention during those two or three weeks," referring to the dip in attention away from the Persian Gulf crisis during the weeks when Congress and the White House were locked in a debilitating struggle over the budget.[74] During that time, President Bush's popularity ratings as well as that of the Republican candidates plummeted.

On November 1, Bush also noted that Saddam Hussein was even more brutal than Hitler, prompting the same reporter to ask him if there was a chance that he "might be exaggerating a bit for effect" in part because elections were one week away. The president, citing reports of atrocities in Kuwait, responded: "I don't think I'm overstating it. I know I'm not overstating the feelings I have about it."[75] Later in the news conference, another reporter asked the president to reveal "what Saddam had done that can be compared to the Holocaust." While noting that he had not invoked the Holocaust, which would be "outrageous" as a comparison, he did assert, with some reservation, that "Hitler did not stake people out against potential military targets and that he did, indeed, respect . . . the legitimacy of Embassies." Bush continued in this vein, saying also that he saw "many similarities" in the way the Iraqi forces "behaved in Kuwait and the Death Head's regiments behaved in Poland." The yoke around the analogy was beginning to break. One reporter noted a certain level of cynicism about Bush elevating the rhetoric against Iraq one week before the elections, noting that it appeared that U.S. diplomats at the embassy in Kuwait were being treated well, while Bush was describing them as being starved and mistreated. Bush said he did not know that they were doing so well, and continued to refer to U.S. hostages and others being mistreated.[76]

Bush found it "infuriating" that he could be accused of using Saddam to call attention away from the recent budget fight.[77] But through the DPM perspective, we would wonder if the timeline raised questions, because heated rhetoric against Saddam seemed to coincide with budget problems. Indeed, as Bush himself recognized, those were the days of his most frequent comparisons of Saddam to Hitler, and the budget crisis had in fact pushed Iraq off the front page. Moreover, Bush's own handlers recognized that he had done far better talking about Saddam than about domestic issues. After he dropped nearly thirty points in the polls in early November, in part as the result of his weak handling of the deficit negotiations, two public relations experts, Roger Ailes and Robert Teeter, told him to quit discussing the budget, emphasize the Persian Gulf and be presidential.[78] Indeed, it was only when Bush was associated with dramatic global events that his polls rose sharply.[79]

While the Munich analogy served its purpose for a while, it slowly began to lose its effect. In part, that was because it oversimplified a complicated crisis. Hitler controlled the strongest state in Europe and possessed enormous industrial and military capability. By comparison, Iraq was much weaker. While Saddam brutalized Iraq's Kurds and Shiite populations, this was a far cry from the shocking horrors of Hitler's genocide. While Hitler went on an ambitious, unprovoked, blatant march toward European and possibly global domination, Saddam had at least some reason to be disgruntled with Kuwait — and could not possibly dominate the whole world.

A Frustrated Administration: Trying to Meet Type 2 Promotional Goals

The crisis may have helped deal with a slate of Type 1 goals, but Washington increasingly became frustrated in its efforts to explain its policy. It realized that it also had what I call promotional goals to meet. As Scowcroft recalls, the administration sought to establish "that this was of vital national interest to the United States and we kept reiterating that over and over and over and the press kept saying 'You haven't explained why it is we're there and why this is a threat to U.S. national interests.' "[80]

The U.S. public and Congress were skeptical about fighting a war to protect oil supplies or to restore the undemocratic Kuwaiti monarchy. By mid-October, Fitzwater recalls, the administration's message was "losing focus," in part because "officials were tired of trying to sell the message over and over again."[81] Press coverage began to sour in early November, and Bush began to be criticized for an unclear and even confusing policy. Partly in response to these pressures, the administration, as Scowcroft points out, tended to react to complaints by expanding the list of U.S. interests to include such things as the new Hitler in the Middle East and the new world order, leading to "charges that each one of the principals had his own reasons and we really didn't have our act together."[82] National

Security Council Middle East Advisor Richard Haass interpreted the president's use of the Munich analogy in part as reflecting "frustration because we felt like we were not galvanizing public support."[83] And, for a time, the analogy worked, before it lost steam. Some officials such as Baker believed that of all the arguments used to convince the public that war was necessary, the one that caught on best was that we could not allow unprovoked aggression "by a large country against a smaller one. That we didn't do anything in the 30's when Hitler started, that this guy had a lot of the same tendencies."[84]

Facing a veritable firestorm of mounting criticism over the decision to double U.S. forces in November, the administration appeared to play up Iraq's nuclear threat. Public opinion polls taken in mid-November indicated national concern about potential Iraqi nuclear capability, which may very well have affected the administration's judgment.[85] Because of the Cold War, the public was concerned about and understood the danger of nuclear weapons, and Saddam Hussein was just the dictator to heighten those concerns. Indeed, studies show that an increase in general support for the war was correlated with increases in negative evaluations of Saddam Hussein, indubitably heightened by efforts at constructing him as problematic and immoral.[86] Bush asserted that Saddam was on the brink of developing nuclear weapons when his advisers believed it was more like five years. Testifying in front of Congress in November, former Defense Secretary James Schlesinger said that economic sanctions were far more effective than had been thought, and he criticized the White House for using nuclear weapons issues for reasons having more to do with public opinion polls than with reality.[87] Senator Al Gore, who was privately briefed by administration officials, suggested that statements that Iraq could have such a weapon within months were misleading.[88]

Facing continuing criticism, Bush chose to fly to Saudi Arabia for Thanksgiving with the troops. While he certainly cared about them, he also used the visit to focus public attention on Saddam's nuclear threat. Scowcroft and Cheney, meanwhile, moved quickly on talk shows to reinforce the president. On ABC's *This Week with David Brinkley*, Scowcroft said that it might be only a matter of months before Saddam obtained a nuclear weapon, suggesting that U.S. forces could face an Iraq with nuclear arms — if the United States waited too long to go to war. While U.N. inspectors discovered after the war that Iraq might have produced a nuclear weapon by April 1991, the administration did not know that at the time. At best we could say that some officials had the right hunch about Iraq's capability, but it is fair to say that the issue was also being exaggerated to some extent.

Perhaps the most controversial effort to explain the stakes involved and the U.S. role had to do with "jobs, jobs, jobs," which is how Baker explained it at a press conference in Bermuda on November 13. Contrary to what a generous Bush would later write in his memoirs, Baker's explanation did differ from those offered by Bush, although on November 15 Bush himself would also say in a CNN interview that "it does mean jobs," perhaps in an effort to cover for Baker.[89]

In the aftermath of witnessing the press jump all over Baker, Fitzwater told the president that it was "not about jobs and men don't die for jobs." As Fitzwater notes, Baker regretted the comment, which was made in an attempt to "draw a connection to the U.S. economy which was facing recession, hoping that would be convincing."[90] In response to Baker's comment—which no one in the group of eight liked—Bush called the group together.[91] In his capacity as the administration's spokesman, Fitzwater argued successfully that everyone should reiterate in their public relations interactions that the United States is in the Persian Gulf for the three original reasons offered by the president, which revolved around protecting regional stability.[92]

The administration had recognized the importance of an "inter-agency effort on public support" for its policy as early as August 7.[93] Intermittently, thereafter, Bush received advice from various notables, including Senate Republican leader Bob Dole, who counseled, in a private letter to Bush, to stay clearly "out front" in obtaining support on the Persian Gulf crisis.[94] However, it was not until after the United Nations set a deadline for Saddam's withdrawal on November 29—and the resulting uproar in Congress over lack of congressional consultation—that Bush and his advisers established a White House working group chaired by David Demarest, Assistant to the President for Communications. It included representatives from various offices of the White House and agencies such as State, Defense, Energy, Veterans Affairs, as well as the Joint Chiefs of Staff. As Scowcroft and Sununu put it in a memo to Bush's key advisers, the group was to be charged "with managing the Administration's public initiatives" on the Persian Gulf crisis, and was a "Presidential priority."[95] It would stitch together a broad public relations plan that would extend until Iraq's deadline for withdrawal on January 15th.[96] The plan involved a concerted effort to communicate to the public, Congress, lobbying groups, foreign leaders and others in key positions why the United States was willing to go to war in the Persian Gulf. But it was clear that within the broader context of an orchestrated public relations effort, Bush still took his own initiatives to construct the crisis. That included copious references to Saddam as Hitler-like and Iraq as a massive threat.

Counter-Construction

One of the individuals likely affected by Bush's construction was Saddam Hussein, though Saddam was as likely as Bush to engage in construction. While Saddam was being constructed as the major threat in Washington, he was constructing himself as the victim who would fight his way to glory, and George Bush as devilish. At various times, he referred to Bush as "Satan," the "Grand Satan," "Unholy," "Criminal Bush," "Loathsome Criminal," "Evil Butcher," and "Satan of the Era."[97] After Saddam declared that Bush was a criminal who should stand trial in Iraq, Bush sent a tongue-in-cheek memo to White House counsel, Boyden Gray, telling him to get a "visa and be ready to go to Baghdad" to defend him.[98] But clearly the war of words was on.

Saddam's attempts to construct the crisis were part of a broader propaganda war directed at his domestic audience, at the Arab world, and at the West.[99] Most of Saddam's efforts revolved around making him appear to be a devout Muslim staring down the imperial Christian West and the Zionist-American conspirators, a modern Saladin who would deal a blow to the returning crusaders. Frequently quoting the Qur'an, Saddam at one point referred to the famous battle of Badr in 624 a.d., in which a small group of Muslims defeated a far larger group of infidels. He reminded Iraqis how Muhammad had blinded the enemy by throwing sand in their eyes and suggested that the battle against the coalition could be similar: "You did not slay them, but God slew them."[100] In his famous "Mother of All Battles" speech, Saddam asserted typically that after Iraq won the war with the "infidels, the Zionists, and the treacherous, shameful rulers, such as the traitor Fahd," the door would then be "wide open" for the liberation of Jerusalem for all Muslims.[101]

As Saddam would have us believe — and perhaps believed himself — the Persian Gulf crisis was no longer about Iraq's invasion, but rather about the ghosts of the past. It was about the messianic, power-hungry, Muslim-hating West that wanted to squash him for his supposed insubordination. Saddam, the blatant secularist, would become a religious warrior, the re-engineered holy hero of al-Qadisiyah, where Arab armies defeated the Sassanian Empire in Persia during the early years of Islam, a battle to which he referred in his speeches during the Iran-Iraq and Persian Gulf Wars.[102]

Unfortunately for Saddam, such efforts did not work as well as he might have anticipated, save in places like Jordan, the West Bank, Algeria, and Yemen. It is true that many in the Arab world replaced their anger at Iraq with hostility towards the West—and towards the United States in particular—as the war approached and the bombs started to fall, but their sympathies were far more with the Iraqi people than with Saddam.[103] Most of the time Saddam botched his public relations stunts. Western hostages placed at military sites, for instance, became "guests" in Saddam's lexicon—a joke by any standard. President Bush even received an unsolicited letter from the former Iranian ambassador to the United Nations about this stunt. In it, he asserted that Saddam's use of "guests" was "entirely against the norms of the Arab world and Islam."[104] Global communications did not help the dictator. In Fitzwater's words, "people can form antagonisms against individuals far faster than against institutions and states, so by carrying Saddam so much, CNN allowed for antagonisms to form against him."[105] And the administration's communication team worked hard, by planning and organizing rebuttals to Saddam's many efforts to portray Iraq as a victim of the West, as a defender of the third world (to which Saddam offered free oil in early September), and as a protector against those who would defile the Muslim holy places.[106]

The DPM and Decision-Making: The Path to War

The DPM offers a perspective on how choices were made. The interest in meeting Type 1 and 2 goals made Bush and other decision makers less likely to give serious consideration to nonwar alternatives. Thus, by August 5 Bush asserted that the invasion would not stand, ruling out the possibility that the United States would contain Iraq and making it clear that the invasion would be reversed. The DPM would explain that behavior by inferring that the president was moved by several motivations, including Type 1 goals. But while Bush was prepared to use force early in the crisis, he was certainly not set on war until later in the crisis. Bush began to demonize Saddam, and a broader public relations effort laid out Iraq as a major threat in order to achieve Type 2 promotional objectives. Iraq's repeated efforts to float negotiated solutions, although half-baked and insufficient from the U.S. perspective, were not only rejected by Bush, but were rejected with bravado. By late September or early October—certainly by October 11—economic sanctions were largely ruled out as an alternative, possibly in a noncompensatory manner wherein such sanctions would fail to meet the crucial goal of meeting domestic-level goals. That was at a time when a confluence of factors was at play, including the budget impasse, recession, looming elections, and the need to sell the war option to the public.

Type 1 and 2 goals, and the lagged effects of earlier efforts at construction, made the administration less likely to consider economic sanctions seriously. Moreover, from the DPM perspective, we would argue that the failure to reach any form of a negotiated solution was not a foregone conclusion, even though the fact that the two states later went to war might make us think so. Rather, the administration's construction of Saddam and Iraq not only made it less likely to take any negotiation seriously, it also made Iraq less inclined to view an unconditional withdrawal as preferable to war (the evidence to support this latter view is laid out in chapter 3). Iraq's perception of U.S. behavior and its counter-response, including counter-constructions, further altered U.S., Iraqi, and global perceptions of the feasibility of such a settlement. The war of words was not mere rhetoric. While it may have served domestic-level goals, it also affected strategic interaction. An action-reaction cycle thus reinforced the administration's tendency to rule out a negotiated settlement. The use of force could further serve Type 1 and Type 2 goals.

Bush's heightened rhetoric against Saddam, including comparisons to Hitler, constructed Saddam and served multiple goals, but it also constructed Bush as the anti-Saddam crusader. Under the DPM, this partly explains why he felt that he had to take Saddam down.[107] Actions taken at one point affected actions at a later point. Bush's own words consigned him to a particular role and a tough path of action. Through his statements and actions, he affected not only his own course of action but also the calculations of all other decision makers who were influenced, willingly or unwillingly, by how he had changed the atmosphere of decision-making. Neither Bush nor members of his inner circle nor allied leaders could argue to offer Saddam a carrot in exchange for withdrawing from Kuwait. Quite the contrary, construction made war look far more sensible — even inevitable — and it decreased Saddam's proclivity to withdraw peacefully from Kuwait. Indeed, Bush created a discursive environment of language and analogies and metaphors through which many actors saw the crisis, and that discursive environment, that shared set of ideas, affected the crisis.

Interestingly, in his bizarre meeting with U.S. chargé d'affaires Joseph Wilson in Baghdad on August 6, Saddam foreshadowed his fate when he warned the Americans against taking "any bold steps that they can not retreat from."[108] By constructing Saddam and, in turn, altering how Saddam was perceived, Bush knowingly or unknowingly may have also boxed himself in and further shut down careful consideration of options, possibly in a noncompensatory manner of decision-making, even as Saddam may have become sufficiently pliable.

Conclusion

The domestic politics perspective yields a different perspective of U.S. behavior in the Persian Gulf crisis and the war than do the book's other perspectives. Yet while the DPM is distinct in its own right, it sits well with one of the broader empirical arguments of this book: by late October, Bush and the group of eight largely preferred war to Iraq's withdrawal from Kuwait. Bush was prepared to go to war from the outset, but he had not committed to this course of action until later. In the interim, his political interests and the question of domestic politics made the alternative of a negotiated approach less likely than it had been earlier in the crisis — though not impossible, were Saddam to become amenable to unconditional withdrawal. The negotiated alternative became all but a chimera later on, partly because of the feedback effects of Bush's own effort to construct Saddam. That made Bush more inclined to prefer war. But a question arises: why was this inclination of Bush's not tempered by members of his inner circle?

CHAPTER FIVE

Elements of Groupthink on the Road to War

The theory of groupthink developed by Irving Janis remains highly influential in explaining how groups make decisions.[1] Prior to Janis, social psychologists explored the implications of small group settings, but not in foreign affairs. While Janis set off a major research tradition that has sought to evaluate, challenge, and expand the theory of groupthink, its nonlaboratory application to political contexts outside of his original analyses is quite limited.[2] In exploring the Persian Gulf case, this chapter seeks to address that gap and to shed new light on why and how the United States went to war.

Groupthink as a Theory

Groupthink is a concurrence-seeking tendency that develops particularly at an early decision-making stage. In such a group, "the members' striving for unanimity override their motivation to realistically appraise alternative courses of action."[3] As Janis points out, when "groupthink dominates, suppression of deviant thoughts takes the form of each person's deciding that his misgivings are not relevant, that the benefit of any doubt should be given to the group consensus."[4] As a result, individuals hesitate to dissent, and conflict avoidance becomes a norm.

Groupthink is most likely to occur in groups that are cohesive or, in other words, exhibit a high level of amiability and esprit de corps among their members. But while high cohesiveness is necessary for groupthink to occur, it is not sufficient. Rather, four structural conditions (represented by box B-1 in Figure 1) also play a crucial role. They are (1.) group insulation from outside sources of information and opinion that could challenge group beliefs, (2.) a lack of tradition of impartial leadership, (3.) lack of norms requiring methodical decision-making procedures for considering evidence and alternative options, and (4.) homogeneity of the members' social background and ideology. These conditions increase the likelihood of groupthink because they predispose group members to

OBSERVABLE CONSEQUENCES

ANTECEDENT CONDITIONS

A

Decision Makers Constitute a Cohesive Group

+

B-1

Structural Faults of the Organization

1. Insulation of the group
2. Lack of tradition of impartial leadership
3. Lack of norms requiring methodical procedures
4. Homogeneity of members' social background and ideology, etc.

+

B-2

Provocative Situational Conflict

1. High stress from external threats with low hope of a better solution than leader's
2. Low self-esteem temporarily induced by:
   a. Recent failures that make member's inadequacies salient
   b. Excessive difficulties on current decision-making tasks that lower each member's sense of self-efficacy
   c. Moral dilemmas: apparent lack of feasible alternatives except ones that violate ethical norms

Concurrence-Seeking (Groupthink) Tendency

C

Symptoms of Groupthink

Type I. Overestimation of the group

1. Illusion of invulnerability
2. Belief in inherent morality of the group

Type II. Closed-mindedness

3. Collective rationalizations
4. Stereotypes of out-groups

Type III. Pressures toward uniformity

5. Self-censorship
6. Illusion of unanimity
7. Direct pressure on dissenters
8. Self-appointed "mind-guards"

D

Symptoms of Defective Decision-Making

1. Incomplete survey of alternatives
2. Incomplete survey of objectives
3. Failure to examine risks of preferred choice
4. Failure to reappraise initially rejected alternatives
5. Poor information search
6. Selective bias in processing information at hand
7. Failure to work out contingency plans

E

Low Probability of Successful Outcome

Figure 1. Theoretical Analysis of Groupthink. Based on Irving Janis and Leon Mann, *Decision Making* (Free Press, 1977).

believe that before all alternatives have been carefully weighed, a prevailing course of action will develop that they should support. The conditions represent "the absence of a potential source of organizational constraint that could help to prevent the members of a cohesive policy-making group from developing a norm of indulging in uncritical conformity."[5]

In addition to cohesiveness and the four structural conditions, Janis identifies a provocative situational context (caused largely by high stress) as contributing to groupthink (represented by Box B-2 in Figure 1). This context contributes to groupthink in part because it makes members of the group more cohesive in addressing the threat or challenge at hand. The antecedent conditions (group cohesiveness, the four structural conditions, and a provocative context) can cause groupthink. Groupthink, in turn, produces symptoms of groupthink or the observable consequences of groupthink (represented by Box C), and symptoms of defective decision-making, of which Janis identifies seven types (represented in Box D).

The Argument of the Chapter

None of the perspectives used so far in this book take us into the inner circle of decision-making to look at group dynamics, nor do we have existing scholarly accounts of these dynamics. We are thus left with a blind spot about not only how decisions were made but also why the United States went to war. The theory of groupthink rectifies this problem. This chapter argues that President Bush's inner circle exhibited significant elements of groupthink, a tendency to agree with each other, sometimes without carefully considering the costs and benefits of various alternatives. It also helps explain why the United States went to war: Bush faced little if any opposition within his inner circle. As we shall see in the balance of this chapter, the antecedent conditions of the groupthink theory (group cohesiveness, the four structural conditions, and a provocative situational context) were present in Bush's inner circle. This contributed to groupthink, and, in turn, to symptoms of groupthink and, technically speaking, defective decision-making.

Group Cohesiveness

Group cohesiveness was in part engendered by Bush's style, and existed to a significant extent. To be sure, it is normal for presidents to choose friends to join their cabinets. Trust and cooperation are well served by doing so, not to speak of managing campaigns and handling scandals. But in the Bush White House, camaraderie was perhaps unprecedented, despite the sometimes confrontational style of Chief of Staff John Sununu and Bush's unabashedly opinionated chief counsel C. Boyden Gray. Cheney, Bush, Gates, and Scowcroft had worked together at least as far back as the Ford administration, and Baker was a longstanding Bush confidant. Scowcroft, who had served in four administrations and had known Bush since the Nixon administration when he was Military Assistant to the President and Bush was at the United Nations, put it in perspective when he said that he had "never seen anything like it before."[6] Gates, another Washington veteran who served under six presidents, put it more interestingly: "I tell professors to throw those text books out, because at crunch time, it is personalities that count. The unique distinction was that the whole inner circle was composed of old friends who went fishing and golfing together. By contrast, as an insider, I can say that by comparison everybody hated everybody under Carter and Reagan."[7]

The group was so closely knit that some meetings seemed like a convivial card game, with feet kicked up and laughs making the rounds, rather than a sober, formal review of options. Cohesiveness was also fueled by norms of loyalty, notions on which Bush had been nursed starting at an early age, and which he proceeded to instill in others.[8]

Group Insulation

The first structural condition deals with group insulation, in this case insulation from the broader foreign policy community. The group of eight was, to some extent, insulated from outside sources of information and opinions, in part because it was structurally exclusive. Neither the group of four, composed of Bush, Quayle, Sununu and Scowcroft who met nearly each morning in regular staff meetings, nor the group of eight relied on outside experts or input, except sporadically from some foreign leaders.[9] The group was also insulated by design in order to avoid leaks to the press.[10] While U.S. Ambassador to Saudi Arabia Chas Freeman criticized U.S. decision-making for not integrating military and political approaches, Scowcroft wrote in his diary on August 6 that he recognized that the "economic side of the house feels excluded from the military options side; and yes, they are by my order. . . . Economics are an important part of this but we are trying to curtail some of the information on a 'need-to-know' basis."[11]

Bush's ability to press the war option was related to exclusive decision-making.

As with the decision to invade Panama, virtually all critical decisions were made by Bush and the group of eight, with the bureaucracy essentially shut out, although administration officials, including Bush, did extensively brief members of Congress and hear their concerns.[12] Despite that, Speaker of the House Thomas Foley was perplexed that he was notified so late of the October 31 decision to double U.S. forces in the Persian Gulf, made publicly only on November 8.[13] It is clear that the administration would have gone to war based on the Korean precedent in which President Truman intervened militarily in a U.N. collective security effort, even had Congress not supported the move.[14]

Lack of a Tradition of Impartial Leadership

The second structural condition exists when a leader does not feel restricted by "any organizational tradition to avoid pushing for his own preferred policies."[15] Under such conditions, the leader is more likely to be "partial," as I refer to it hereafter. Such partiality can be exercised through overt pressures or through subtle constraints on open expression. When a determined leader announces a certain decision, others are likely to accept it "somewhat uncritically, as though it were equivalent to a group norm."[16] While that does not transform them into sycophants, it makes them reluctant to express openly their doubts or to consider alternatives fully.[17]

It is abundantly clear that partial leadership was at play. From the outset, President Bush steered others toward his unyielding view that Iraq would face massive war if it did not withdraw unconditionally from Kuwait, and that it should be constrained even if it were to withdraw. While Bush acknowledged that the "Reagan style of 'collegial' management encouraged outspokenness at Cabinet meetings, with the president listening to a spectrum of opinion," his approach in the Persian Gulf crisis differed.[18] It also differed from presidents such as Dwight Eisenhower, who encouraged others at NSC meetings to challenge his position so as to explore options more systematically, and Nixon, who, in instituting a new NSC system, stressed that he wanted the bureaucracy to present clear alternatives, irrespective of what his key advisers were recommending.[19]

Bush at times did encourage open discussions and debate, but his approach did not place a high priority on each member airing doubts and raising objections. He certainly did not refrain from stating his preferences early on, sometimes in quite stark terms. He did not assign anyone the role of devil's advocate or ensure that all alternatives were carefully considered, which might have offset leadership bias, a dynamic we will cover in more detail later in this chapter.[20]

Lack of Norms for Methodical Procedures

The group of eight lacked procedures for evaluating alternatives (such as carefully considering the pros and cons of each available option). This is in stark contrast, for instance, to President Kennedy's decision-making group during the Cuban missile crisis, which laid out at least ten alternatives and discussed each methodically.[21] No available evidence exists that anyone even referred to the desirability of using methodical decision-making procedures in the Persian Gulf crisis.

Several factors can explain why such approaches were largely absent, especially on the more significant decisions. First, while Bush, as Powell described him in his earlier days, tended to be a cautious, information gatherer, in the Persian Gulf crisis he was sometimes more impetuous.[22] This was reflected in his bold and surprising statement that the invasion would not stand, in his emotional response to Kuwaiti atrocities, in his fiery and repeated use of the Munich analogy, and in his personalization of the conflict with Saddam.[23] It was also exhibited at times when he appeared to seek a pretext for attacking Iraq, such as in August when he wanted to enforce the naval blockade against Iraq, and Scowcroft dissuaded him from using force.[24]

Second, the president frequently knew what he wanted in advance of group of eight meetings, either through independent, bilateral, or group of four meetings.[25] As Sununu put it, a "lot of opinion shaping took place on a one-on-one basis and was then firmed in the group of four meetings, before impacting the group of eight as a whole."[26] Scowcroft understood "Bush's mind better than anyone else" and was central in pushing the "engine of government" that implemented Bush's views.[27] He encouraged Bush to shape his views privately sometimes.[28] This type of decision-making increased the president's power by decreasing the unpredictability of group meetings and helping shape group consensus. In this sense, in the Persian Gulf crisis at least, Bush was a bit like President Lyndon Johnson, who funneled and received information through McGeorge Bundy, his special assistant for National Security Affairs, and who used closed meetings with no established staff process for evaluating options.[29]

Scowcroft in particular spent much time privately with Bush, during which

Bush tested ideas on him and shared concerns.[30] Scowcroft was critical to the process in a way that Bush himself said history may never know.[31] Other than Henry Kissinger, we may be hard-pressed to find a national security advisor as influential as Scowcroft. Bush and Scowcroft had the close contact that Kissinger and Nixon established, with the added dimensions of implicit trust and deep friendship. Scowcroft had access to the president at any time, without an appointment, on virtually any issue. As Quayle put it, if the president did not decide an issue immediately, that usually "meant that Brent Scowcroft was going to get his way, and you could pretty much count on whatever position you'd just heard him argue being the one that would prevail."[32]

During the crisis, there were innumerable ways by which decisions could have been more methodical.[33] But Bush, buoyed by Scowcroft, often knew what he wanted to do, and given the group dynamics, could do so. To a lesser extent, Bush also confided in Baker on a one-on-one basis. Other officials, according to Colin Powell, did not even know what was going on in these bilateral meetings because Bush, they surmised, shared certain views only with Baker.[34] When it served particular goals, even Baker may have been excluded, either intentionally or unintentionally, from key decisions. In Freeman's view, "Baker played the role the president wanted him to play, which reflected poorly on the president's notion of the relationship between war and diplomacy. He cut Baker out of the military planning. Baker had no real idea of military planning. He did not understand the air campaign and he thought it would be one week long — ignorance that surprised me."[35] Schwarzkopf also was sometimes unaware of the decisions made in Washington.[36] That, in turn, meant that the Saudis were often in the dark. Indeed, Saudi General Sultan even went so far in one of his daily meetings with Schwarzkopf in December to suggest plans for an attack on Iraq that would start in Turkey, rather than Saudi Arabia, just to provoke a response from Schwarzkopf that might provide some insight into U.S. plans.[37]

Third, the complexities and time pressures of decision-making, particularly in periods of crisis, meant that decision-making perforce was often *ad hoc*. As Scowcroft recalls: "If there was time, I would talk to Cheney and Baker to gauge their mood. If a lot of space existed between their views, their principals would meet without the President and we would hash out differences or sharpen them to see where all of us were, so we wouldn't waste the President's time and then have one or more meetings with him at which he would then decide the big issues. For immediate issues, we called the Gang together but I hated to do that because it wasted the President's time. I tried to make meetings more efficient."[38]

Homogeneity of Members' Social Background and Ideology

Group insulation was enhanced by the homogeneity of social and ideological views within the group of eight. Bush and Scowcroft were not only close friends, but they also saw reality in general and Saddam in particular similarly. Scowcroft, moreover, viewed one of his core tasks as generating and maintaining harmony among the president's key advisers, which in his estimation had a "common world view" and shared "broad consensus about policy."[39] By contrast, in past administrations, the general world view itself was in question. Under President Carter, National Security Advisor Zbigniew Brzezinski and Secretary of State Cyrus Vance disagreed fundamentally on how to deal with Moscow. Vance argued for lowering tensions and Brzezinski for pursuing a tougher line, especially on global competition.[40] In Scowcroft's view, based on firsthand knowledge of both situations, the "Bush team wasn't anything like Cy Vance and Brzezinski, Weinberger and Shultz under Reagan, or even Kissinger and Rogers under Nixon."[41]

Moreover, the group had similar social backgrounds. Bush and Baker were old Texas friends who were also doubles partners in tennis; Gates, Scowcroft, Cheney, Baker, and Bush were old government hands, having been molded for two or more decades in the Washington milieu by virtue of their shared experiences.[42]

Provocative Situational Context

We can now examine the third and final antecedent condition — a provocative situational context (Box B-2 in Figure 1). The first aspect of this context is high stress from external threats. They arise chiefly when members are concerned about the risk of personal or organizational setbacks and losses from whatever option is chosen. Such threats can unify the group. While Janis emphasizes that high stress alone is neither a necessary nor a sufficient condition for groupthink, the social psychology literature indicates that stress adds to it.[43]

In the Persian Gulf War case, decision makers were not under constant pressure and stress, as was the case in the much shorter, thirteen-day Cuban missile crisis. But they did experience stress, which they often tried to relieve through jokes and raucous laughter.[44] In particular, they faced significant stress in the first weeks after the invasion, when an Iraqi invasion of Saudi Arabia was possible and could have threatened the first arriving U.S. forces.[45]

Meanwhile, developments that we take for granted in retrospect were not clear at the outset. It was unclear if the Saudis would grant access — and maintain that access — to the U.S.-led forces, if such forces could arrive to the Persian Gulf in a timely fashion, if Washington could effectively develop and maintain a coalition, and if Iraq could be evicted from Kuwait without massive casualties.[46] Bush and the group of eight were clearly able to deal with, but at the same time highly pressured by, the tough task of addressing the threat at the international level while dealing simultaneously with domestic opposition and politics.[47]

Stress took a visible toll. Scowcroft's many all-nighters, starting on August 2 when he awakened President Bush and the First Lady at 5 a.m. to fill them in on the invasion, at times left him dozing at meetings. This prompted Bush, in a gesture of affection, to bestow the "Scowcroft award" on anyone who fell asleep during meetings — a ritual that added to group cohesiveness. At certain junctures, however, Bush was quite concerned about Scowcroft's health, and that of others. As Bush recalls in his diary on January 24: "Everybody's got the shivers. I worry about Brent Scowcroft. He's been up all night — many, many nights and I worry about him. I call the doctor and the doctor goes down and talks to him and says he's got a fever and the flu and the guy just won't go home and take care of himself."[48]

Baker recalls that Bush agonized over potential casualties and understood that the crisis could bring down his presidency, a prospect that Baker and Quayle seriously contemplated as well, one with negative implications for all of the members of the group of eight.[49] As noted earlier in the book, the administration also faced a slate of evolving domestic problems, including a serious economic recession that higher oil prices would have exacerbated if the crisis were mishandled.

A second aspect of the provocative situational context is a temporary lack of self-esteem. It is an internal source of stress that is based much more on the self-perceptions of group members. This can be caused by (1.) recent failures that make members' inadequacies salient, (2.) excessive difficulties in making decisions that lower the members sense of self-efficacy, and (3.) moral dilemmas of having to choose an option that violates ethical standards of conduct. Such factors can bring the group closer together to cope with the challenge at hand. This condition is difficult to test because it requires knowledge about the psychology of decision makers that they may not themselves understand. We do know from the previous chapter that Bush was viewed as a "wimp" in some political quarters — a label at which he chafed; that an October 1990 budget showdown with Congress loomed and would push Bush to renege on his "no new taxes" pledge, damaging his credibility; and that decision-making was taxing.[50] But it is not clear how that affected the group's sense of efficacy. Finally, the group did face moral dilemmas associated with the decision to go to war, but they were not notably forced toward an option that they felt violated their sense of ethics, at least insofar as we can infer.

Concurrence-Seeking (Groupthink) Tendency

In brief, the group of eight was highly cohesive, the four structural conditions existed, and there was a provocative situational context. While no votes were taken at meetings, the record suggests that few individuals challenged the consensus that developed on the central decisions leading to war. We can contrast that with dynamics during other crises, such as the problem of Lebanon during President Reagan's first term, when core decision makers disagreed bitterly on the basic nature of U.S. policy, or even during the Cuban missile crisis.[51]

Symptoms of Groupthink

The antecedent conditions for groupthink largely existed, and, as Janis theorizes, their presence generates groupthink and its key symptoms: overestimation of the group's abilities and morality, closed-mindedness, and pressures toward uniformity. An aspect of overestimation is a belief in the inherent morality of the group, such that it views its motives and actions as just.[52] The members of the group of eight saw its motives as just. While differences existed, they felt that Saddam was an egregious transgressor who had to be checked and even punished. Moreover, the closed-mindedness of the group, which Janis identifies as an important symptom, was reflected in stereotyped views of rivals as too evil to negotiate with or too lame to be a serious challenge.[53] The group, and Bush in particular, did not view Saddam as a potential negotiating partner. And to some extent, that no doubt was related to the image of Saddam as evil. As Scowcroft noted of Bush: "I think he in his own mind demonized Saddam Hussein. And it's not hard to do. . . . When the reports came in about the way Kuwait was being treated, or just the way Saddam treated his own people in different circumstances, it took on a good versus evil kind of quality to it."[54] The administration refused not only to negotiate with Saddam, but also to give him even the semblance of a face-saving withdrawal. Iraq's aggression, of course, made negotiation problematic, even without stereotypes at play.

In the groupthink theory, pressures toward uniformity are manifested in four symptoms: self-censorship, an illusion of unanimity, direct pressure on any member who dissents or argues against any of the group's views, and the emergence of self-appointed "mind guards" who protect the group from adverse ideas or information that can undermine consensus.[55]

Self-censorship, as well as group pressure, is indicated by the fact that key group members agreed with Bush in the group, despite their own doubts about his approach outside it. Like Nixon, who, according to Kissinger, was opposed to settling "disagreements face-to-face" and "abhorred large meetings, especially those in which he might be asked to arbitrate between conflicting points of view," Bush himself hated confrontation.[56] As Quayle notes, Bush "wanted to avoid friction. He didn't mind debate in his administration, but he was very bothered by any report of people not getting along," so much so that he refused to settle disagreements among officials.[57] That predilection affected the decision-making atmosphere.

Bush preferred to generate consensus, and on some issues Scowcroft and others even screened the debate before it reached the president, thus injecting direct pressures on group members.[58] While Bush was much more likely to encourage debate on domestic issues, he was inclined to eschew it on foreign affairs, particularly in the Persian Gulf crisis case.[59] This proclivity, when combined with Bush's strong views and the general mood of harmony and loyalty discussed earlier, made members of the group of eight less likely to question him. Such an atmosphere may have also created the type of tacit peer pressure that made deviance from the norm more difficult. That was reflected in the high level of agreement in the group. As Cheney put it, while some disagreement arose, by and large the mood of the crisis was one of "cooperation and moving in sync and agreeing 90% of the time."[60] While there were instances of questioning who was giving the president bad advice, cooperation was strong.

Bush set the tone for consensus, and Powell, Baker, and Schwarzkopf voiced at most muted or transient concerns, despite their own views. As Scowcroft saw it, almost from the outset, "Powell was much less convinced about the importance of the invasion. That was manifested on several occasions. Powell was wedded to the notion that you used armed forces when the country is behind it, a function of his Vietnam experience which flavored Colin's approach."[61]

At the second NSC meeting on August 3, Powell lightly questioned whether it was worth going to war to liberate Kuwait, later admitting that the question was inappropriate, given that he was only supposed to give military advice.[62] Indeed, Cheney would reprimand him for precisely that. As Powell recalls, such questions annoyed Cheney enough that he cautioned him to "just do the military options. Don't be the Secretary of State or the Secretary of Defense or the National Security Adviser."[63] While that may have been motivated in part by turf issues, it also suggests direct pressure to control Powell's dissent.

Inasmuch as dissent existed, it did not cause serious disagreements on key questions. Bush helped ensure that "people acted in the bounds that he thought were appropriate," and the group of eight eventually fell in line with the move toward war.[64]

Symptoms of Defective Decision-Making

Groupthink can generate seven types of defective decision-making. It is vital to note that the theory does not require that all or even a majority of them occur. The most important symptom is that the group does not effectively discuss alternatives or options. This is especially problematic if a leader seeks to push an agenda on the group and reveals a favored policy alternative early in the decision-making process, before other alternatives can be discussed fully.[65]

Without opening up the black box of decision-making and delving into the inner workings of a unitary actor, we could reconstruct the crisis, as the Rational Actor Model would guide us, as one in which the United States weighed alternatives at the broadest level. That is, we would tend to explain the war decision as following a calculated approach in which it first tried diplomatic and economic means and military threats to get Saddam out of Kuwait before going to war. Inside the black box, we would also assume that aspects of decision-making reflected careful consideration of alternatives, an approach that some decision makers believed was, in some measure, executed. In Scowcroft's view, "while the President and I talked about the crisis frequently and were on the same wavelength, no *fait accompli* were presented to the group."[66]

However, these qualifications notwithstanding, the record strongly suggests that alternatives were not carefully evaluated on key decisions. At the first NSC meeting on August 2, 1990, which, as Scowcroft put it, some questioned the seriousness of the invasion and the necessity of a strong response from Washington.[67] In Scowcroft's view, it was treated "as if it were a *fait accompli* and as if it was hard to do anything about it."[68] Had the president, as Scowcroft points out, followed that sentiment, the U.S. approach would probably have been very different, aimed less at reversing Iraq's aggression than at preventing an invasion of Saudi Arabia.[69] Indeed, Colin Powell argued that United States should defend Saudi Arabia but not save Kuwait, prompting U.S. Ambassador to the U.N.

Thomas Pickering to respond that the result would be a loss of U.S. credibility with allies and friends.[70]

Bush and Scowcroft, however, decided to alter how the crisis was interpreted and treated and to foreclose that option.[71] Bush opened the second NSC meeting on August 3 with a few stern remarks and remained largely quiet thereafter; then Scowcroft asserted that the invasion was a critical threat to U.S. and global interests, one that could not be tolerated. Members present believed that Scowcroft sought to get others to fall in line, and indeed Scowcroft asserted that accommodating Iraq "should not be a policy option."[72]

Lawrence Eagleburger, aware of Bush's and Scowcroft's strong position, pounded the table and said, "Absolutely right," asserting that Saudi Arabia and then Israel would be Saddam's next targets.[73] As Scowcroft recalls and as Bush confirms, Eagleburger as well as Cheney helped to "reinforce solidarity for the larger group," contributing to a significant shift in "tone" from the first NSC meeting.[74] Bush, who had been somewhat reserved, concluded the meeting by asserting that the invasion was "an issue of great importance for the United States" and that "he expected everybody to treat it as such."[75] Powell was largely quiet, despite preferring to protect Saudi Arabia rather than to reverse the invasion.[76]

On August 5, when Bush asserted in public that Iraq's invasion would not stand, he effectively eliminated the alternative that the United States would allow Iraq to remain in Kuwait. Bush's statement was made outside the group setting, but it shaped group dynamics. An emerging norm for taking a strong, uncompromising stand began to develop in which Iraq would be removed by force if it did not withdraw unconditionally and totally. That contrasted sharply with the approach of President Kennedy in the Cuban missile crisis of October 1962. He wanted some meetings held without him, after learning that doing so motivated more spirited debate, and he purposefully made certain that his first moves did not shut down options for either side.[77]

Scowcroft, who was not consulted on Bush's statement despite being Bush's closest confidant in the crisis, was surprised at how early in the crisis Bush made it.[78] In Powell's view, the president had suddenly moved from "not discussing intervention" to a "line in the sand," which seemed impetuous.[79] At the time, U.S. forces were not ready for such intervention, and would not be ready for war until November, if not later. Powell viewed Bush's statement as altering U.S. options from protecting Saudi Arabia to evicting Iraq from Kuwait.[80] Stopping Iraq from invading Saudi Arabia was one thing, but Bush's statement seemed to amount to declaring war on Iraq, which, as even Bush recognized, was "a widespread reaction" to it.[81] Bush's August 5 statement was particularly powerful because the chief focus at Camp David the weekend before was defending Saudi Arabia rather than on evicting Iraqi forces from Kuwait.[82]

While Powell and Baker realized that there had been little debate on the options of deploying forces to Saudi Arabia and reversing the invasion, Powell did not question the move at the NSC meeting on the evening of August 5.[83] From the outset, Powell's attitude was that the "President should not be just looking at a single option of invading at the end of a time"; indeed, Powell "felt it was important that he look at all options available to him."[84] He presented Bush with roughly that position on September 24 in a brief meeting, only to be rebuffed in short order.[85]

As described by Scowcroft, Gates, and Fitzwater, Powell's opposition during the crisis was "subliminal."[86] As Fitzwater recalled, starting from the first day "Powell never offered a word of reluctance about the approach, or even suggested reservations about not using economic sanctions longer, despite our many discussions on it."[87] Gates, who was at most of the group of eight meetings, further confirms that point: "I never heard Colin Powell try and deflect the President from his course of action or to argue in front of the President for containment. I don't recall any such thing. He would at times in the privacy of Scowcroft's office, sometimes with Cheney there, sometimes with Cheney and Baker both there make those points."[88]

Like Powell, Baker was concerned about the path toward war. As Eagleburger observed, Baker "in his gut, preferred not to do any of this."[89] Baker informed Powell early on in the crisis, after Powell had contacted him to express concern over the march to war, that the State Department was preparing a report on the advantages of waiting for economic sanctions to work.[90] Baker was concerned that the United States would assume major commitments without considering all of the consequences, and he wanted to give economic sanctions a chance.[91] However, no evidence at hand suggests that he raised that option seriously, if at all, at meetings. As Gates recalled, "Baker's reservations were never done in meetings — perhaps privately with the President, since he hoped that diplomacy would work to get Saddam out."[92]

Schwarzkopf, who believed that Washington was moving too quickly toward force, also preferred other options.[93] However, his opposition in and outside meetings with the group of eight was low-key, except for a single press conference, in which he expressed his misgivings about the option of moving toward war in lieu of pursuing economic sanctions.[94] Even later in the crisis, when speaking to Bush, he voiced no objections to ending the war earlier, although he in fact strongly believed that more time was needed to crush Saddam's Republican Guard.[95]

By invoking the Munich analogy of failed appeasement and repeatedly comparing Saddam Hussein to Hitler, Bush also clipped the potential for the group of eight to consider even a veiled face-saving withdrawal for Iraq as an option. In this sense, cognitive influences were related to groupthink by motivating the partial behavior of the group leader. If Saddam was Hitler and Iraq was a major threat to regional and world peace, then it must be treated firmly, even punished. That meant that economic sanctions were dubious, a view that Bush may have started to develop tentatively as early as August 3, but more definitively thereafter.[96] At an October 11 meeting, the president and the group of eight agreed that military action, and not sanctions, would almost certainly be needed to evict Iraq from Kuwait.[97]

The exclusive nature of the group of eight and the rejection of methodical decision-making procedures both contributed to groupthink and made it easier for Bush and Scowcroft to advance the war option without carefully considering the costs and benefits of other alternatives. The group of eight had slowly coalesced, behind its strong and partial group leader, around the notion that economic sanctions would fail. While Powell and Baker had voiced some dissent outside the group, there had "never been," as Michael Gordon and Bernard Trainor point out, "much of a debate" on that score, or, for that matter, on the decision to double U.S. forces in the Persian Gulf, which was made at an October 31 NSC meeting.[98] Bush insisted on that decision ahead of most of his advisers, and it was adopted without consulting the most senior U.S. generals and admirals, including Powell, who was disturbed by it, and Schwarzkopf, who was furious about it.[99] Freeman, who played a fundamental role with Schwarzkopf in the field and was in communication with Washington, asserted his view that "the record will show that a lot of issues were not fully discussed."[100]

Key members of Congress also objected to what they viewed as a hasty move away from economic sanctions.[101] Members of the group of eight fell in line, despite their private reservations; by November, even Baker, who had wanted to give sanctions a chance, joined the group of eight in arguing that an "ultimatum, plus a major force build-up, would make it clear we're serious," although he thought "ultimatum" was the wrong word to use.[102] That ultimatum was issued on November 8, triggering congressional hearings of the Foreign Relations and

Armed Services Committees and allowing for a serious, sustained challenge to the administration's approach. "The chorus," Bush recalled, was still to "let sanctions work."[103] Bush's approval rating on the crisis dropped from 75 percent in August to 50 percent, reflecting a public that remembered that Vietnam was also supposed to be a short war.[104]

Some members of the Joint Chiefs of Staff, with whom Bush met on December 1, were also surprised about being shut out of the decision-making process.[105] While Bush informed them of his plans, like Congress they were not consulted beforehand. Even the offer to send Baker to Baghdad, driven partly by concern about weakening public support for war, was made quickly and with barely any discussion, other than with Cheney, who did not mind, and Scowcroft, who was displeased because of the message he thought it would send regarding Bush's resolve.[106]

Other Manifestations of Defective Decision-Making

Not only did the group of eight sometimes fail to evaluate options, it also engaged in an incomplete survey of objectives. As Scowcroft testifies, the administration tried to generate public support, which had begun to flag in November, by expanding the list of U.S. interests to include such things as stopping the next Hitler, protecting jobs, and creating a new world order. The administration's shifting objectives confused the public and necessitated the development of a coordinated public relations plan.[107] The goal was to make sure that all of the group of eight members and their assistants hammered home the same objectives in their speeches.[108]

On some issues, moreover, the group of eight also failed to explore the risks of decisions. For instance, Bush's statement that the invasion would not stand or his myriad efforts to describe Saddam in Hitlerian terms were not discussed in the group to assess their risks, even though some found them problematic. Thus, Powell described Bush's August 5 statement as policymaking "on the hoof," while even Scowcroft told Bush privately that the use of the Hitler analogy was problematic.[109]

Some of Bush's independent actions, as well as the strong decisions made by consensus in the group, also made it difficult to reappraise alternatives. Thus, the administration early on asserted that it was seeking an unconditional withdrawal by Iraq from Kuwait as a requisite for ending the crisis. This made it hard for the group of eight to consider, for instance, the alternative of offering Iraq a veiled face-saving withdrawal in order to avoid war, despite the fact that Saddam appeared to become more willing—albeit probably not sufficiently willing—to meet U.S. demands as the crisis proceeded. No evidence suggests that the benefits of such an approach, or the continued use of economic sanctions, were reconsidered in the group of eight. In fact, the evidence suggests precisely the opposite.

This may be partly because of biases in processing information. Such a bias results when information that challenges the group's decisions or consensus is screened out. Biases result from many different processes, but, as discussed in chapter 3, one cognitive bias that was clearly at play in the Persian Gulf crisis was historical analogy.

Conclusion

The theory of groupthink helps explain how President Bush could advance the war option in a setting where key military officials, core members of Congress, foreign leaders, significant elements of the public, and members of Bush's inner circle believed that other alternatives should be given greater consideration. Longstanding friendships and a culture of consensus did exist in the group of eight, as well as strong loyalty to the president. That made it extraordinarily cohesive. As a highly partial leader, Bush pushed for the war option in a decision-making process that was fairly insulated from outside input, generally lacked methodical procedures for appraisal, and was marked by a high level of homogeneity in views and background among the decision makers. Stressful conditions added to group cohesiveness. While Bush faced public and congressional opposition, he did not encounter many challenges within his collegial and cohesive inner circle. The president's partial and strong role, combined with some implicit and explicit pressures toward uniformity, further decreased potential challenges.

CHAPTER SIX

Government Politics

Not Much, Actually

In *Essence of Decision*, Graham Allison applied three decision-making models to the Cuban missile crisis of October 1962, when the superpowers edged toward nuclear war. One of them was the government politics model, which he helped develop, and which was recently revised in an updated edition of the book.[1] (I will refer to government politics as GP, which is what the model assumes is prevalent in the reality of government behavior, and to the model as the GPM.) Allison's work was a classic in part because it presented alternative models, the GPM as well as the organizational process model, which illuminated state behavior that appeared too irrational and/or complex to be explained by the dominant RAM. In this sense, he offered a basis for challenging the preeminent RAM. Subsequently, the GPM has proven to be of cross-disciplinary influence, and it has illuminated decision-making. Indeed, a rare study commissioned by President Carter about decision-making in eight of his administration's key domestic and foreign policies revealed the prevalence of GP, thus confirming the model.[2] Much work of value exists on the GPM, but scholars have largely failed to take up Allison's challenge to test and build the theory.[3] Insofar as they have done so, for the most part they have not sought to use interviews with key decision makers, or to test the theory systematically.[4]

The Finding of This Chapter

Of all of the perspectives, the GPM performed poorly enough in explaining how and why the United States went to war that there is no real sense in presenting it as a potentially useful perspective. Nonetheless, the work in this chapter is important. It develops an approach for testing the model that is lacking in the literature, and it shows why and how it failed. This is useful because, as the integrated approach suggests, we need to run reality through multiple perspectives. Testing the GPM also reveals important aspects of the crisis. In failing, it helps us better understand the factors that were most crucially at play and provides some insight into the model itself. It shows, for instance, that individual decision makers largely did not engage in petty bureaucratic politics and rivalry, and that government politics was not prevalent in part because President Bush helped preempt such politics. Unlike any of the other perspectives, it also draws our attention to the committee dynamics of the deputies group, on which little work has been done. I will discuss the deputies group in more detail later in the chapter.

The Government Politics Model

I derive four assumptions of the GPM from the most authoritative account of the model by Allison and Zelikow, and contrast them with the assumptions of the RAM.[5] The goal here is not to illuminate the nuances of these models, which is not necessary to the present work, but rather to lay them out clearly enough to make the GPM testable.

First, while the present version of the RAM assumes that decisions are made out of concern for national interests (as the decision makers perceive them), the GPM assumes that decision makers are affected by and act as advocates for their particular bureaucracies. They share some concern about national interests, but they have quite different interests, priorities, and questions in mind that arise mainly from the departments they represent.[6] This leads to the notion that where you stand is "substantially affected by" where you sit.[7] It follows that if we know the propensities and priorities stemming from each decision maker's roles and positions, we can predict each person's stand on a range of issues. Behavior is determined, that is, mainly by the office and position rather than by peculiarities associated with the individual.

While players assume preferences and adopt stands based on "parochial priorities and perceptions," each player's impact on results will be centrally a function of relative bargaining power among the players. That power derives from bargaining advantages and the skill and will to use them, as well as from how the players perceive those advantages. The nature of interaction among particular actors will also be affected by the broader political context. Bargaining does not occur in a vacuum. Rather, actors need to be adept at using action-channels or regularized means for taking government action on particular issues. Knowing how to use and exploit institutionalized procedures for facilitating or implementing decisions is an important asset, as is an understanding of the rules of the game. These rules stem from domestic laws and statutes, which can influence how bureaucratic politics are played.[8]

Second, while the RAM portrays decisions as resulting from a process of careful cost-benefit calculations of potential options, the GPM assumes that they result from conflict, confusion, bargaining, and compromise among individuals in a broader bureaucratic setting. Since individual views and recommendations differ, each player "pulls and hauls with the power at his discretion for outcomes that will advance his conception of national, organizational, group, and personal interests."[9] As David Welch points out, the GPM does not assume that players behave irrationally in the games in which they partake, but rather that the sum total of those games produces an outcome that does not conform with what a unitary rational actor would have chosen.[10]

Third, bargaining is not limited to a particular group of individuals or to lower-level actors. It occurs among all group members, which must include the president, who uses his bargaining advantages to try to alter the interests of others to what he wants — a task that requires much skill.[11]

Fourth, under the GPM, while the individual players are viewed as rational, the outcome of their interaction does not reflect a careful cost-benefit analysis, but rather a collage. This collage reflects the decisions and actions of individuals and groups of players in multiple interactions, the bargaining among individuals who represent particular agencies in a committee setting, and the relative influence of central actors or subsets of actors in more specific circumstances. Thus, the U.S. decision to quarantine Cuba during the missile crisis could be viewed as a collage whose "pieces included the president's initial decision that something forceful had to be done; the resistance of McNamara and others to a surprise air strike. . . . To get from those impulses to a government decision that combined both the blockade and air strike approaches required an effort to forge the synthesis."[12]

Typically, as the notion of a collage suggests, the final decision is not an intended outcome of the group and will not reflect the preferred option of any one individual or leader. In this sense, knowledge of the president's position or that of any salient leader is, by itself, "rarely a sufficient guide for explanation or prediction."[13]

The Persian Gulf War Case

With respect to the Persian Gulf case, this chapter focuses on two types of decisions. I refer to the first type as the "whether to" decisions because they eliminated key alternatives on the road to war. They include President Bush's assertion on August 5, 1990, that the invasion would not stand, the move away from economic sanctions as a way of forcing Iraq to withdraw from Kuwait, the doubling of U.S. forces in the region in November, and the decision to go to war. While I focus on these decisions because of their gravity, this chapter also explores the "how to" questions. They refer to how decisions, once made, would be implemented. They include decisions such as how to stop tankers headed for Iraq, how to deal with Iraq diplomatically, and how to execute militarily the decision to attack Iraq. Examining both types of questions allows added insight into whether model performance is influenced by the type of decision.

Testing the Model

The need for more tests of the GPM is abundantly clear. Heretofore, analyses of this model have been largely theoretical rather than empirical.[14] That may be because, as several scholars have pointed out, the GPM is so complex that it is not clear, as it stands, what would falsify its predictions.[15] One way to do so is to infer from the model a specific and narrowly defined behavior that would confirm or disconfirm it, such as expectations that budgeting decisions in the U.S. Navy would reflect GP.[16] A second way is to distill from it core assumptions, infer from them a set of expected behaviors, and match them against the facts. Both approaches are valid, but this chapter uses the latter to set up a general test that may be used by others, and which I will apply in the Persian Gulf War case. While theories can be useful even if their assumptions are unrealistic, it is recognized that one way to test theory is to determine significant facts and match them against the theory.[17]

The four assumptions elaborated upon below are crucial to the model. The *first assumption* is that players' stands or views on issues will derive chiefly from role and position. We can test that aspect of the model in an innovative manner. Indeed, if bureaucracy truly shapes and influences the stands of players, which is a core assumption of the model, then we would expect players from different bureaucracies to assume different stands and players from the same bureaucracy to assume similar stands.[18] Testing the model in this way is advantageous. It obviates the need to infer the expected stands of players — a point upon which scholars may disagree. Indeed, we need not infer what we would expect actors to do in order to compare their actual behavior. That comparison itself provides testing leverage, without the potential problems of inference. A question arises, however: which actors do we compare in any case?

We need to search for key actors from similar and different bureaucracies who influenced decision-making, especially in a committee setting. Based on that, the first best test in the Persian Gulf War case is to compare the views of Secretary of Defense Richard Cheney and Secretary of State James Baker. They played critical roles, and we can infer from the model, as Allison and Zelikow point out, that they will "differ radically" based in part on the pressure and nature of their positions.[19]

The second test is to compare the stands of the Secretary of Defense and the Chairman of the Joint Chiefs of Staff. To be sure, they do face somewhat different bureaucratic pressures within the Department of Defense, and so we would not predict that they will have the same stands on all key issues.[20] However, if bureaucracy does matter fundamentally in shaping and influencing stands, we certainly should not expect them to take significantly different stands.

That brings us to a third test. By and large, we also should not expect a greater difference in stands between the Secretary of Defense and the Chairman of the Joint Chiefs of Staff, than between the Chairman and the Secretary of State. This is because the bureaucratic milieu and pressures that Powell and Cheney faced within the Department of Defense were more similar than those that Powell faced compared to Baker, or that Cheney faced compared to Baker. This largely holds, notwithstanding the fact that the Chairman and Defense Secretary do face different bureaucratic realities, risks, and interests within the Department of Defense. Based on the foregoing discussion, it is fair to say that we would expect the following three propositions to be true:

1. Cheney and Baker took different stands.
2. Cheney and Powell took similar stands.
3. Cheney and Powell were closer in their stands than were Powell and Baker.

The GPM is based on a *second key assumption*. Players will not only hold different stands, they will also promote different recommendations, bargain over outcomes, and generate conflict. The real question, however, is not whether they will do so, but to what extent. One way to explore that question is to place bargaining on a "continuum" of actions that represent increasing levels of GP (hereafter referred to as the continuum). As conceived herein, this continuum begins with explanation and ends with rivalry.

1. Explanation: the effort to communicate information about, or ideas that emanate from, the player's bureaucracy.
2. Bargaining: the use of give-and-take approaches to achieve compromise such that players are inclined to assent to one option only on condition of another.[21]

3.   Advocacy: the active pursuit of the interests of the bureaucracy.
4.   Rivalry: extended, structural competition.

While these actions overlap, they are quite different, as discussed later in this chapter. The Persian Gulf War case actually provides us with two sub-cases for testing such levels of GP: the group of eight or Bush's inner circle, and the deputies committee, which I will define below. If the GPM is revealing, we would expect the continuum to manifest itself there.

The *third assumption* is a more specific form of the second one. While we may not think of presidents as bargainers, in fact they sometimes are, something the model clearly assumes.[22] In the Persian Gulf War case, we would infer from the model that Bush:

1.   Argued with his senior staff about key decisions.
2.   Offered give-and-take solutions.
3.   Faced at least some bureaucratic resistance, which might have pushed him to bargain.

The *fourth assumption* is that the decision-making process will produce decisions that represent collages. Collages are typically a combination of inputs, representing the views and stands of different players. They reflect the varied brushstrokes that "when stuck to the same canvas, constitute government behavior relevant to an issue."[23] If decisions take the form of collages, then we would not expect them to:

1.   Reflect President Bush's imprimatur.
2.   Be intended by any one individual.
3.   Cause surprise among the decision makers.

Indeed, since collages represent multiple, competing, and sometimes *ad hoc* inputs that result from bargaining and compromise, no one actor is expected to dominate the collage or to be able to predict the outcome. Rather, the outcome is a function of loose, bureaucratic politics. If decisions represent a collage, we would not expect them to surprise players, because a collage is a combined effort. Players are largely aware of their participation in generating a collage. By contrast, individual or noncommittee decision-making can take place unbeknownst to others and produce decisions that surprise those not privy to the decision-making process. As with the second assumption of the model, we can test the GPM by exploring both the group of eight and the deputies committee.

While several committees composed of deputies played a role, the main deputies committee, which framed many of the key issues and papers for the group of eight, consisted of six core individuals who represented members of the group of eight and, thus, acted as their deputies: Gates, who chaired the deputies committee; Paul Wolfowitz, Assistant Secretary of Defense for Policy; Robert Kimmitt, Under Secretary of State for Political Affairs; Richard Kerr of the CIA; Admiral David Jeremiah, Powell's deputy; and Richard Haass, Special Assistant to the President for Near East and South Asian Affairs, who drafted most of the papers and worked closely with Brent Scowcroft. The committee usually met in the West Wing conference room in the White House. It aimed to improve coordination among various agencies, which was viewed as lacking in the decision to go through with the December 1989 invasion of Panama that ousted the drug lord and dictator, Manuel Noriega.[24]

Government Politics and the Persian Gulf Crisis

Did players behave in a manner that suggests that their stand depended substantially on where they sat — the first key assumption of the model? We can test the first three propositions in order to explore that question, by first examining the stands of Powell, Cheney and Baker.

Powell's Stand

Powell viewed the crisis largely in military terms and offered military options, and the executive branch stayed out of that process, with the not insignificant exception of vetoing the military's original plan for a frontal attack on Iraqi forces.[25] But, as noted in the previous chapter, while Powell did not try to influence Baker on diplomacy, he did overstep his mandate at times by questioning the nature and clarity of U.S. political goals.[26]

In military terms, Powell sought overwhelming military capability to meet goals. Indeed, he was concerned when Bush stated dramatically on August 5 that Iraq's invasion would not stand. As discussed earlier in the book, for Powell, that statement created a new "direction" for the crisis and a "new mission."[27] Cheney, by contrast, approved of Bush's resolve.

As noted earlier, Powell went out of his way to meet with the president on September 24 in order to present the case for long-term economic sanctions and containment as an alternative to war. Unimpressed, the president told Powell "that's all, very, very interesting. It's good to consider all options but I just don't think we're going to have time for sanctions to work."[28] While Powell preferred to run economic sanctions longer, he wanted the ability to launch a massive and decisive attack, if war was to be the president's decision. Powell supported Bush's decision to double U.S. forces in the Persian Gulf in November, but that was because Bush had already dismissed economic sanctions as not viable. Powell, however, was very reluctant, leading Gates to assert in retrospect that the "biggest doves in Washington wear uniforms."[29]

Moreover, Powell repeatedly emphasized the potential for casualties, feeling, as Gates recalls, "an enormous sense of responsibility for the troops — worried that they were being pushed into conflict."[30] Even in the last meeting prior to the attack on Iraq, Powell told Bush that war was messy and that the casualties could be many, perhaps playing his post-Vietnam role of reminding civilian leaders that war was serious business.[31] Powell reluctantly supported the move toward war after the potential for casualties was understood, military capability matched the goals laid out by the administration, and Bush committed himself to going to war.

Unlike Cheney, who did not even want Bush to seek formal congressional approval on January 9 for the use of force, Powell would have preferred to run economic sanctions much longer. While the president never had much faith in sanctions, it took Powell until mid-October to accept that they would not "work in any kind of reasonable time."[32] In his own words, Powell was a "reluctant warrior."[33]

Baker's Stand

Like Powell, Baker did not assume a hawkish stand. He largely pushed diplomatic options at the United Nations and repeatedly sought U.S.-Soviet cooperation in order to generate a peaceful outcome. Baker had greater faith in that approach than did most others on the group of eight.[34] As discussed earlier in the book, Baker was also more inclined than Scowcroft, Cheney, or the president to allow Saddam a face-saving withdrawal, albeit a very modest and ambiguous one.[35] Like Powell, Baker also was concerned about the potentially perilous path toward war, shifting to support that path when it became increasingly clear that the president was committed it.[36]

Cheney's Stand

Cheney's stand is not particularly hard to track. He was as hawkish as Bush and Scowcroft on a range of issues. As Scowcroft recalls and Bush confirms, from the first NSC meetings, such as the one on August 3, Cheney take a very strong stance on Iraq.[37] Unlike Powell, he strongly favored Bush's statement that the invasion would not stand, and stoked his resolve.[38] He also did not favor continuing economic sanctions against Iraq, strongly supported the doubling of forces in

Table 2. Key Decisions

	"Will Not Stand"	Economic Sanctions	Doubling Forces	Launching War
Powell	Not favored	Favored	Reluctant support	Cautious support
Baker	Concerned	Favored	Concerned	Support
Cheney	Strongly favored	Not favored	Strongly favored	Strongly favored

the Persian Gulf in November and the decision to go to war, and even, as mentioned above, was opposed to seeking formal congressional approval on January 9 for the use of force.[39]

Analysis

The foregoing discussion allows for clear tests of our three propositions. The first proposition is strongly confirmed. Cheney and Baker held different positions, as we would expect. The second is strongly disconfirmed. Cheney and Powell did not hold similar positions. While Powell and Cheney, to be sure, faced somewhat different influences within the defense establishment, we would not expect their views to be so dissimilar, as Cheney himself recognized they were, if bureaucratic influences played a significant role.[40]

The third proposition is also strongly disconfirmed. As Table 2 shows, the differences between Cheney and Powell were far greater than the distance between Powell and Baker. In fact, Baker and Powell were both concerned that the United States was moving toward war too quickly (a concern heightened by Bush's statement that the invasion would not stand) and preferred to continue economic sanctions against Iraq longer in lieu of using force.[41] While Powell and Baker both supported doubling U.S. forces in the Persian Gulf in November, and giving Iraq an ultimatum prior to going to war, Baker to some extent and Powell to a greater extent were far more cautious about these decisions than Bush, Scowcroft, and Cheney.[42]

Bargaining and the Continuum of Government Politics

While we can compare the stands of players, it is also important to explore how they behave in a group or committee setting. The evidence at hand suggests that it would be misleading to argue that players were not consciously or subconsciously influenced by their position or role, and did not at certain junctures present and explain what was occurring in their departments or try to elucidate their department's position, insofar as one existed. But while such efforts at "explanation" confirm the GPM in a rudimentary way, they do not confirm it alone. As suggested by the continuum developed earlier in this chapter, explanation is the least intense of GP behaviors. We must also explore the other parts of the continuum: bargaining, advocacy, and outright rivalry.

Indeed, players can communicate information about, or ideas that emanate from, the bureaucracies they represent and seek to explain their aggregate positions on issues, without bargaining. Bargaining is far more competitive. It involves a strategic interaction where actors seek to do their best, given the positions and likely responses of others. Bargaining creates the potential for conflict, acrimony, and even rivalry, if it breaks repeatedly.

Advocacy, meanwhile, is even more intense than bargaining. That is because advocates who push a bureaucratic objective are less likely to make the tradeoffs necessary for successful compromise. They may decide to lean towards advocacy in lieu of bargaining for myriad reasons, including self-righteousness, a sense that their departments are dominant enough not to have to bargain much, or because of a directive from their departments not to bargain or their perception of such a proclivity. Whatever the case, they are likely to play a rougher game of GP. It may even assume the dimensions of rivalry when they see themselves as being caught in a more enduring struggle that begins to resemble aspects of a zero-sum game.

The differences between the behaviors identified on the continuum are quite meaningful, both for understanding the Persian Gulf War case and the general thrust of the GPM. They help identify gradations of GP, and help us explore not whether it exists, but rather to what extent. As analyzed below, in the Persian Gulf War case, decision makers did present and explain what was transpiring in their respective departments and at times did communicate the general position held by those departments, especially in the deputies committee. Less frequently, they also argued on behalf of their departments. But little evidence at hand reflects any serious bargaining, much less advocacy or rivalry. At a minimum, these findings also suggest that actors did not focus much attention on non-national interests, suggesting but not confirming that they focused on the process of achieving national goals, however they perceived them.

The Deputies Committee

A clear emphasis was placed on having the players explain their departments' positions, but this was done largely by design, in order to obtain perspective. Indeed, as Gates observes, we "expanded the group to get people who could commit their departments, who could vote their department's stock in a sense."[43] Committee members identified solutions to problems that made sense across agencies and departments, and, in so doing, aimed to avoid the turf wars and miscommunication that often plague inter-agency relations.[44]

Furthermore, many factors influenced the deputies beyond departmental motivations. Gates observed that "he never heard people advocate or push the views of their department"; they were "much more likely to argue the position of their principal, which was more personal than departmental."[45] In Haass's view, "they were influenced by many factors in how they thought and acted. People are pretty well entrenched in their views by that age. I have to run it by people is what they would say. You should know where my building is coming from, they would point out. But that was to provide input."[46] While members did try to present how their departments would view a certain decision, they did not argue and bargain much based on where they sat.[47] Reflecting broader reality in the group, Kimmitt observed that, while he did present some State Department views on issues, he was "neither sent into a meeting as an advocate for State nor played that part when there."[48]

Rather than bargaining and conflict, consensus also tended to prevail. For instance, the group believed by September or October that economic sanctions could not be sustained and were not affecting Saddam, and that the United States could not produce an intrusive enough process to stop his development of nuclear weapons. Thus, the committee members were comfortable with the idea of using force.[49] In any event, they were unlikely to challenge the group of eight because they represented its members and because their mandate was essentially limited to providing background studies to the group of eight. In Haass's words, "if we thought the issue was above our pay grade, we kicked it upstairs but first checked with our principals."[50]

If the GPM predicted a collage of decisions, the metaphor for the deputies group may have been bed-making. As Jeremiah put it: "I thought about decision-making as a sheet and if you pull on one side then it all falls apart, so you need to pull on all sides and produce a process."[51] Indeed, the deputies committee consciously focused on U.S. national goals, although it sometimes did so with more concern for department stands than at other times. Thus, when deciding how to stop tankers headed for Iraq in defiance of the embargo, the group, as Jeremiah points out, "went around the circle and asked which of several options should we pursue . . . and wanted to make sure that it made sense to all the respective departments in order to maximize inter-agency cooperation for key goals."[52] The process, as described separately by all of the interviewees, involved explanation but little bargaining and even less advocacy or rivalry.

The Group of Eight

The process in the group of eight was not dissimilar, both in intensity and duration. The members did present departmental views and input. Thus, at the second NSC meeting on August 3, Eagleburger, sitting in for Baker who was abroad, did suggest that the United States work through the United Nations to authorize economic and military force, when it appeared as if Iraq might invade Saudi Arabia. Meanwhile, Powell and Cheney did present military options.[53]

Members of the group of eight sometimes also argued the views of their departments at the beginning of discussions, although "half way through you would hear their individual views come through, after they did their responsibility to their agency."[54] Their actions, thus, were limited in duration. While differences arose, and although there were instances of questioning who was giving the president bad advice, cooperation was strong. As Sununu put it, in talking to "previous chiefs of staff, I realized that our staff and agency chiefs were extremely harmonious."[55] Even outside his inner circle, Bush's advisory team was viewed as unusually cooperative by Washington standards.[56]

Bush's strong role also helped generate consensus and decreased challenges to his position. Bush doubted the value of economic sanctions as early as August 3 in describing their record as "spotty"; both he and Scowcroft put little faith in them.[57] Yet at no point did Powell, Baker, and Schwarzkopf argue together for continuing economic sanctions. In Powell's words, "in our democracy, it is the President, not generals, who make decisions about going to war. . . . If the President was right, if he decided that it must be war, then my job was to make sure we were ready to go in and win."[58] Over time, the group of eight fell in line with the move toward war, and each core agency carried out its duties, despite privately held differences in view.

When serious questions were raised, such as why economic sanctions were not given more time, they were either stated privately or in a muted way, rather than highlighted in bargaining among the key decision makers. Powell, for instance, pushed economic sanctions with the president in just one meeting on September 24, as noted earlier.[59]

While members of the group of eight rarely bargained or acted as advocates, rivalry was even more rare. Scowcroft was quite influential with Bush, but he was also careful in general about rivaling State or Defense, or about trying to steal the limelight.[60] In the Carter administration, by contrast, NSC and State were intense rivals, exacerbating turf battles and GP, even in crises.[61] Brzezinski and Vance disagreed on how to deal with Moscow, and clearly rivaled each other to the point that Vance even "warned" Carter that Brzezinski's public pronouncements were undermining his own, thus harming U.S. interests.[62]

Bush himself disliked confrontation, although he was more likely to encourage debate on domestic issues than on foreign affairs.[63] By contrast, as Vance saw it, Carter "encouraged frankness and accepted disagreement from his advisers. He did not want to be shielded from unpleasant facts, hard options, or difficult decisions."[64]

The President as a Bargainer

While it is not fully clear to what extent President Kennedy was a bargainer in the Cuban missile crisis, little evidence, if any, suggests that Bush was one.[65] If he were one, we would expect to see evidence that he argued with his senior staff about key decisions and/or offered give-and-take solutions to key problems. We have no such evidence at hand.

As laid out earlier in the book, from the earliest NSC meetings with his advisers, Bush felt strongly about reversing the invasion, and the real question then became how it would be done.[66] The fact that from the outset Bush was far more "forceful and convinced" than many of his advisers decreased the range of debate on how to approach Iraq, and set the parameters of the agenda on the issue.[67]

As another example, it is quite notable, as discussed earlier in the study, that Powell's opposition to Bush's preference to move more quickly to a war footing was extremely muted.[68] There was no bargaining, no give and take, except for Powell's brief exchange with Bush on September 24. In fact, Bush was the opposite of a bargainer. He did not stray from his belief that Iraq must withdraw unconditionally from Kuwait and be contained. Even his comparisons of Saddam to Adolf Hitler, which Scowcroft and Gates tried to check and which they, along with Fitzwater, viewed as counterproductive, were not tempered.[69] Bush did not bargain on the issue. He did not seek a compromise. He proceeded with the comparisons.

Actors sometimes bargain because they face resistance. If we viewed bureaucratic opposition of any kind to the president, we might infer at least a potential need or motive to bargain away that resistance. However, no available evidence suggests that bureaucracies ignored or obstructed presidential instructions in a parochial, exclusive, and self-interested manner, as the Navy arguably did in the Cuban missile crisis, for instance.[70]

A Collage of Views?

The major decisions reached in the Persian Gulf War case did not reflect a collage. They largely reflected Bush's views and, to a lesser degree, Scowcroft's. While presidents often play a more major role in crises, the extent of their role differs. Bush was particularly preeminent, although vigorous discussions ensued, especially between Cheney and Baker, on the less significant "how to" issues.[71]

We cannot, for instance, say that Bush's critical assertion on August 5, 1990, that the invasion would not stand represented a collage. No group of advisers debated that question. Quite the contrary, it surprised some of them, such as Powell, who believed that it set a new course for the crisis.[72] Nor did the decision to double U.S. forces in the Persian Gulf in November result from a combination of views and actions. Although some discussion transpired on the question, Bush and Scowcroft were central in making that decision, one that left Powell and Schwarzkopf surprised and displeased (in part because they were not consulted), and Baker puzzled by the failure to consult Congress.[73] That reflects top-down decision-making far more than it does the makings of a collage. No evidence exists, moreover, that those who favored economic sanctions over the move toward war brokered a deal that reflected elements of both approaches.

The decision to issue Saddam an ultimatum to leave Kuwait or face war is another case in point. By that time, the group of eight was in full agreement, except perhaps for differences over the term "ultimatum."[74] The decision in mid-October that shaped that consensus, in any event, was made primarily by Bush and Scowcroft, with support from British Prime Minister Margaret Thatcher. Given his view that time was running out, Bush did not believe in "the luxury of waiting for sanctions to work" and "staunchly believed that a provocation" was all the coalition needed to use force, but Scowcroft, as Bush points out, argued effectively that we had to be "sure we could continue to get international political support to go in on the ground to kick Saddam out of Kuwait."[75]

Bush also spearheaded the decision that Baker should meet with Aziz prior to war.[76] As early as November 10, in the midst of a congressional uproar over his decision to double U.S. forces without having consulted Congress, Bush told Scowcroft that the United States might "want to show we are going the extra mile for peace," by perhaps inviting Aziz to the White House for a meeting, although without making any face-saving concessions to Saddam in the process.[77] On November 30, the day after the U.N. passed the resolution on using force against Iraq, Bush shocked many observers by announcing his plan. Scowcroft had told Prince Bandar of Saudi Arabia as early as December that Bush's desire for talks constituted window-dressing and that Bush had already decided to be absolutely unyielding.[78] Scowcroft points out that while some in the inner circle thought that meeting with the Iraqis might send Saddam a message of weakness, "the president felt that to go to war without having a direct meeting with the Iraqis would not be a good idea."[79] It was largely Bush's decision, one that even the supportive Scowcroft believed should have been given more thought.[80] Had it been the case that Baker or Scowcroft initiated the idea to meet the Iraqis, and had Bush been reluctant, that would be evidence for a collage in the making, but the facts suggest nearly the opposite.

If the GPM were an accurate guide, we would also have to infer from the notion of a collage that the decisions discussed above were unintended by President Bush. But there is no evidence to support the view that he preferred other options or that the outcomes surprised him. Quite the contrary, he usually produced the outcomes that he desired, despite the myriad and varied constraints he faced. While many critical decisions were made in the context of the group of eight, the president knew what he wanted "going into these meetings."[81]

Conclusion

This chapter developed an approach for testing the GPM, based on identifying the key assumptions of the model and inferring expected behavior from them. This transformed the variable of "bargaining," which is central to the model, into one existing on a continuum. That helped explore behaviors that do not clearly fall into the model's current purview, but that are relevant to understanding the realities that it purports to explain. Generating a continuum helped delineate the gradient of complex behaviors that reflect varying degrees of GP.

With regard to the Persian Gulf War case in particular, the best evidence available strongly suggests that the GPM performed poorly in explaining U.S. decision-making (with the qualification dealing with the "how to" versus "whether to" decisions). While Cheney and Baker held different views, as the model would have largely predicted, Powell and Cheney held quite different views, despite similar bureaucratic influences, and their positions were far more different than those of Powell and Baker. But it is not here that the model was weakest.

Rather, as we draw on the concept of the continuum developed in this chapter, we see that while decision makers did engage in explanation, they rarely bargained, acted as advocates, or rivaled each other. Moreover, while we cannot establish that they focused on national interests, they did not appear to push departmental goals. Little if any evidence, moreover, suggests that the president engaged in bargaining. Decisions were shaped by multiple inputs, but they reflected Bush's imprimatur, along with that of Scowcroft, far more than they suggested a collage. That helps explain why no evidence at hand suggests that Bush was ever surprised by them.

It is worth making one last point here before proceeding to test the other perspectives of this book. This point is about another famous model of decision-making, one that is in the general genre of the GPM: the organizational process model. Some readers might wonder why it was not included in this book, so it is worth sketching the model here and explaining why.

This model focuses on the behavior of organizations such, as the Departments of Defense and State. It downplays individual choice and instead examines the organization as a whole. It tries to explain decisions by emphasizing the role, behavior, needs, standard operating procedures, and culture of such organizations, and by viewing them as caught in rivalry with other organizations or parts of organizations. Unlike the GPM, it downplays the role of particular individuals who bargain in committee settings and instead focuses on how bulky, slow, methodical, turf-conscious organizations behave as a whole in a complex decision-making process. An organizational process model argument for how and why the United States went to war might look like this: Particular branches of the military saw the Persian Gulf War as a way of establishing their importance against rival military branches, and vying for postwar budgetary consideration. This pushed them to favor the war option, and in particular to push for a larger combat role for their branch of the military. Despite all the bluster about the level of Saddam's threat, in fact, it was inter-service rivalry, military culture, and the military's interest in dealing Iraq a good blow that fundamentally shaped U.S. decisions.

To be sure, the model may explain other elements of the crisis, such as the manner by which U.S. forces were dispatched to the region, or the decision to launch a particular form of attack. It might even explain why the military presented a war plan based on a direct, frontal assault on Iraqi positions in Kuwait rather than the sweeping attack from the west that was eventually used. One might say the military was following its general routine, but that personalities also had something to do with it. That some in the Air Force argued that air power alone could win the war — without the use of ground forces — can also be accounted for in the model.

While the integrated approach allows for using this model in general, it was not used in this book because it was even less useful than the GPM as a guide for explaining government behavior. The behavior of organizations meant little in terms of how and why the United States went to war. This yields a proposition for further thought: the greater the role and influence of the president, the less likely we can rely on the organizational process and government politics models to yield insights into decision-making. Thus, in cases where we have established that significant presidential influence exists, it may be sensible to look for other models for explaining major decisions.

CHAPTER SEVEN

Mirror, Mirror, on the Wall

Evaluating the Perspectives

Scholars have repeatedly called for tests of the different models of government behavior, but to no great avail.[1] While numerous models compete to explain how countries make decisions, they are rarely explored against real cases to test and improve them, to explain the cases, and to examine how decisions are actually made.[2] This is not so surprising. Testing theory is challenging and forces us to confront a number of questions. To what extent can we or should we test it? How can we do so sensibly? When can a theory be useful, even if it is unrealistic as a guide to reality? Volumes have been written on these questions, to which I can add little, but I will test the remaining four perspectives of the book.

To be sure, there is no ironclad manner by which to test any of the perspectives, but we can draw on the foregoing chapters to do so sensibly, if imperfectly, in a manner similar to the previous chapter. All the while we should remain mindful that strong arguments have been made that perspectives that fail tests can nevertheless be quite useful, that unrealistic assumptions can serve crucial theoretical goals, and that entire paradigms, like more specific models and theories, can still perform vital tasks such as unlocking puzzles.[3]

Testing the Theory of Groupthink

Scholars from various disciplines have repeatedly called for groupthink theory to be tested comprehensively, but this call has largely gone unheeded, notwithstanding many useful partial tests of the theory.[4] The advantage of this book is that it offers the potential for a comprehensive test. As such, it differs from the other tests herein, insofar as it examines all of the conditions of the theory in lieu of using inference and draws partly on the guidelines for testing the theory provided by Irving Janis.[5] I stress here that Janis does not require that all of the conditions of the theory be met, nor did he discriminate among them, except for cohesiveness of the decision-making group which was necessary but not sufficient.

Chapter 5 went some way towards a comprehensive test, because it provided an accurate portrayal, albeit not a complete one, of group decision-making. Enough conditions of the theory are present to conclude that groupthink was at play, a rare finding.[6] Crucially, the antecedent conditions for groupthink existed, and they contributed to a concurrence-seeking tendency, and to some important symptoms of groupthink: self-censorship, an illusion of unanimity, and pressure on dissenting members, although not a proclivity to overestimate abilities or rationalize to discount warnings or information (see Figure 1 in chapter 5).[7] Bush, Quayle, Baker, and others saw the potential peril in the crisis, even to the presidency.[8] Groupthink also led to some of the seven symptoms of defective decision-making. Most importantly, we did observe an incomplete survey of the alternatives. This is a crucial factor in evaluating decision-making, because it lies at the very heart of what we mean academically by rational processes. Some of Bush's independent actions, as well as the strong decisions made by consensus in the group, made it difficult to reappraise alternatives.[9]

However, while the inner circle did demonstrate a selective bias in processing information, it did not appear to engage in a poor information search outside of this bias. While President Bush did make some quick decisions, evidence also suggests that the group of eight did seek sufficient information to make decisions, including background reports on the effectiveness of economic sanctions, on Iraq's developing weapons programs, and on the views of coalition partners.[10] Each agency also conducted significant research and evaluation. Secretary Cheney, for instance, was briefed dozens of times on various options for warfare.[11] Moreover, the administration did not appear to fail to make contingency plans to deal with potentially changed circumstances. Indeed, decision makers did, for instance, create contingency plans in the event that Iraq withdrew fully or partially from Kuwait.[12]

Some evidence also suggests a failure to evaluate risks, but it is unclear to what extent that was central in the group itself. Moreover, the group appeared to fail seriously to survey objectives, partly because it was fishing for the best strategy to sell the war. However, privately it largely understood that the key objective was to check Iraq and evict it from Kuwait if necessary, although the members differed on the value of economic sanctions and the timing of when to evict Iraq.

The evidence at hand also suggests that the group of eight did explore the risks involved in going to war with Iraq and took them seriously. Powell in particular emphasized them. On the day before the war, for instance, he warned everyone, as he had done before, that war was "hell" and that "unpredictable consequences" would result, that "once it has started, the President was no longer in control."[13]

On some issues, however, Bush did act quickly without closely consulting others to explore the risks. Thus, Powell described Bush's August 5 statement that he would not allow the invasion to stand as policymaking "on the hoof," while even Scowcroft told Bush privately that the use of the Hitler analogy was problematic.[14]

The Individual-Group Interaction Question

There is another aspect of the theory of groupthink that we need to discuss here. The theory at the same time subordinates the individual to the group and elevates the group leader in importance. This raises what I conceive of here as the individual-group interaction question, a question not well addressed in the literature regarding the theory heretofore: when does a partial group leader, like Bush, become so powerful that the theory of groupthink fails the test, and that the best perspective of explanation is no longer group dynamics as a whole as groupthink would posit, but the individual as an individual actor? In this section, I offer six interpretations of the evidence presented in this book that bears on that question, thus helping illuminate the question in theory and in the Persian Gulf War case.

The first interpretation is that this question is not problematic, because the theory does not attempt to distinguish sufficiently between individual and group causation. Janis does not ascribe causal gravity to any of the antecedent conditions, although he emphasizes cohesiveness. Thus it would be inappropriate to presuppose such gravity, and better to explore each of the conditions and infer groupthink on that basis. Concurrence-seeking, in any event, is crucial to the theory and yet, as Alexander George puts it, "generally not accessible to direct observation."[15] Under this interpretation, we could argue that specific cause-effect relationships between the individual and group are subject more to future work than present analysis, that the individual-group interaction question does not matter greatly.

The second interpretation is similar to the first in that it does not see a major problem, but for a different reason. It argues that the theory does, in fact, account for very strong leadership. Indeed, as some scholars observe, the antecedent condition that addresses leadership "refers to situations where a leader has too much influence on the decision-making processes used by the group."[16] Interpretations of groupthink have placed significant emphasis on assertive, directive leadership as leading to premature concurrence-seeking, or on leaders who manipulate group dynamics.[17] For his part, Janis clearly sees a strong leader as vital. Indeed, most of his suggestions about preventing groupthink, and suggestions by subsequent thinkers, are directed at checking leader bias and influence.[18] In his own case studies, moreover, Janis's groups had powerful leaders and some subsequent case studies viewed groupthink as generated by such leaders.[19] Under this interpretation, we might even distinguish leader- or peer-directed groupthink based on the notion that groupthink can be reached through different routes, a notion that Paul't Hart demonstrates in his revision of the theory.[20]

The third interpretation is that at some point very strong leadership becomes problematic for Janis's theory because of its focus on the group as a whole. If a leader were too dominant, groupthink could no longer be viewed as a strong explanation or would at least have to be subordinated to other explanations. However, depending on how we interpret Janis, we might still cite Janis's view that the theory can still be confirmed, even if one or more of its conditions are not met.

The fourth interpretation is that we can infer from Janis that the theory does not allow for explaining outcomes by attributing them entirely to one powerful, stubborn person. That is the one-person explanation, as Janis puts it, which is akin to the individual level of foreign policy analysis.[21] Janis offers limited clues as to how to distinguish between one-person and groupthink explanations, for example asserting that if the president did not make decisions alone and his key aides were not mere yes-men, then the one-person rule hypothesis is unlikely to be explanatory.[22] Importantly, the Persian Gulf War case largely passes that test. The record suggests that members of the group of eight were not simple yes-men, nor did Bush act simply as a sole decision maker on many key questions. Being a strong group leader and acting alone are too different phenomena, though in select instances Bush did act outside the group, as I will discuss below.

Fifth, one might argue that agreement in the group of eight resulted not because of compliance induced by a proclivity to suppress private doubts, but because the members accepted the correctness of key decisions, many of which were promoted by Bush. But in the view of Clark McCauley and Fritz Gaenslen, we could interpret Janis's conception to be a phenomenon of either or both of these dynamics.[23] That is, groupthink could be said to exist regardless of how the group achieves consensus. Arguably, a better test for group effects is to see if members held different views inside and outside the group, something the present work reveals did, in fact, occur.

The sixth interpretation is that the individual-group problem is a serious one, but that we can disaggregate an event and test the theory against separate decisions. This approach is potentially promising, partly because it obviates the need to generalize across an entire event about whether the individual or group dynamic was more salient. But it also raises problems. Neither Janis's theory nor his cases address disaggregation, making it unclear if doing so is a legitimate test of the theory of groupthink. Moreover, since decisions in a broader case sometimes overlap and merge, and since their effects can affect any part of the causal chain laid out by Janis, we must wonder if we can identify discrete units for analysis. Groupthink, furthermore, is expected to result earlier in an event for Janis. If a case is disaggregated, what constitutes early and late?

Disaggregation is enticing, but may require a reinterpretation of how to test the theory. That said, it is fair to make two related but different points. The first is that future work should do more to consider the potential of groupthink versus non-groupthink explanations at certain junctures in an event. The second is that short of a separate test of the theory on each decision, this book supports the finding that elements of groupthink, along with and related to strong partial leadership, depended to some extent on the type of decision made. Elements of groupthink existed more on the major decisions that eliminated key alternatives on the road to war and were crucial in driving Washington into war (the "whether to" decisions) than on the less major ones (the "how to" issues).

Thus, Baker and Cheney, for instance, did disagree, but mainly on questions of approach, such as on whether the United States should go to the U.N. first before taking a particular action.[24] Options were spelled out on issues such as how to go to Congress to obtain a war resolution were considered and spelled out in various memos, and alternatives were explored, at least initially, on how to invade Iraq.[25]

All six interpretations may appear plausible in one way or another. But it appears that only the fourth interpretation could bedevil the present argument. While that interpretation deserves our consideration because some evidence certainly corroborates it, this chapter argues that the evidence fits another conclusion better. That is, in broader group dynamics and the larger decision-making environment, groupthink was at play, but it was only one of several phenomena affecting decision-making.[26]

Within the context of a discussion about individual-group dynamics, we can identify several ways by which Bush affected outcomes, which can provide a more nuanced view of individual and group dynamics and their interaction in the Persian Gulf War case, and alert us to similar dynamics in other cases. Bush acted (1.) outside the group in a sole capacity, (2.) outside the group setting with one or more advisers, (3.) outside the group in a manner that influenced the antecedent conditions of the theory, (4.) inside the group as a group leader, (5.) inside the group as one member among many subject to group dynamics, and (6.) inside the group as a directive leader so strong that he made group decisions apart from group dynamics.[27] Behaviors 1 and 2 are exogenous to the theory, and do not disconfirm it but rather point to its explanatory limits. The theory cannot account for behavior 3, but it may buttress its conditions nonetheless. Behaviors 4 and 5 are consonant with the theory. While behavior 6 contradicts the theory, groupthink and a one-person explanation are not mutually exclusive in broader explanations of decision-making. They may both help explain a case.

The analysis here points to three areas of future work. The first is to link the agent-structure literature more formally to the theory of groupthink. That literature explores how structures like the group influence agents like the individual, and vice versa.[28] The second is to cross-fertilize a topology of leadership style, attributes, and behavior into the theory and interpret what that means for its predictions. Some scholars have explored variables such as open versus closed leadership style, and a gigantic literature on that subject could inform such an effort.[29] The third is to explore events using multiple models — one thrust of this book. Concomitantly, we could do more to examine how the leader's activity outside the group setting feeds back into group dynamics. That can illuminate issues related to the theory, such as the individual-group interaction question. These various areas of future study hold promise.

The Domestic Politics Model

The DPM, like the other perspectives, is parsimonious and does little to explain either the broader strategic picture or the cognitive, group, and bureaucratic factors that influence government behavior.[30] But, unlike the other perspectives, it does highlight how domestic-level goals can affect such behavior. It may help us explain Bush's personalization of the crisis, and his multiple efforts to paint the crisis as particularly threatening at critical junctures when that may have served domestic-level goals. It may also offer a more cynical explanation for the use of the Hitler analogy, in which the analogy was simply manipulated to exaggerate the threat and to gain public support. And it may challenge the RAM's focus on national interests and rational processes.

If the DPM is telling, we would expect evidence of:

1. A serious public relations campaign, including exaggerations of the challenge at hand;
2. Type 1 (personal, institutional and diversionary) and Type 2 goals (promotional);
3. A rise in rhetoric corresponding with the appearance of domestic problems or challenges;
4. Some discussion of domestic issues in decision-making deliberations;
5. Statements by decision makers that indicate that they are constrained by their own previous behaviors.

Let us briefly look at these guideposts and the evidence. It is abundantly clear that the administration had an organized public relations campaign and that President Bush engaged in efforts to construct the crisis. Moreover, it is clear that Bush and the administration had addressed Type 1 and 2 goals in some fashion. In particular, there is no doubt that the administration faced significant domestic problems and challenges, including a recession and the budget impasse. While we cannot know how important all of the Type 1 and 2 goals were, a motive certainly did exist for engaging in construction. While chapter 4 did submit evidence on that score, a problem with the model arises: Had they been more concerned about public opinion, wouldn't decision makers have consulted Congress before doubling troop strength in the Persian Gulf in November? When that decision produced an uproar in Congress and public approval slipped approximately eight percentage points below pre-crisis levels, would they not have changed their approach? Quite the contrary, Bush repeatedly told close advisers that congressional and public support was desirable, but that he would go to war without it, if need be.[31] If domestic considerations were so crucial, why was the administration more pro-war than the public, thus risking domestic-level costs?

We could try to explain away this behavior by noting that Bush did better in the polls when he focused on the Persian Gulf conflict than on other issues, that highlighting the conflict could also draw attention from domestic problems and perhaps meet other Type 1 and 2 goals, and that the war in fact did cause not only a surge in consumer confidence but also in Bush's popularity. But such behavior still raises questions.

While public opinion did not appear to affect key decisions, Bush and others in his administration clearly sought to shape public opinion. They put considerable time into convincing the public that war might be necessary and important. In that effort, members of the administration were hardly reluctant to exaggerate aspects of the crisis. Thus, for instance, when polls indicated that Americans were concerned about nuclear weapons, the administration highlighted that threat significantly. While it was a potential threat at the time, it was only discovered after the war just how serious it was. Bush also did suggest that he wanted to move ahead with war because Americans might not tolerate an appearance of stalemate for long. He would express this view to CNN on November 15, when he noted that "holding public opinion forever in any country is very difficult to do. . . . In any country, I think there is a ticking of the clock."[32]

We would also expect to see at least some serious discussion of domestic issues in decision-making deliberations, despite the fact that decision makers would obviously be reluctant to explain foreign behavior overtly in terms of Type 1 and 2 goals. On this score, we do know that domestic concerns were discussed at the end of group of four meetings, in group of eight meetings, and in the communications group assigned to the task of public relations. But these discussions focused largely on how to explain the potential for war to the public and on how to combat Saddam's efforts at construction. Beyond that, little evidence is confirmatory, unless we resort to generous inference.

If previous efforts at construction produced constraining effects, we might expect to see decision makers comment upon them, if they understood the lagged effect of construction on their own behavior and if they were comfortable noting it. Any evidence of it, in any event, would be useful. Unfortunately, we have no evidence at hand to support that notion, nor do we have a strong basis for inferring it. That does not mean that it did not exist, but rather that we cannot establish it.

A look at the evidence presented in chapter 4, and to some extent in the rest of the book, does not suggest that the DPM is disconfirmed, but rather that it is partly confirmed, partly disconfirmed, and partly nonconfirmable in this case. We have no "smoking gun" that key decisions were made because of domestic reasons. At most we can say that Type 1 and 2 motivations probably contributed at some level to the elimination and nonconsideration of alternatives, that construction was an important part of selling the war option, and that the effects of construction may have affected future decisions in the lagged manner that the DPM predicts. Even so, it would remain unclear if Bush purposefully used construction to signal that his options were now self-limited, as RAM would explain it, or whether he was limited unintentionally and driven toward a course of action that he and others may not have preferred. In any event, Bush's efforts at construction may very well have helped convince Saddam that war was Bush's preferred option.

The Cognitive Perspective

The cognitive perspective was unique in drawing attention to analogies and their impact on decision-making, but how telling was it? We can focus here chiefly on the Munich analogy. If the cognitive perspective was telling, we would expect:

1. Significant references to Hitler and World War II in public discourse and in private, among advisers and others;
2. Such references to affect important decisions;
3. Advisers close to the president to identify the connection between the analogy and decision-making.

We can discuss these indicators and summarize the evidence briefly. If an analogy were at play, we would expect it to be invoked somewhat frequently, adjusting for its possible political use. Moreover, exploring to see if it was involved in private discourse among decision makers is important, because it allows insight into whether it was a genuine factor on a personal, cognitive level rather than a public relations move, as the DPM might posit. On this score, it is indisputable that innumerable references were made to Munich and World War II by Bush and others, both privately and in public. The far harder issue is what this meant for decision-making.

Even stronger confirmatory evidence would focus on whether the analogy was actually connected to key decisions. That helps rule out the possibility that it was used gratuitously. On this score, the evidence suggests that it is unclear if it affected all decisions, but did affect some of them. As noted earlier, once Bush asserted that Saddam was like Hitler, it became "clear" to him, as he would later recall, that "the goal was the removal of Iraq from Kuwait."[33] Bush repeatedly cited Munich in buttressing his stance against any face-saving withdrawal for Iraq, and in favor of a tougher stance.

If the president were strongly affected by the analogy, we would also expect to see some evidence that advisers commented on that effect. On that score, our expectations would be confirmed. Advisers repeatedly noted the impact of Munich and World War II on the president's thinking. Since they had no particular reason to do so, and in fact some found his use of the analogy problematic, that is telling.

Evaluating the Rational Actor Model

While the RAM black boxed domestic factors, it did yield important insights into the broader international environment and into U.S.-Iraqi strategic interaction, insights the other perspectives could not muster. It was thus important in explaining U.S. decision-making and why war was not avoided. Regarding rationality in particular, we should reemphasize here that it is never easy to judge rationality, a concept that varies in meaning depending on such things as the discipline in question (economics, political science, and the humanities), the issue under study (deterrence, economic cooperation, and personal consumption) and the level of analysis (individual, group, and state).[34] But in exploring rationality, we should avoid the many interpretations of the model where disagreement is strong.[35] As I observed in chapter 2, most versions of rationality regarding any actor view the failure to compare options as compromising rational behavior. This may result from such things as impetuous action, in which options are not even identified; or an overhasty cycling through options; or negligence in assessing alternatives, once they are identified.

If attempts were being made to weigh and compare alternatives carefully, we would expect to see:

1. No plausible alternative neglected;
2. Little discouragement of dissenting opinion;
3. A high rather than low level of integrative complexity among decision makers.

Looking at the evidence, it becomes clear that nonrational behavior was prominent in the decision-making process, with important qualifications. Let us look at our guideposts.

A failure to weigh a plausible alternative obviously makes it hard to attempt to weigh all plausible alternatives. While we cannot assert definitively that such a failure occurred, the analysis in the groupthink chapter strongly suggests that it did. To be sure, while that evidence focused on group dynamics in particular, it also reflected how the decisions that we observed were made, with the possible proviso that Bush may have carefully considered alternatives outside the group setting before joining the group, where he pushed his view in a way that seemed to conflict with the group's ability to evaluate alternatives. The evidence presented in the cognitive perspective further raises doubts about the evaluation of alternatives.

The potential for analogies to complement or challenge the RAM may be highlighted by the differing effects of the Vietnam and Munich analogies. The Munich analogy did more to impair efforts to weigh alternatives on the way to war than did the Vietnam analogy, which did more to influence decision makers to choose a massive attack and a quick exit strategy once the decision to go to war was made. This may be because Bush, the critical decision maker on the "whether to" questions on the road to war, was affected by the Munich analogy, while the less critical decision makers, such as Schwarzkopf and Powell, who played a larger role in deciding "how to" launch the war, were affected more by the Vietnam analogy. Thus, their activity was less likely to affect consideration of alternatives. We might surmise that if the roles had been reversed and the Vietnam generation had been more influential, the Vietnam analogy would not only have affected the way the United States prepared for and carried out the war, but also the proclivity to go to war in the first place.

The Munich analogy pointed to the costs of appeasing or of appearing to appease an aggressor; in this sense it complemented the RAM explanation. But the analogy did not simply add one more perceived cost to war avoidance. Strong evidence suggests that it was also central in pushing Bush to personalize the conflict and to shut down consideration of alternatives to war, such as the use of economic sanctions, before they were fully considered.

We can now look at dissenting opinion — our second indicator. When dissenting opinion is discouraged, it is far harder to weigh alternatives, because ideas and information about the costs and benefits of alternatives may never arise. Enough evidence exists to suggest that key decision makers, including Powell, Baker, and Schwarzkopf, were reluctant to express their views strongly and to introduce analyses, for instance, of the benefits of the economic sanctions alternative.

In terms of the last indicator, integrative complexity is an attribute of information processing that generally indicates the extent to which decision makers search for information, weigh options, and consider multiple potential strategies. In particular, the groupthink chapter provides evidence that problems existed in evaluating options, as do aspects of the other chapters in this book. We can also note that one study showed that Presidents Bush and Hussein showed generally lower complexity than leaders of nations less involved in the conflict.[36]

The upshot of this analysis is that nonrational processes were prominent. It follows that the assumption that the observed decisions and behaviors resulted from a rational approach would be at least partly misleading. But this conclusion needs serious qualification.

Contingent Rationality

We must qualify the finding presented above in several ways. First, the extent to which we would be misled if we assumed that decisions were made through a rational process depends on the importance of the issue that decision makers faced. By and large, if we identified state behavior that resulted from the more important decisions of the crisis (the "whether to" questions), and tried to explain that behavior in terms of the RAM, we would more likely be misled than if we tried to explain the observed behavior that resulted from less significant decisions (the "how to" questions), using the RAM. Witness, for instance, that Bush's decision to assert on August 5 that the invasion would not stand did not occur after a discussion weighing the pros and cons of doing so. Quite the contrary, it surprised some of his advisers. Using the RAM, we would have explained it in this way: The United States, after evaluating the costs and benefits of all alternatives, decided that it would commit not only to protecting Saudi Arabia in Desert Shield, but to evicting Iraqi forces from Kuwait. But this is not what transpired.

The second distinction has to do with the political entity in question, such as a committee or agency. A unitary actor model would lead us to explain any observed decision, regardless of where it arose in the policy process, as a function of rational processes. Yet, in exploring both the group of eight and the deputies committees, it became clear that the latter was more methodical and inclined to weigh costs and benefits carefully than was the group of eight. Thus, for instance, Admiral Jeremiah notes that the deputies "thought through alternatives well in advance of the time required, including how to pull together elements of the Middle East peace process."[37] Were we to learn of the decisions that emanated from the deputies committee on television, and to recreate the process that produced them in terms of the RAM, we would be less likely to be misled than if we did the same regarding decisions emanating chiefly from the group of eight.

The third distinction is about timing. The ability of any theory of decision-making to explain the Persian Gulf crisis changes depending on when during the crisis it is applied. For instance, early in the crisis, the United States preferred that Iraq withdraw peacefully from Kuwait. Later in the crisis, it began to prefer war as a means of checking Iraq's military power. If we observed that Bush used charged rhetoric against Saddam, which made Iraq less likely to withdraw from Kuwait early in the crisis, that would be far less rational than if it were done toward the end of the crisis, after Bush had shifted his preferences. At the later time, we could at least argue that his apparently emotive behavior had a strategic rationale. That is, he aimed to antagonize Iraq, so that it would not withdraw and so that the United States would have the chance to weaken significantly and possibly eliminate the Iraqi dictator. Similarly, characterizing U.S. decision-making as being affected by important elements of groupthink would be fair — provided that appropriate qualifications are attached — but groupthink was just one of many phenomena at play. Focusing on groupthink explanations, thus, might push us to miss variations in the overall case over time. All of this is not to say that we could or should test all of the models decision by decision. Groupthink, for instance, is too much of a process model to do so. But we should be sensitive to the varying levels of explanatory potential that these models bring to bear, which are partly decision-dependent.

The upshot is that it is unwise to categorize cases as falling into one or another perspective. Breaking them down into discrete units or time periods can yield better insights, not only into what happened in those periods but also into how those periods relate sequentially as well as how our perspectives might explain them.

The final distinction is between the rational behavior of individuals and governments. It is important to distinguish individual and government rationality, because, in basic terms, the government is a different entity, even though it is made up of individuals.

The state-centric rational actor model seeks to model the behavior of governments, not complex individuals subject to myriad motivated and nonmotivated biases and shortcomings. While individuals compose governments, it is not the same thing to explore the multitude of pressures that they face as it is to delve into the pressures that influence a state as a whole. The RAM treats the state as a single actor endowed with one set of preferences and goals, which it pursues rationally and seeks to promote in world affairs. This is termed the "national interest." While the RAM interprets the state's actions in that light, individuals can and usually do have different goals, interests, and preferences than states do, and they are affected by different phenomena. By black boxing reality, the RAM may "explain" the behavior of a government, even if particular individuals display irrational behavior. Conversely, individuals may be rational, even if the overall process at the governmental level does not proceed as the RAM would have us believe. That logic is similar for groups. Thus, as Kenneth Arrow demonstrated with the "Impossibility Theorem," even as few as three actors will not be able to reach a decision that meets the minimum transitivity requirements of rational choice, e.g., sharing a common rationale. Individuals then can be described as rational, but that question is quite different regarding a group.[38]

The more interesting question is how the behavior of all actors, when considered together, produced the actions and decisions that we observe. Each perspective offers a different view on that issue, with the RAM emphasizing rationality, and the other perspectives offering varying levels of potential challenges to that view.

The GPM and the Theory of Groupthink

The analysis yields several general insights about the groupthink and government politics perspectives. We saw relatively little GP at play, with a key qualification. The evidence suggests that on the "how to" questions, we saw less evidence confirming what the GPM would lead us to expect than on the "whether to" questions. While the theory of groupthink is largely confirmed, we can also note that insofar as it is sensible to explore the theory in particular decisions, we did see less confirmation of groupthink on the "how to" questions than on the "whether to" questions.

The second point follows from the first. The GPM and groupthink are sometimes mistakenly conflated, but they carry quite different assumptions.[39] Indeed, these models are so different that testing them in one book offers more leverage than testing them separately. If the theory of groupthink is confirmed, the evidence that confirms it is also likely to disconfirm the GPM, and vice versa. Thus, bargaining among individuals in a committee and bureaucratic setting is crucial to the GPM, but largely disconfirms the theory of groupthink. Meanwhile, camaraderie and concurrence-seeking is central to the theory of groupthink, but would tend to disconfirm the GPM, although not outright. And if we observe that the outcome of decision-making was a "collage," that points to GP but not to the theory of groupthink.

The third point has to do with the role of the individual, where the findings regarding both the groupthink and GPM perspectives intersect. In the theory of groupthink, a "partial leader" helps drive and shape consensus within a group setting. Bush's crucial role satisfied that condition of the theory, but it raised the individual-group interaction question. In the GPM, the strong leader, in this case Bush, did not help confirm the theory, but rather helped disconfirm it. As a strong leader, Bush preempted bargaining and conflict and placed his imprimatur on key decisions that otherwise may have looked like the collage that the GPM would predict.

The fourth point is that theory-building, as we shall see in chapter 10, is facilitated by exploring both models within one case.

Reconciling Explanations

The use of multiple perspectives inevitably raises questions about contradictory explanations. One question arises as to how we can reconcile the description of the Iraqi threat in the RAM chapter with the notion that it was constructed in chapter 4. One answer is simple. They are different perspectives. Beyond that, we can say that this is because the threat was both real and created. Chapter 4 helps explain how Iraq could be routed in war, while having been described as a major power before it. That is in part because its capability was exaggerated. Thus, while the United States viewed Iraq as a legitimate threat, and had good reason to do so, it also tended to exaggerate the threat for political effect. Hence, we could see in the RAM perspective how the threat was serious and in the DPM how it was elevated significantly for political effect.

The second question is how we can reconcile the RAM explanation in chapter 2, which appeared persuasive, with the notion that decision-making on the whole was marked by significant nonrational processes. The way to do so can be stated in both simple and complex terms. The simple answer is that RAM reconstructs the decision as if it were conducted by a unitary actor. By black boxing out a significant aspect of the picture, it can paint a convincing portrait of rationality. The more complex answer is that the picture was not black and white. Decisions that we may have explained solely in rationalist terms were a function of a mixture of decision-making behaviors that varied in texture depending on a plethora of factors.

The third question has to do with the cognitive and DPM perspectives, insofar as they relate to the RAM. The cognitive perspective pointed to the costs and benefits of any accommodation of Saddam, while the DPM underscored, among other things, how construction could help sell a preferred alternative. Some evidence also suggests that U.S. diplomacy, by some time in October, was not intended to lead to a compromise with Iraq, or even to generate Iraq's withdrawal. It was intended to inflame Saddam and make his recalcitrance a justification for a war that was recognized as in the U.S. interest. Insofar as the cognitive and DPM perspectives help explain this behavior, both perspectives captured key elements of the crisis that were consonant with rationalist accounts. Both models, however, pointed to nonrational dimensions as well, and explained phenomena from different angles than did the RAM. It is entirely legitimate to view them as vehicles for both complementing and challenging the RAM.

Finally, we can reconcile individual level explanations with elements of groupthink. Two key ways are worth reemphasizing. The first is that the theory of groupthink allows for a strong group leader, despite its emphasis on group dynamics. The second is that President Bush sometimes acted outside the group in important ways. Groupthink dynamics and individual influence, thus, can both be parts of an overall explanation.

Conclusion

This book addresses two questions: how and why the United States went to war. With respect to how decisions were made, chapter 6 found the GPM wanting. This chapter, by contrast, reveals that important elements of groupthink were at play, with appropriate qualifications. The cognitive perspective also fares well in that the Munich analogy and World War II experience did shape and influence President Bush's behavior. The DPM, meanwhile, did not perform altogether well, but it did call attention to the potential at least for domestic politics to have affected some decisions, especially insofar as the administration did indeed make significant efforts to sell the war to the public. While construction can serve a range of rational goals, it can also undermine rationality if it boxes in decision makers so that they ignore or fail seriously to consider certain options. Moreover, the DPM reminds us that what we may regard as objective, based on our inclination to think in terms of the RAM, can be partly or fully constructed by leaders who have personal and other interests. Thus, without running reality through this model, it can be misleading to recreate the behaviors as if they were based on an effort to maximize national interests.

The weight of these findings yields some insight into the rational actor model. Decisions were made through a mix of rational and nonrational behaviors. Key decisions were based far more on concern for national interests, as the RAM would have us believe, than on parochial, departmental interests, as GPM would have us believe. Decision makers, moreover, did not bargain much as representatives of competing bureaucracies, particularly not at the expense of collective, national goals. Numerous efforts also were made to get Iraq out of Kuwait prior to the use of force, demonstrating that at some broad level, the process was reasoned and measured. At some critical junctures, decision makers did discuss options in detail, especially in the deputies group, which should be distinguished in its behavior from the group of eight. However, if we reproduced decisions as if they were made through rational processes, we would frequently be misled. In fact, we would guided better by the theory of groupthink.

This book asks a second, central question: why did the United States go to war? The RAM fares far better in providing insights to answer this question than into how decisions were made. It is highly useful for explaining the broader international context and strategic interaction, chiefly that between Iraq and the United States. But even here the RAM was limited by its inability to account for domestic factors. This was revealed by the subsequent perspectives, which helped paint a fuller picture.

The cognitive perspective largely stands as accurate. Bush was influenced by historical experiences, which made him more determined to go to war and less likely to preside over careful consideration of nonwar alternatives, such as offering Saddam any face-saving formula for his withdrawal, or running economic sanctions longer. Moreover, it may well have motivated U.S. efforts to try to undermine myriad efforts by others at compromise with Saddam, and helped frame Saddam as a significant threat against which a strong stand was necessary.

While the Munich analogy pointed to the costs of any form of compromise, an effect that was consonant with the rationality assumption of the RAM, it also inclined Bush to personalize the conflict and to ignore or downplay options that clashed with the message encoded in it.

The DPM, for its part, did not perform very well, but did suggest that in selling the war to the public, Bush also became more determined against Iraq and sent signals to Iraq that only war, and perhaps Saddam's removal, would satisfy him. This, along with the Munich factor, made negotiations less desirable — indeed, it made their success almost impossible. It probably made it harder for Saddam, proud and powerful in his own mind, to step down from his self-inflated perch. That made Bush even angrier, in what became a cycle of mutual recriminations that Bush may not have intended at first, but later appeared to encourage, once war appeared to him to be preferable to Iraq's withdrawal. Once a "Hitler" is identified and constructed, he cannot be treated with civility. He must be vanquished.

The theory of groupthink, meanwhile, helps explain why Bush faced so little opposition in his inner circle. Once Saddam threatened the United States, and once Bush resolved to get him out of Kuwait (with Saddam proving stubborn), few brakes existed on the road to war, in part because others in Bush's inner circle were reluctant or unable to question seriously the move to war.

The analysis in this chapter and in the foregoing chapters is important in its own right. It helps us understand the extent to which the perspectives of this book were useful in the Persian Gulf War case, and, in turn, forces us to think about what these perspectives really mean as well. However, in the process, evaluating the perspectives also yields insights that we can integrate into a more complete tale of the crisis, a task to which we now turn.

CHAPTER EIGHT

Threading the Tale

While enjoying the serenity of Camp David during one of the Saturday meetings conducted by the president throughout the fall, Dan Quayle asked James Baker an intriguing question: "Would you put your presidency on the line for this?" Quayle recalls that neither of them had an answer.[1] The question alone, however, underscores the possibility that other presidents would have behaved differently, and raises a related question: how much does the individual matter in driving history?

The failures and successes of the multiple perspectives illuminate President Bush's crucial role in the Persian Gulf War case, and, more importantly, how and why he was vital. As stated in the last chapter, the RAM is heuristic insofar as it lays out the broader strategic picture of the crisis, but it is not designed to account for the particular characteristics of individuals. The cognitive perspective underscored how the historical and psychological factors particular to Bush were at play in affecting his reaction to the crisis. For its part, the domestic politics model to some extent highlighted the relationship between the interests of individuals as politicians and the foreign policy event that they face. Meanwhile, the theory of groupthink emphasized Bush's role as a partial leader in the group of eight. And the government politics model failed, partly because Bush preempted the type of politics and bargaining, the "collages" of decisions, and the unintended results that the model assumes will be fundamentally at play.

But if the different perspectives, through their successes and failures, highlighted the individual, how do these insights help us tell a more complete tale of the crisis? This chapter seeks to tell that tale. The first part of the chapter discusses how to assess individual importance in general. It applies this analysis to President Bush, all the while integrating insights from previous chapters to tell the story of the crisis more fully. The second part adds another dimension to round out the story of the crisis. It continues to draw on multiple perspectives to build on the RAM explanation of how U.S.-Iraqi dynamics and strategic interaction contributed to the U.S.'s decision to go to war and to clarify why war was not avoided. It shows how and why the preferences of Iraq and the United States never coincided and actually tended to close any window of opportunity for a peaceful outcome.

Exploring the Importance of the Individual

History is replete with thinkers who question the importance of the individual and stress impersonal forces. Nineteenth-century social determinists, for instance, held that the apparently significant consequences of individual behavior could be "antecedently inferred from a quite different set of considerations."[2] In his comprehensive philosophy of history, Hegel theorized that the iron laws of social evolution dwarfed the role of the individual. For their part, philosophical determinists such as Schopenhauer have held that individuals are defined by environment and history, making free will an illusion. Sociologists have argued in various forms that group dynamics shape the individual. Biologists have focused on nature over nurture, political scientists on structures such as the socializing effects of global anarchy and on impersonal forces such as the balance of power, macro-economists on market effects, and historical determinists on the underlying forces in history.

If individual influence, even that of a president in crisis, is hardly assured, then under what conditions are individuals more likely to be able to be important and influential? That question is so grand that we cannot explore its many dimensions here, but we can explore it in general terms and then in the Persian Gulf War case. To that end, we can ask a few basic questions: (1.) to what extent did the person manifest special personal characteristics and capabilities, (2.) take critical initiatives ahead of others, (3.) face and overcome opposition, (4.) act over and above what his/her role or the situation required, (5.) and surmount historical chance circumstances and factors?[3] For the purposes of this inquiry, "special personal capabilities and characteristics" refers to historical experiences and knowledge; political or personal motivations; personality characteristics and diplomatic skill relevant to handling the issue in question, whether domestic or foreign. "Initiatives" refers to statements or actions that the individual makes that surprise those around him/her, cut against the consensus or prevailing views, and alter the course of the situation. "Opposition" refers to direct and indirect efforts to impede or undermine the individual's beliefs or goals. Meanwhile, acting over and beyond what one's role requires means that the individual exceeded the powers accorded him/her in law or statute.

A "historical chance factor," I posit, is one that the individual did not produce or affect but rather inherited, that evolved over time in the historical process, and that benefited or undermined the individual fortuitously in his/her effort to take successful action. Individuals who play their cards effectively despite poor chance, are more influential, all other things being equal, than those who have been dealt a great hand and have serendipity on their side. Naturally, given continuity in history, it is not easy to separate what an individual inherited from what he or she created or affected. Nonetheless, some things are clearer than others. Bush, for instance, inherited the huge strategic infrastructure in Saudi Arabia, from which he benefited enormously. And he was probably a marginal figure in ending the Cold War, which resulted from a concatenation of multiple profound factors.

1. Personal Capabilities and Characteristics

Let us look at the variables mentioned above in order. Examining them can at least offer a more systematic way of examining Bush's role in the crisis. We start with special personal capabilities and characteristics.

Experience and Knowledge: Back to the Past

The first aspect of special personal characteristics and capabilities is experience and knowledge. As shown in chapter 3, using the lens of Munich, Bush saw Saddam as evil, implacable, rapacious, as a leader who had to be cut down to size. Merely generating Iraq's withdrawal could not meet that goal. At some point, war became the best option.[4] On Christmas Eve, Bush wrote in his diary: "I think of the evil of this man. He has to not only be checked, but punished, and then we worry about how we handle our relations with the Arab countries."[5]

While Munich did help frame the crisis, sometimes in stronger terms than the situation warranted, it also helped sort out the costs and benefits of different approaches. In this sense, it fed into rational thinking. It helped Bush and others assess the costs of not taking a strong stand against Saddam, and predisposed him toward war. At times, he also used it to construct the crisis, so that we could say that the analogy was both heartfelt by a president who experienced World War II and used to advance the war option.

While Bush's experience in World War II shaped his approach, so did his knowledge of and experience in the Middle East. In U.S. Ambassador to Saudi Arabia Chas Freeman's view, Bush "was ideally suited for the moment—combative and knowledgeable as the only president that I know who had been out to the region."[6] In fact, Bush had traveled extensively throughout the region.

Bush probably knew more about the Middle East than any other president in history. He began learning about the region long before becoming president, during his early days in the oil business. After graduating from Yale, Bush decided to pass on a nine-to-five business career on the East Coast, and instead headed off to Midland, Texas, to begin a career in oil. You couldn't survive in the oil business unless you understood something about the oil industry in the Middle East and the broader environment that affected supply and demand, especially in the postwar period when the terrain was relatively uncharted.

Bush also learned about the Middle East through his roles as CIA director, UN ambassador, and vice president. In the latter role, he faced the Iran-Contra scandal, the 1982 attack on U.S. Marines in Lebanon, and the Iran-Iraq War. Interestingly, he also edged out Secretary of State Alexander Haig for the job of managing international crises under President Reagan's watch, which included presiding over senior officials in the process of framing and addressing such crises. It is hard to imagine better preparation for the Persian Gulf crisis than that. One adviser, noting his experience, observed that "he was attached to and aware of Gulf politics and acted on the basis of knowledge."[7] A skilled and experienced group leader decreases the negative impact on decision-making that a lack of methodical procedures can have. In Gates's view, the success of Desert Shield and Storm made Bush's effort appear less significant in retrospect, but in fact he managed multiple complicated diplomatic tasks in ways that were "hard to replicate."[8]

Global Politicking and Personal Relations

Bush's personal relations proved vital in the Persian Gulf crisis. He knew dozens of world leaders before they took power, through his positions as CIA director, U.S. ambassador to the UN, and vice president. He had unknowingly laid the groundwork for successful diplomacy in the Persian Gulf long before Saddam's invasion. As one high-level official put it, "he was potent in part because of his foreign policy background."[9]

Bush's excellent relationship with President Mitterrand, for example, was no accident. Bush invited him to Kennebunkport shortly after taking office with the precise goal of shoring up U.S.-French relations, which were strained at the time, in the event that France was needed in a future crisis.[10] France eventually proved crucial to U.S. influence in the UN Security Council and Europe, and contributed 16,000 soldiers and important air assets to the U.S.-led coalition.

Bush also cultivated other leaders, including Gorbachev, with whom he had warm relations long before he actually became president, and such Persian Gulf leaders as President Zayid bin Sultan an-Nahayan of the United Arab Emirates and Sultan Qabus bin Said of Oman. Bush also befriended King Fahd and Prince Bandar of Saudi Arabia while Bush was CIA director and Bandar was sharpening his lobbying skills in Washington. That would prove quite handy, because Bandar, who was sometimes referred to as "an Arab Great Gatsby" for his proclivity to entertain, was King Fahd's western-educated favorite nephew. As Saudi ambassador to the United States, Bandar helped Bush convince King Fahd to allow U.S. forces into the kingdom. After getting assurances from Bush of U.S. resolve, Bandar told Fahd that he had talked to the "Big Man" — meaning Bush: "Your Majesty knows George Bush very well and you know that he is a man who always keeps his word."[11]

Bush's foreign contacts also went beyond heads of state. On one trip to Japan, for instance, it was clear to his advisers that he was well known. To their surprise, he even knew spouses and kids by name and asked them personal questions about their lives, which created a rare level of intimacy.[12]

Beyond his knowledge of the region, Bush was skillful in global affairs. To be sure, he had much help from Baker and his State Department team. They laid the groundwork for effective UN action even before the crisis occurred. Indeed, U.S. Ambassador to the United Nations Thomas Pickering, along with other UN diplomats, helped turn the UN Security Council from a moribund group that rarely met to one that by August 1990 met around the clock.[13] But Bush's global contacts were crucial in creating and maintaining the coalition, which was composed of some strange bedfellows and strong-willed countries.

Crises, in particular, put a high premium on trust. The combination of time pressures and high stakes mean that personal commitments and promises must count. Foreign leaders trusted and respected Bush. That made them more willing to go out on a limb for him and facilitated his effort to enlist the scores of leaders that he called personally in the early days of the crisis. As Sununu saw it, Bush's personal relations led leaders to help him in ways that they "never thought they would."[14] A president without such strong relations would have faced far greater difficulty holding the coalition together. In that effort, as Cheney notes, he often made phone calls and "greased the skids" for his key advisers ahead of their visits to various countries.[15] In the first days of the crisis Bush, Cheney recalls, called key Arab leaders prior to Cheney's discussions with them, which allowed for "some very important understandings and arrangements" to develop.[16]

Other presidents, to be sure, also had strong relationships with foreign leaders. Nixon's China connection comes to mind, as does Reagan's relationship with Margaret Thatcher. But as Webster, who knew Reagan and Bush very well, noted: "Reagan didn't know leaders like Bush did. He did not have so many one on ones with them. Overall, not many people in the world could have done what Bush did with the coalition."[17] Most presidents were not particularly strong in foreign affairs, literally learning the trade on the job. Lyndon Johnson worked the phone effectively. But he was not trusted, as Bush was, by such a wide range of foreign leaders and diplomats.[18] To bring China aboard and to prevent it from using its UN Security Council veto to torpedo U.S.-led efforts against Iraq, Bush personally and effectively handled relations with Beijing, based on years of experience with the Chinese.[19] He had, after all, lived in China in the mid-1970s as chief of the U.S. Liaison Office, a position that indoctrinated him about the ways of China and allowed him to make important connections.

While Bush had major global connections, his influence was also enhanced by personal relations in his own inner circle, as laid out in chapter 5.

2. Taking the Initiative

Regarding the variable of taking initiative, Bush spearheaded a number of critical initiatives that to some extent have already been discussed in the body of this book, but are elaborated upon in the following eight sections of this chapter.

The First Days of the Crisis

At first, Bush was willing but reluctant to let Arab leaders solve the problem so long as they did not give Saddam any carrots, but he changed course largely because he thought Saddam was exploiting these efforts to consolidate his hold on Kuwait.[20] Bush's propensity to take bold initiatives was clear from the outset to his advisers and is manifest in the record. He repeatedly asserted that Saddam's brutality must be punished. It was Bush, not his public relations team or aides, who decided to use forceful rhetoric against Saddam, rewriting speeches for that purpose. Summing up the sentiment of his closest advisers, Baker asserted that "Bush was absolutely critical. He made a visceral decision to reverse the invasion and he was out in front of all his advisers."[21] The real question was which option would get Iraq out of Kuwait, not whether it should be done.

Why Economic Sanctions Were Rejected

While some of Bush's actions reflected an impetuous bent, it would be misleading to say that he awoke one day to an epiphany about war. Rather, as Scowcroft points out, the president "hoped that economic sanctions would work, but he made up his mind fairly early on that force would be used if necessary and that planning should be based on the assumption that sanctions would fail."[22] The ultimate decision to use massive force was reached slowly, though some of the decisions that led up to it were reached quickly. Earlier in the crisis, in fact, Bush appeared ready to go to war on a pretext. When it appeared that two Iraqi ships, the *Khanaqin* and the *Baba Gurgur*, would attempt on August 18 to break the U.S.-led embargo, Bush wanted to sink them, even though some of his advisers argued that the United States was not ready for war, and even though states such as the Soviet Union were urging the United States to avoid such moves and to allow Arab and UN diplomacy to work.[23] Later, on August 23, the day Washington shut down its embassy in Kuwait, Bush and Scowcroft went fishing for bluefish near Walker's Point, Maine — their first real chance to unwind and talk. Bush seemed eager to consider force. He even noted that the Iraqis, who were using human shields like cowards, were not so tough. But Scowcroft, Bush recalls, was "less certain that we could destroy Saddam's spread-out tanks and planes in one sweep."[24]

Nonetheless, Bush noted in his diary on August 23 for the first time that he could "not see" how the United States would "remove Saddam Hussein from Kuwait without using force." That was a critical juncture, caused, Bush asserted, by the "cumulative effect" of his worries about Iraq's ability to withstand sanctions and the dangers of waiting for them to work.[25] While the reasons appear to have been more complex than that, Bush's position contrasted with that of Baker and Powell. They wanted to give sanctions a chance, but, as discussed in chapter 5, did little in group settings to actually push that position.

The dominant reasons for why, though not how, the United States went to war in the Persian Gulf are highlighted by the RAM perspective. Beyond dominant oil concerns and the question of setting a positive precedent for the post–Cold War world, real concerns arose that time was running out for nonwar options. While the coalition was giving sanctions a chance, Iraq could finish dismantling Kuwait, the coalition might split, Iraq might develop weapons of mass destruction, and burgeoning democracies around the world could falter under the economic pressures of higher oil prices. By late October, these pressures started to mount. Bush actually contemplated the use of force even in response to minor incidents, such as over the besieged U.S. embassy in Kuwait. In his diary, he entered these interesting words: "The news is saying some members of Congress feel I might use a minor incident to go to war, and they may be right. We must get this over with. The longer it goes, the longer the erosion."[26] At the time, talk was again making the rounds about negotiating with Saddam —

which Bush totally rejected — and Bush's credibility had also been hurt by the budget struggle with Congress, a looming recession, and other domestic problems noted in chapter 4.

Making a War Plan

Bush began to press strongly for an offensive option far sooner than his military officers had wanted. He wanted to send Saddam a "clear, clarion signal" that Washington meant business in getting Iraq "out of Kuwait" and in protecting American citizens and the world economic system.[27] But while Bush drove policy at some critical junctures, he did not dictate how U.S. goals should be accomplished. Military policy was largely left to the military brass, their assistants, and Secretary Cheney. As Powell notes, "Bush never told me what to do militarily," with one key exception.[28] On October 11, the NSC core group met in the Situation Room, only to learn that the military planned a frontal assault into Kuwait. While the plan was being unveiled, Bush, Scowcroft, and Sununu rolled their eyes in a bit of silent communication.[29] Scowcroft, who was "appalled," was the first to shoot it down, and Bush became convinced that the military had a long way to go before it was "gung ho" and felt we "had the means to accomplish our mission expeditiously."[30]

After the meeting, Sununu told Bush and Scowcroft that the plan sounded like something out of one of Woody Hayes's football strategy books at Ohio State University, where the idea was to knock as many people down as possible, in head-on attacks. With strong backing from Bush and Sununu, Scowcroft, according to one account, recommended that the generals consider a flanking maneuver, which they eventually adopted as the strategy underlying Desert Storm, after failing to revise their plan effectively two times.[31] The frontal attack plan was created on the basis of the force level at hand in the Persian Gulf in early October, which was recognized, according to Schwarzkopf, as being deficient for more ambitious strategies.[32] Whether or not one agrees with that assessment, the group of eight did agree that the flanking plan would require substantially more force, and by the end of October, Powell and others who had preferred a go-slow approach began to recognize that time was running out.[33] The crisis was in a new stage. To be massive and decisive, in contrast to Vietnam, Desert Storm required that U.S. forces be doubled in the Persian Gulf.

Seeking a Peaceful Solution

At a broad level, the controversial decision of October 31 to double U.S. forces in the Persian Gulf reflected mixed motives: to use force and seek peace. Bush's inclination toward force was matched by some hope earlier on that U.S. saber rattling would convince Saddam to withdraw. Failure to show resolve could encourage the dictator — a type of thinking that was consonant with the message of the Munich analogy. It is too simple to say that Bush was on an unmitigated warpath. In fact, he was also angling to see if he could force a humiliating Iraqi withdrawal on his quite strict terms. That was clear in a number of official and unofficial documents underscoring his position with foreign and domestic leaders.[34]

In a scribbled private note to former Secretary of State George Shultz on December 14, Bush observed that "Saddam still does not grasp what he's up against and he still does not feel force will be used. I'm convinced on both these points."[35] When asked if the president believed that Saddam did not understand the situation, Fitzwater asserted on January 4 that "we can't believe that he would continue to put his country and his people at such great risk if he did not understand it."[36] In meetings with members of Congress, Bush repeatedly asserted that the only way to avoid war was to convince Saddam that we were ready for one.[37] And in fact, Bush did not forget that Saddam had told President Ozal of Turkey on August 5 that he planned to annex Kuwait and believed that the West was "bluffing."[38]

Seeking War, after All

The official line in U.S. diplomacy with its allies and with Iraq was that there could be no reward for Iraq's aggression. In effect, that meant that Saddam would not be punished if he withdrew from Kuwait. However, while it was never broached publicly, or even at a group of eight meeting, and although Bush did hold out the prospect of an Iraqi withdrawal, Bush and key members of the group of eight increasingly began to view war not just as likely, but as preferable to Iraqi withdrawal.[39] Their perceptions on this score were clear, very similar, and important to understand. As Gates put it, war was "absolutely preferable. One of our real worries was that Saddam would make a tactical move that would pre-empt our attack; that would allow him to loot the country, and not get punished, and remain a major menace."[40] The group of eight, spearheaded by Bush, also believed that the United States either had to go to war at some point or stand down, which was unthinkable. Perhaps Scowcroft put it most clearly, in saying that "both Baker and Powell argued for sanctions. I took the position that we couldn't afford not to have a conflict. We had to continue forward. The force was larger than we needed and we could not keep it in place if he withdrew. We would have had to withdraw."[41] Bush, in particular, strongly believed that Saddam would return another day as a more serious threat, if he were able to withdraw with his army intact. Munich clearly affected the extent to which Bush would consider options short of war.

Scowcroft, like Bush, believed that it would be "far more costly to fight another day. Someone would have to pay the price if Saddam were allowed out of this."[42] That widely-held view was generated in large part by the fact that Saddam, as Webster points out, "gave a big signal of what other things might lie out there in the future, so we thought we should reduce the number of toys he had to terrorize the neighborhood."[43]

For its part, the deputies group gamed numerous scenarios ranging from Iraq's partial to full withdrawal; in Haass's view, "war was far less worse than the alternatives."[44] A full withdrawal would have been problematic, but a partial one could have been even worse by making it harder to justify an attack on Iraq, while Saddam was able to maintain a threatening posture. The committee, Haass recalls, established a number of tests that Iraq would have to pass, even if it withdrew partially, and it was prepared to release them publicly. The goal was to prevent Saddam from changing the political atmosphere so that by withdrawing, he could still control parts of Kuwait.[45] Ambassador Pickering and others proposed that the UN establish an occupation zone in Kuwait in the event that Iraq withdrew partially or fully from Kuwait, or in Iraq itself after the war concluded. However, that approach, which Pickering thought he could get through the UN Security Council, was dismissed by Powell and Schwarzkopf, and could not have been viewed positively by Bush and Scowcroft.[46] Such proposals had to be broached to deal with a potential ongoing threat from Iraq, but the goal was clearly to cut Iraq down to size, while maintaining U.S. control of the overall effort.

Bush viewed the potential for a successful war as high, despite the Defense Department's talk of thousands of body bags, and despite his deep concern about casualties. He later characterized his state of mind in late August as follows: "I thought the Defense Department overestimated Iraq's strength and resolve. Despite the size of their army, I just didn't see the Iraqis as being so tough. They had been unable to defeat Iran; they had never fought over long supply lines, or at any time when they did not control the air."[47] In mid-October, when the president was literally looking for a pretext or provocation to attack Iraq, he thought to himself that overwhelming U.S. air power would "smash Saddam's military threat and wipe out Iraq's nuclear, chemical, and biological weapons facilities."[48] He increasingly believed that force could be used successfully.[49] By Thanksgiving, after getting a briefing from Schwarzkopf, Bush noted in his diary that he was "more convinced than ever that we can knock Saddam Hussein out early."[50]

Bush had the military infrastructure in the region, the forces in place, a strong coalition, and superior technology on his side. Factoring these elements into the equation made war all the more preferable to a situation where Saddam could return another day after the coalition had disbanded, the U.S. force level in the region and military readiness had decreased, and Iraq possibly had nuclear capability. Finally, while war always had the potential of cutting Saddam's army and ambitions down to size, we need at least to consider that it tended to bolster Bush's legacy as well as his efforts to divert attention from domestic problems. Purportedly, Sununu was telling people that a short, successful war would be pure political gold for the president — would guarantee his re-election.[51] The image of Bush as a wimp with little vision might also be erased in the sands of Arabia, and the ghosts of Vietnam exorcised.

None of this means that the United States definitely wanted a war from day one. As Pickering perceived it, U.S. decision makers saw "no good negotiated solution to the crisis, but if Saddam withdrew completely and early on from Kuwait, the United States probably would have had no choice but to accept that outcome because it would have complied with UN resolutions."[52] War was not avoided not only because Washington preferred it, but also because Iraq would not back down.

Banging Heads in Geneva: Too Much Baggage

On November 30, Bush shocked many observers when he announced his plan for going the extra mile to avoid war. While it was partly window-dressing for war, the president, as Scowcroft recalled, "felt that to go to war without having a direct meeting with the Iraqis would not be a good idea."[53] It was Bush's decision, one that even the supportive Scowcroft believed should have been given more thought.[54]

After much wrangling, Iraqi officials agreed to meet on January 9 in Geneva.[55] In an effort to pressure Congress before its historic debate on the war, a resolved and strident Bush sent a letter to congressional leaders the day before the Geneva meeting. He criticized Congress for not sending Saddam a clear signal of American unity. The letter argued that Congress could help Baker in Geneva if it endorsed the November decision by the United Nations setting a January 15 deadline, after which "all necessary means" could be used to get Iraq out of Kuwait. Bush also asserted that no compromise would take place and that Saddam posed a future threat as well, even if he withdrew.[56]

As discussed in chapter 3, Bush rejected even a semblance of a veiled negotiated deal with Iraq. Bush's January 8 letter warned the international community to resist pressures "now building" to negotiate with Iraq, arguing that such negotiation would only feed Saddam's "appetite for conquest" and "be paid many times over in greater sacrifice and suffering" at a later time when he might even have nuclear weapons.[57] Bush was resolved to act and far from sanguine that Saddam could withdraw in time. On January 12, he noted that while "an instant commencement of a large-scale removal of troops with no condition, no concession, and just heading out could well be the best and only way to avert war, I would say almost impossible [*sic*] to comply fully with the United Nations resolutions."[58] Perhaps in response to Bush's statements, or for other reasons, Aziz warned on the night before the Baker meeting that "Iraq does not yield to pressure," although he also emphasized that he had come in "good faith, open-minded, ready to conduct positive, constructive talks."[59]

Why Iraq Did Not Withdraw

We may never know fully why Iraq stood its ground, but several factors were likely at play. It may very well have doubted U.S. resolve, partly due to a misreading of the impact of the Vietnam experience, as chapter 3 discussed in some detail. U.S. negotiators at Geneva sensed that Iraq's diplomats felt that the United States still carried the baggage of Vietnam, that the public could not handle a major war, and that Congress was wishy-washy on war.[60] Saddam may very well have believed that, as Freeman put it, the United States would "fold if the going got rough."[61] He did assert in a speech to the Islamic Conference in Baghdad in January 1991 that Iraqis are "not people who speak on the basis of books: we are people with experience in fighting."[62]

Saddam may have sporadically considered withdrawing from Kuwait. Soviet Foreign Minister Yevgeny Primakov said, for instance, that when he told Saddam in October that he must leave Kuwait, Saddam balked — but then when Primakov asserted that if he didn't withdraw "there will be a military strike against you," Saddam showed that he was in a position to change his approach.[63] This may suggest that Saddam was flexible. He may have wanted to stand up to the coalition to score political points at home and on the Arab Street — although not to the point of a full-scale war — but did not manage this balancing act effectively. He may have thought that he could bargain with Bush as the crisis proceeded, or force his hand in a bloody war. Yet, as the crisis proceeded, Saddam's bargaining hand weakened and Bush's strengthened, further bolstered by his Munich-inspired determination. Saddam, in this sense, misestimated the strategic interaction between Iraq and the United States. Washington, in fact, had lower opportunity costs from noncooperation. It wasn't just that it could afford to tolerate no agreement on Iraqi withdrawal, it preferred that outcome, which put it in a very powerful bargaining position.

That Saddam was surrounded by "yes-men" was also important. As Primakov told a disturbed Bush on October 19 about his visit to Baghdad, Saddam was "poorly informed" and was "hearing more about his support than about his political isolation."[64] If Saddam did not think that the United States would launch a major war, he also could not discount the possibility that, short of war, it would harass him. Or that it might even try to have him killed, given his international pariah status, even if he withdrew.[65] Tariq Aziz captured this dynamic perhaps most effectively when he described how he felt following the failed Geneva summit on January 9, days before the war: "We were expecting a war. I, I tell you frankly and responsibly, we were expecting an Israeli aggression or an American aggression, or both, during that period, regardless of what we do. Margaret Thatcher and George Bush spoke about dismantling Iraq's military power, even if Iraq withdraws from Kuwait. So what does that mean? It means some sort of a war. With or without Kuwait. Damned if you do it, damned if you don't."[66] Saddam also alluded to such a dynamic in interviews and speeches, such as when he noted, in response to questions in late December about whether Iraq would withdraw, that such an act would be difficult to achieve "when a peace-loving human being surrenders to the wolf in the forest, or when a massacre occurs because that human being has become his prey?"[67]

Such fears, insofar as they accurately reflect Saddam's mindset, may not have been fully clear to U.S. decision makers. They knew that they could not attack Iraq outright if Saddam withdrew and may have assumed that Saddam understood that—a fairly common assumption among leaders who seek to understand how others perceive them. Indeed, studies show that actors tend to simplify their operational environment; in particular, they assume that they are virtuous, and, more importantly, that the adversary recognizes their virtue.[68] Leaders tend to believe that they understand the other side's view of the world, and thus they assume that their own messages have been received and interpreted as intended. This predisposes them to believe—erroneously—that others will view their behavior as less threatening than it is in reality.[69]

Even at the outset of the crisis, both Saddam and his officials repeatedly asserted that they viewed U.S. action in the Persian Gulf as offensive, as an effort to dominate the region.[70] Virtually each time a Western diplomat visited Baghdad, Saddam would not just mention but habitually discuss the "Zionist-American conspiracy" that he faced.[71] By early November, when talk of compromise was in the air, he wanted guarantees that the United States would not attack him if Iraq withdrew from Kuwait. He once again wanted such assurances at the end of the war. Saddam's notion of a Zionist-American conspiracy was baseless, but from his perspective he had some reasons to doubt U.S. intentions. Among them, he remembered that the United States had offered his archenemy, Iran, arms for hostages during the Iran-Iraq War, when he thought he had U.S. support; according to Tariq Aziz, Saddam did not trust Washington thereafter.[72]

During the Persian Gulf crisis, moreover, Bush suggested on November 1 that Iraq's chemical and biological weapons would have to be checked even if Saddam withdrew because they posed a threat to regional security.[73] The next day, Quayle went further, stating that they had to be dismantled, and, in an interview in late December, Scowcroft said that they would have to be "dealt with one way or another."[74] At a minimum, as one internal memo suggested, economic sanctions would have been continued to "ensure that Iraq cannot again pose a threat to the Gulf"; and another suggested on January 10 that "if we fail to stop Saddam now, we will have to at some point down the road when it will be that more much [*sic*] difficult and expensive."[75] Clearly, Bush and his key advisers were not interested in "returning to the *status quo ante*," if Saddam withdrew.[76] We might argue that Saddam was unaware of such proclivities, but that is not very likely, since Aziz was acutely conscious of them.[77] And the cosmopolitan, well-traveled, and cultured Aziz, despite being a Christian Arab in Saddam's predominantly Sunni Muslim regime, was quite loyal to Saddam.

There was also a rising chorus to try Saddam as a war criminal, which must have decreased his incentive to negotiate or withdraw.[78] To try to guarantee the safety of British hostages through deterrence, Thatcher earlier in the crisis raised the specter of Nuremberg-like trials after the war. That struck a responsive chord with Bush, although the State Department thought it was a bad idea.[79] When the crisis is over, Bush said, the "world will hold him accountable, just as it held Adolph Hitler accountable in the wake of the destruction of World War II."[80] Indeed, Bush's legal office researched that prospect and offered talking points for the president on war crimes trials on February 4, 1991.[81]

For his part, Saddam was fully aware of Iraq's glorious Babylonian past, and exalted himself in that light, despite his disastrous record of war. Iraqis had "the honor," as Saddam would say in a letter to Bush and Gorbachev, "to show humanity the right path to its humanity when they taught it the alphabet and writing 6,000 years ago, and when they taught it law 4,500 years ago."[82] From the outset on August 5, Saddam appeared to some extent conflicted. Throughout the crisis, he sometimes simultaneously put forth proposals for a negotiated settlement — which Washington found wanting — and showed elements of profound defiance. Whether Aziz agreed with Saddam's approach is hard to tell, but he acted as if he did. Thus, when Gorbachev told Aziz in Helsinki on September 5 that Iraq was acting as if in a "vacuum, in unreality," Aziz asserted that Iraq was "not afraid — neither of the world conflict nor of the Americans."[83] That led Gorbachev to tell an annoyed Bush in Helsinki a few days later that Saddam must be allowed to save face.[84]

Later, on October 19, after his earlier trip to Baghdad, Primakov informed Bush of chilling comments made by Saddam, a man clearly struggling with the clash between his ego and fate: "I'd die before leaving. I'm prepared to die, but this battle is not confined to one country alone. I am a realist. I know I must leave Kuwait, but I simply can't leave."[85] Saddam was defiant enough that Primakov described his behavior as in line with a Masada complex — an odd reference to the unwavering and doomed stand on Masada, a plateau overlooking the Dead Sea, that a small band of Jews made against Roman legions in the first century; when asked by Primakov, Saddam agreed that he did have a conspiratorial view and such a complex.[86] While Primakov was initially hopeful about a negotiated breakthrough after his October 4 trip to Baghdad, that would change after his trip at the end of October. The cables he sent to Moscow at that time were viewed in Moscow as "discouraging."[87]

The streak of defiance in Saddam's personality would continue to express itself sporadically until the bombs fell.[88] Thus, on the night the war started, he lambasted Bush in a letter for, among other things, his "arrogant style" in addressing him and the Iraqi people, describing Bush as one who took the "devil" as his "colleague."[89] Indeed, Iraq commonly referred with disdain to what it perceived as Bush's arrogant style during the crisis.[90] On January 10, Iraqi First Deputy Prime Minister Taha Yasin Ramadan laid out Iraq's position in a long speech, emphasizing the longstanding "grand conspiracy against the lands of Arabs and Islam" dating back centuries.[91] A few days later in a letter to Gorbachev, Saddam reasserted the common theme that Iraq rejects the "US law of hegemony and domination."[92] The Rubicon appeared to have been crossed. Bush warned of catastrophe for Iraq if Saddam stayed in Kuwait. Saddam warned that rivers of blood would flow if the United States challenged Iraq militarily. "I know I am going to lose," Saddam told French diplomats, but "at least I will have the death of a hero."[93] It is unclear to what extent this reflected bravado more than heartfelt emotion.

At Geneva, Aziz repeatedly asserted that Iraq would not be intimidated and that Saddam was too tough to back down to threats. In long arguments, he spoke with charged rhetoric about a variety of issues, emphasizing Iraq's resolve and dignity while questioning that of the United States.[94] Aziz even refused to take a letter, carried by Baker, from Bush to Saddam, which informed Saddam that, among other things, dire consequences would follow if he refused to withdraw. Baker recalls that Aziz, one of Saddam's most dependable allies, took "maybe 10 minutes or so to read the letter and he said 'I cannot accept this letter, it's not written in the language that is appropriate for communications between heads of state.' "[95] Aziz in fact later described the letter as one "of threat" which he could not even give to his President.[96] The letter simply sat on the table for six to seven hours, out of neither sight nor mind of the negotiating teams on both sides of the long, oval table. While it was strongly worded and warned that the American people would demand vengeance if Iraq were to use weapons of mass destruction, it did hold out the prospect of Iraq rejoining the international community.[97] Bush's previous rhetoric may have affected how Aziz perceived the letter. And Aziz's repeated refusal to take it to Saddam probably had much to do with concern about bringing Saddam any potentially humiliating statements from Washington. Americans who negotiated with Saddam's advisers perceived this fear in them, and believed, quite sensibly, that such fear inclined them to allow Saddam to overestimate Iraq's strength.[98]

The reluctance to take Bush's letter to Saddam may have also stemmed from the view that Saddam by January 9 viewed war as preferable anyhow, in the absence of a face-saving withdrawal or at least acceptable assurances that Iraq would not be attacked. In fact, it is possible that even before Geneva, Iraq had decided to go to war and to press the Palestinian issue in order to gain some sympathy in the Arab world. On January 8, Ramadan gave a spirited speech emphasizing the importance to Iraq of the Palestinian cause.[99] At Geneva, the Palestinian cause dominated Aziz's position and statements, to the point that he did not even mention Iraq's invasion of Kuwait in his long opening statement.[100]

While the U.S. team at Geneva knew that only Saddam could give them assurances of Iraqi withdrawal, they thought Aziz might show at least a hint of flexibility, or, as one U.S. official in Geneva said, we "hoped he would at least blink!"[101] But, rather than being compliant, Iraq argued that all allied forces must be replaced with a UN-directed, all-Arab force, that all politico-economic sanctions against Iraq must end, and that Iraq's withdrawal must be met with similar action by Syria in Lebanon and Israel in the occupied territories. Aziz told Baker that if "you are ready to bring about peace to the region, comprehensive, lasting, just peace to the whole region of the Middle East, we are ready to cooperate."[102] Even if such demands could have been met, the oft-stated U.S. position was clear to Aziz, that Iraq must withdraw unconditionally to avoid war. At the end of the meeting, Baker once again asked Aziz if he would take the letter Bush wrote to Saddam, to which he tersely replied "No."[103]

3. Facing Opposition

The previous sections of this chapter explored initiative as a crucial factor in assessing the importance of the individual, but it is equally vital to examine the level of opposition the individual faced. As discussed in the introduction and sporadically thereafter, Bush faced much opposition outside his inner circle and many challenges on the road to war. They came from Congress, the American public, prominent former U.S. military leaders, foreign leaders, and even his own presiding bishop.[104] That opposition, however, was most significant from August through November.

However, as we saw in chapter 6, Bush also benefited from little bureaucratic politics, which have bedeviled other presidents. Elements of groupthink also worked to his advantage. Apart from such group dynamics, his key advisers also worked hard for him, protected his interests, and carried out his directives. That cannot be underestimated, especially because many presidents lacked such support. As Sununu saw it, "We had a President whom we trusted, admired, and wanted to work hard for, and who viewed us similarly, and that climate of operation was extremely critical."[105] That Bush received some significant support from foreign leaders further enhanced his ability to carry out a desired set of decisions and to achieve success in U.S.-Iraqi strategic interaction.

4. Exceeding Role Play

Beyond assessing the opposition that an individual faces, we need to explore the extent to which the individual takes actions *beyond what his/her role* or the situation requires. As president, was Bush required to take such a strong, energetic, and unyielding stand? According to their formal and informal roles, presidents are generally more influential in foreign affairs, and, as commander in chief, in foreign military matters than in other matters of the state. Thus, we would have expected any president to play an important role in the Persian Gulf crisis. It was a military crisis in a foreign land where the United States has vital interests.

Yet, although the crisis required a strong leadership role, it is not at all clear that any leader would have taken as strong a stand against Saddam as did Bush. While presidents are sometimes exalted in the public eye as all-powerful, they often must work hard to get others to do what they want, even in crises, and may face a plethora of constraints. These range from time and information limitations to a potentially uncooperative bureaucracy and a hostile public. As President Kennedy's aide Theodore Sorensen points out, "the President is not omnipotent. Choices within his control may be altered by events beyond his control."[106]

As discussed in the introduction of this book, innumerable other decisions and outcomes were possible. Other presidents, for instance, might have given Saddam a face-saving way out of Kuwait, to avoid what at the outset appeared to be a crisis with unpredictable results. Or, more quietly, they could have given France, the U.S.S.R., or Jordan the nod to arrange a *quid pro quo* behind closed doors. Or Saddam might have accepted France's last-minute effort to advance a face-saving Iraqi withdrawal — thus putting Washington in a pickle — and, as mentioned earlier, Saddam could also have withdrawn partly from Kuwait, thus altering the crisis altogether. Other presidents might have decided to avoid war by running economic sanctions and using containment indefinitely, as was U.S. policy toward Iraq in the 1990s. Or they might have stood their ground but allowed economic sanctions to run far longer, thus possibly changing the outcome of the crisis. Or, if that failed, they could have opted for a war of attrition over a major war, the likes of which we periodically saw in the 1990s, as Washington sought to impose U.N. sanctions on a defiant Iraq. Literally thousands of other changes in approach at virtually any time were also possible, which alone or together would have altered the confluence of events.

The fact that Bush played the role of president is not enough to explain U.S. behavior. Reflecting broader opinion in the group of eight, Baker asserted the view that the war would not have been possible with a president other than Bush, adding that Bush "set the standard . . . and had the resolve and the determination and the leadership qualities that made all of this possible."[107] While structuralists would question that view, for his part, Gates, who was himself a historian who had worked in three administrations before becoming deputy national security advisor, claimed that he could "absolutely see another outcome with a different president" because Bush was hard to replicate in three ways. Namely, his "utter conviction," his oft-repeated willingness to be "impeached" and to "gamble everything which other presidents don't do," and his management of the military and diplomatic side of the crisis.[108] Whatever we think of such personal testimony, all of Bush's advisers took similar views. They believed that he played a role up and beyond what his office called for, a view that they need not have shared to such an extent.

5. The Chance Factor

Chance benefited Bush. Politically, Bush and Baker were crucial in securing Soviet cooperation against Iraq, but the end of the Cold War and Moscow's need for Western economic support made that possible. The world had changed in ways that made Iraq a liability more than a regional asset for Moscow. Meanwhile, the end of the Cold War meant that Moscow would be less likely to veto U.S. efforts at the UN, despite the fact that, as Gorbachev told Baker and Bush, it would be very hard for him to sell a vote in favor of U.S. force against a longtime ally in the Persian Gulf to his military and political elite.[109] The end of the Cold War also altered the nature of Middle East affairs to Bush's favor. With Moscow's star waning and the Cold War fading, the U.S.S.R.'s former clients, like Syria, were more inclined to join the coalition. In earlier decades, when anti-American radicalism was at a higher pitch and Moscow was supporting its regional allies, the crisis would have been far more complicated. Bush would likely have run into far more serious problems getting Arab support for the coalition, and Saddam might have had more allies, or at least sympathizers.

Strategically, only a decade earlier, President Carter had to consider the use of nuclear weapons when the Soviets invaded Afghanistan in 1979, because the United States lacked a conventional response. But over the next decade, the United States significantly improved its ability to project its forces to the Persian Gulf. That was critical because Desert Shield would involve the largest movement of forces in U.S. history. In 1980, movement even of minimal U.S. forces to the Persian Gulf would have taken many weeks.[110] From 1980 to 1987, American airlift capabilities increased from 26.9 to 39.6 million-ton-miles per day. The United States also enhanced the Military Sealift Command active fleet from 44 to 57 ships, and the Ready Reserve Force from 27 to 82 ships. Overall, the Defense Department spent over $7 billion to improve sealift capabilities in the 1980s. Key improvements included a prepositioned force of 25 ships, some of which provided the first supplies during the Persian Gulf crisis, 8 fast sealift ships especially suited to transport heavy Army unit equipment, and an additional increase in the Ready Reserve Force to 96 ships.

Moreover, the Iran-Iraq War increased Saudi interest in funding and building an estimated $200 billion military infrastructure for the entry of massive American forces. That infrastructure served all U.S. and all allied forces and housed U.S. Central Command (CENTCOM). Commanded by General Schwarzkopf, it had been headquartered in Tampa but moved to Saudi Arabia during the crisis.[111] Despite improvements in U.S. force projection, sealift in particular was still lacking and U.S. forces were vulnerable for the first two months.[112] Nonetheless, the improvements on the U.S. side and in the Saudi military infrastructure made Desert Shield and Storm possible. In 1980 there had only been two major non-oil docks in Saudi Arabia, each capable of unloading only one ship at a time. By 1990, dozens of ships could be unloaded simultaneously at nine major ports. Saudi airfields became significantly more sophisticated and had doubled in number. The Saudis also integrated their ground-based radar missile systems, fighter bases, fighters, and command-communication posts into a single network. Military roads, emergency fuel storage facilities, air-conditioned bunkers, and nuclear-proof command posts all became part of this elaborate military infrastructure.

Schwarzkopf stated that had this infrastructure not existed, U.S. CENTCOM, which prior to 1983 had been called the U.S. Rapid Deployment force, would not have recommended sending in such a substantial American force.[113] And, in fact, had it not been for U.S. advances in the 1980s, there would not have even been a big force to send in, outside of U.S. forces drawn from Europe. In this sense, Bush was quite lucky. He was the first president who had the military capability and regional position to mount operations as complex as Desert Shield and Desert Storm, and to transfer U.S. divisions from Europe, where they had stared down the Soviet army, to the Persian Gulf. The ending of the Cold War made that possible. That was no insignificant factor. It gave Washington the confidence to challenge Saddam, to draw on the best American tanks, and to launch a ground war.

Saddam was also clumsy and ineffective — politically, strategically, and militarily. If anything, he helped Bush spearhead the move toward war. And Bush was also lucky in that Saddam chose to invade Kuwait before acquiring nuclear weapons; in retrospect, we know that Saddam was possibly just a year away from obtaining them. A nuclear-armed Iraq probably would have made it impossible for any president to send hundreds of thousands of American troops into harm's way, and would have forced another strategy altogether. Chance again smiled on Bush.

A Brief or Nonexistent Window

The foregoing analysis helps thread different insights into one tale and helps place Bush's individual role in better perspective. However, there is another dimension to the story of how and why the United States went to war that deserves to be laid out more fully. The second part of this chapter does just that, by expanding on U.S.-Iraqi strategic interaction.

No natural laws of the human condition dictate that war must occur. History's twists and turns offer windows of opportunity where the preferences of otherwise irreconcilable actors may meet, thus avoiding conflict. In the Persian Gulf crisis, however, that window either stayed open very temporarily or never opened at all. By "window," I refer to the potential for withdrawal by Iraq in exchange for veiled concessions to Saddam by the United States, or in exchange for convincing promises that Iraq would not be harassed or attacked if it withdrew from Kuwait unconditionally. The window thesis was introduced in chapter 2 in noting that the *de facto* bargaining range where agreement could arise between the actors was too limited, if it existed at all, to avoid war.[114] But we need to draw on the other perspectives and analyses presented in this book in order to obtain a more developed answer. I turn to this task below.

As the months wore on, Bush focused on Saddam so much that even Powell was struck by how much it affected Bush's policymaking. Even Baker expressed concern to aides that the White House was speeding toward an armed confrontation with Saddam.[115] The war may have been avoided at critical junctures, but Saddam was unwilling to lose face by withdrawing unconditionally from Kuwait, and Bush was unwilling to let Saddam save face by compromising, even in a veiled manner. But the dynamics were more complicated than that. Saddam and Bush exhibited a propensity to be intransigent from the start, but, as suggested in the introduction of this book, over time Saddam became more pliable and less inclined toward full-scale war, and Bush became more intransigent and more inclined toward full-scale war — both with some exceptions.

Immediately after the invasion, Saddam was defiant and cocksure. But after facing UN sanctions, Arab League condemnations, and U.S. military deployments, on August 12 he floated a plan to defuse the crisis, though it was viewed as unrealistic by the United States and many Arab leaders. Bush, meanwhile, was prepared to go to war in this time period, but, by and large, that was not his preference. By October, Saddam moved farther ahead in contemplating a withdrawal in exchange for territorial concessions, though he was still far short of U.S. demands. By November, he dropped some demands for territorial concessions and appeared to want some assurances, chiefly that he would not be attacked, if he withdrew. The air war seemed to shift Saddam's position further. Indeed, with the ground war pending in February, he appeared to move even closer to accepting U.S. conditions, presumably because he realized that the United States was stronger and more determined than he had anticipated.

It is true that Saddam did reject U.S. overtures to meet in December and January, before the two sides agreed to meet on January 9 in Geneva. It is also true that Aziz was uncompromising in Geneva. This period does not fit into the present thesis, insofar as Bush appeared to be seeking a peaceful outcome and Iraq was intransigent. Yet we should also consider the following. While some evidence suggests that Bush was serious about seeking a peaceful Iraqi withdrawal at Geneva, other evidence suggests that he was merely going the last mile to gain support for a war he preferred. However, a month earlier, in December, the administration's rhetoric against Saddam could only have been viewed as offputting to Saddam, perhaps intentionally. He was ridiculed for using hostages in a cowardly way, his desire to save face was rejected, and he, in essence, was told to withdraw from Kuwait with no dignity at all — or else. This could account for his more strident position in late December and at Geneva on January 9. For both sides, talking tough may have been perceived as serving the purpose of intimidating the enemy into concessions and, if that failed, preparing for war as well.

Meanwhile, as chapter 4 suggested, the *de facto* bargaining range was closed further because Bush's rhetoric, as well as his talk of Nuremberg-like trials, must have raised concerns in Baghdad that even were Iraq to withdraw, it might still be attacked. Primakov had reported since November that his conversations with Saddam indicated that Iraq might be forthcoming if Saddam received assurances that he would not be attacked subsequent to a withdrawal. Based on Primakov's reports, Mitterrand was willing to send Michel Vauzelle, Chairman of the France's National Assembly's Foreign Affairs Committee, to assess whether Saddam might be willing to resolve the crisis along the general guidelines of UN resolutions. However, when the two met in Baghdad on January 5, Saddam asserted, after repeating his usual conspiracy theories, that he had not rejected all negotiations, but sought an official envoy from France with whom to talk.[116] It appears that if he was going to make what he considered concessions, he wanted the act itself to be worth the political risk. Having the imprimatur of a government that could deliver on any promises could serve that goal. Even so, Saddam still had to wonder if the

United States would accept. The answer to that became clear in the strong U.S. rhetoric prior to the January 9 meeting in Geneva and certainly on January 9 itself. Baker indicated that nothing short of unconditional withdrawal would do. That included no references to a Middle East conference, to an "Arab solution" after the crisis, and so forth. This may explain why a private French initiative one day after the Baker-Aziz meeting proved futile. Aziz ignored the initiative, which called for an Iraqi withdrawal followed by an "Arab solution" to the Iraq-Kuwait problem thereafter — a concession to Saddam, perhaps, but one that Bush would reject.[117]

While the air war phase of the broader war was in motion, Algeria and Iran tried unsuccessfully to broker a peace deal at the start of February. Iraq's Minister of State for Foreign Affairs Saadoun Hammadi did not show any new flexibility on Iraq's part, although he agreed to take the peace plan of Iran's President Hashemi Rafsanjani to Saddam Hussein, a plan that failed.[118] Enter Moscow.

Gorbachev, facing heightened pressure from his defense ministry and increasing criticism that he had gone too far in supporting U.S. action in the Persian Gulf, sought to take action to avoid a wider U.S.-led ground war. Primakov was sent to Baghdad and met Saddam on February 12. He reported that Saddam in fact was considering withdrawal and that Saddam again pressed Primakov about whether Iraq would be attacked if it withdrew. Unfortunately, while Primakov was optimistic about the meeting, Saddam subsequently asserted that Iraq might withdraw within the context of addressing the region's other problems.[119] On February 15, Baghdad radio announced that Iraq was prepared to "deal with Resolution 660," a major statement indicating a willingness to withdraw without conditions. But once again Saddam emerged to add conditions to the statement.[120]

On February 18, Aziz and Hammadi arrived in Moscow, where they met with Gorbachev. One insider privy to the records of Gorbachev's lengthy conversations with Aziz just before the start of the U.S. ground war expressed his amazement at how Gorbachev was succeeding in getting Aziz to accept all the terms on which Washington insisted publicly, and noted that Bush rebuffed Gorbachev when he indicated that Iraq was softening its position.[121] Sometime between February 22 and 23, when Gorbachev had two conversations with Bush, Saddam actually agreed, according to this account, to total and unconditional withdrawal — a white flag, as Gorbachev described it to Bush. But Gorbachev was rebuffed again by Bush, who asserted that Iraq had not, in fact, accepted an unconditional withdrawal — a point by Bush that Moscow viewed as unconvincing.[122] In a speech on February 24, Saddam described himself as supporting the

Soviet peace initiative and described Bush as "treacherous" and as one whose objective, along with others in the coalition, would now become "known to all who have not known their objective so far."[123]

While the Soviet account presents Bush as committed to war, irrespective of Iraq's position, the U.S. account suggests that Iraq was noncompliant and that Soviet or Iraqi negotiators could not be trusted. Despite the fact that Moscow's ties to Baghdad could have colored Moscow's account, the evidence tends to support both accounts, in part. It is true that Saddam was becoming more pliant. He did agree to a full withdrawal in exchange for assurances that his regime would not be threatened thereafter, but the sticking points were that he also sought to have all UN economic sanctions lifted once Iraq had withdrawn two-thirds of its forces from Kuwait, and to have all UN Security Council resolutions voided upon the conclusion of the withdrawal.[124] The United States team objected to lifting all sanctions on Iraq, partly because it sought unconditional withdrawal, but also because it sought to contain Iraq even if it did withdraw from Kuwait.[125] Bush was willing to allow Gorbachev some more time to press Iraq, but in the midst of these discussions, on February 22, Iraq lit the Kuwaiti oil wells on fire. While the cause of this action is unclear, it made the ground war inevitable.

By and large, however, Iraq did become inconsistently but increasingly more pliant from August to February, dropping some preconditions for its withdrawal. When Bush may have been more pliant in August and even September, Iraq was more recalcitrant. By the time Iraq became more pliable, Bush had become first implacable, then resigned to war as the least worst alternative by October or November, and then of the mind that, short of very strict conditions of compliance by Iraq, war would produce a positive outcome. The analysis above suggests that Saddam's position in February may have met Bush's position in August. Bush became more intransigent and more inclined toward using force over time, not only because of Iraq's recalcitrance, but also for a related reason — because the expected utility of the use of force, as chapter 2 showed, became more positive over time.

We can infer from the evidence that the *de facto* bargaining range, moreover, was cut down from the U.S. side by several factors. The Munich analogy changed the context in which the crisis was interpreted, both by genuinely affecting how alternatives were viewed, and also by offering images and symbols by which Bush altered the narrative for political reasons. Bush used it as a genuine description of Saddam, in line with the cognitive perspective, and as part and parcel of a broader effort to degrade Saddam and sell the war to the public, in line with the domestic politics perspective. Yet, while the use of the Munich analogy had different motivations, it produced a not dissimilar end. Words have meaning. They affected the likelihood that the crisis would end with Iraq's unconditional withdrawal. The effects of constructing Iraq did not restrain Bush by making him wholly unable to accept less than a full withdrawal, but it made him rather less likely to consider nonwar options short of that. In other words, it made him less inclined to continue sanctions.

Inasmuch as Bush subscribed to the Munich analogy and as Saddam seemed to subscribe to the Vietnam analogy, they developed inconsistent expectations. That made it harder, as I noted in chapter 3, for a shared framework of interpretation to develop within which good-faith negotiations could proceed.

As a result of multiple factors at different levels of analysis, the preference orderings of Bush and Saddam differed significantly; indeed, they never really lined up enough for any movement toward a negotiated withdrawal. Thus, while it may have been rational for the United States to offer Iraq a carrot for withdrawal earlier in the crisis, that became less rational toward the end. This is not only because the United States had put extraordinary effort into the crisis by then, but also because its prospects for military success were much higher. In assessing the reaction of its allies to its attack — as well as the reaction of Iraq, or of the U.S. public — it must have expected a better outcome on January 9 than it would have earlier.

It would be useful here to sketch briefly the positions of the United States and Iraq, as gleaned from the discussion above and the foregoing chapters. By and large, Bush became increasingly more steadfast and Saddam somewhat, though inconsistently, more pliable over time. The record seems to support that Bush preferred to:

— send massive U.S. forces rather than appease Saddam with carrots such as modest Kuwaiti territorial concessions (August 3).
— reverse the invasion rather than just defend Saudi Arabia (August 5).
— pursue war over a peaceful withdrawal, unless Bush could totally humiliate Saddam in the process and construct post-crisis containment of Iraq (mid-late October).
— move toward war and away from economic sanctions (October 31).
— pursue a ground war over an unconditional Iraqi withdrawal (February 22).

Saddam's positions are harder to discern. However, based on the analysis in the foregoing chapters, on the statements of Saddam and Aziz, on testimony from third parties and U.S. officials that negotiated with Iraq, and on Saddam's various peace proposals, we can offer a general picture of his evolving positions. He seemed to prefer to:

— cooperate with the United States in oil pricing if he could keep Kuwait and dominate the region, rather to confront the United States (immediately after the invasion, until it was clear that such a strategy could never work).

— confront the United States rather than withdraw from Kuwait and restore the Kuwaiti royal family (until August 12).

— withdraw from Kuwait (partially or fully is not clear) if Israel withdrew from all occupied territories and Syria from Lebanon (August 12).

— withdraw from Kuwait and restore the Kuwaiti government, in exchange for a reduction of U.S. forces and an agreement to follow up by holding an international conference on peace in the Middle East (September 9). It is useful to note here that on September 30, in response to French diplomacy, for the first time Saddam backed away from asserting that the invasion was irreversible, although he appeared to change course again by mid-October.

— withdraw, possibly, if he could receive the small islands of Warba and Bubiyan in exchange — they block Iraq's access to the Persian Gulf — and the southern section of the Rumaila oil field over which Iraq and Kuwait had a dispute preceding the invasion (mid-to late October).

— go to war, absent the following conditions: all allied forces be replaced with a UN-directed, all-Arab force; all political-economic sanctions against Iraq end; and Iraq's withdrawal be met with similar action by Syria in Lebanon and Israel in the occupied territories (January 9 at Geneva).

— withdraw from Kuwait, if the United States agreed to lift all UN sanctions thereafter and not to attack Iraq (February 23).

Conclusion

The use of multiple perspectives in this book directly and indirectly serves several goals. Among them, it shows how, why, and when Bush was a crucial actor, without ignoring the many factors that constrained him, or could have constrained him. Bush may or may not have been wishy-washy on some domestic issues, but he clearly evidenced unique personal characteristics and capabilities that affected crisis decision-making. And he took critical initiatives, sometimes far ahead of his advisers, that put the United States on the path to war. He also had to surmount serious domestic and international support for using diplomacy or economic sanctions, either in lieu of war or in lieu of war on his timetable. While we would have expected any president to take a stand in such a crisis situation, Bush also seemed to act above and beyond what his role or the situation required.

While Bush was unique in many ways, he did benefit not only from Scowcroft's indefatigable support in particular and the group of eight and deputies group, but also from a synergy of historical chance circumstances. Chance did not work against Bush; it elevated and enabled him. In the broader scheme of things, that takes away from Bush's role as an individual, by making the job of taking the country into a successful military campaign easier.

Easier, however, does not mean easy. It has never been popular, with the exception of the war against the Taliban in Afghanistan launched in 2001 by President George W. Bush, to take the United States into a major war in or near the Middle East. Yet Bush managed to do precisely that.

We can think of history, as Joseph Nye suggests, as a funnel that widens and narrows as a function of myriad factors, some intended and others fortuitous.[126] In that process, the individual plays a role, with varying levels of importance in each case. Saddam started the crisis and is thus chiefly responsible for the war and for the strategic context that Bush and his colleagues faced on August 2, 1990. But we can say that after Saddam set history in motion, Bush narrowed the funnel. He did so when he drew a line in the sand, eliminating the possibility that Washington would not send massive force to the Persian Gulf. By asserting that the invasion would not stand, he eliminated the possibility that the United States would allow Iraq to remain in Kuwait.

By invoking Munich and engaging in construction, he repeatedly helped clip the potential for any face-saving withdrawal to be arranged, especially in August and September, and probably for Iraq to withdraw from Kuwait, even unconditionally. The massive U.S.-led buildup in November, driven in part by recollections of Munich and Vietnam, could have compelled an aggressor to stand down, but in Saddam's case, it may just have convinced him to prepare for an inevitable war, thus pitting two large armies against each other — a historical recipe for war.

When Bush offered to go the extra mile by sending Baker to Baghdad, he widened the funnel a bit. But Saddam did not respond, and, in fact, the funnel had already narrowed to such a degree that Bush's action had little chance of success, barring a major change in Saddam's mindset.

It would be presumptuous to assume that another president would have handled matters similarly, even though in retrospect we might view the course of events as eminently logical. While any president would probably have been forced to try to mount Desert Shield because of the longstanding U.S. commitment to Saudi Arabia and the massive ramifications of Iraq's invasion of Kuwait in an oil-rich region, this is less true of Desert Storm.

Bush's role clearly meant that even veiled face-saving measures that might otherwise have generated Iraq's withdrawal from Kuwait would be rejected. It also meant that attempts to offer such measures by states such as France, Russia, and Jordan would also be rejected and even undermined, that economic sanctions would be viewed as ineffective fairly early in the crisis, that an atmosphere not conducive even to an unconditional withdrawal by Iraq would be at least partly at play, that U.S.-Iraqi strategic interaction would not be conducive to finding an alternative short of war that both would prefer to war, and that war would be viewed as preferable to Iraq's withdrawal in the period of October 1990.

Bush's crucial role in the drive to war should not obfuscate some simple facts. It was Saddam who invaded and annexed Kuwait. He led his soldiers into unspeakable ruin on the battlefield, by invading first Iran in 1980 and then Kuwait in 1990. His tenure is quintessential testimony to how a country with great riches, fine human resources, and a bright future can be stunted for decades by ill-advised wars. But Saddam's fate was hardly predetermined when he invaded Kuwait. This book strongly suggests that the challenges the United States faced when Iraq invaded Kuwait would not have been met similarly by past Republican or Democratic presidents and administrations. There was a unique confluence of historical, global, regional, bureaucratic, group and, above all, individual dynamics at play here that help explain how and why the United States went to war.

The powerful role of the president may suggest something about the presidency as well. Historically, we have viewed presidents from Abraham Lincoln to Franklin Delano Roosevelt as very influential. Yet for the past two decades, as Marcia Lynn Whicker points out, a major theme of presidential scholars has been that presidents have limited power. This may be because of the increasing complexity of world affairs, fragmented and loosely defined political parties that create democratic gridlock, fragmented government, checks and balances writ large, an uncooperative bureaucracy, a challenging media, poor public relations skills, and poor information and advice.[127] While the notion of limited presidential power may or may not be illuminating in general, it clashes with the present argument. Even if we separate Bush the person from Bush the president, and even if we account for the fact that presidents do enjoy greater power in crises, we can still say that the Persian Gulf War case reflects the significant powers of the presidency.

While the founding fathers set up a system of checks and balances, Congress had almost no serious check on the executive branch. It was largely shut out of the big decisions. Although the decision to go to war against Iraq was put to a vote in Congress, a negative vote most probably would not have stopped the president from launching war. Foreign crises in particular tend to highlight executive powers, but the Persian Gulf War case is extreme in that regard. Bush's individual characteristics, when combined with presidential powers on paper, produced a powerful result.

CHAPTER NINE

Tackling Puzzles and Developing Theory

This chapter launches a foray into the more theory-oriented part of the book. Now that we have presented and tested the perspectives and synthesized the insights into a more complete empirical account of the Persian Gulf War case, we are in a better position to address three puzzles, a task I tackle in the next three sections of this chapter.

Beyond Groupthink: Creating the Non-Fiasco Theory

To presume the existence of groupthink from a policy fiasco or its absence from a positive outcome verges on tautology.[1] As Irving Janis recognizes and Clark McCauley emphasizes, the link between groupthink and failure is probabilistic, rather than deterministic.[2] Yet the theory is designed to explain fiascoes — and all of Janis's cases were fiascoes, raising questions about a suspicious fit. If the theory largely predicts a fiasco, and if elements of groupthink existed in the Persian Gulf War case, then the puzzle is why failure was avoided. We have no answer to that puzzle, in part because no study pairs groupthink with a positive outcome or non-fiasco, and no effort has been made to develop what I call a "non-fiasco theory" related to groupthink. While we cannot rely on one case to develop a theory, it is better to theorize with at least some guidance from one case, than with no guidance at all.

In investigating this puzzle, it is *crucial* to note that, while innumerable variables can explain policy success or failure, the task here is to find variables that can cause groupthink (only the antecedent conditions in the theory already described in Figure 1 in chapter 5) and a positive outcome. These variables *must* serve both causal purposes to constitute the basis of a non-fiasco theory. This narrows the field of salient variables significantly, by eliminating variables or explanations that may serve one causal goal but not the other.[3] The present theory is based on two antecedent conditions: the absence of a tradition of impartial leadership, which in effect allows for partial leadership, and the external threat faced by the group.

Leadership is a good variable upon which to build this theory. Janis assumes that a lack of tradition of impartial leadership is one of four antecedent conditions that contribute to groupthink, but concedes that "considerable empirical support" exists establishing that partial leadership can, under some conditions, enhance group performance or at least be nonnegative in its impact.[4] That raises an intriguing question: when can partial leadership contribute to a positive decision-making outcome?

In the present theory, partial leadership assumes different dimensions. The crucial one is the leader's level of experience and skill. Studies have shown that these characteristics are associated with providing the wherewithal for enhanced decision-making.[5] A skilled and experienced partial leader may or may not contribute to the existence of the other antecedent conditions and symptoms of the theory, but he or she is more likely to mitigate their negative impact. Thus, group insulation and a lack of norms requiring methodical procedures may result in a failure to consider alternatives, but that may not be problematic if the leader is experienced and skilled and can negotiate such defective decision-making.[6] By contrast, a partial leader lacking those attributes may contribute to the other antecedent conditions, and fail to mitigate them. This suggests that it is not enough to know if a leader is partial or impartial to explain outcomes. We also need to know more about the leader's disposition and characteristics. Fortunately, there is a large body of theory-oriented literature that is useful for that purpose.[7]

The second key variable is external threat, which is especially important in groupthink theory because it contributes to stress and cohesiveness, which is, as Paul 't Hart points out, the "sole group-level factor that he [Janis] singles out as a substantive, independent cause of groupthink."[8] Moreover, much evidence conditionally supports the stress-cohesiveness connection.[9]

The present theory assumes that group members will form a perception of threat at the outset of the event. That perception may vary among the members of the group, and, like the variable of partial leadership, can take different forms. Janis sees external threat perception as contributing to stress and groupthink, but there is reason to believe that some types of perception may cause stress and contribute to groupthink, but not to failure. In the present theory, external threat perception ranges from significantly overestimated to significantly underestimated. Overestimation of threat is always possible because decision makers can feel threatened irrespective of the objective level of threat. That is especially true under certain conditions, such as if cognitive biases derived from analogies highlight the threatening aspects of the situation, if decision makers face stress-inducing uncertainties, or if they are risk-averse and thus more likely to experience stress.[10]

While overestimation of threat is always possible, so is the potential for change in the situation confronting the group, between the outset of the event (T_1) and the period when the group actually addresses or confronts the challenge at hand (T_2). In the present case, T_1 occurred in early August when Iraq invaded Kuwait and T_2 occurred when the U.S.-led forces launched Operation Desert Storm on January 16. Two key changes are highlighted by the theory: the group may become more able to address the challenge, partly because its own overestimation of the challenge motivates it to prepare for it in some ways, and the challenge itself may become less formidable. The group, however, cannot predict these changes at T_1, although it becomes clear at T_2 to what extent the threat was over- or underestimated.

From the foregoing analysis, we can observe that when the threat at hand is overestimated at T_1, groupthink is likely to occur. Overestimation will contribute to stress, cohesiveness, and, in turn, groupthink. As Janis puts it, groupthink "tendencies are increased when the situational context at the time the group starts its deliberations is such that the members are undergoing high stress from external threats or losses to be expected."[11]

However, departing from Janis, we can observe that while the threat was overestimated at T_1, it did not contribute to failure at T_2. This is because overestimation will place the group under stress at T_1, but the challenge will not materialize to the expected extent in reality at T_2. By contrast, we can hypothesize that when the threat is underestimated, groupthink will be less likely to develop at T_1—although it may be generated by other conditions—but the challenge the group faces at T_2 will be more serious than originally estimated at T_1.

The theory is illustrated in Table 3. Drawing on the variables of partial leadership and threat, four hypothesized outcomes are identified. The most salient of them is that when a partial leader is highly experienced and the threat is significantly overestimated in T_1, groupthink is more likely to occur but a fiasco is less likely. By contrast, when a partial leader lacks these characteristics and the threat is significantly underestimated, groupthink will be less likely due to the lowered levels of initial stress, but the leader will either contribute to failure or be less likely to prevent it, *ceteris paribus*.

Table 3. Groupthink: Experience vs. Threat Perception

	Partial Leader	
Perception of Threat	Highly Experienced	Highly Inexperienced
Underestimated	Mixed outcome	Groupthink less likely; fiasco more likely
Overestimated	Groupthink more likely; fiasco less likely	Mixed outcome

The present theory, like all theories, is parsimonious. Future work could thicken it, for instance, by elaborating the enabling conditions for misestimation of threat and by adding auxiliary assumptions about when changes in the situation will militate in favor of a positive, counterintuitive outcome.

The Theory and the Persian Gulf War Case

In the Persian Gulf War case, failure was avoided in part because Bush was both partial and highly experienced and skillful in the subject matter at hand. As discussed earlier, Bush knew many leaders around the world quite well and had more foreign policy experience and knowledge than probably any other president.

While Bush's role helped in avoiding failure, failure was also avoided in part due to the dynamic of overestimation. As discussed in chapter 5, the group feared an Iraqi invasion of Saudi Arabia, an inability to gain access to the Saudi strategic infrastructure, a potential rout of vulnerable U.S. forces at the hands of the Iraqi army, and an inability to develop and maintain a coalition and gain world support. Indeed, as noted earlier, the group of eight members recognized that the crisis could undermine the Bush presidency.[12]

Such concerns and realities, however, shifted over time — a dynamic that the theory of groupthink does not account for theoretically. Bush, Powell, and others were "deeply preoccupied" with potential casualties.[13] As Gates observes, his "entire demeanor" started to change around October from "joking and kidding" around with the group of eight to a more serious one when the prospect of war increased significantly.[14] Nonetheless, Bush and most members of the group of eight increasingly did not believe the Defense Department's estimate of 10,000 body bags was realistic.[15] Bush had become, as he put it in an internal memo to Fitzwater, "more and more convinced that we could use force and be successful."[16] Over time, the United States, in part motivated by its overestimation of the threat, built an impressive coalition and military capability in the region. By November, it had a U.N. mandate to use force and, on January 9, from the U.S. Congress as well. Support from the Soviet Union, which even included information about its military cooperation with Iraq, removed a large stumbling block.[17]

We should also consider another major change over time. While Iraq initially was very threatening, Saddam did not effectively translate his capabilities into real political and strategic gains. Rather, in reality and as perceived by the group of eight, Saddam's use of human shields, atrocities in Kuwait, and hostile rhetoric helped unify the U.S.-led coalition and isolate him worldwide through U.N. economic, diplomatic, and military sanctions.[18] He also failed to withdraw partially from Kuwait, which would have made it harder to attack Iraq and even to preserve the coalition while leaving Iraq in control of parts of Kuwait. That is why decision makers called it "the nightmare scenario," viewed it as quite likely, and prepared contingency plans for it.[19]

When war finally erupted, the Iraqi challenge would prove far less serious than most members of the group of eight, and certainly Bush and Scowcroft, estimated in early August. Iraq proved militarily ineffective. Several days into the air war, the allied airforce dominated the skies. The ground war would also prove far easier than anyone would have expected.

At the theoretical level, we have paired groupthink with a positive outcome, or at least a non-fiasco, and sought to explain that result theoretically. We may in fact find groupthink and positive outcomes to be far more prevalent than the theory predicts, if we begin to explore the conditions of the theory in such overlooked cases.

Now that we have addressed the first puzzle of the chapter, we can turn to the second: how can we explain that there was so little government politics on the road to war? No existing theory explains when we can expect government politics to be less prevalent, and, in turn, the GPM to be less explanatory. I move to develop one below.

A Theory of Government Politics (TGP)

In general, we should expect less GP in crises than in noncrises, in part because decision makers are more likely to perceive threats to national interests. However, we need to know much more than the nature of the event (crisis versus noncrisis) to explain, predict, or identify in retrospect the level of GP. That is in part because some crises at least partly confirm the GPM or elements of it, while some noncrises will not be marked much by GP.[20] The real question is: under what conditions are we less or more likely to observe GP? At the outset, disagreement existed in President Bush's inner circle, for instance at the August 2 NSC meeting, about the importance of the invasion and about how to deal with it.[21] Such differences could have spawned GP among players from different agencies, but they did not. Why?

The TGP that I develop in this chapter is based on five conditions. They are theorized here to decrease the probability of GP, or, in other words, decrease the probability that decision-making will be characterized by (1a) the "where you stand" notion, (1b) conflict and bargaining, (1c) presidential involvement and bargaining, and (1d) collage formation. These five conditions are (2a) decision-making procedures, (2b) the president's experience and skill, (2c) similarity of cognitive maps and professional experience of key decision makers, (2d) the nature of the threat, and (2e) the nature of the question that decision makers address ("how to" versus "whether to"). The section below draws connections among the variables of the theory, using the simple numerical designations attached to them.

The Five Conditions of the Theory

The first condition is that the less that clear procedures are used in governing decision-making, the less likely GP is. It is well recognized that such procedures, which vary in each case, can affect the nature of decision-making.[22]

In the TGP, this condition is theorized to affect three factors. First, the less such procedures are used, the more likely it is that key decisions will be made outside the group or committee setting. Indeed, lax procedures will allow for decisions to be made where and how the opinion leaders (such as Bush and Scowcroft) see fit. The more decisions are made outside the group, the more likely a few individuals will be able to agree on a course of action and to convince each other to change views, given that they will not be in the spotlight of a larger, open group where it may be more necessary to play GP.[23] They will, thus, be more able to bypass the bargaining, conflict, and collage effects that occur in the group or committee setting.

Second, the less such procedures are used, the more likely decisions will take place in smaller groups. This is important, in theory, because the smaller the group, the less chance there is for bargaining (1b, 1c) and for a collage-like effect (1d) resulting from the fingerprints of many competing individuals. Certainly it is harder to play GP when one lacks access to the site where the decisions are made, and it is harder to generate a collage when fewer players are involved.

Third, the less such procedures are used, the greater the power of the president is likely to be. Procedures will be less likely to place a direct or indirect check on his preferences or to allow others to challenge his positions.

In the Persian Gulf War case, procedures, insofar as they were even used, clearly lacked the structure that some might associate with formalistic style.[24] There is no available evidence that anyone even referred to using such procedures. Discussions did take place in group meetings, but crucial decisions were sometimes made privately. Moreover, Scowcroft not only played the key advisory role, but he also helped shape the decision-making process partly so that some key decisions would be private. In this way, the type of argumentation and bargaining that we saw, for instance, in the Cuban missile crisis, was preempted. As Scowcroft put it, "I always urged the President not to make decisions in meetings — to listen, but to reserve his decisions to a more quiet time period. He was good at drawing people out, at asking reaching questions. I always made it a point to advise him of the different points of view ahead of meetings."[25] While that approach increased efficiency, it also enhanced Bush's already significant power by helping him think through key questions without facing the unpredictability of group meetings. It also decreased the potential for individuals to be departmental advocates because the main context in which GP would take place was, to some extent, bypassed.

The TGP posits a second condition. The greater the president's level of skill and experience for the task at hand, the less likely GP is. This condition of the theory is likely to generate three key consequences that diminish GP. The first is that the president's imprimatur on decision-making is likely to be more significant, thus decreasing prospects for a collage-like effect (1d). That is because high levels of skill and experience increase the likelihood that the president will have the confidence and foresight to make good decisions, and also that he will in fact do so, even against the wishes of his advisers.[26] He can rely more on himself. The second, related, effect is that the president will be more able to preempt bargaining by others (1b). The third is that decisions will more likely be made in a small group, and sometimes outside the group altogether. The president will be more able to control where policy is made.[27]

Bush's skill and experience in foreign affairs ranked among the best for U.S. presidents, especially regarding the Middle East. In part because of that, Bush was particularly crucial at critical junctures in the Persian Gulf crisis when history could have gone down another path. Of Bush, Scowcroft would later observe: "He was absolutely essential, a pillar of strength. . . . He realized early on what was required and determined to do it and simply kept on course."[28] He was both the "spark plug and fuel," according to Powell, for Desert Shield and Storm.[29] In fact, Bush would have gone to war with or without congressional approval.[30] While he preferred even a narrow vote of support in Congress to none at all, he sought very hard to avoid any action in Congress that "seeks to tie our hands."[31]

The president's critical role decreased the utility of, and in some ways obviated the need for, individual bargaining by others. He usurped elements of the roles regularly played by his advisers.

The president's role also decreased the utility of bargaining in another way. Others around him understood that he was willing and able to play a predominant role. They must have factored that into their calculations. Indeed, it is one thing to bargain and advocate the interests of an agency when there is no clear directive from above, quite another thing to do so when there is one.[32] In the latter case, the potential costs of bargaining must be viewed as higher and the potential payoffs lower. Decision makers could not be sanguine about bargaining with a determined president, or, for that matter, with colleagues who were following the president's lead. And they could be even less sanguine about engaging in actions further along the continuum such as rivalry. Gates put it rather succinctly in describing the deputies committee and, to some extent, the group of eight: "There was little bargaining among us or with the President because we knew what we would do. The President decided and we executed."[33]

The president's role also decreased the potential that he himself would bargain. As noted at the outset, the GPM assumes that bargaining occurs among all the members in a group, which must include the president, and yet there is no evidence to suggest that Bush was a bargainer.[34] Even when he did not participate in group meetings, such as in the case of the deputies committee, his influence worked its way down to the deputies group serving the group of eight.[35] In this sense, indirect influence obviated a direct presidential presence. Interestingly, Gates would note that, having served under four presidents, he "learned that when you have strong guidance, like in the Gulf case, government politics is much weaker."[36]

That Bush played the decisive role is telling in another way as well. The GPM assumes that bureaucracies define individual stands and actions. Emphasis is placed much more on the context so as to downplay the influence and impact of any one individual. But again Bush and Scowcroft clearly defined the bureau-cratic context more than it defined their behavior.

The third condition of the theory is that the more decision makers share similar cognitive maps and professional socialization, the less likely GP will be. This is because we can surmise that the more similar their cognitive maps, the more likely they will view the problem and solutions to it similarly, and the less conflict we can expect. Many decision makers shared the analogy of appeasement at Munich in 1938, especially Bush and the other leaders of that generation, and it was quite influential in affecting how they saw the crisis and made key decisions.[37]

Like cognition, professional socialization is also associated with generating a similar frame of reference and a similar orientation and disposition towards issues.[38] The notion that a shared cultural tradition, a common code of sorts, increases prospects for solidarity and collective action has been promoted from Emile Durkheim and Talcott Parsons to the work of modern sociologists.[39] That similar professional socialization may also generate friendship is also a point to consider.

If cognitive and socializing influences generate common beliefs and attitudes, we can theorize about two key effects. The first is that such similarities will decrease the likelihood of bargaining, advocacy, and rivalry, which are central to GP on the continuum laid out earlier in the chapter.[40] Second, the president's influence and role is likely to be increased because he is likely to be challenged under such conditions. For both reasons, we are also less likely to see collage-like effects (1d).

In the Persian Gulf War case, Bush, Scowcroft, Cheney, and Baker had worked together in past administrations and were establishment players (rather than academic outsiders, for instance), and thus received part of their professional socialization in that context. Even in the deputies group, Gates and Robert Kim-mitt had worked for the NSC under Ford and Carter. Kimmitt and Haass had also worked together, as had Kimmitt and Wolfowitz under Reagan for eight years. That background, as Kimmitt observes, made the deputies group "highly col-legial compared to past administrations in which I worked where bureaucratic in-fighting between State, Defense, Intelligence, and the NSC was more serious."[41]

Interestingly, Powell and Schwarzkopf were most inclined to push for the continued use of economic sanctions and to question the president's actions, albeit in a muted manner. This may be in part, because they shared Vietnam, rather than World War II, as a key cognitive reference point and did not share administrative experience as much as others in Bush's inner circle. What this suggests is that the cognitive approach carries more weight in explaining the preferences of actors than the GPM. In any event, virtually all decision makers, many of whom served in other Republican administrations and could thus compare their experiences to previous cases, stressed an unprecedented camaraderie in the group of eight and deputies group.[42]

The fourth condition of the theory deals with the nature of the event. The theory puts forth that we are less likely to observe GP in crises than in noncrises, and in military crises than in political or economic crises. This is largely because crises generate more real or perceived threats to national interests than noncrises. The higher the threat, the smaller the decision-making group is likely to be. That is a widely accepted correlation, although exceptions exist.[43] Moreover, while the players may still explain the views of their departments, they will be less likely to engage in serious bargaining, advocacy or rivalry (1b). Why? If each player must, in theory, engage in a tradeoff of concern from parochial to national interests, we can expect a greater emphasis on national interests as the level of real or perceived threat increases. This is because the threat will focus greater attention, within and outside the group, on each player's parochial behavior. It will appear more unseemly for a player to advance bureaucratic interests.

Moreover, the higher the level of threat, the more likely that actors will realize meaningfully that such parochialism may yield short-term gains, but that the pursuit of individual best strategies will leave all worse off in the long run. High-level threat not only makes it harder to mask GP, but if the threat worsens because of such politics, all the players may be affected or blamed for it. Failure in conditions when the stakes are lower may be more easily forgotten, but less so if the stakes are high and much attention is focused on the problem. This is particularly true because the higher the level of threat, the less inclined the president will be to bargain with others (1c). All other things equal, the president will be more inclined to ensure that national interests are not subject to politics.

Furthermore, we can theorize that players are likely to view others as similarly predisposed against playing GP. If expectations of outcomes cause outcomes, as game theory illuminates, then such similar expectations are likely to generate an outcome that protects national over parochial interests. By contrast, inconsistent expectations would make that more difficult to attain.

In the Persian Gulf War case, the stakes involved were high, particularly at the outset, when it appeared as if Iraq might invade Saudi Arabia, and later, when war approached. Nonetheless, *ceteris paribus*, in other domestic cases or foreign exigencies where the perceived threat is lower, turf battles may be viewed as more acceptable, given that major national interests are not at stake, and because the president or other high level officials are less likely to be heavily engaged. Thus, in debates during the same administration about removing restrictions on the export of U.S. digital software, Commerce and State would invariably favor it, and Defense and the CIA would take a far more conservative position because they thought it was not in their department's interest.[44]

The fifth condition of the theory is that GP will be less likely in the "whether to" questions than in the "how to" questions. Since they are usually far weightier, the "whether to" questions are more likely to involve the president, thus creating the potential that he will attempt to preempt aspects of GP. Moreover, fewer players are likely to have input into the "whether to" questions than into the "how to" questions, which deal with execution of a decision and thus require greater discussion and involvement.

In the Persian Gulf War case, we saw relatively little GP on the "whether to" questions, but some manifestations of GP arose on the "how to" questions.[45] For instance, in trying to execute the decision to enforce U.N. economic sanctions, the group of eight had to assess "how to" deal with a sanctions-busting Iraqi oil tanker steaming toward South Yemen in late August. Cheney, Powell, Scowcroft, and Gates argued to hit the ship. They feared that failure to do so would send Saddam a message of weakness at the outset. They also believed that Article 51 of the U.N. charter allowing for collective defense gave the U.S. the right to do so, provided Kuwait requested the support. Meanwhile, Baker wanted to obtain Soviet support first and preserve diplomatic relations. That was an argument, Gates recalls, that Baker largely won. The Soviets did sign on to U.N. Resolution 665.[46]

Decision-making on this "how to" question reflected more GP than in the decision-making for most other questions. The outcome, for instance, reflected somewhat of a collage. The preference of Defense and the NSC was to take strong action, independent of the Soviets, while the preference of State was to use diplomacy. Indeed, U.N. Resolution 665, pushed by Washington, would allow the United States and others to disable ships that refused to stop to have their cargoes checked, as the more hawkish decision makers wanted, but it also reflected and built U.S.-Soviet cooperation, as Baker sought. The deputies committee, for its part, did far more to sound out the positions of different departments than did the group of eight. Even though it did not manifest much of the continuum, a greater awareness of departmental interests and motivations existed on the "how to" questions that it addressed, such as on how to stop tankers headed for Iraq in defiance of the embargo.[47]

For his part, Baker did not openly question whether to go to war, but he did float a proposal on "how to" possibly bring it to a close, which linked a cease-fire to negotiations on the Palestinian question. While we would largely expect the Secretary of State to push diplomatic solutions that highlight the role and influence of the State Department, Bush, Cheney and Scowcroft did not like Baker's approach much.[48]

We can also point to another example. As noted earlier in this chapter, in order to deal with the question of "how to" evict Iraqi forces from Kuwait, military leaders presented a frontal attack plan for the ground war. They did so largely because their existing force levels allowed for that plan to be executed, but not for more ambitious ones, such as the eventual attack that used massive firepower chiefly in a "left hook" maneuver from the west. We would expect military leaders to be concerned about force levels matching mission goals.[49] Their plan, however, was vetoed, as noted earlier, in a decision made chiefly by Bush and Scowcroft.[50]

The TGP and the Persian Gulf and Cuban Missile Crises

The TGP, as laid out above, is probabilistic. It theorizes that the greater the extent to which its five conditions exist, the less prominent GP is likely to be. No single condition is sufficient or necessary. Explanatory and predictive power is enhanced by considering the conditions *in toto*. A comparison of the Persian Gulf and Cuban missile crises can serve to illustrate this point, and further highlight the TGP.

For example, the fourth condition of the TGP — the nature of the event (crisis versus noncrisis) can tell us only so much about GP. If we focus only on that condition, we are sure to find exceptions to the TGP. The real question is whether some or many of these exceptions can be explained away by the other conditions of the TGP.

The 1962 crisis is a case in point. Based only on the condition of the nature of the event (crisis versus noncrisis), we would predict that the 1962 case would have a low level of GP. Allison's finding of a high level of GP in that case would prove us wrong. However, in testing the missile crisis case against the other conditions of the TGP, we would discover another outcome. The TGP seems to explain quite well why the missile crisis case had a high level of GP, while the Persian Gulf War case did not. As I will discuss below, three of the four key conditions of the TGP were absent in the 1962 crisis but present in the Persian Gulf War case, while the fifth condition ("how to" versus "whether to") was inconclusive.

The first condition of the TGP is that the less decision-making procedures are used, the less likely GP is. As noted earlier, stringent decision-making procedures were used in the missile crisis case, quite unlike in the Persian Gulf War case.[51]

The second condition of the TGP is that the greater the president's level of skill and experience for the task at hand, the less likely GP is. President Kennedy was not nearly as experienced or skilled in foreign affairs as Bush was. Some observers even described him as being educated by crises, which he was not good at avoiding, rather than bringing his education to them.[52] Kennedy's first major foreign policy initiative was the disastrous effort to overthrow Cuban leader Fidel Castro in the Bay of Pigs invasion of April 1961, which raised serious doubts about his judgment.[53] Clearly, Kennedy came to office as a relative novice compared to Bush, and he was far less conversant with the issues germane to a nuclear showdown than Bush was with the strategic, military, and political dimensions of reversing Iraq's invasion of Kuwait. Even though he ultimately made good decisions and helped resolve the Cuban missile crisis effectively, the account provided by Allison and Zelikow suggests that GP was certainly at play along the way and was not preempted much by President Kennedy.

The third condition of the TGP is that the more decision makers share similar cognitive maps and professional socialization, the less likely GP will be. The Persian Gulf War case fulfilled that condition perhaps unprecedentedly well, as demonstrated earlier in this study, and, arguably, far more so than in the missile crisis case.[54] To be sure, some members of the EXCOM shared professional socialization, but by and large they came from more varied backgrounds (business, military, government, and academia) than the Bush team and had worked with each other less than the Bush team had.

The fifth condition of the TGP is that GP will be less likely on the "whether to" questions than on the "how to" questions. It is fairly hard to compare the Persian Gulf War and missile crisis cases on that score. Allison and Zelikow did not draw distinctions between these types of questions when presenting the missile crisis case, nor does the GPM deal with it in theory. Nonetheless, two points are worth making. It would be interesting to revisit the missile crisis case with this distinction in mind, and to see if there were higher levels of GP on the "whether to" as opposed to the "how to" questions. Drawing on the TGP, we may propose that the difference in the level of GP found in both cases is partly related to a greater emphasis in the Persian Gulf War case on the "whether to" questions as compared to the "how to" questions, and a greater emphasis in the missile crisis case on the "how to" as compared to the "whether to" questions.

But, again, to understand both cases, we would need to look at all of the conditions of the TGP.

As a closing point on theory, the reader may notice that some of the conditions both make GP less likely and groupthink more likely. In particular, similar beliefs and socialization are likely to increase camaraderie and, in turn, decrease GP. However, according to the theory of groupthink, camaraderie increases the potential for groupthink or a concurrence-seeking tendency among members of a group.[55] That suggests, at a minimum, that whether camaraderie produces a negative effect (groupthink) or a positive effect (decreasing GP) depends on the conditions that accompany it. If accompanied by the conditions specified in the TGP, presuming the theory is on target, it is likely to decrease GP. If accompanied by the conditions identified in the theory of groupthink, presuming that theory is on target, it is likely to produce groupthink. However, as a lone variable, it has an indeterminate impact on outcomes in both theories.

Nonrational Processes and a Nonnegative Outcome?

Under the definition of rationality often used by economists, the actor picks the right alternative every time. By contrast, if we assume a modified rationality, as is the case in this book, we create the potential for nonrational processes to be paired with a nonnegative or positive outcome. This creates an interesting puzzle. Unless we creatively argue that outcomes are unrelated to the process of decision-making, we would expect rational behavior to be likely to produce positive outcomes and nonrational behavior to be likely to produce negative outcomes. If so, we should contemplate the following question: how can we explain that the outcome was positive, or at least nonnegative? I will develop several interpretations below, and then identify my favored one.

The first interpretation reflects skepticism about the question itself. It argues that rationality is highly contingent, as discussed in chapter 7, which makes it hard to assert that the decision-making process or any decision-making process was nonrational. The more important question may be: under what conditions was it more likely to be rational?

The second interpretation takes a different tack, which is important to consider. It argues that decision-making only *appeared* to be marked by significant nonrational elements. This argument is based on the notion that action may be rational from the standpoint of a particular decision maker, but not from the perspective of the state. Thus, if we presume that a decision maker is not a simple extension of the state, what is rational for the individual may not be so if we evaluate that behavior from the standpoint of the state.

On that score, we can further argue that Bush and Scowcroft weighed the costs and benefits of alternatives carefully and quickly and, as a result of a process that reflected individual rationality, knew what they wanted in ways that are not discernible in the record. The task then became to implement their already considered decisions in a broader governmental setting, rather than to expose those decisions to much debate.

Under this interpretation, the most important reason for why decision-making at the governmental level was exclusive, *ad hoc*, and often failed to consider all alternatives methodically was partly because the alternatives were already "deemed inadequate" by Bush and Scowcroft.[56] That Bush's preferences clashed with those of others adds to the impression that Bush was impetuous and did not see or consider all alternatives. In fact, while Bush did at times fit that description, he and Scowcroft sometimes also decided what they believed had to be done, based on innumerable factors discussed in the foregoing chapters, and carried it out unyieldingly. Future work might explore Bush by drawing on various conceptions of individual rationality available in the literature.

The fourth interpretation is that human logic and reason may not allow us to know with any great confidence what would have transpired in history had certain variables been different. However, we can argue that the outcome that resulted in the Persian Gulf War case was far more negative than it initially appeared to be, if we consider its consequences over the long term. In effect, then, our puzzle is not really a puzzle at all. Decision-making that was marked by nonrational processes did produce a negative outcome. It just took some time for that outcome to manifest itself. Since this book seeks to stay largely focused on the events leading up to the war, I will extend the analysis of the postwar period and this question of postwar consequences in the Postscript.

The fifth interpretation is that the outcome was not highly positive, but that it was somewhat positive, or at least nonnegative. That view is based on the notions that the United States met most of its stated goals in the Persian Gulf crisis, especially with respect to reversing the invasion and containing Iraq, and that meeting such goals should be the yardstick for success. That does not mean that long-term consequences are not relevant, merely that too many intervening variables emerge over time, which complicate the effort to assess causality between the crisis and its possible long-term consequences.

The sixth interpretation is that the crisis was indeed marked by nonrational processes, although not on all decisions; that the outcome of U.S. decision-making, if we focus on the short term, was positive or at least nonnegative; and that mitigating factors allowed for that outcome to occur, despite nonrational processes. Four mitigating factors are key in this interpretation.

The first is leadership. That variable was laid out in discussing how group-think can be paired with a non-fiasco. The second is the level of resources that could be commanded. The United States had immense economic, political, military, and human resources at its disposal. Thus, it could afford not to carefully consider alternatives because its margin of error was large. The third is allies. Sometimes allies matter more than at other times, but on the whole, the actor that can draw on allied support has a significant edge. Such allies can help secure a positive outcome or avoid a negative outcome, even if decision-making is non-rational. In the Persian Gulf War case, the United States had a massive coalition servicing its interests. It helped ensure that if the United States chose a certain course of action, it would succeed. Thus, while the decision to reverse Iraq's decision was not weighed carefully against other alternatives, numerous other countries were ready to execute it.

The fourth factor is the difficulty of the challenge. As discussed in chapter 5, one of the reasons that the United States could meet most of its stated goals is that the challenge appeared to be greater at the outset of the crisis than it turned out to be. Iraq proved highly ineffective in complicating the opposition's military plans.

Each of the six interpretations presented above has some merit, and some of the interpretations cannot be ruled out. However, the argument of this book favors the sixth interpretation. Mitigating factors certainly did intervene between process and outcome to contribute significantly to a positive or at least nonnegative short-term outcome. We should, however, hold out the Persian Gulf War case as a cautionary tale. We cannot count on mitigating factors to be at play in each foreign policy case. We cannot count on leaders with significant foreign policy experience and skill, on massive resources, on our fairly solid allies, on dubious adversaries, and on a little bit of luck. Indeed, we should be more inclined to count on precisely the opposite set of conditions, if only to guard against our own optimism and sporadic myopia.

At a minimum, methodological procedures should be emphasized by the president and other important leaders for purposes of generating and evaluating alternative options for problem-solving, and for engaging in all the tasks that are necessary for doing so. This does not mean that decision-making should be overintellectualized or that countless hours should be spent examining each minute cost and benefit pertaining to various alternatives. However, it does mean that such procedures can prevent certain alternatives from being rejected even before they are considered, and others being adopted more quickly than is optimal.[57] The less we can count on mitigating factors, the more important it will be to have a decision-making process that employs methodical procedures and pays careful attention to evaluating alternative courses of action.

Conclusion

The integrated approach facilitates theory-building because it situates different perspectives and tests them against the evidence. This chapter has sought chiefly to develop theory that enhances our understanding of groupthink and the government politics model. These theories, which are suited for broader application to foreign policy cases, also share something in common. They both show that the particular characteristics of individuals would generate different outcomes, even under similar structural constraints. Thus, in the theory of groupthink, a partial leader helps drive and shape consensus within a group setting. But knowing that a leader is partial and strong is not enough to determine the outcome of groupthink. Not only do we need to consider the individual-group interaction question that I introduced in chapter 7, but also what type of group leader is at work. In generating theory about the non-fiasco theory, the characteristics of the group leader became crucial—over and above the fact that the group leader was influential. That was also true about the conditions under which the GPM is less likely to be telling. A strong, experienced, and knowledgeable leader was related theoretically to a decrease in government politics. In the Persian Gulf War case, Bush's role did not help confirm the theory, but rather disconfirmed it.

CHAPTER TEN

Understanding Government Behavior

Integrating Process, Choice, and Outcome

The goal of this chapter is to tackle a fundamental question raised in the introduction: how can we integrate areas of study—domestic and international theory—that are often treated as separate? While chapter 8 integrated insights derived from using and testing multiple perspectives in order to tell a more complete empirical tale, this chapter builds on the previous one to see how we can combine these insights in a theory-oriented manner. We can seek to bridge domestic and international theory by thinking about the three central areas of foreign policy: process, choice, and outcome. I first elaborate upon them, and then proceed to show how multiple perspectives allow us to integrate them. I then approach integration from another angle by introducing what I call "layered thinking" and generating some theoretical propositions for further study.

Dichotomies of Thought and International Relations Theory

While the RAM is not equipped to account for factors internal to states in the effort to explain government behavior, it is also limited in another sense. It is designed to explain just one of the two central dimensions of decision-making: "choice." In basic terms, the RAM tells us how actors choose. It tells us that when faced with a choice between alternatives, actors will take (or try to take) the option that promises the best outcome.

The present version of the RAM, however, ignores the second central aspect of decision-making: process.[1] Process in this book refers to the nature, content, and origin of the beliefs, and the perceptions, preferences, and objectives of the actors. It is what happens in decision-making prior to choice. The RAM treats these elements of process as givens, and then tells us how choices will be made. They are assumed rather than established through research and analysis. But what if, for instance, we seek to understand how actors form their preferences in the first place, or, in other words, why they prefer certain policies over others, such as free trade over protectionism, economic sanctions over negotiation, and war over economic sanctions?[2]

RAM is not the only theory that assumes away process for purposes of parsimony. While neorealists actually "come close" to believing that states' identities, preferences, and interests are, in fact, given and fixed, as John Gerard Ruggie puts it, neoliberal institutionalists also approach reality in this manner at least as a "convenient assumption."[3] Andrew Moravcsik views this proclivity as a fundamental problem with international relations theory, so much so that he develops a liberal international relations theory that explicates "domestic" preference formation. He sees preference formation as a prerequisite to international relations theory, because it defines the conditions under which the assumptions of the two main theoretical schools hold — that is to say, realism/neorealism and neo-institutionalism. Moravscik thus privileges domestic-level variables that provide insight into preference formation.[4] To be sure, Waltz rejects the notion that neorealism is a theory of foreign policy that explores process, and black boxes decision-making.[5] Nonetheless, process is a vital part of decision-making and deserves explanation, and it is integral to informing international relations theory as well.[6] Decision makers respond to the opportunities and constraints that they face at the international level, but they may do so in quite different ways. Structure may give us good clues but not outright answers. To explain outcomes, we must also consider preference as a key aspect of process. But that returns us to our bigger question: what is the best conceptual approach for trying to capture process, choice, and outcome?[7]

Process as a Key Aspect of Decision-Making

The integrated approach of this book is simple conceptually, while allowing for complex analysis and synthesis. It provides a vehicle for understanding the origins and contents of beliefs and perceptions, an important aspect of process.[8] The RAM tells us that perceptions of national interest do matter profoundly, but it does not tell us much about the origins and content of beliefs and perceptions, especially insofar as they arise at the domestic level. The cognitive approach can provide insight on that score. In the Persian Gulf War case, it instructs us that Bush viewed the Persian Gulf crisis partly through the prism of the Munich analogy. That helps explain the perception that Saddam was like Adolf Hitler, and the resulting tendency to believe that Iraq could pose a threat not just to Kuwait but to Saudi Arabia and even to the global order. The RAM cannot offer such insight into perceptions and belief, simply because it ignores such phenomena.

The origin and content of beliefs and perceptions can also be shaped through group dynamics. Just as analogies can shape perceptions and beliefs by operating on the way individuals process information, group dynamics can do so through socialization or group pressures. The theory of groupthink reflects a particular type of group dynamic that generates similar beliefs about the adversary among its members. In the Persian Gulf War case, the group eventually shared the belief of a dangerous Iraq led by an evil leader. Group dynamics promoted consensus on key perceptions and beliefs. The cognitive influence and the group dynamic reinforced each other. They both helped shape the perceptions and beliefs of actors, either through their independent effects or because the cognitive factor affected Bush mainly as a group leader who then influenced group dynamics.

All of the perspectives offer insight at different levels of analysis into preference formation as well. It is not true that the RAM ignores the origin of preferences outright. The RAM tells us that states will focus on security and national welfare and that such invariant preferences arise from international factors. However, it tells us nothing about a range of potential preferences, or how preferences form out of domestic-level factors. While a literature has developed to trace the development of state preference formation, it traces them largely to certain elites.[9] It cannot account for the varied ways that preferences can arise, ways highlighted by multiple perspectives. The cognitive approach yields insight into preference formation. This book shows how analogies can be a source of preferences, how certain policies are preferred because they accommodate the historical lesson or message provided by the analogy. Others are less preferred because they clash with the lesson or message of the analogy. The analogy, in this way, acts as a prism through which preferences can be formed, downgraded in importance, and even rejected if the analogy is particularly powerful in its impact.

The DPM tells us that preferences cannot simply be presumed to be national and largely invariant in nature. They may arise from the personal interests of leaders or organizations. The DPM also suggests that preferences can form as a function of the discursive environment created by decision makers who seek to construct the adversary, but in the process alter that environment as well. The environment, then, can push leaders to prefer certain policies over others. Although the DPM was not especially telling in this book, it may be more illuminating in other cases.

While the DPM highlights preference formation, so can group dynamics. The theory of groupthink offers one take on group dynamics. If confirmed, it tells us that the preferences around which consensus forms early in an event will prevail. Other preferences will either not form or be downgraded in importance. This occurs largely through group dynamics driven in part by a partial group leader whose preferences can prevail in part because of groupthink dynamics.

The GPM, moreover, allows us to see what factors may shape each player's perceptions, preferences, and likely course of action. The GPM informs us that preferences will be formed based on the bureaucracies that individuals represent and as a result of bargaining among individuals. These interests, in competition, may ultimately shape the international behavior of actors. While RAM analysts will explain behavior in terms of the national interests that the analyst assumes are at play, the GPM clearly takes a different tack. Bureaucratic interest and politics shape preferences more than concern for some perceived national interests. This was not the case in the Persian Gulf crisis, but it may be so in other cases.

The cognitive, DPM, and GPM perspectives yield different insights into how individual preferences are shaped in the first place, but we gain insight into how they are aggregated into collective or even national choice by exploring group and bureaucratic dynamics. The theory of groupthink and the GPM offer different answers. Unlike groupthink, the GPM posits that preferences are aggregated, sometimes into national policy through conflict and bargaining, with actors promoting and being shaped by their bureaucracies. In the Persian Gulf War case, group dynamics, driven by an influential group leader, were a better explanation for how preferences were aggregated than was the GPM. Bush as an individual also aggregated preferences outside the group through construction, personal lobbying, and strength of personality.

While RAM tells us how actors pick among options, group or institutional dynamics yield insight into how hard or easy it may be to execute the group leader's preferred option. If government politics are at play, we would expect it to be harder. If, by contrast, the groupthink dynamics are at play, we would expect it to be easier, with a spectrum of outcomes lying in between.

Choice as the Other Key Aspect of Decision-Making

The integrated approach provides a more complete picture of process, but it also offers angles on exploring choice. For the RAM, the actor is treated as one single entity with one set of perceived choices, and a single estimate of the costs and benefits of each alternative for any given question. The RAM posits that actors seek to choose based on a rational process.

The other perspectives offer different explanations for choice. The theory of groupthink emphasizes nonrational processes, partly by highlighting the potential for alternatives not to be considered carefully. The cognitive approach and DPM allow for either rational and/or nonrational choice. Meanwhile, the GPM assumes that individual actors are rational but that outcomes are unlikely to be. What does all this mean? The different explanations of choice allow us to explain one or more choices chiefly in terms of one perspective. Raising the level of complexity, it also allows us either to complement or challenge rationalist explanations of choice. This book, in testing the perspectives, found that nonrational processes were prominent, but also revealed a complex continuum of behaviors, some rational and some not, some quasi-rational and some simply ambiguous or opaque.

Using multiple perspectives yields other insights into choice. If the reader recalls, noncompensatory decision-making occurs when a certain alternative is deemed to be unacceptable in a given dimension, and cannot be saved by a high score in another dimension. That is, decision makers value one objective so much that if an option does not meet it, they will reject that option even if the option can meet other objectives quite well. Alex Mintz and Nehemia Geva focus on cognitive factors as generating such behavior in their poliheuristic model.[10] However, the multiple perspectives of this book offer other explanations as well, which can enhance our understanding of the crisis and build on the theoretical notion of noncompensatory decision-making.

In part, I argue that one explanation for noncompensatory behavior that has not been advanced in the literature arises from group dynamics. In the Persian Gulf War case, one or more nonwar options were eliminated because they failed in the dimension of the need for group consensus. High scores for these options on other dimensions could not save them from elimination. The record as reflected in chapter 5 supports such an interpretation in the Persian Gulf War case and may help us see more general connections between group dynamics and noncompensatory decision-making.[11]

Explaining Outcomes

So far, we have discussed process and choice in light of the other perspectives. Now we can turn attention to the related aspect of outcomes. If process and choice are the two key aspects of decision-making by one actor, outcome is about the result of interactions with other actors. It is about the outcomes of interactions between two or more actors. The decision-theoretic aspect of the RAM tells us that actors seek to maximize utility without concern for what others are expected to do. It deals with choice. The game-theoretic aspect of the RAM informs us that A's choice will be affected by what A expects B to do in response to A's actions, and that A's ability to realize its preference will depend to a significant extent on what B does. It lays out how choice will be affected by strategic interaction, how choice will be affected by expectations of outcomes.

In this section, I seek to show how all five perspectives of this book can provide insight into outcomes, and in particular how they can inform the game-theoretic dimension of the RAM. To be sure, scholars have begun to draw on various research traditions for this purpose. Some important research on perceptions, ideas, norms, and the social construction of identity, for instance, has moved in that direction.[12] Using multiple perspectives allows us to approach this task more systematically in three ways. The first two ways cross-fertilize the RAM and non-RAM perspectives of this book, and the third integrates their insights without cross-fertilizing them.

The first line of analysis draws on the cognitive approach. The cognitive perspective revealed that analogical thinking not only affected how decisions were made but also what the actors expected of each other. Indeed, it is quite plausible to argue that the Munich analogy led the United States to believe that Iraq would become even more threatening if Washington did not cut its army down to size, while the Vietnam analogy pushed Iraq to expect that the United States would retreat if Iraq killed enough American soldiers. In this sense, war was more likely than a negotiated outcome or continued economic sanctions because of inconsistent expectations between the United States and Iraq. Expectations of war, expectations of what the other side would do, and expectations of outcomes were shaped in part by cognitive factors, by analogies.

The second intersection can be found in the domestic politics model explanation. That model alerts us to the potential for counter-construction, a situation where one actor seeking to achieve domestic level goals will construct the adversary, who in turn seeks to engage in counter-construction. That dynamic is not just relevant to explaining decision-making, it is relevant to understanding strategic interaction. Expectations of outcomes at the international level can be shaped in part by the intended or unintended impact of domestic-level behavior on interaction among nations. Chapter 4 showed the potential for that dynamic in the

Persian Gulf War case. If in meeting domestic goals, actor A contributes to a cycle of mutual recrimination between A and B, or decreased trust in certain outcomes on the part of B, that fundamentally alters their strategic interaction. It decreases prospects for cooperation and makes noncooperative outcomes more likely.

Moreover, we can say that while the lagged effects of construction can undermine rational processes, that need not always be the case. The rational choice element of the RAM could explain construction as a way of engaging in self-binding commitments, preventing the choice of undesirable alternatives at a later date. As Jon Elster points out, "rational behavior at time 1 may involve precautionary measures to prevent the choice of B at time 2, or at least to make that choice less likely."[13] The DPM could be perfectly consistent with a rationalist explanation, although not a state-centric RAM. It could argue that decision makers construct the adversary to signal their commitment to be tough against the adversary. In theory, such action would alert the adversary, as James Fearon models it, that democratically elected decision makers would face high domestic costs if they backed down or appeared any less committed to being tough. Such costs would include not being re-elected, for instance. That, in turn, would increase bargaining leverage with the adversary.[14] In the Persian Gulf War case, unfortunately, Saddam did not think that the domestic audience would take such action, but rather considered it more pacific than President Bush. Hence, we might argue that we first must know what domestic preferences are, as a rough aggregate, before Fearon's model above can predict how useful signalling can be in a bargaining situation.[15]

The third intersection has already been developed at the end of chapter 7. Chapter 2 showed how we could draw on the game-theoretic aspect of the RAM to explain not only why the two sides went to war, but why they could not reach an agreement to avoid war. In drawing on the other perspectives and analyses presented in this book, we obtained a more developed answer to that dimension of strategic interaction, i.e., why the window of opportunity was closed or did not remain open for long. This is less about cross-fertilizing the perspectives than it is about integrating their insights.

Generating Propositions

The integrated approach allows us to generate myriad propositions that can further understanding about how to integrate process, choice, and outcome. A number of generalizations were already used to build the theories in chapter 9.

Here, we can offer the following added propositions as examples in order to spur thought and future study:

P1: The greater the presence of groupthink in the central decision-making group, the easier it will be for the group leader to aggregate preferences into a preferred outcome (reasoning: the leader will face less opposition).

P2: The greater the presence of groupthink, the less likely a state will bargain with an adversary (reasoning: groupthink is partly caused by a negative view of the adversary and results in greater resolve against the adversary).

P3: Strategic interactions that resemble a noniterated Prisoner's Dilemma are more likely to generate groupthink (reasoning: the external threat will be higher when the interaction between two players is expected to be short — usually the case when the interaction is iterated; external threat, in turn, contributes to groupthink).

P4: Analogizing back to an historic event that induces fear among decision makers will increase the potential for groupthink (reasoning: it will generate stress, which is linked to groupthink).

P5: The higher the level of government politics, the harder it will be for the president to aggregate preferences into a preferred outcome (reasoning: the president will face more opposition in a high-conflict atmosphere of decision-making).

P6: The higher the level of GP in a government, the less bargaining leverage that government will have at the international level (reasoning: it will be harder to generate resolve when GP dynamics are at play).

P7: The greater the emphasis on Type 1 and 2 goals in decision-making, as conceptualized in the DPM, the less a state will try to bargain seriously with another to avoid conflict (reasoning: its incentive decreases because the conflict yields domestic-level benefits).

P8: The more a president constructs the adversary for public consumption, the stronger his bargaining hand will be at the international level, if he has majority public support (reasoning: such construction communicates to the adversary that he has little room for bargaining).

Layered Thinking

While we have integrated insights across some areas of process, choice, and outcomes, we can also offer one more cut at the question of integration. I call it layered thinking, and I introduce it here in a preliminary fashion. The aim is to stimulate further thought on the subject in the future.

In contrast to many studies and approaches that focus on specific episodes or decisions without regard to how they are linked, the layered approach treats decisions in an event as linked. It explores sequential decision-making in a conventional manner, but also seeks to explain different time periods of decision-making with different perspectives, something that is not often done.[16]

Using multiple perspectives in this manner does not mean that the perspectives would apply only to a particular time period within a broader case, but rather that perspectives or aspects of them may be most insightful at particular junctures in an event. In the Persian Gulf War case, for instance, decision makers largely began with behaviors consonant chiefly with the RAM. Thereafter, decision-making could best be explained by layering additional insights from the other perspectives used in this book.

Future work might explore the idea of the layered approach in other cases, and if that proves useful, examine the prospect for exploring additional sequences and processes within each time period of a decision-making episode. For present purposes, I will limit myself to laying out a process of sequences with respect to U.S. decision-making in the Persian Gulf War case.

Identification and RAM

Foreign policy scholars have long recognized the importance of the initial stages of decision-making, which involve understanding the strategic problem at hand. These are crucial stages because that is often when the foreign policy problem is defined. We would not be especially misled about what was occurring in the black box of decision-making if we used the RAM as a guide to this first stage of the crisis. In fact, in the black box, decision makers were inclined initially to engage in identification by asking the following types of questions: What is the problem the country faces? What are the facts of the situation? Who are the players involved or potentially involved? What are the national stakes for the country? In essence, they sought to determine the objective parameters of the situation, chiefly in light of national interests, before wrestling with what they meant. That was quite clear in the CIA and NSC briefings that the president was given beginning on August 1, when a troubled Scowcroft, along with Haass, informed him that an invasion may take place. It was also clear, in part, at the first two NSC meetings on August 2 and 3, and at Camp David the following weekend when the group of eight determined the level of threat that Saudi Arabia faced (number of Iraqi troops, position, direction, and intent) and how it might be addressed (how many forces needed; Saudi compliance required to allow U.S. forces in). But while the RAM was revealing at the outset, albeit also at other junctures, other dimensions of decision-making were soon added to the mix.

Evaluation: Adding Cognition

After identifying the problem at hand, decision makers edged quickly toward inquiring more deeply about its meaning. The early encounter with the facts of the situation served as a basis for drawing inferences about what they meant. To do so, they drew, in part, on their experiences and background. In this sense, they were engaging in "process" or in an effort to interpret the situation, to assess the information that was bombarding them, and to frame or disregard certain options. While they continued to engage in identification and to carry with them initial views of the facts, they also needed to manage the complex situation in their minds. For Bush in particular, this is where the Munich analogy came in. While pushing him to see the crisis in emotive ways that clashed with rational behavior, it also pointed to the costs of alternatives other than war. As Yuen Foong Khong points out, analogies in that sense sometimes help decision makers see the costs of alternatives better than they otherwise could.[17] The cognitive dimension thus was added to the mix of factors at play.

Public Relations: Adding Construction

While decision makers continued to engage in identification and evaluation, carrying their previous interpretations and inferences into the decision-making process, over time they also needed to answer the following questions: Now that we have a sense of the problem and of our objectives, how can the situation be framed and presented to various constituencies to meet these objectives? What Type 1 and Type 2 objectives can we realize in the process? The DPM, in part, helps explore this question. Public relations was important from day one, but it became vital later in the crisis when the administration sought to explain U.S. policy better and to sell the war option. That is when the president, recognizing this need, established a committee designed to accomplish it, which worked feverishly. Constructing Saddam may have also served some domestic goals that took shape as the crisis proceeded.

Execution: Adding Group Dynamics

Bush and Scowcroft also had to execute their will in a complex political setting composed of competing and overlapping bureaucracies and diverse individuals with their own views. What type of group dynamics would they face? Could they push their ideas through? How would they be implemented? Such questions were relevant throughout the crisis, but they were especially germane as time proceeded, and particularly after Bush, Scowcroft, and then others in the group of eight came to the realization, which developed slowly over time, that war was the best outcome. That elements of groupthink developed earlier in the crisis and that group dynamics were amenable to a partial leader made it easier to execute the move to war. The models of groupthink and GPM can provide insight into such dynamics because they model factors that affect the questions of advancing and executing ideas in a group or bureaucratic setting. In the Persian Gulf War case, elements of groupthink provided a better guide to answering these questions than did the GPM.

Feedback

Decisions made during the crisis produced consequences that in turn affected each one of the previous stages cited above in different ways. Thus, once Desert Shield was in place, the Iraqi threat to Saudi Arabia diminished, as, in turn, did perceptions of threat to national interests. And when it became clear that Saddam was unlikely to withdraw and added his own vitriol to an atmosphere of construction and counter-construction, public relations and execution became easier, as well as seeing Saddam through the filter of the 1930s. Had Saddam, for instance, withdrawn partly from Kuwait, the feedback effects would have been significant on all the phases discussed above. Iraq's objective threat would have decreased, as well as the ability to see or construct Saddam in Hitler-like terms. Public relations also would have been less effective and execution would have been more challenging. And group dynamics may have become less agreeable if Iraq's partial withdrawal had split those who had preferred a go-slow approach toward Iraq but were reluctant to express it from those more inclined toward war and toward weakening Iraq so that it could not be a significant future threat.

In effect, the layered approach helps us see better why partial withdrawal was viewed as a nightmare scenario in the White House. It would have thrown a monkey wrench into the process that allowed the United States to cut Saddam and his over-sized military down to size.

Conclusion

This chapter builds on the previous chapters to show how we can integrate insights across areas of study that are often treated as separate. By laying out five perspectives side by side in one book, we open vistas for cross-fertilization and we can try to explain outcomes through a variety of combinations of insights derived from the perspectives. We also hold out the prospect of developing a grand theory of government behavior. Such an endeavor, however, would have to side-step the contradictory assumptions of some of the perspectives, or find particular variables across various perspectives that lend themselves to logical, theoretical integration on a broad scale. That is an effort better left to future work.

CHAPTER ELEVEN

Beyond the Gulf

Foreign Policy and World Politics

The questions of how states make decisions, and what results in world affairs from those decisions, transcend time, place and culture. All states face, in an existential sense, the intended and unintended consequences of their own decisions. In history, states have risen and fallen because of key decisions, as have empires and entire civilizations. Understanding how decisions are made, therefore, can offer a window on history and insight into a timeless dimension of the human condition.

Such a window is of great importance with regard to the United States and the Middle East, a region which has defined important contours of global affairs. In the past two decades, the Persian Gulf region alone has suffered through the disastrous eight-year Iran-Iraq War, which, in history's ongoing chain of events, set the backdrop to Iraq's invasion of Kuwait. That tragic event, in turn, created the conditions for the Persian Gulf War, which has set the stage for war in Iraq more than a decade later.

In trying to understand government behavior, this book began with the notion that an integrated approach could prove useful. It then sketched and developed this approach and applied it to the Persian Gulf War case. It first presented multiple perspectives on government behavior, and then used them to shed light on how and why the United States went to war, taking into account U.S.-Iraqi strategic interaction within the broader context of Middle East and world politics. After doing so, it evaluated these perspectives against the available evidence, and then proceeded to integrate the resulting insights into a more complex tale and to draw on them to develop theory.

While this book applied the integrated approach to the Persian Gulf War case, a question arises as to whether it can be applied to other cases. The thrust of the book strongly suggests that it can, but it would be useful in closing to elaborate on this point.

The integrated approach is broadly applicable because it uses multiple perspectives emerging from several disciplines, each of which captures essential aspects of government behavior. Indeed, as laid out in the introduction and throughout the book, each perspective offers an alternative take on government behavior, emphasizing different levels of analysis and types of decision-making.

However, while the integrated approach is widely applicable, it does not apply equally to all foreign policy cases. It will tend to be most useful in cases where important national interests are at stake, but where the wheels of government are given some time to turn. This will allow for dynamics to transpire, which these perspectives attempt to capture. Government behavior in minor cases may be handled in just one part of the government, and with some alacrity, thus not evidencing a broad range of complex dynamics.

While the integrated approach will tend to be more useful in important foreign policy cases, such as those involving the threat, display, and use of force, it can also be applied to cases of economic or diplomatic statecraft, if they involve issues of major importance. Such cases range from the Smoot-Hawley tariff of 1930 that raised taxes on imported goods by as much as 60 percent to how to respond to France's challenges to U.S. policy towards Iraq preceding the Iraq War in 2003.

The integrated approach can also be useful in routine foreign policy cases, but less so. In such cases, the government politics or organizational process models could potentially be telling, but probably not the theory of groupthink, which requires stressful conditions; the rational actor model, which is most useful in highlighting the broader strategic context and the dynamics among nations; or the domestic politics model, which presumes that the leadership will use a foreign policy event to divert attention from domestic problems or, as conceived herein, to meet other personal or institutional goals. Less significant foreign policy behavior does not usually serve such goals because it is not important enough to divert attention. Overall, it is fair to say that the more significant the behavior, the more leverage we would obtain by using the integrated approach.

However, a plethora of goals commonly pursued by scholars, students, and decision makers can also be met within the context of a scaled-back version of the integrated approach. Some thinkers may want to use the perspectives only as heuristic devices, as explanatory engines that generate different views and insights about government behavior, without testing them against the record or developing theory. Thumbnail sketches of this kind do not involve heavy research and are useful explanatory forays. Indeed, we could imagine students doing such thumbnail sketches on different cases, trying to thread them into sensible explanations of decision-making as a whole.

At a rudimentary level, thinkers may only be interested in what two particular perspectives tell us about government behavior. They may be tasked, for instance, with laying out RAM and cognitive explanations for why India significantly increased its military forces against Pakistan in May-June 2002 or why the United States bombed Cambodia during the Vietnam War. Such an effort may also involve comparing and contrasting these two different explanations in order to gain insight into the cases.

At a higher level of complexity, thinkers may be interested in seeing how narratives drawn from two or more perspectives fare against the evidence. They can then generate insights that can be synthesized into a single, more effective tale of an event. Moving beyond the empirical, they may also seek to advance theory. As an example, chapter 9 developed a theory of government politics that laid out the conditions under which we would not expect to see government politics at play. That theory helped explain why we saw far less government politics in the Persian Gulf War case as compared to the 1962 Cuban missile crisis case. The use of multiple perspectives also creates the potential for exploring the extent to which the perspectives are contradictory or complementary. Inasmuch as they are complementary, they may be fit for cross-fertilization at different levels of analysis.

Beyond the theoretical, the practical implications of the approach are important. The wisdom of decision makers depends fundamentally on avoiding closed-mindedness, seeing the different dimensions and shades of phenomena, and understanding the implications of their own governmental behavior. Indeed, disasters great and small in world affairs, disasters which have sent nations to war, stunted economic growth, and caused cultural clashes, have occurred in the absence of such insight.

The perspective that decision makers use either consciously or subconsciously will alter how they interpret the motivations and goals of their counterparts in world affairs, and how those counterparts respond. This can make the difference between cooperation and conflict in world affairs. For instance, in the post–Cold War period, the United States did not want Russia to sell Iran arms and repeatedly pressured Moscow on that score. Through the conscious or subconscious prism of the rational actor model, the analyst would be more likely to see such Russian arms sales as quite provocative. They would appear to be intended and calculated — even bold and defiant — as if Russian leaders carefully explored the costs and benefits of the sales and decided to risk confronting Washington on purpose. By contrast, seen through the government politics perspective, these arms sales would not be viewed necessarily as intentionally provocative behavior on the part of the Russian government, but rather as the artifice of self-interested bureaucrats and bureaucracies pushing for the interests of their bureaucracies, in a manner not easily controlled by Moscow. The outcome would be viewed as the unintended output of the grinding, competitive bureaucratic wheels of government. The American response would likely be different depending on the perspective that it used to evaluate the same situation.

The integrated approach can also take a postmodern turn. Multiple perspectives could yield explanations and narratives that are held out against each other without being tested, based on the postmodern notion that perspectives are what really count, because it is doubtful that we can identify, much less understand, "objective" reality. Thus, it would make sense to use multiple perspectives in line with the first part of the integrated approach, but to eschew its positivist effort to see how they fare against the evidence and what they suggest about theory.

Of course, the integrated approach is not cast in cement in terms of the perspectives used. Other models/theories could be applied as well, so long as they cover different levels of analysis and modes of decision-making.

Conclusion

The integrated approach seeks to enhance our ability to understand the complex, ubiquitous behaviors that shape our lives, the trajectories of states, and the historical process itself. While it was used in this book to explore a case of high politics where major security interests were at stake, it can apply to other cases as well. Indeed, what it seeks to do is to force the consideration and study of a variety of sometimes contradictory and sometimes complementary ways of thinking about theory as well as historical cases. That these perspectives are drawn from multiple disciplines ensures that a diversity of approaches are considered in explaining events and also enhances the potential for a theoretical dialogue across disciplines.

Postscript: From War to War

The saga of wars in the Persian Gulf did not end with the cease-fire in the Persian Gulf War. As with any drama, there was more to come — a war to end a regime and to start a different era for Iraqis. This book has focused on why and how the United States went to war in 1991, but it would be useful here to explore briefly the U.S. decisions that ended the 1991 war, the immediate postwar period, and some of the consequences of the war. In this context, we can also examine an important question: to what extent was the military operation in the Persian Gulf a success?

Following this discussion, it would also be useful to explore the Iraq War of 2003, which has altered Iraqi and regional dynamics in profound ways. I will offer brief sketches of how the integrated approach might explain U.S. decision-making on the road to this war.

To What Extent was the Military Operation a Success?

Many critics of the Persian Gulf war not only questioned whether the United States should have gone to war, but pointed to its short- and long-term political, economic, and human consequences, and Saddam's survival, as evidence that the war was a failure.[1] It is important here to distinguish between judging the success of statecraft in terms of meeting stated objectives, as has been the approach in this book, or in terms of its short- and long-term consequences.

The administration largely did meet its stated goals. President Bush asserted that the United States had four main objectives. The first was the unconditional withdrawal of all Iraqi forces from Kuwait. That was accomplished. The second was the restoration of Kuwait's legitimate government, which was also achieved. The third was the maintenance of the security and the stability of the region, while the fourth was the protection of the lives of Americans abroad. The United States achieved the third and fourth objectives if we focus on the short run. The picture becomes less clear as we extend the time period of examination.

The Immediate Postwar Period

While the United States did meet most of its stated objectives in the short run, difficulties began to arise for Washington toward the end of the war. Three decisions at the end of the war are particularly salient to explore.

Political pundits, the U.S. public, and some scholars and Arab leaders argued in retrospect that the U.S.-led coalition should have marched into Baghdad.[2] Such criticisms regained momentum in 2002–03, when the administration of George W. Bush once again appeared to be on the path to war with Iraq, with regime change as its ultimate goal. Critics asserted that such a goal should have been accomplished by George H.W. Bush.

However, the march on Baghdad scenario was never seriously considered in 1991, for several reasons. The U.N. mandate that governed Operations Desert Shield and Storm did not allow for such action, and America's Arab allies, some of whom would not even fight Iraq during the war, would have opposed it. Therefore, U.S. decision makers were concerned that Washington would have been acting without international support. As one member of Bush's small coterie of advisers put it, "the idea of going to Baghdad was not a hot prospect — even Egyptian President Hosni Mubarak reiterated opposition to this idea in March 1996."[3] Moreover, it was widely believed that Saddam would be hard to find, that such an operation would have entailed unacceptable potential casualties, and that, even if successful, finding an alternative Iraqi regime to lead a post-Saddam Iraq would be difficult. As Colin Powell asserted and James Baker confirmed, the administration believed that it had "no assurance that someone other than Saddam would be better than Saddam."[4] The administration was also concerned about dismembering Iraq. As both Powell and Scowcroft made clear, the balance of power in the region was considered insofar as the United States did not want to split Iraq apart, a prospect that might lead to Iran emerging as a dominant power in the region.[5]

While there were good reasons not to march on Baghdad and while no one in Bush's inner circle appeared to consider that prospect seriously, it was certainly perceived by some as a military option at that point. As General Schwarzkopf pointed out from the field, if it had "been our intention to overrun the country, we could have done it unopposed, for all intents and purposes."[6]

Short of marching on Baghdad, the administration had the choice of when to end the war. It chose to end it at approximately a hundred hours. As one official put it, "there was a legitimate debate about going another 24-48 hours against Iraq's Republican Guard divisions."[7] In retrospect, the administration was widely criticized for ending the war too soon. Even Schwarzkopf warned that he needed more time to finish the job. In fact, Bush did believe that Iraqi forces were more devastated than they were, and was concerned about exceeding the coalition's mandate. His advisers were also concerned that more attacks, after the surrender of thousands of Iraqi soldiers, would look like a massacre and, in Powell's words, would not only be "un-American" and but also "unchivalrous."[8] That was a prominent motive.

The United States also had to decide how to terminate the war once it was decided that it should be ended. While U.S. Ambassador to Saudi Arabia Chas Freeman pressed the Bush administration for a war-termination strategy, no real action was taken because, in Freeman's view, the administration was concerned that the coalition would break down if such a strategy were formulated and leaked. For his part, Schwarzkopf was very "agitated" when he received little direction from Washington regarding the cease-fire talks at Safwan. Iraqi generals must have "walked out of Safwan with smiles on their faces, wondering why the U.S. position was so apolitical." Schwarzkopf wanted instructions from Washington on how to negotiate, and, absent such direction, was forced to treat the talks in military rather than political terms.[9] One overriding concern was to avoid getting stuck in the Persian Gulf. This concern "seriously affected the war-termination approach" because, as one decision maker put it, "after achieving our critical objectives, Bush did not want to stick around and lose Arab support and get into the types of troubles that U.S. forces faced in the terror bombings in Saudi Arabia in 1996."[10] Concern about terrorism was a chief motive.

Whatever the motivations for U.S. decisions at the end of the war, the outcome was somewhat problematic. Bush encouraged the Shia in the South and the Kurds in the North to rise up against Saddam, which they did, but the U.S. did not support them militarily, believing with some reason at the time that they could topple the shaky regime. Iraq, in fact, was not precluded by the cease-fire agreement with Washington from flying helicopters, and it used them as well as its best military divisions, which had survived the war, to crush the rebellions. In the postwar period, Saddam survived onerous economic sanctions, the most intrusive postwar U.N. inspection regime in history, unwavering U.S. military containment, and virtually unending global scrutiny. Not only did he survive all that, but he almost certainly continued to develop deliverable weapons of mass destruction. It is sobering to imagine his progress on that front had the war and postwar U.N. inspections not substantially reduced his capabilities.

Exploring Some Possible Long-Term Consequences

The Persian Gulf War certainly cut Iraq's military down and set back Saddam's effort to develop weapons of mass destruction. But some might argue that one negative long-term consequence to consider is that the Persian Gulf War contributed to the September 11 terrorist attacks. Osama bin Laden did point to the Persian Gulf War and the continuing presence of U.S. forces in Saudi Arabia as a primary grievance. He repeatedly asserted that "infidel" forces in the land of Mecca and Medina, Islam's two holiest sites, was blasphemous, unacceptable, "not permitted," and he even offered to fight off potential Iraqi invaders with his own small forces.[11] Detractors might argue that the Persian Gulf War and 9/11 were unrelated, that bin Laden was so deranged that he would have become a major terrorist anyway or that the real causes of terrorism have little to do with U.S. foreign policy. Still others might say that the events may be linked, but that if Iraq had not been attacked in 1991 by U.S.-led forces, the threat of terrorism a decade later would have been even more severe, because a strong Saddam could have played a larger role in it.

Conclusions

The extent to which one views U.S. decisions and the subsequent initiation of war to have been successful depends in part on perspective. If one believes that we should measure the success of statecraft in terms of meeting stated objectives, then the U.S.-led operation was largely a success. The coalition met most of its objectives with minimum casualties. If one believes that we should measure success, and can measure success, by looking at longer-term consequences, then the picture of success becomes somewhat murkier. Ultimately, the best question is not whether the operations produced success, but whether the outcome of not having attacked Iraq in 1991 would have been better than going to war. While that question is beyond the scope of this book, one thing is clear: the Persian Gulf War weakened Iraq economically, politically, and militarily — despite all that, the Iraq problem still persisted to the point that another showdown with Saddam was seen as necessary by the administration of President George W. Bush more than a decade later, a showdown I investigate in the next section.

The Iraq War of 2003

In April 2003, dozens of statues of Iraq's ubiquitous dictator came crashing down at the hands of Iraqi civilians and U.S. military forces, forming an indelible image for the ages, unleashing a sense that a new dawn was perhaps at hand for Iraq. Saddam and his sons were either dead, hiding, or on the run. The Baathist regime was history.

The Persian Gulf War of 1991 and the Iraq War of 2003 etched the Persian Gulf region into the American mind with a firebrand, and, in their own strange way, reflected all things American at the outset of the twenty-first century. They were fast for a people that values alacrity, and not too overtly messy and inconvenient for a people that values convenience. And, of course, they were antiseptic to the point of being almost surreal. Both wars reflected American technological prowess in an age of great optimism in machines that few understood but that seemed to make enemies go away. The wars at once celebrated the destructive precision of smart bombs and the humanitarian dimension of their ability to not kill civilians. Americans could thus revel in their virtuous self-image, while also getting the job done.

But just as fast as the euphoria of military victory came, it went away, to be replaced by stark realities. In 1991, Operation Desert Storm was a success, but the patient lived — and proceeded to suppress brutally the Kurdish and Shia uprisings. And in the Iraq War, Washington faces the profound challenges of rebuilding a nation frozen in time by a cold, oppressive regime that had resisted change and hijacked a nation for its own narrow interests.

At the time of this writing, there is no telling how post-Saddam Iraq will unfold. It may take a year, or ten, or even a hundred to really answer that question. Nation-building does not occur overnight, nor does it presage its own direction. Historians may look back at the Iraq War and consider it to be the opening salvo of a "Golden Age of Democratization" in Iraq, or they may see it as a successful military victory that produced no broader changes of this kind. The truth is likely to lie somewhere in between, as it so often does.

But while the future is hard to predict, we can continue to tell the ongoing story of wars in the Middle East. As that story goes, the Persian Gulf War left Saddam in power and able to continue to develop weapons of mass destruction

(WMD) in defiance of U.N. Resolution 687, passed on April 2, 1991, shortly after the war's end. Referred to as the "mother of all resolutions" for its great length, it mandated full disclosure of all of Iraq's ballistic missile stocks and production facilities (over 150 kilometers in range), all nuclear materials, all chemical and biological weapons and facilities, and cooperation in their destruction. Paragraphs 10 through 12, furthermore, required Iraq to "unconditionally undertake not to use, develop, construct, or acquire" WMD. Resolution 687 also forced Iraq to accept the U.N. demarcated border with Kuwait, the inviolability of Kuwaiti territory, and the existence of U.N. peacekeepers on the Iraq-Kuwait border, and intrusive U.N. arms inspections aimed at ridding Iraq of its ability to produce WMD. Iraqi compliance with Resolution 687 was a prerequisite for lifting or reducing sanctions against it.[12]

All in all, seventeen U.N. resolutions, including Resolution 687, would be passed between 1991 and 2002 mandating Iraq's full compliance. In effect, the United States was in conflict with Iraq from the time it drove Iraq's army from Kuwait in 1991 and imposed no-fly zones over two-thirds of Iraq. Throughout the 1990s, it periodically attacked Iraq to punish its defiance of U.N. resolutions, and tried to overthrow the dictator outright using CIA-led operations. By 1998, regime change in Iraq had already become official U.S. policy, well before George W. Bush took office. But it was not until after the September 11, 2001, attacks by the terrorist group Al Qaeda that the Bush administration repeatedly expressed a strong and determined will to remove Saddam from power, by force if necessary, as part of the global war on terrorism and as a way to rid Iraq of WMD. In his State of the Union address on January 29, 2002, President Bush identified Iraq, Iran, and North Korea as forming an "Axis of Evil." In a speech given at the U.S. Military Academy at West Point on June 1, he added that Washington would preempt threats from such rogue regimes and transnational terror groups before they could actually become imminent and massive dangers to the United States. Such statements eventually formed the core of a Bush doctrine of preemption which contrasted with the previous emphasis in American foreign policy on containing threats.[13]

On November 8, 2002, after two months of intense negotiation, all fifteen members of the U.N. Security Council signed Resolution 1441, the seventeenth U.N. resolution against Iraq.[14] It required Baghdad to admit U.N. inspectors from the U.N. Monitoring, Verification, and Inspection Commission (UNMOVIC) and the International Atomic Energy Agency and to comply fully with all U.N. resolutions. In Washington's view, Resolution 1441 also allowed for the use of force against Iraq because it indicated that "serious consequences" would follow if Baghdad failed to cooperate.

It is interesting, then, that as of early June 2003, Saddam's WMD had yet to be found. Two trailers were found that appeared to be equipped to produce WMD, but there was disagreement within the U.S. intelligence community about their exact purpose, and no "smoking gun" weapons were actually found in the trailers. In fact, after weeks of extensive searching, U.S. teams could find no actual WMD. This raised some interesting questions worldwide: did the Bush administration fabricate or exaggerate the WMD threat in order to gain support for a war that it thought was important for non-WMD reasons, such as reshaping the Middle East, liberating the Iraqi people, preempting any future WMD potential in Iraq, or, as the cynical view would have it, enhancing the president's re-election chances? Was the intelligence offered to the president inaccurate or selective? Were WMD simply hard to find in such a large country, offering the prospect that they would be discovered in due time, along with the understanding that perhaps Saddam's generals did not want to use these weapons for fear that they would be prosecuted for doing so, in a war they were sure to lose? Had Saddam or his generals spirited the key weapons out of the country before the war, possibly to use at a later time, to sell to terrorists, or to elude U.N. weapons inspectors?

In compliance with Resolution 1441, on December 7, 2002, Iraq gave the U.N. a report of more than 12,000 pages and several compact discs that purportedly described the country's arms program before and after 1990. In effect, the report asserted that Iraq had no WMD, raising suspicions in Washington and elsewhere in the world that Baghdad was obfuscating its capabilities. Serious doubts arose because Iraq itself had admitted to U.N. weapons inspectors that it had produced such weapons, including 8,500 liters of anthrax and a few tons of the nerve agent VX. U.N. inspectors, world leaders, and especially U.S. officials were thus curious as to what had happened to these weapons. Since Iraq refused to provide an acceptable answer — other than to say that they did not exist — many leaders around the world, not just in the United States, assumed the worst.

Subsequently, Iraq allowed U.N. inspectors to search the country for weapons; they found no "smoking gun" but were not satisfied with Iraq's cooperation. The United States, meanwhile, released intelligence information, including tape-recorded conversations among Iraqis, indicating that Iraq possessed WMD and was trying to hide it from U.N. inspectors. Up until the war, Iraq repeatedly denied that it had WMD, as if the allegation were an outright fabrication by a war-hungry United States. It also treated U.S. accusations of its connection to Al Qaeda as nothing more than a pretext for war.

After weeks of strained negotiations among members of the U.N. Security Council, the United States and Britain moved to present the eighteenth U.N. resolution against Iraq. In contrast to the position of France, Russia, and China, who sought a period of months for continued U.N. inspections, the eighteenth resolution pushed openly for using force should Iraq not immediately comply. After France threatened to veto the resolution, a move that might have received support from Russia and China, and after Washington and London failed to secure the votes of the smaller countries on the Security Council, the two allies decided that Resolution 1441 provided sufficient basis for the use of force, even without the eighteenth resolution.

After providing Saddam, his sons, and key Iraqi leaders with an ultimatum to leave Iraq in forty-eight hours or face war, the United States proceeded to launch Operation Iraqi Freedom. It was supported by British forces and some Australian troops, and was backed by a broader "coalition of the willing," as the United States and Britain referred to it. However, unlike George H.W. Bush, the younger Bush faced harsh criticism that American foreign policy had become unilateral and arrogant, and that he had been much less successful in forming a highly engaged coalition.

On March 19, President Bush announced that the Iraq War had begun, with a precision strike on a bunker suspected of containing Iraq's leadership, a strike that some believed had killed Saddam Hussein and his top aides and could lead to Iraq's quick surrender. After Iraq did not surrender, the United States launched a massive air attack referred to as the "Shock and Awe" campaign, which was followed by a large ground attack mostly launched from Kuwait. Special forces worked within Iraq to undermine Saddam's regime using subversion and psychological operations, and the U.S. Air Force continued to bomb key Iraqi targets as American and British forces proceeded on the ground. At first, they faced unexpected resistance from Saddam's Fedayeen fighters, backed by some elements of Saddam's Republican Guards, in cities such as Basra and Nasiriyah.

Eventually, the Iraqi opposition was suppressed and U.S. forces marched toward Baghdad, in the process destroying Iraq's Republican Guard. The fall of Baghdad came much more quickly than most had expected, ending the main military phase of the war in about three weeks and revealing in stark relief that Saddam's rule was one of horror, gangsterism, and brutality. Iraq's regime appeared to scatter into thin air, but neither Saddam nor his sons were confirmed dead. In the following months, many Iraqi leaders either were killed or surrendered to American forces, and the United States faced the daunting task of rebuilding Iraq, providing internal security against looting and thievery, and laying down the roots of democratic government — tasks that many critics doubted could be accomplished effectively.

The Iraq War and the Integrated Approach

Given that this book has sought to illuminate the Persian Gulf War using the integrated approach, it is tempting here to see how we might begin to do the same with the Iraq War. A sensible place to start is to offer thumbnail sketches from multiple perspectives, each explaining how and why the U.S. made the decision to go to war and why war was not avoided.

Rational Acting

Through the lens of the rational actor model, we would re-create the decisions to attack Iraq as an effort to protect and advance U.S. national interests. On that score, we could say that the United States viewed Iraq as a threat even before September 11. This is because Iraq had not complied fully with U.N. resolutions requiring it to dismantle and forswear WMD. Were Iraq to provide terrorists with biological or chemical weapons, the destruction of September 11 would pale by comparison. If 9/11 taught the U.S. any lessons, it was that terrorists could not be allowed to obtain WMD, because they would surely use them, thus altering the course of U.S. and possibly world history. The United States could not take the chance of letting such a scenario transpire.

Moreover, if Iraq obtained a nuclear weapon, Washington would have a hard time sending U.S. forces to the Persian Gulf to deal with Iraq's growing power. Such troops could, after all, be vaporized if Iraq were to use a nuclear weapon. In addition, all of the Middle East countries, but particularly Saudi Arabia and Kuwait, would be severely intimidated by Iraq. Thus, they would be much less likely to put more oil on the market to stabilize prices, if Iraq took a hawkish position on oil pricing. Iraq's influence over the global economy, which depends on reasonably priced oil, would rise, giving it the potential to cause a global recession and blackmail other nations to its own ends.

Rather than allowing such potential threats to develop, the United States could eliminate Iraq's regime, destroy its potential as a base of operations or support for terrorists, and free Iraqis from tyranny. Democratization in Iraq might spark more regional democratization, based on the notion that Middle Easterners, contrary to the warnings of critics, yearned for inalienable rights just as much as individuals anywhere else.

From the RAM perspective, we would re-create the decision to go to war as resulting from the calculation that the benefits minus the costs of war exceeded those of continued containment. Costly and prolonged containment would not have caused regime change, nor would it have eliminated Iraq's WMD, its connection to terrorism, or its oppression of its own people. War was also preferable to another option: continuing U.N. inspections of Iraq for many months, as France, Russia, Germany, and China wanted. Iraq could hide its weapons from inspectors indefinitely, while providing sporadic cooperation, thus delaying war for months, perhaps years. And U.N. inspections would not achieve regime change, even if Iraq did cooperate fully. Quite the contrary, inspections could lead to greater international legitimacy for the regime, if Iraq indeed were somehow given a clean bill of health. The United States had to take a lead role, and was, in President Bush's words, in a "unique position" to act as a global leader, to lay out a vision, because the "vision thing matters."[15]

As an added benefit, regime change in Iraq would decrease U.S. dependence on Saudi Arabia as a site for military bases. A liberated Iraq would be less threatening, thus making such bases less important, and Washington might have access to military sites in Iraq itself. A U.S. withdrawal from Saudi Arabia — which was in fact announced in late April 2003 — could decrease political internal pressures on the Saudi regime and deprive terrorists of a key reason to focus their hatred on the United States. Meanwhile, if Iraq became more friendly towards Washington than the Baathist regime had been, and began pumping more oil (once its oil infrastructure was rebuilt), U.S. and global dependence on the Saudi ability to pump extra oil in times of crisis or oil shortages might decrease. The overall decrease in U.S. dependence on Saudi Arabia would give it more freedom to pressure the royal family to crack down on potential terrorists and terrorist sympathizers in the kingdom.

A final benefit could arise for Israel. Saddam Hussein had paid Palestinian suicide bombers approximately 10 to 25 thousand dollars each for killing Israelis, and Iraq's WMD programs could have targeted Israel as well. With regime change, America's ally would feel more secure and be more willing to make concessions for peace, and the Arab parties would feel more pressure to do the same, now that a stalwart opponent of the peace process had been removed.

Of course, war carried the unknown costs of American and civilian casualties. However, the U.S. ability to use precision-guided and other weapons had increased so significantly since the 1991 war, and Iraq had become so weakened by wars and sanctions, that quick victory was likely, at a relatively low cost. Even if civilian casualties were high, the fact was that Iraqi civilians, according to the U.N., were dying each year by the thousands under the U.N. economic sanctions, due to the regime's brutality and neglect. Removing Saddam from power would also result in the lifting of U.N. economic sanctions.

War might have been avoided had Iraq fully complied with the U.S. demands, but, at some point, the United States preferred war to compliance, because if Iraq had complied, it could just come back another day to develop WMD, threaten the region, and possibly provide terrorists with the ability to attack the United States. For this reason, Washington's bargaining position with Iraq became quite tough.

Meanwhile, Iraq not only wanted to retain its weapons and its sense of national pride, it also did not trust Washington not to attack, even if it were to comply fully. This is because the United States talked about regime change at least as much as Iraqi compliance. If the regime was the real target, then war was coming anyway, which contributed to Iraq's reluctance to cooperate with U.N. inspectors. It did not want to be the sucker, in the terms of the Prisoner's Dilemma, that cooperated with an agreement to disarm, while the United States proceeded to attack or otherwise seek the regime's removal anyway. The probability of such an outcome made Iraq far less willing to seek a diplomatic outcome. In this sense, the nature of U.S.-Iraqi strategic interaction, as in the Persian Gulf War, contributed to war.

The Cognitive Dimension

While the rational actor model stresses the strategic context and careful decision-making, the cognitive dimension takes us into the minds of decision makers. We might say that President Bush analogized back to the 1991 Persian Gulf War. He had learned from his father's experience that attacking Iraq can succeed quite well, despite the warnings of doomsayers. After all, Iraq's forces were not all that tough. After taking some serious air bombardment in 1991, they folded in a one-hundred-hour ground war. If anything, Iraq was far weaker in conventional military capability in 2003 than in 1991, due to twelve years of American containment and punishing air strikes, as well as U.N. sanctions and global isolation.

What failed to happen in 1991, however, was that Washington did not go far enough in eliminating the regime, and Saddam resurrected himself politically and reasserted his control over Iraq. Moreover, the vengeful dictator proceeded to try to assassinate George H.W. Bush in 1993, which prompted President Clinton to order a cruise-missile attack against his intelligence headquarters in Baghdad. George W. Bush remembered that well. As he pointed out to the press, Saddam was the guy that tried to kill his "daddy." No proud Texan of what was a growing political dynasty was willing to let a no-good dictator with a hearty appetite for nasty weapons take a potshot at his father and get away with it. Analogizing back to the 1991 war taught the lessons that beating Iraq was not difficult and that eliminating Saddam was necessary for ultimate victory, both for country and for family.

From Iraq's side, we might speculate that analogies were also at play. Indeed, Saddam may have believed that if he imposed many casualties on U.S. forces, Washington would retreat as it had in Somalia, Lebanon, or Vietnam, or sue for some type of peace that left Saddam effectively in power — a dictator's main goal. While the 1991 war did not allow for imposing large numbers of casualties, a war in 2003 very well could have, because the possibility of urban warfare, possibly in the heart of Baghdad for many weeks, was high.

Domestic Politics

The rational actor and cognitive models may provide some insights, but they ignore what all politicians think about: the home front and re-election.

Using the domestic politics model, we would thread together an explanation for war which emphasized domestic motives. Attacking Iraq could serve to divert attention from profound economic problems. Indeed, the Wall Street market bubble had burst, leaving Americans with a third of their 401(k) plans. Meanwhile, unemployment had hit nearly six percent, and the gross domestic product was barely inching along — problems that the Bush administration was trying to address with massive tax cuts. The only thing that appeared to be rising significantly was a lack of confidence on the part of consumers, whose spending accounts for two-thirds of the nation's economy. By February 2003, consumer confidence had dropped to a nine-year low.[16] A good war might do wonders in diverting attention from these domestic problems, which could threaten the president's re-election chances.

As conceived herein, painting Iraq as a grand threat and Saddam as evil incarnate in order to lay the groundwork for war, may very well have boxed President

Bush into the path to war. So that when he faced unexpected global opposition, he still felt it necessary to go to war in lieu of pursuing U.N. inspections longer or switching to a containment strategy. Bush's war rhetoric, aimed primarily for domestic consumption, may have also convinced Saddam that he had nothing to lose by being more belligerent because the United States was resolved to attack Iraq and eliminate his regime. As this book suggests, there is evidence to suggest that this was partly at play in influencing Iraq's behavior prior to the 1991 Persian Gulf War, a war that Washington saw as necessary in diminishing Iraq's military threat.

An even more cynical interpretation of the road to war features the notion that the president and vice president had strong contacts in the oil industry. War with Iraq would bring American firms big contracts to rebuild Iraq's oil industry and other basic functions. U.S. firms that were allotted such contracts would be more inclined to fund the administration's re-election campaign and that of other Republicans, and, in any event, such work would decrease the unemployment rate. The large contracts awarded to Vice President Cheney's former company Halliburton during the conflict added fuel to this line of thinking.

Groupthink Dynamics

The theory of groupthink would give us another take altogether. It would suggest that the dynamics in Bush's inner circle did not favor a serious evaluation of different options for dealing with Iraq. Quite the contrary, the group was driven partly by President Bush as a partial group leader who saw Saddam as an evil man atop a horrid regime that had to be removed by force. Other group members, facing stressful conditions and a determined position taken by the president and other key decision makers, were reluctant to voice serious objections to the course toward war, even if they thought that continued containment of Iraq or other options made better sense. Thus, early on, a concurrence-seeking tendency developed in which the road to war was not challenged within the decision-making group. War prevailed as an option because other options were not seriously considered and advanced in the inner circle.

Government Politics

In sharp contrast, the government politics model, in a nutshell, would explain the decision as a function of bargaining among individuals representing different bureaucracies. One possible explanation drawn from this perspective would be that Secretary of Defense Donald Rumsfeld viewed the removal of Saddam, possibly by a war with Iraq, as in line with the imperatives and interests of the Department of Defense (and possibly U.S. interests as well).

Rumsfeld prevailed at committee meetings in pushing this option because he is a good bargainer who understands the channels of power and effectively lobbies for his department and position. Moreover, the military success in removing the Taliban regime and dealing Al Qaeda a major blow in Afghanistan in response to the 9/11 attacks increased the influence of the Department of Defense in the bureaucratic sphere as well as Rumsfeld's influence in Bush's inner circle. His position on Iraq, then, gained greatest currency in an overall approach that was a collage of competing interests.

Comparative Foreign Policy

The thumbnail sketch of each perspective offered above could be developed much further to offer competing, and possibly complementary, insights into the case. Additional perspectives could be added as well if there was evidence to suggest that generating them would be helpful. Using multiple perspectives could offer the basis for a more complete understanding of the decision, even without detailed information about it. However, they become even more useful once more is known about the case and the perspectives can be evaluated against the evidence.

It is, of course, far too early to evaluate the relative merits of the different perspectives, or even to sketch them more fully, but some speculation is worthwhile about decision-making in the two wars. Pending further research, three points at least seem promising to consider at this point. Naturally, myriad others may arise as we learn more about the Iraq War.

Decisions by Analogy

We can speculate fairly that, unlike in the Persian Gulf War, decision-making by analogy was either less important in the Iraq War, or quite different in nature. President George H.W. Bush repeatedly referred to Munich and to World War II, both in private and public discourse. By comparison, George W. Bush scarcely mentioned Munich, perhaps because the Iraq War was one of preemption, thus not fitting the 1930s analogy. After all, Saddam had not invaded another country in the recent past, nor did he threaten to create a domino-like effect of aggression through the region, as some thought he might in 1990. Nor was the Vietnam analogy prominent, though critics of the war did raise the specter of Vietnam.

Perhaps this is because the ghost of Vietnam had already been dealt with in the 1991 war, not to mention in Kosovo and in Afghanistan after the 9/11 attacks.

Of course, we may find that decision makers did draw on other analogies, such as the experience in the 1991 war. But, that would represent a different analogy at work than in the 1991 case, with different lessons.

Government Politics and Groupthink: A Brief Comparison

Disagreements among decision makers about various courses of actions do not, in and of themselves, disconfirm the theory of groupthink. This is because the theory allows for discord outside the group context, even if it is muted within the group itself. However, it appears that greater disagreement existed, even within the group, in the Iraq War case than in the Persian Gulf War.[17] At a minimum, Rumsfeld was more hawkish about going to war against Iraq and eschewing an effort to gain U.N. approval than was Secretary of State Colin Powell. While Secretary of State James Baker and Secretary of Defense Richard Cheney also preferred different routes in the Persian Gulf War, we may find that their level and intensity of disagreement, and the extent to which it permeated their bureaucracies, was much lower than that between Powell and Rumsfeld.

Moreover, we may also find that George W. Bush, unlike his father, was more likely to be swayed by discussions among group members than to shape group consensus, at least on key issues. For instance, George W. Bush asserted that it was his team of advisers who "convinced him" of the sensibility of the war plan, not vice versa.[18] If future work confirms that disagreement did occur among his advisers and that he did less to shape group dynamics than his father, groupthink will prove an unsuitable explanation. That will set up an interesting comparison to the Persian Gulf War case. Why did significant elements of groupthink arise in the Persian Gulf War case, but not in the Iraq War case? In particular, it would be profitable to explore if, in the Iraq War case, the level of camaraderie was lower; if George W. Bush pushed less for his own preferred approach than his father did; and if more attention was paid to evaluating options (norms for methodical procedures).

We may also find that the Iraq War case offers more evidence of bureaucratic politics than the Persian Gulf War case. Disagreements among inner circle members certainly do not confirm that government politics was at play. We would have to know much more about the case. What, for instance, drove the disagreements? Were the motivations bureaucratic or not? Did they occur in a committee setting or outside it? However, the existence of disagreements and, possibly, turf warfare at least creates the potential for bureaucratic politics to have been at play.

Individuals Making History

While these two wars were different in important ways, they were similar in others. Above all, perhaps, President George W. Bush, like his father, played a vital role in defining the road to war. How, when, and to what extent his role was defining, as compared to other influences on foreign policy, will have to await future work. But it certainly seems possible that he fundamentally drove Washington towards war in lieu of continued containment of Iraq. Indeed, the Iraq War was more optional for Washington than was the Persian Gulf War. This is because it was preemptive rather than reactionary. And few would have criticized George W. Bush for continuing a strategy of containing Iraq.

Historians, like many in other disciplines, have struggled to understand the causal role of the individual versus non-individual forces. They have preferred in recent times to downplay the individual and play up systemic and deterministic forces, as well as such things as culture, geography, and even technology. However, the roles of George H.W. Bush and George W. Bush seem to support the "Great Man" theory of history. Contrary to its name, this theory or notion ascribes neither greatness nor heroism nor rightness to the individual. Rather, it posits that few individuals — in some cases, one individual — can be causally crucial.[19] By emphasizing free will, the hero-in-history theory downplays factors that limit or eliminate the ability of individuals to take bold, defining action.

While this book supports this "Great Man" notion, its use of multiple perspectives also suggests that it is too simplistic. It attributes variation in history chiefly to one source — the individual — and downgrades the importance of other factors. That is a problem because none of us can escape life's arrows; the day's challenge; the unpredictable combination of forces that can conspire to slow us down. It is within these limits, some laid out by the multiple perspectives, that individuals make their mark — or are marked. But, that said, the role of the two presidents in these two wars should give any determinist some pause. While a number of factors shape the behavior of individuals, they also differ quite significantly in how they respond to these factors, thus making it vital to understand those factors, the uniqueness of the individual, and the interaction between the two.

Into the Future

The Iraq War was over in a flash, and with it passed a seemingly interminable era, the Saddam era, an era of tyranny for Iraqis and terror for Iraq's immediate neighbors, an era whose end would have seemed like an unlikely fiction to many in the Middle East and around the world just months before. Of course, history is littered with fallen dictators and emperors, but rarely does it treat us to a ringside seat for the precipitous fall of a tyrant whom so many saw as a permanent fixture in the Middle East landscape.

And yet, so much remains unanswered. Will Iraqis forge a democracy? Can Washington maintain its commitment to Iraq's democratic experiment? Will democracy spread in the Middle East? Should the United States actively seek to remake the Middle East? Will Iraq split apart over time? Will a Shia-led clerical government take hold in Iraq, or parts of it? Will Iran co-opt Iraq's Shias or gain influence over Iraq? Will Kurdish factions try to be part of a federated Iraq or eventually seek their own state — and can Washington allow that outcome? Can remnants of Saddam's regime reassert control in parts of Iraq in the coming years, thus forcing the United States to revisit Iraq militarily? Will transnational terrorists, working either with or apart from remnants of Saddam's defunct regime, strike at the United States, thus raising the possibility that the Iraq War provoked them, or will they be weakened by the war?

As these questions suggest, Saddam's precipitous end is not the end of the Persian Gulf story. It is a story in which the United States has become increasingly important, a story that is likely to continue to define important contours of the Middle East well into the twenty-first century, a story that inevitably will offer us a plethora of future foreign policy cases to explore as it continues to be cast in history's crucible.

Appendix: Core Interviews

James Baker, Secretary of State. Washington, D.C. 4 June 1996.

Abdullah Bishara, former Secretary General, Gulf Cooperation Council. Kuwait City, Kuwait. 6 August 1998.

Sandra Charles, Deputy National Security Advisor. Washington, D.C. 5 June 1996.

Richard Cheney, Secretary of Defense. For background purposes only, not for citation.

Lawrence Eagleburger, Deputy Secretary of State. Phone interview. 23 July 1996.

Marlin Fitzwater, White House Press Secretary. Phone interview. 21 June and 12 July 1999.

Chas W. Freeman Jr., U.S. Ambassador to Saudi Arabia. Washington, D.C. 26 June 1996, 19 February 1999.

Robert Gates, Deputy National Security Advisor. Phone interview. 24 June 1999.

Richard Haass, Special Assistant to the President for Near East and South Asian Affairs. Washington, D.C. 26 June 1996, 19 February 1999.

David Jeremiah, Vice Chairman, Joint Chiefs of Staff. Rockville, Maryland. 26 June 1996.

Kenneth Juster, Under Secretary for Commerce. Phone interview. 29 July 1999.

Bobbie Kilberg, Deputy Assistant to the President for Public Liaison. Phone interview. 1 October 1999.

Robert Kimmitt, Under Secretary of State for Political Affairs. Phone interview. 25 January 2002.

Robert Pelletreau, State Department official. Washington, D.C. 6 March 2001.

Thomas Pickering, U.S. Ambassador to the United Nations. Washington, D.C. 2 March 2001.

Colin Powell, Chairman, Joint Chiefs of Staff. Alexandria, Virginia. 30 May 1996.

Mohammad al-Rumaihi, Political analyst, (Kuwait). Kuwait City, Kuwait. 6 August 1999.

Mohammad al-Sabah, Kuwaiti Ambassador to the United States. Washington D.C. 27 June 1996, 17 September 1999.

Brent Scowcroft, National Security Advisor. Washington D.C. 26 June 1996, 18 February 1999.

Prince Bandar bin Sultan, Saudi Ambassador to the United States. Washington, D.C. 12 October 1997.

John Sununu, White House Chief-of-Staff. Phone interview. 11 August 1999.

William Webster, Director of Central Intelligence. Washington D.C. 1 October 1999.

Some interviewees requested to remain off the record altogether.

Notes

Introduction

1. On Saddam's background, see al-Khalil, *The Republic of Fear* and Miller and Mylroie, *Saddam Hussein and the Crisis in the Gulf*.

2. Author interview with Baker.

3. The Defense Department did not view Executive Order 12333 as prohibiting Saddam's assassination, as he was central to Iraq's military machine. Memorandum from J. H. Binford Peay III, Lieutenant General (Colin Powell Papers).

4. Author interview with Bishara.

5. Allison and Zelikow, *Essence of Decision*, 13, 15–17. See also Byman and Pollack, "Let Us Now Praise Great Men," esp. 107–14.

6. The observation that this is how we tend to view decision-making was advanced famously by Graham Allison in the original edition of *Essence of Decision* and then more recently in the updated edition. See Allison and Zelikow, *Essence of Decision*, 13, 15–17. On perceptions of rationality in Western civilization, see Hybel, *Power Over Rationality*, 2–4, chap. 2.

7. Allison offered one of the first challenges to the RAM on the basis of domestic political processes. On the revision of this work, see Allison and Zelikow, *Essence of Decision*.

8. The term "perspective" downplays pretension to theory insofar as it does not necessarily connote the ability to generate or falsify predictions, while not precluding the potential for doing so.

9. Brecher, "International Studies in the Twentieth Century and Beyond," 232–33.

10. Bennett and Stam, "A Universal Test of an Expected Utility Theory of War," 453–54.

11. For instance, see Hart et al., *Beyond Groupthink*, 25–26; Bernstein, "Understanding Decisionmaking," 141, 145, 148; Welch, "The Organizational Process," 114; Paulus, "Developing Consensus about Groupthink," 370–71; and Fuller and Adlag, "Organizational Tonypandy," 163–84.

12. Hudson, "Foreign Policy Analysis," 229.

13. Brecher, "International Studies in the Twentieth Century and Beyond," 229.

14. On the value of doing so, see Patomaki and Wight, "After Postpositivism?" 232–33.

15. Drezner, "Ideas, Bureaucratic Politics, and the Crafting of Foreign Policy," 733–49.

16. Fearon, "Domestic Politics," 289–313; Elman, "Horses For Courses."

17. For a good discussion, see Allison and Zelikow, *Essence of Decision*.

18. Colin Powell described Bush's statement that the invasion would not stand as *ad hoc*. *Frontline* interview with Brent Scowcroft; author interview with Scowcroft.

19. Schafer and Crichlow, "The Process-Outcome Connection," 45.

20. *Frontline* interview with Mikhail Gorbachev.

21. Ibid.

22. Byman and Pollack, "Let Us Now Praise Great Men," 108–9.

23. For a good discussion, see Berlin, *The Hedgehog and the Fox*.

24. For an excellent review of these areas, see Hudson, "Foreign Policy Analysis" and Fearon, "Domestic Politics," 307.

25. Waltz, *Theory of International Politics*.

26. Neorealism is not intended by Waltz to be a theory of foreign policy, although some scholars believe that it can be viewed as one. See Elman, "Horses For Courses," 10–11. For Waltz's rebuttal of Elman, see Waltz, "International Politics Is Not Foreign Policy," 54–57.

27. Waltz, *Theory of International Politics*, esp. 93–97.

28. Bueno de Mesquita and Lalman, *War and Reason*.

29. Milner, "Rationalizing Politics," 766–68.

30. Moravcsik, "Taking Preferences Seriously."

31. Schafer and Crichlow, "The Process-Outcome Connection," 46.

32. Milner, "Rationalizing Politics," 759. See also Moravcsik, "Taking Preferences Seriously," esp. 516.

33. For instance, see Fearon, "Domestic Politics"; Putnam, "Diplomacy and Domestic Politics," 430–60; Garrett, "Global Markets and National Politics," 787–824; and Snyder, *Myths of Empire*.

34. This paragraph is based on the author's interviews with Scowcroft and Sununu.

35. Author interview with Fitzwater.

36. For a brief analysis of the literature on crises, see Haney, *Organizing for Foreign Policy Crises*, chap. 1., esp. 9–10.

37. Gordon and Trainor, *The General's War*; Woodward, *The Commanders*.

38. Allison and Zelikow, *Essence of Decision*.

39. In any case, they treat groupthink as part of the broader family of models into which the government politics model falls. I treat them as different perspectives altogether.

CHAPTER ONE: The United States, Iraq, and the Crisis

1. Walter Pincus, "Secret Presidential Pledges Over Years Erected U.S. Shield for Saudis," *Washington Post*, 9 February 1992, A20.

2. On the Nixon and Carter doctrines, see Palmer, *Guardians of the Gulf*, 85–111.

3. In Ronald Reagan, *Public Papers of the Presidents of the United States* (*PPP*) (Washington, D.C.: GPO, 1981), 873; clarification of this statement, 952.

4. For a detailed analysis, see Karsh and Rautsi, *Saddam Hussein*, chap. 6. On the broader origins and development of the crisis, see Dannreuther, *The Gulf Conflict* and al-Khalidi, "The Gulf Crisis." For the most developed Saudi perspective, see Sultan, *Desert Warrior*, esp. 19, 189.

5. *Cairo MENA*, in Foreign Broadcast Information Service (FBIS): Near East and South Asia (NESA), 13 August 1990, 5.

6. In a letter to Iran's President Hashemi Rafsanjani on August 15, Saddam even called

on Iran to help Iraq confront the "evil doers who seek to inflict evil on Muslims and the Arab nation." Baghdad, Republic of Iraq Radio, 15 August 1990 in BBC Summary of World Broadcasts (16 August 1990).

7. For an excellent background analysis, see Schofield, *Kuwait and Iraq*.

8. On Iraq's view, see the Aziz statement in *Baghdad AL-THAWRAH*, FBIS: NESA, 12 September 1990, 26–32.

9. Quoted in Bengio, *Saddam's Word*, 37.

10. Quoted in ibid., 155.

11. Iraq recognized that Kuwait did change its position but said that Kuwait's behavior suggested it was a ploy. See interview with Iraqi First Deputy Prime Minister Taha Yasin Ramadan, in *London AL-TADAMUN*, FBIS: NESA, 30 October 1990, 24; speech by Saddam Hussein to the Arab Summit Conference in Baghdad, in FBIS: NESA, 29 May 1990, 5.

12. On Iraq's view, see the Aziz statement in *Baghdad AL-THAWRAH*, FBIS: NESA, 12 September 1990, 30–31.

13. Quoted in "Saddam Says He Won The War," in *APS Diplomat Recorder* 54 (20 January 2001).

14. BBC Special Report, "The Gulf War," 16 January 1991.

15. For the text of the transcript of the Glaspie meeting, see "Excerpts from Iraqi Document on Meeting with U.S. Envoy," *New York Times*, 23 September 1990, A19.

16. On Saddam's perceptions of the situation, see Baram, "The Iraqi Invasion of Kuwait," 21–25.

17. For an in-depth analysis, see ibid.

18. *Frontline* interview with Richard Haass. See also *Iraqgate*. For a more extensive analysis on this period, see Karabell, "Backfire," esp. 32–38.

19. See Saddam Hussein's speech to the Arab Cooperation Council, in FBIS: NESA, 27 February 1990; Aziz statement in *Baghdad AL-THAWRAH*, FBIS: NESA, 12 September 1990, 30; Telhami, "Middle East Politics in the Post Cold War Era"; "Excerpts from Iraqi Document on Meeting with U.S. Envoy." On Saddam's concerns about U.S. hegemony, see text of interview with Saddam, *Mexico City XEW Television Network*, FBIS: NESA, 26 December 1990, 20.

20. This is made clear in critical staff reports, *Chemical Weapons* and *Kurdistan* (to the US Senate. Committee on Foreign Relations).

21. Cited in Sifry and Cerf, *The Gulf War Reader*, 102.

22. Ibid.

23. See Speech by Saddam Hussein to the Arab Summit Conference in Baghdad, in FBIS: NESA, 29 May 1990, 5.

24. Aziz recounting Saddam's 16 July 1990 speech, in *Baghdad AL-THAWRAH*, FBIS: NESA, 12 September 1990, 30.

25. *Frontline* interview with General Powell.

26. *Frontline* interview with Robert Gates.

27. *Frontline* interview with James Baker.

28. Gordon and Trainor, *The General's War*, 11–13.

29. Ibid.

30. Author interview with off-the-record source.

31. For a brief recapitulation of this approach, see Karabell, "Backfire," esp. 31–33.

32. Author interview with Charles.

33. Author interview with Juster.

34. Kelly, *U.S. Relations with Iraq.*

35. Tetlock and Belkin, *Counterfactual Thought Experiments In World Politics,* 15.

36. One sophisticated model settled on precisely this outcome. On Kugler's model, see Mintz, "The Decision to Attack Iraq," 604–5.

37. Author interviews with Bishara and al-Rumaihi. See Speech by Boutros-Ghali, Egypt's Minister of State for Foreign Affairs, at the U.N. General Assembly, 4 October 1990. See also Heikal, *Illusions of Triumph,* 330. On the "historical Arab propensity," see Bush and Scowcroft, *A World Transformed,* 321.

38. *Frontline* interview with Colin Powell.

39. Author interviews with Scowcroft and Haass.

40. On public support for the war, see Kelman, "The Reaction of Mass Publics to the Gulf War," 253–54.

41. On these polls and the general mood, see Ann Devroy and Dan Balz, "Bush Says Time Is Limited For Peaceful Gulf Solution," *Washington Post,* 16 November 1990, A1, A24.

42. Quoted in *The Road to War.*

43. "Letter from Wellstone to Bush."

44. "Memo from Fred McClure to Assistant Secretaries for Legislative Affairs."

45. Author interviews with Sununu and Gates.

46. Persian Gulf Working Group (GBPL).

47. Ann Devroy, "President on Inexorable Course," *Washington Post,* 24 February 1991, A1.

48. Quoted in David Hoffman, "Gulf Crisis Tests Baker as Diplomat, Politician," *New York Times,* 2 November 1990, A16.

CHAPTER TWO: The Rational Actor Model

1. As Mary Zey observes, it is called "public choice" by political scientists, "neoclassicism" or "rational choice theory" by economists, "expected utility" by psychologists, and "rational choice theory" by sociologists. Zey, *Rational Choice Theory,* 1.

2. Bendor and Hammond, "Rethinking Allison's Models," 306.

3. Waltz, *Theory of International Politics.*

4. See Bendor and Hammond, "Rethinking Allison's Models," 305–9.

5. If the person is indifferent about A/B and B/C, then the person is also indifferent about A/C. The preferences, we should add, are also consistent in that if A is preferred to B, then B cannot be preferred to A.

6. For a discussion of this topic, see Grafstein, *Choice-Free Rationality.* Noncooperative game theory predicts that the outcome of strategic interaction will be a Nash equilibrium, wherein both actors feel that they are doing as well as they can do, given the choices of the other actor.

7. On the importance of considering incomplete information and uncertainty, see Bendor and Hammond, "Rethinking Allison's Models," esp. 303, 306.

8. At the same time, the version of rationality that I use is more stringent than the model of bounded rationality developed by Herbert Simon, which accounts for myriad inescapable limitations on decision-making, ranging from cognitive variables to values and beliefs. See Simon, *Models of Bounded Rationality.* For a brief analysis, see Allison and Zelikow, *Essence of Decision,* 19–21.

9. On these other dimensions, see Bendor and Hammond, "Rethinking Allison's Models"; Farkas, "Evolutionary Models in Foreign Policy Analysis," 343–61; and Kahler, "Rationality in International Relations."

10. Mintz and Geva, "The Poliheuristic Theory of Foreign Policy Decisionmaking," 84–85.

11. See, for example, Harold Brown, "Protecting U.S. Interests in the Persian Gulf Region," *Department of State Bulletin* (DSB) 80 (May 1980): 63; DSB 81 (June 1981): 43; DSB 85 (May 1985): 25; DSB 87 (July 1987): 64. See also U.S. Senate, General H. Norman Schwarzkopf.

12. See Karsh and Rautsi, *Saddam Hussein*, 57–109; al-Khalil, *The Republic of Fear*; and Miller and Mylroie, *Saddam Hussein and the Crisis in the Gulf.*

13. Sultan, *Desert Warrior*, esp. 19.

14. See Hiro, *Desert Shield to Desert Storm*, 114–15 and *Baghdad INA*, in FBIS: NESA, 12 September 1990, 32.

15. Sultan, *Desert Warrior*, esp. 19, 189.

16. Author interview with Bishara.

17. Fahd Speech on the Gulf Crisis, broadcast on 9 August 1990, *The Middle East*, 371–72. Also, see Brian Lamb interview with General Schwarzkopf (C-SPAN 2, *Book TV*, 1 October 1990) who interacted closely with the Saudis in theater.

18. Author interview with Webster.

19. Author interview with Powell.

20. Author interview with Bandar.

21. "Casting their lot": Scowcroft interview in *The Road to War*. "Stay the course": *The Road to War*.

22. In fact, he had conferred with elders in various tribes and they decided in the first two days to hold off on inviting U.S. forces in, although the younger leaders (twenties to forties) did want Fahd to do so. Heikal, *Illusions of Triumph*.

23. Bush and Scowcroft, *A World Transformed*, 328–29.

24. Author interview with off-the-record source.

25. Author interview with Jeremiah.

26. Author interview with Freeman.

27. Fahd was also aware of Saddam's Machiavellian nature. After all, he suggested to Fahd twice in the 1980s that they divide the small Arab Gulf states between them. See *The Road to War*.

28. Author interview with Freeman.

29. Bush interview with Sir David Frost, PBS, 16 January 1996.

30. Author interview with Fitzwater.

31. "Press Conference by the President."

32. "Letter from Bush to Foley," 9 August 1990.

33. Goldberg, "Saudi Arabia," 127–28.

34. Address to the Nation.

35. Excerpts From President's News Conference on Gulf Crisis, *New York Times*, 31 August 1990, A11. "Our Troops are giving Bush all his options," *USA Today*, 18 December 1990. Baker interview in ABC News, "This Week With David Brinkley," 12 August 1990.

36. Author interview with Scowcroft. *Frontline* interview with Scowcroft. Statement by the Honorable Richard Cheney (GBPL).

37. *Frontline* interview with James Baker.

38. "Statement by Secretary of State James A. Baker, III To The U.N. Security Council."

39. Author interview with Scowcroft. For a discussion of the key elements of the new world order, see Miller and Yetiv, "The New World Order in Theory and Practice."

40. Interview with a Russian diplomat (Washington, D.C.: 6 March 2001).

41. Author interview with Pickering.

42. Bush, *PPP,* 1990, 1030.

43. Ibid., 307.

44. Baker, *The Politics Of Diplomacy,* 71–72, 151–56.

45. Bush and Scowcroft, *A World Transformed,* 363.

46. Presidential Address to Congress, "Gulf Crisis an Opportunity For a'New World Order,' " *Congressional Quarterly,* 15 September 1990, 2953.

47. Author interview with Eagleburger. On Bush's use of the "new world order" trope throughout the crisis, see Tucker and Hendrickson, *The Imperial Temptation,* chap. 2.

48. Author interview with Sununu.

49. This prospect disturbed Bush and Scowcroft. Author interview with Scowcroft.

50. On their different approaches, see Lesch, "Contrasting Reactions to the Persian Gulf Crisis."

51. The Saudi-led GCC was formed in May of 1981 and is composed of Saudi Arabia, Kuwait, Oman, Bahrain, Qatar, and the United Arab Emirates.

52. The text of this resolution appears in FBIS: NESA, 13 August 1990, 1–2.

53. Saddam's proposal appears in *Baghdad Radio,* in FBIS: NESA, 13 August 1990, 48.

54. Ibid.

55. Hiro, *Desert Shield to Desert Storm,* 180–83. See also Ali Khamenei speech in *Tehran Domestic Service,* FBIS: NESA, 10 January 1991, 53. Senior official Mohammad Javad Larijani quoted in *Tehran IRNA,* FBIS: NESA, 26 December 1990, 39.

56. See text of the Rafsanjani interview and a speech, in *Tehran International Service,* FBIS: NESA, 15 October 1990, 63. See also *Paris AFP* in FBIS: NESA, 17 September 1990, 56.

57. "Rafsanjani waits for dust to settle," *Middle East Economic Digest* (8 March 1991), 21–22; "Rafsanjani makes bid for diplomatic solution," *Middle East Economic Digest* (15 February 1991), 12–13.

58. Tehran, Voice of the Islamic Republic of Iran, 24 August 1990 in BBC Summary of World Broadcasts/Middle East (27 August 1990). See statement by Iranian Foreign Minister Velayati, *Tehran Domestic Service,* in FBIS: NESA, 20 September 1990, 46. See also Khamenei speech, referred to in the cited text as the leader of the Islamic revolution, in *Tehran Domestic Service,* FBIS: NESA, 10 January 1991, 53.

59. On Jordan's approach, see the account of the Minister of Foreign Affairs (appointed in September 1990) in Jaber, "Jordan and the Gulf War."

60. On the Saudi view of his position, see "Excerpts From King Fahd's Speech to Saudis," *New York Times,* 10 August 1990, A10.

61. On this view, see press conference in FBIS: NESA, 20 August 1990, 33.

62. Author interview with Baker.

63. Ibid.

64. For an account from Moscow's perspective, see Palaczenko, *My Years With Gorbachev and Shevardnadze,* 230–34. When Yemen voted on November 29 against the U.N. resolution allowing the coalition to use force against Iraq, the United States promptly cut its aid the next day — a threat that Baker had made on a recent trip to Yemen. See *The Road to War.*

65. This paragraph is based on the author's interview with Baker.

66. Author interview with Baker.

67. On the Saudi role, see Sultan, *Desert Warrior*, chap. 14.

68. On Syrian motivations, see Lesch, "Contrasting Reactions To The Persian Gulf Crisis," 41–43.

69. See Speech by Boutros-Ghali, Egypt's Minister of State for Foreign Affairs, at the U.N. General Assembly, 4 October 1990.

70. "Excerpts From the TV Talk By Mubarak to the Egyptians," *New York Times*, 9 August 1990, A18.

71. See President Mubarak's press conference on Cairo radio in FBIS: NESA, 8 August 1990.

72. Author interview with Scowcroft.

73. US Department of State Dispatch, "Operation Desert Storm Launched," 21 January 1991, 37.

74. Author interview with Scowcroft.

75. See Bush letter to the Emir of Kuwait (GBPL).

76. Author interview with Bishara.

77. Author interview with Scowcroft; Sultan, *Desert Warrior*, esp. 19, 189; author interview with Sununu.

78. For an excellent analysis of Saddam's speeches and his manipulation of Islam, see Bengio, *Saddam's Word*, 155.

79. Ibid., 187.

80. See *Baghdad INA* in FBIS: NESA, 20 September 1990, 21.

81. For example, see statements by Israeli Defense Minister Arens and Ambassador to the U.S., Zalman Shoval, *Jerusalem Post*, 30 December 1990. See also Peled, "The Gulf Crisis." The United States spent significant time ensuring that Israel would stay out of the conflict. Numerous interviews with U.S. officials.

82. On the failure of the Israeli card, see Freedman and Karsh, *The Gulf Conflict*, chap. 24.

83. Author interview with Pelletreau.

84. Bush and Scowcroft, *A World Transformed*, 385–86.

85. "Interview with Yevgenni Primakov," in FBIS: NESA-91-021, 11.

86. Thatcher, *The Path to Power*, 499.

87. Webster document (GBPL).

88. George Bush, interview with Sir David Frost, PBS, 16 January 1996.

89. Author interview with Haass.

90. In fact, this links the game-theoretic dimension of expectations of the behavior of others and the decision-theoretic aspect of expected utility.

91. Based on a review of these documents at the GBPL.

92. Michael R. Gordon, "C.I.A. Fears Iraq Could Deploy Biological Arms by Early 1991," *New York Times*, 29 September 1990.

93. Author interview with Jeremiah.

94. Text of Bush's Radio Address (GBPL).

95. Author interview with Freeman.

96. Author interview with Scowcroft. See also Bush and Scowcroft, *A World Transformed*, 406.

97. ABC News interview with Iraq's Ambassador to the U.N., "This Week With David Brinkley," 12 August 1990.

98. Author interview with Jeremiah.

99. Author interviews with Gates, Haass, and Scowcroft. Webster, as well as other officials such as the (at the time) more dovish Baker, tended to dismiss the usefulness of sanctions in congressional testimony in December. Baker memo on his testimony to President Bush; Memo from Baker to Bush (GBPL).

100. Author interview with Webster.

101. Letter from Webster to Les Aspin (GBPL).

102. Letter from Bush to House Speaker, Tom Foley (GBPL).

103. Sultan, *Desert Warrior,* 187–88.

104. Quoted in Dan Balz, "Letter Requests Endorsement of U.N. Deadline," *Washington Post,* 9 January 1991, A16.

105. *Frontline* interview with James Baker.

106. Ibid.

107. Presidential Statement with noted memo revisions (GBPL).

108. Kelly, quoted in *The Road to War.*

109. Bush and Scowcroft, *A World Transformed,* 337.

110. *New York Times,* 28 March 1991.

111. Author's multiple interviews.

112. "Address to the Nation Announcing Allied Military Action in the Persian Gulf," 16 January 1991, 43.

113. Bush and Scowcroft, *A World Transformed,* 353; memo from Bush to Fitzwater (GBPL).

114. Author interviews with Scowcroft, Haass, and one off-the-record source. Bush and Scowcroft, *A World Transformed,* 416.

115. See FBIS: USSR, 23 August 1990, 18–19.

116. On the increased tendency of democracies to anticipate military success in comparison to non-democracies, see Clark and Reed, "A Unified Model of War Onset and Outcome."

117. On how such a condition makes war more likely, see Bueno de Mesquita, *The War Trap.*

118. "Speech to the Islamic Conference," FBIS: NESA, 91–009, 20–24.

119. Fearon, "Rationalist Explanations for War," 380.

120. Ibid., 390.

121. Many scholars have discussed bargaining problems of this kind, but John F. Nash is original in this regard. See Nash, "The Bargaining Problem," 155–62.

122. We can represent this range by an interval, and we can model mathematically how various phenomena can narrow it. See Fearon, "Rationalist Explanations for War," esp. 403.

123. On the theoretical tendency for rational states to fight rather than negotiate, see ibid.

124. Fearon, "Bargaining, Enforcement, and International Cooperation," 269–305.

125. On bargaining, PD, and game theory, see Camerer, *Behavioral Game Theory.*

CHAPTER THREE: A Cognitive Compass

1. See introduction, note 18.

2. Author interview with Scowcroft.

3. Prospect theory, not covered in this book, also differs from the RAM. At its core, it combines an understanding of cognitive biases with how decision makers view the international situation they face, in order to explain and predict how they will make decisions. See McDermott and Kugler, "Comparing Rational Choice and Prospect Theory Analyses," 49–85.

4. For a good, brief discussion of the cognitive approach, see Hybel, *Power Over Rationality*, 19–25. See also Herrmann et al., "Images in International Relations," 403–33.

5. Khong, *Analogies at War*, 14, 25.

6. Mintz, "Foreign Policy Decisionmaking," 2.

7. Ibid., 3.

8. Khong, *Analogies At War*, 9.

9. Ibid., 25.

10. See George, *Presidential Decisionmaking*; Jervis, *Perception and Misperception*; May, *Lessons of the Past*; Neustadt and May, *Thinking in time*; and Khong, *Analogies at War*, esp. 252.

11. Jervis, *Perception and Misperception*, 237.

12. Nisbett and Ross, *Human Inference*, 17–42.

13. For an excellent analysis of this point, see Sylvan and Voss, eds., *Problem Representation in Foreign Policy Decision Making*.

14. Khong, *Analogies at War*, 7.

15. Mintz, "Foreign Policy Decisionmaking," 84–85. See also Lake and Powell, eds., *Strategic Choice*, 30.

16. A goal upon which there was consensus in the Lake and Powell volume mentioned in note 15.

17. Kahler, "Rationality in International Relations," 919–941.

18. I thank Phil Tetlock for these insights (author's correspondence, 17 July 2001).

19. On that debate, see Green and Shapiro, *Pathologies of Rational Choice Theory* and Levy, "Prospect Theory and the Cognitive-Rational Debate," 41–47.

20. Bernstein, "Understanding Decisionmaking," 152.

21. Quoted in Kahler, "Rationality in International Relations," 927. Bayes's rule provides a game-theoretical approach that accounts for learning, according to which probabilities are changed on the observation of conditional events.

22. See Khong, *Analogies at War*, 10. For conditions under which cognitive factors such as historical analogies are likely to be influential in decision-making, see George, *Presidential Decisionmaking*, chaps. 2 & 3. Also, Neustadt and May, *Thinking in Time*.

23. On the literature about the undermining of rational processes, see Wallace et al., "Political Rhetoric of Leaders Under Stress in the Gulf Crisis," 95–96. On the impact of stress, see Janis and Mann, *Decision Making*. For a good, brief analysis of the power of analogies, see Hybel, *Power Over Rationality*, 5, 19–25. On how analogies are used and misused, see Vertzberger, *The World in Their Minds*, esp. chap. 6; and Jervis, *Perception and Misperception*, esp. 220, 237.

24. On these skeptics, see Khong, *Analogies At War*, chap. 1, esp. 15–16.

25. Quoted in Neustadt and May, *Thinking in time*, 36, 37–43.

26. Hirschbein, *What if They Gave a Crisis and Nobody Came?* 11.

27. Quoted in Jervis, *Perception and Misperception*, 223.

28. Ibid., 219.

29. Author interview with Fitzwater.

30. Original letter. Bush Presidential Museum (Texas A&M University, College Station, Texas).

31. *Frontline* interview with Richard Cheney.

32. Author interview with Webster.

33. Author interview with Sununu.

34. "The Burden of Decision," *Newsweek*, 29 October 1990, 32.

35. Jervis, *Perception and Misperception*, 253, 266.

36. Author interview with Freeman.

37. Author interview with Gates.

38. Bush and Scowcroft, *A World Transformed*, 340.

39. Hirschbein, *What if They Gave a Crisis and Nobody Came?* 18.

40. Bush and Scowcroft, *A World Transformed*, 320.

41. Goldberg, "Saudi Arabia," 117–18.

42. See speech by Fahd, Saudi TV, 5 March 1991, in FBIS: NESA, 6 March 1991.

43. *Frontline* interview with Margaret Thatcher.

44. Bush interview with Bernard Shaw, CNN, 2 March 1996; Thatcher, *Downing Street Years*, 818.

45. Thatcher, *Downing Street Years*, 818; interview with Charles Powell, *The Road to War*.

46. Bush and Scowcroft, *A World Transformed*, 318–19.

47. Ibid., 326.

48. Hirschbein, *What if They Gave a Crisis and Nobody Came?* 17.

49. Remarks for the Republican National Committee (GBPL).

50. This paragraph is based on Hiro, *Desert Shield to Desert Storm*, 118.

51. Glad, "Figuring Out Saddam Hussein," 66.

52. On this proposal, see *Baghdad Domestic Service* in FBIS: NESA, 13 August 1990, 48.

53. Text of Saddam Husayn's Reply to Soviet Leader, 20 January 1991 in Bengio, *Saddam Speaks*, 173.

54. Hiro, *Desert Shield to Desert Storm*, 146.

55. Bush and Scowcroft, *A World Transformed*, 348.

56. See the account of Jordan's Minister of Foreign Affairs (appointed in September 1990). Jaber, "Jordan and the Gulf War." For the letter, see interview with King Hussein, "The Great Survivor," *Time* (22 July 1991), 14.

57. See "Transcript of News Session by Bush and 2 Officials on Mideast," *New York Times*, 23 August 1990, A17.

58. "Excerpts From'Open Letter' To Bush by President of Iraq," *New York Times*, 17 August 1990, A11.

59. See, for instance, *Baghdad INA*, in FBIS: NESA, 17 September 1990, 24–25.

60. Excerpts From President's News Conference on Gulf Crisis, *New York Times*, 31 August 1990, A11.

61. Bush and Scowcroft, *A World Transformed*, 358.

62. Ibid., 365.

63. Ibid., 366.

64. "Interview with Yevgenni Primakov," in FBIS: NESA-91–021, 11.

65. For one instance, see Palazchenko, *My Years With Gorbachev and Shevardnadze*, 230.

66. Ibid., 215.

67. See Aziz interview in *London Al-Tadamun*, FBIS: NESA, 26 September 1990, esp. 32.

68. Judith Miller, "Iraq's Seesaw Diplomacy: Threats and Entreaties," *New York Times,* 17 October 1990, A12.

69. Text of Aziz comments, in *Baghdad INA,* FBIS: NESA, 30 October 1990, 20; Ramadan interview, *London AL-TADAMUN,* FBIS: NESA, 30 October 1990, 23.

70. See text of statement by Taha Yasin Ramadan, high-level member of Iraq's Revolutionary Command Council, who reflected Iraq's views, in *Baghdad INA* in FBIS: NESA, 11 October 1990, 28–29.

71. See Aziz interview in *London Al-Tadamun,* FBIS: NESA, 26 September 1990, 29–32.

72. Letter from Bush to King Hussein in Bush, *All the Best, George Bush,* 484.

73. Quoted in Freedman and Karsh, *The Gulf Conflict,* 217.

74. Author interview with Scowcroft; Quayle, *Standing Firm,* 219.

75. Author interview with Scowcroft; letter from Bush to the Emir of Kuwait (GBPL).

76. Remarks at a Republican Fundraising Breakfast in Burlington, Vermont, 23 October 1990 in Bush, *PPP,* 1990, 1443.

77. Author interviews with off-the-record sources.

78. On Primakov's trip, see Freedman, "Moscow And The Iraqi Invasion Of Kuwait," 90–91.

79. See Palazchenko, *My Years with Gorbachev and Shevardnadze,* 219–23.

80. *The Road to War.*

81. Ibid.; Bush and Scowcroft, *A World Transformed,* 377–78.

82. Author interview with high-level Arab official who wished to remain anonymous. See also Youssef M. Ibrahim, "Saudis' Quandary," *New York Times,* 24 October 1990, A10.

83. Quoted in Heikal, *Illusions of Triumph,* 330.

84. Author interviews with Bishara, al-Rumaihi, and Al Sabah.

85. Quoted in *Washington Post,* 2 December 1990, A33.

86. Cited in Hiro, *Desert Shield to Desert Storm,* 231.

87. Freedman and Karsh, *The Gulf Conflict,* 246.

88. Quoted in Rowland Evans and Robert Novak, "St. George and His Dragon," *Washington Post,* 17 December 1990, A11.

89. Text of interview in *Ankara Anatolia* in FBIS: NESA, 21 September 1990, 20.

90. Quoted in Bengio, *Saddam's Word,* 155.

91. Schwarzkopf, *It Doesn't Take A Hero,* 316.

92. Ibid., 317.

93. Drew, "Letter from Washington," 4 February 1991, 83.

94. Statement by Secretary of State James A. Baker, II (GBPL).

95. The *Independent,* 14 February 1991.

96. Quoted in Freedman and Karsh, *The Gulf Conflict,* 270; author interview with Baker.

97. Gates, *From the Shadows,* 499.

98. On efforts at negotiation, see Freedman and Karsh, *The Gulf Conflict,* 266–73.

99. Letters from members of Congress repeatedly urged Bush not to link the Palestinian question to the Gulf. This was clear from innumerable documents in the GBPL, Whorm files-general.

100. On this episode, see Bush and Scowcroft, *A World Transformed,* 460–61. Gates also describes this gaffe as a mistake, as Baker "getting carried away." Author interviews with Gates and Fitzwater.

101. Author interview with Gates.

102. Powell, *My American Journey*, 478.

103. Campbell, "The 'Let's Deal' President," 206.

104. Author interview with Scowcroft.

105. Author interviews with Gates and Fitzwater. Indeed, Bush was not advised to use the analogy in any memo that I saw in the process of researching thirty-six boxes of materials on the crisis at the GBPL.

106. Author interview with Fitzwater.

107. Glad, "Figuring Out Saddam Hussein," 80.

108. John F. Burns, "Hussein Warns Nation Of Possible U.S. Attack," *New York Times*, 31 October 1990, A8.

109. Quoted in *Baghdad Domestic Service* in FBIS, 6 December 1990, 13.

110. ABC News, "This Week With David Brinkley," 12 August 1990.

111. Betty Glad argued that, drawing on Munich and his own experiences in World War II, Bush personalized the conflict with Saddam, which made war more likely. Glad, "Figuring Out Saddam." On the effect of analogies, see Jervis, *Perception and Misperception*, 217.

112. For instance, see Note from Bush to Dan Rostenkowski (GBPL).

113. Voss et al., "Representations of the Gulf Crisis as Derived from the U.S. Senate Debate," 289.

114. Excerpt From Remarks To Republican National Committee (GBPL).

115. Quoted in Freedman and Karsh, *The Gulf Conflict*, 59.

116. See the Aziz statement in *Baghdad AL-THAWRAH*, FBIS: NESA, 12 September 1990, esp. 31.

117. See ABC News, "This Week With David Brinkley, 12 August 1990.

118. See interview with Mohammed al-Mashat, Iraq's ambassador to the United States, ABC News, "This Week With David Brinkley," 19 August 1990, 6, 10.

119. "Excerpts From the TV Talk By Mubarak to the Egyptians," *New York Times*, 9 August 1990, A18.

120. See Algosaibi, *The Gulf Crisis*.

121. Press Conference by the President (GBPL).

122. See Hybel, *Power Over Rationality*, 9.

123. Jowett, "Toward a Propaganda Analysis of the Gulf War," 77.

124. Author interview with Fitzwater.

125. *Frontline* interview with James Baker.

126. Woodward, *The Commanders*, 324.

127. *Frontline* interview with James Baker.

128. See *Baghdad Domestic Service*, in FBIS: NESA, 6 September 1990, 29. Iraqi Transcript of the Meeting Between President Saddam Hussein and U.S. Ambassador April Glaspie. *New York Times*, 23 September 1990.

129. Text of interview in *Ankara Anatolia* in FBIS: NESA, 21 September 1990, 20.

130. Mattar, "The PLO And The Gulf Crisis," 37.

131. *Frontline* interview with Tariq Aziz.

132. Freedman, "Moscow And The Iraqi Invasion Of Kuwait," 100–101.

133. *Baghdad Domestic Service*, in FBIS: NESA, 6 September 1990, 29.

134. On miscalculation, see Fearon, "Rationalist Explanations for War," 393–95.

135. *Frontline* interview with Tariq Aziz.

136. Memo from Bush to Fitzwater (GBPL).

137. The President's News Conference With Regional Reporters, 18 December 1990, in Bush, *PPP,* 1804.

138. Exchange With Reporters in Kennebunkport, Maine, 17 February 1991, in Bush, *PPP,* 151.

139. Lally Weymouth, "How Bush Went to War," *Washington Post,* 31 March 1991, B4. Also, Remarks to Veterans Service Organizations, 4 March 1991, 207.

140. Author interview with Scowcroft.

CHAPTER FOUR: Constructing the Threat

1. On the process of enhancing political standing, see Bostdorff, The Presidency and the Rhetoric of Foreign Crisis. For a related but different model that explains how options can be weighed against the goal of assuring a domestic political consensus, see Farnham, *Roosevelt And The Munich Crisis,* chap. 2.

2. On construction in crises, see Bostdorff, *The Presidency and the Rhetoric of Foreign Crisis,* esp. 205 and chapter 8. Also, see Edelman, *Constructing the Political Spectacle,* 31.

3. See Morgan and Bickers, "Domestic Discontent and the External Use of Force," 27. For a good discussion of the evolution of diversionary theory and outcome of myriad efforts to test it, see DeRouen, "Presidents and the Diversionary Use of Force," esp. 317–19, 325–26. For a brief analysis and cited evidence, see Mintz, "The Decision to Attack Iraq," 608–9.

4. Ibid.; DeRouen, "Presidents and the Diversionary Use of Force," 319.

5. The sociological literature on strategic framing highlights how actors can frame issues for important effects, such as mobilizing followers or agenda setting, but do little to model lagged effects in the manner done herein. For an interesting application to the behavior of Arab leaders, see Barnett, *Dialogues in Arab Politics,* chap. 2. Tarrow, *Power in Movement,* chap. 7.

6. Mintz and Geva, "The Poliheuristic Theory of Foreign Policy Decisionmaking," 84–85. See also Redd, "The Influence of Advisers."

7. This is in contrast to expected utility models that posit a careful consideration of many criteria, or the cybernetic model that posits that an alternative will be chosen that "satisfices" certain criteria.

8. For work that models the impact of domestic audience costs, see Fearon, "Domestic Political Audiences," 577–92.

9. If so, an alternative will be eliminated based on the political dimension, even though this may well result in diminished utility in terms of substantive values. In simple terms, expected utility is undermined.

10. This is borrowed from the poliheuristic model developed by Alex Mintz and Nehemia Geva. For subsequent work on this model, see Alex Mintz, ed., *Integrating Cognitive and Rational Theories of Foreign Policy.*

11. McDermott, *Risk-Taking in International Politics,* 21.

12. Smith and some others argue that Bush was trying to address the "wimp" image problem as well. Smith, *George Bush's War,* 233.

13. For the literature on crisis rhetoric and construction by presidents, see Kiewe, *The Modern Presidency and Crisis Rhetoric,* esp. introduction.

14. Ibid.

15. "The Mother Of All Battles" speech on Baghdad Radio (translated by Reuters), 20 January 1991.

16. Dorman and Livingston, "News and Historical Content," 67–70.

17. Hiebert, "Public Relations as a Weapon of Modern Warfare," 30, but the whole volume is useful on the role of the media.

18. Clark, *The Fire This Time*, 3.

19. See Mustafa M. Zein, "Losing the Rumor War," *Washington Post*, 16 December 1990; ABC News, "This Week With David Brinkley," 12 August 1990. See also interview with Mohammed al-Mashat, Iraq's ambassador to the United States, ABC News, "This Week With David Brinkley," 19 August 1990.

20. Baram, "The Iraqi Invasion of Kuwait," 22.

21. Quoted in Hiro, *Desert Shield to Desert Storm*, 114. See also Baram, "The Iraqi Invasion of Kuwait," 120–21.

22. Bush and Scowcroft, *A World Transformed*, 328.

23. Author interview with Fitzwater.

24. Author interview with Bishara.

25. Manheim, "Strategic Public Diplomacy," 138–40.

26. Bush, *PPP*, "Address Before the 45th Session of the United Nations General Assembly in New York," 1 October 1990, 1332.

27. Ibid.

28. Heikal, *Illusions of Triumph*, 271–73.

29. Hearings Before the Senate Armed Services Committee, 192.

30. Sultan, *Desert Warrior*, 311.

31. Primakov's firsthand account, as relayed to Bush, in Bush and Scowcroft, *A World Transformed*, 377.

32. Author's interviews (Kuwait City, Kuwait: 5–8 August 1998).

33. Jensen, "Fighting Objectivity."

34. Quoted in Bengio, *Saddam's Word*, 125.

35. Author interview with Scowcroft.

36. Margaret Garrard Warner, "Bush Battles the'Wimp Factor,'" *Newsweek*, 19 October 1987, 28–35.

37. Kenneth T. Walsh, "Bushwhacking the'wimp factor,'" *U.S. News and World Report*, 30 March 1987, 36.

38. George F. Will, "George Bush: The Sound of a Lapdog," *Washington Post*, 30 January 1986, A25.

39. Rozell, *The Press and the Bush Presidency*, 73–75.

40. This view was popular in parts of the Arab world as well as in left-leaning quarters in the US. See Khadduri and Ghareeb, *War in the Gulf, 1990–91*, 257.

41. R.W. Apple Jr., "Bush's Two Audiences," *New York Times*, 12 September 1990, A21.

42. "The First Test of Our Mettle," *Newsweek*, 24 September 1990, 26.

43. Quoted in "From Pit Bull to President," *Newsweek*, 12 November 1990, 30.

44. Tom Wicker, "Bush's Double Gamble," *New York Times*, 13 August 1990, A15.

45. Andrew Rosenthal, "The Golf Cart Crisis," *New York Times*, 26 August 1990, A16.

46. On the press coverage, see Rozell, *The Press and the Bush Presidency*, esp. 92–93.

47. Graubard, *Mr. Bush's War*, xi.

48. *Newsweek*, 24 September 1990, 26.

49. Fred Barnes, *The New Republic*, 7 January 1991, 10.

50. Bush and Scowcroft, *A World Transformed*, 427.

51. Author interview with Scowcroft.

52. Ibid.

53. Author interview with Gates.

54. Ibid.

55. *U.S. Department of State Dispatch*, "Operation Desert Storm Launched," 21 January 1991, 37.

56. Author interview with Eagleburger.

57. On the new world order, see Miller and Yetiv, "The New World Order in Theory and Practice."

58. This paragraph is based on Duffy and Goodgame, *Marching in Place*, 136.

59. Berman and Jentleson, "Bush and the Post-Cold-War World," 98–99.

60. Dan Goodgame, "What if We Do Nothing?" *Time*, 7 January 1991, 22.

61. Quoted in Heikal, *Illusions of Triumph*, 352.

62. For extensive analysis of polling numbers, see Krosnick and Brannon, "The Media and the Foundations of Presidential Support."

63. Author interview with Fitzwater.

64. Ibid.

65. Woodward, *The Commanders*, 311–12.

66. Bush and Scowcroft, *A World Transformed*, 363.

67. For evidence of this connection, see Mintz and Russett, "The dual economy," 181.

68. On these conditions, see Council of Economic Advisers.

69. For analysis and data, see Mueller, *Policy and Opinion in the Gulf War*, 92–95 and 379, figure 7.

70. Ibid., 151.

71. Cited in the *Wall Street Journal*, 16 November 1990.

72. Cited in Hiro, *Desert Shield to Desert Storm*, 191.

73. The President's News Conference in Orlando, Florida, 1 November 1990 in Bush, *PPP*, 1515.

74. Quoted in Michael Oreskes, "Bush Trying A New Topic," *New York Times*, 31 October 1990, A21.

75. The President's News Conference in Orlando, Florida, 1 November 1990 in Bush, *PPP*, 1514.

76. Paragraph is based on ibid., 1517.

77. Bush and Scowcroft, *A World Transformed*, 388.

78. "From Pit Bull to President," *Newsweek*, 12 November 1990, 30.

79. Brace and Hinckley, *Follow the Leader*, 155.

80. *Frontline* interview with Brent Scowcroft.

81. Author interview with Fitzwater.

82. Bush and Scowcroft, *A World Transformed*, 400.

83. Author interview with Haass.

84. *Frontline* interview with James Baker.

85. See Freedman and Karsh, *The Gulf Conflict*, 224. See also Smith, *George Bush's War*, 210–11.

86. Spellman et al., "A Coherence Model of Cognitive Consistency."

87. Hearings Before the Senate Armed Services Committee, 193–95.

88. Press Conference By The President (GBPL).

89. Bush and Scowcroft, *A World Transformed*, 399; excerpts from the CNN interview, published in the *Washington Post*, 16 November 1999, A24.

90. Author interview with Fitzwater.

91. Author interview with Gates.

92. Author interview with Fitzwater.

93. Memo from Bruce Gelb to James Baker (GBPL).

94. Letter from Dole to Bush (GBPL).

95. Memo from Sununu and Scowcroft (GBPL).

96. Author interview with Fitzwater.

97. See Bengio, *Saddam Speaks*.

98. Memo from Bush to Gray, 9 September 1990 in Bush, *All the Best, George Bush*, 479.

99. On symbolism and construction in inter-Arab politics, see Barnett, *Dialogues in Arab Politics*.

100. See Bengio, *Saddam's Word*, 182.

101. "The Mother Of All Battles" speech on Baghdad Radio (translated by Reuters), 20 January 1991.

102. See *Baghdad Domestic Service*, in FBIS: NESA, 6 September 1990, 27. See also Saddam's speech on Baghdad Radio on 24 February 1991, "Acts of Treachery Against Iraq's Struggling Forces," translated by Reuters; and Bengio, *Saddam's Word*, 172–75, 205–6.

103. Ebert, "The Gulf War and Its Aftermath," 84–88.

104. Letter from Bush to Fereydoun (GBPL).

105. Author interview with Fitzwater.

106. See text of speech, in *Baghdad Television Service*, 12 September 1990, 26; letter from David Demarest to John Sununu (GBPL).

107. Edelman, *Constructing the Political Spectacle*, 112, 114.

108. Quoted in Baram, "The Iraqi Invasion of Kuwait," 22.

CHAPTER FIVE: Elements of Groupthink on the Road to War

1. Janis, *Groupthink*, 9.

2. This literature is discussed throughout this chapter, but is covered in Hart et al., *Beyond Groupthink*, esp. chaps. 2 and 3; Park, "A Review of Research on Groupthink"; Paulus, "Developing Consensus about Groupthink," 370–71; Mohamed and Wiebe, "Toward a Process Theory of Groupthink," 416–30.

3. Janis, *Groupthink*, 9.

4. Ibid., 247.

5. Ibid., 249.

6. Author interview with Scowcroft.

7. Author interview with Gates.

8. John Sununu, Speech on Bush Presidency, and Question and Answer session (C-SPAN 2, 31 December 1991).

9. Author interview with Fitzwater.

10. Author interviews with Sununu and Scowcroft.

11. Bush and Scowcroft, *A World Transformed*, 338.

12. For a brief, authoritative sketch, see David Hoffman, "The Politics of Timidity," *Washington Post*, 23–29 October 1989, A6, national weekly edition; report, Meetings on the Persian Gulf (GBPL).

13. *The Road to War.*

14. Author interview with Scowcroft.

15. Janis, *Groupthink,* 249.

16. Janis and Mann, *Decision Making,* 131.

17. Ibid., 3.

18. Bush, *Looking Forward,* 231.

19. Haney, *Organizing for Foreign Policy Crises,* 65. On Eisenhower's style, see Bowie and Immerman, *Waging Peace,* esp. 256. On Nixon, see Halperin, *Bureaucratic Politics and Foreign Policy,* 109.

20. Janis, *Groupthink,* 267.

21. Ibid., 143.

22. Parmet, *George Bush,* 455.

23. They had a major impact on him. Author interview with Scowcroft.

24. Ibid.

25. Author interviews with Gates and Sununu.

26. Author interview with Sununu.

27. Author interview with Gates.

28. Author interview with Scowcroft.

29. On Johnson, see Haney, *Organizing for Foreign Policy Crises,* 70; and Humphrey, "Tuesday Lunch at the Johnson White House," 81–101.

30. Author interviews with Scowcroft and Gates.

31. Bush and Scowcroft, *A World Transformed,* 303.

32. Quayle, *Standing Firm,* 102.

33. Pffifner, "Presidential Policy-Making and the Gulf War," 7–8.

34. Author interview with Powell.

35. Author interview with Freeman.

36. Ibid.

37. Sultan, *Desert Warrior,* 327–31.

38. Author interview with Scowcroft.

39. Ibid.

40. See Vance, *Hard Choices,* 36.

41. Author interview with Scowcroft.

42. Professional socialization is associated with generating a similar frame of reference, a similar orientation and disposition towards issues. See DiMaggio and Powell, "The Iron Cage Revisited," esp. 71–72.

43. Janis, *Groupthink,* 250; Hensley and Griffin, "Victims of Groupthink," 511.

44. Author interview with Sununu.

45. This paragraph is based on the author's interviews with Scowcroft, Powell, Baker, and Webster.

46. Hiro, *Desert Shield to Desert Storm,* 110–11; Gordon and Trainor, *The General's War,* 57–66.

47. *Frontline* interview with Richard Cheney. Author interviews with Scowcroft, Haass, and Fitzwater.

48. Bush and Scowcroft, *A World Transformed,* 459.

49. Baker, *The Politics of Diplomacy;* Quayle, *Standing Firm,* 208.

50. Author interview with Scowcroft.

51. See May and Zelikow, eds., *The Kennedy Tapes.*

52. Janis, *Groupthink,* 174.

53. Ibid.

54. *Frontline* interview with Scowcroft.

55. Janis, *Groupthink*, 175.

56. Kissinger, *Years of Renewal*, 68.

57. Quayle, *Standing Firm*, 93.

58. Author interview with Scowcroft.

59. Burke, *The Institutional Presidency*, esp. 162–63.

60. *Frontline* interview with Richard Cheney.

61. Author interview with Scowcroft.

62. Powell, *My American Journey*, 465–66.

63. *Frontline* interview with Colin Powell.

64. Author interview with Sununu.

65. See McCauley, "The Nature of Social Influence in Groupthink," 250–60.

66. Author interview with Scowcroft.

67. Author interviews with Scowcroft and Haass.

68. Author interview with Scowcroft.

69. Ibid.

70. Author interview with Pickering.

71. On the vital importance of problem representation, see Sylvan and Voss, eds., *Problem Representation in Foreign Policy Decision Making*.

72. Bush and Scowcroft, *A World Transformed*, 323.

73. Author interviews with Scowcroft and Fitzwater. Also, see Freedman and Karsh, *The Gulf Conflict*, 76.

74. Author interviews with Scowcroft and Haass. Bush and Scowcroft, *A World Transformed*, 322–23.

75. Based in part on a *Frontline* interview with Scowcroft.

76. Gordon and Trainor, *The General's War*, 35–37.

77. Sorensen, *Decision-Making In The White House*, 20–21.

78. Author interview with Scowcroft.

79. Powell, *My American Journey*, 466–67; *Frontline* interview with Brent Scowcroft.

80. *Frontline* interview with Colin Powell.

81. Bush and Scowcroft, *A World Transformed*, 333.

82. Quayle, *Standing Firm*, 206–7.

83. Woodward, *The Commanders*, 261–62.

84. *Frontline* interview with Colin Powell.

85. Author interview with Scowcroft. *Frontline* interview with Colin Powell.

86. Author interviews with Scowcroft, Gates, and Fitzwater.

87. Author interview with Fitzwater.

88. Author interview with Gates.

89. Author interview with Eagleburger.

90. Woodward, *The Commanders*, 299–303.

91. Thomas L. Friedman, "Baker Seen as a Balance To Bush on Crisis in Gulf," *New York Times*, 3 November 1990, A1.

92. Author interview with Gates. Webster observes that he also never saw Baker argue against military action; author interview with Webster.

93. Lamb interview with Schwarzkopf (C-SPAN 2, 1 October 1992).

94. Freedman and Karsh, *The Gulf Conflict*, 204.

95. Ibid., 405.

96. Remarks by the President (GBPL).

97. Author interview with Scowcroft. Gordon and Trainor, *The General's War*, 139.

98. Ibid., 153–58.

99. Author interview with Gates; Woodward, *The Commanders*, 312–13.

100. Author interview with Freeman.

101. Bush and Scowcroft, *A World Transformed*, 390.

102. Quoted in ibid., 394.

103. Ibid., 396.

104. CBS/New York Times telephone poll, 13–15 November 1990 (New York: CBS News, 1990).

105. Rick Atkinson and Bob Woodward, "Gulf Turning Points: Strategy, Diplomacy," *Washington Post*, 2 December 1990, A1.

106. Freedman and Karsh, *The Gulf Conflict*, 235–37.

107. Author interviews with Fitzwater and Scowcroft.

108. Author interview with Fitzwater. See also "Memo from Sununu and Scowcroft."

109. Author interview with Scowcroft.

CHAPTER SIX: Government Politics

1. Allison and Zelikow, *Essence of Decision*.

2. Burke, *The Institutional Presidency*, 132.

3. For more recent work, see Yetiv, "Testing the Government Politics Model"; Allison and Zelikow, *Essence of Decision*; Bendor and Hammond, "Rethinking Allison's Models"; Welch, "The Organizational Process"; Bernstein, "Understanding Decisionmaking." On Allison's challenge, see Welch, "The Organizational Process," 114.

4. For an exception, see Rhodes, "Do Bureaucratic Politics Matter?" He uses a fairly systematic test, although without interviews.

5. Allison and Zelikow, *Essence of Decision*.

6. For an elaboration on this model, see Allison and Zelikow, *Essence of Decision*, esp. 294–313. See also Morton H. Halperin, *Bureaucratic Politics and Foreign Policy*.

7. "Substantially" is a clarification made in the revised edition. Allison and Zelikow, *Essence of Decision*, 307.

8. This entire paragraph is based on ibid., 294–304.

9. Ibid., 302–4.

10. Welch, "The Organizational Process," 118.

11. Allison and Zelikow, *Essence of Decision*, chap. 5. See also Bendor and Hammond, "Rethinking Allison's Models," 315.

12. Allison and Zelikow, *Essence of Decision*, 346.

13. Ibid., 258.

14. For two different ways to test the model, see Rhodes, "Do Bureaucratic Politics Matter?" 4–7. See also Welch, "The Organizational Process."

15. See Bernstein, "Understanding Decisionmaking," 141, 145, 148. Smith, "Allison and the Cuban Missile Crisis," esp. 32–35.

16. As conducted by Rhodes, "Do Bureaucratic Politics Matter?"

17. Welch, "The Organizational Process," 119–25.

18. Allison and Zelikow, *Essence of Decision*, chap. 5. For a similar interpretation from a critical perspective, see Krasner, "Are Bureaucracies Important?"

19. Allison and Zelikow, *Essence of Decision*, 311.

20. Hays et al., *American Defense Policy*, esp. chap. 5. The methods have disagreed even about some exceptional cases. For instance, on troop withdrawals from Vietnam, see Halperin, *Bureaucratic Politics and Foreign Policy*, 186–87.

21. Welch, "The Organizational Process," 132–33.

22. Halperin, *Bureaucratic Politics*, 298–99. See also Neustadt, *Presidential Power and the Modern Presidents*.

23. Allison and Zelikow, *Essence of Decision*, 257.

24. Author interview with Webster.

25. Author interviews with Sununu and Scowcroft.

26. Powell, *My American Journey*, 465–66. *Frontline* interview with Colin Powell.

27. *Frontline* interview with Colin Powell.

28. *Frontline* interview with Colin Powell. Author interview with Scowcroft.

29. *Frontline* interview with Robert Gates. Author interview with Gates.

30. Author interviews with Fitzwater and Gates.

31. Author interview with Gates.

32. *Frontline* interview with Colin Powell.

33. Powell, *My American Journey*, 480. Compare his position, for instance, with that of the Joint Chiefs of Staff during the Cuban missile crisis, who pushed strongly for an air attack on Cuba over a quarantine in the absence of a Presidential imprimatur. Or with the position of David Jones, Joint Chiefs Chairman under Carter, who advocated a military rescue of U.S. hostages in Iran. Smith, "Policy Preferences," 129–33.

34. Author interviews with Fitzwater and Scowcroft. *Frontline* interview with James Baker.

35. See, for instance, Bush and Scowcroft, *A World Transformed*, 460–61.

36. Author interviews with Gates and Fitzwater; Bush and Scowcroft, *A World Transformed*, 394.

37. Ibid., 322–23. Author interview with Scowcroft.

38. *Frontline* interview with Colin Powell.

39. *Frontline* interview with Colin Powell. Author interviews with Gates and Eagleburger.

40. *Frontline* interview with Richard Cheney.

41. *Frontline* interview with Colin Powell. Author interview with Eagleburger.

42. Author interviews with Sununu, Scowcroft, and Gates.

43. "Scowcroft and Gates: A Team Rivals Baker," *New York Times*, 21 February 1991, A14.

44. Author interview with Jeremiah.

45. Author interviews with Gates and Jeremiah.

46. Author interview with Haaas.

47. Author interviews with Haass and Kimmitt.

48. Author interview with Kimmitt.

49. Author interviews with Jeremiah and Haass.

50. Author interview with Haass.

51. Author interview with Jeremiah.

52. Ibid.

53. Powell, *My American Journey*, 464.

54. Author interviews with Fitzwater and Gates.

55. Speech by John Sununu and Question and Answer Session on the Bush Presidency (C-SPAN 2: 31 December 1991).

56. Crabb and Mulcahy, *American National Security*, chap. 10.

57. Remarks by the President (GBPL); *Frontline* interview with Brent Scowcroft.

58. Powell, *My American Journey*, 480.

59. *Frontline* interview with Colin Powell.

60. Burke, *The Institutional Presidency*, 169–70.

61. Ibid., 138. Author interview with Scowcroft.

62. Vance, *Hard Choices*, 36.

63. Quayle, *Standing Firm*, 93; Burke, *The Institutional Presidency*, esp. 162–63.

64. Vance, *Hard Choices*, 35.

65. Bernstein, "Understanding Decisionmaking," esp. 158.

66. Author interview with Scowcroft.

67. Author interviews with Eagleburger and Scowcroft.

68. Author interviews with Scowcroft, Gates, and Fitzwater.

69. Author interviews with Scowcroft and Fitzwater.

70. Halperin, *Bureaucratic Politics and Foreign Policy*, 279–80.

71. Author interviews with Fitzwater and Gates.

72. Author interview with Powell.

73. Author interviews with Baker, Scowcroft, Gates, and one off-the-record source; letter from Bush to Foley (GBPL). The letter inadvertently and indirectly emphasized how Congress was not consulted.

74. Author interview with Baker.

75. Bush and Scowcroft, *A World Transformed*, 385–87.

76. *Frontline* interviews with Scowcroft and Baker.

77. Bush and Scowcroft, *A World Transformed*, 397.

78. Smith, *George Bush's War*, 222.

79. Author interview with Scowcroft.

80. Woodward, *The Commanders*, 336.

81. Author interview with Gates.

CHAPTER SEVEN: Mirror, Mirror, on the Wall

1. See note 11 of the introduction.

2. See Mintz and Geva, "The Poliheuristic Theory of Foreign Policy Decisionmaking," 81. Hart et al., *Beyond Groupthink*, 25–26.

3. This argument was made most famously in Friedman, *Essays in Positive Economics*. On subsequent challenges to that notion, see Farkas, "Evolutionary Models in Foreign Policy Analysis," 343–44. On the puzzle-solving aspects of paradigms, see Welch, "The Organizational Process," 112–46.

4. Sixteen partial tests were conducted across disciplines prior to 1991. See Park, "A Review of Research on Groupthink," 229–45. A consensus among scholars on the need for more systematic and partial tests was identified in Paulus, "Developing Consensus about Groupthink," 370–71. See also Fuller and Adlag, "Organizational Tonypandy," 163–84; and Neck and Moorhead, "Groupthink Remodeled," 554.

5. Janis identifies three key methodological concerns. The first concern is objectivity. Individuals involved in the subject matter or recently affected by it may be less objective. That is not the case here. The second concern deals with the requirements used for the acceptance or rejection of the theory. Chapter 5 of this book uses multiple sources before determining if a crucial condition of the theory was present. The third concern is sources of information. Janis was limited to secondary sources in testing the occurrence of group-

think, which he recognized to be a limitation. See Janis, *Groupthink*, viii–ix. The present work uses primary sources.

6. Paulus, "Developing Consensus About Groupthink," 368.

7. Ibid., 174.

8. Author interviews with Gates and Fitzwater. Quayle, *Standing Firm*, 208.

9. Author interview with Gates.

10. This is evident from numerous documents at the GBPL.

11. Author interview with Powell.

12. Author interviews with Haass and Jeremiah.

13. *Frontline* interview with Robert Gates.

14. Author interview with Scowcroft.

15. George, "From Groupthink to Contextual Analysis of Policy-making Groups," 39.

16. Moorhead et al., "The Tendency toward Defective Decision Making," 338–39.

17. Stern and Sundelius, "The Essence of Groupthink," 103; Hoyt and Garrison, "Political Manipulation within the Small Group," 249–74.

18. Park, "A Review of Research on Groupthink," 237; Janis, *Groupthink*, 262–71.

19. Janis, *Groupthink*. See also Adlag and Fuller, "Beyond Fiasco," 541.

20. Hart hints modestly in this direction by referring to "leader-centered or peers-centered conformity." Hart, *Groupthink In Government*, 31, 62.

21. Janis, *Groupthink*, 69.

22. Ibid., 210–11, 235–36.

23. McCauley, "The Nature of Social Influence," 250. Gaenslen, "Decision-Making Groups," 170.

24. Author interview with Fitzwater.

25. Memo from Stephen Rademaker to Scowcroft (GBPL). On the alternatives explored, see Gordon and Trainor, *The General's War*, 142–52.

26. This is evident in Hart et al., *Beyond Groupthink*.

27. On the impact of the group leader on such conditions, see Preston, "Following the Leader," in Hart et al., *Beyond Groupthink*, esp. 192–95.

28. See Hart et al., *Beyond Groupthink*, 25–29, on the various approaches that could be fruitful. See also Carlsnaes, "The Agency-Structure Problem in Foreign Policy Analysis," 245–70. For an interesting effort to explore individual-versus group-level processes, see Greitemeyer and Schulz-Hardt, "Preference-Consistent Evaluation."

29. Hermann and Preston, "Presidents, Advisors, and Foreign Policy," 75–96; Neck and Moorhead, "Groupthink Remodeled," esp. 550–51; Preston, "Following the Leader."

30. For recent work that emphasizes international over domestic factors, see Moore and Lanoue, "Domestic Politics and U.S. Foreign Policy."

31. Author interviews with Scowcroft and Kilberg.

32. Excerpts from CNN interview, published in the *Washington Post*, 16 November 1990, A24.

33. Memo from Bush to Marlin Fitzwater (GBPL).

34. Even in a particular area such rational deterrence, differences of view abound. See the series of articles in *World Politics* 16 (January 1989).

35. Mintz and Geva, "The Poliheuristic Theory of Foreign Policy Decisionmaking," 84–85.

36. Suedfeld et al., "Changes in Integrative Complexity Among Middle East Leaders During the Persian Gulf Crisis."

37. Author interview with Jeremiah.
38. Allison and Zelikow, *Essence of Decision*, 271.
39. Welch, "The Organizational Process," 118.

CHAPTER EIGHT: Threading the Tale

1. Quayle, *Standing Firm*, 208.
2. Hook, *The Hero In History*, 60.
3. On the ability of individuals to shape foreign policy decisions, see Hermann, ed., *A Psychological Examination of Political Leaders;* Falkowski, ed., *Psychological Models in International Politics.* For a good synopsis of case studies of individual leaders, see Winter, "Personality and Foreign Policy," esp. 85–86.
4. On this decision, see Woodward, *The Shadow*, 184–88.
5. Bush and Scowcroft, *A World Transformed*, 434.
6. Author interview with Freeman.
7. Author interview with Charles.
8. Author interview with Gates.
9. Author interview with off-the-record source.
10. Author interview with Sununu.
11. Quoted in Heikal, *Illusions of Triumph*, 270.
12. Author interview with Kilberg.
13. Author interviews with Pickering and Baker.
14. Author interview with Sununu.
15. *The Road to War.*
16. Cheney, *From Cold War to New World Order,* 483.
17. Author interview with Webster.
18. Ibid.
19. Author interview with Baker.
20. Author interview with Charles.
21. Author interview with Baker.
22. Author interview with Scowcroft.
23. See, for instance, FBIS: USSR, 17 August 1990, 18.
24. Bush and Scowcroft, *A World Transformed*, 354.
25. Ibid., 353.
26. Ibid., 382.
27. Excerpts of Bush's interview with CNN, "Bush Says Time Is Limited For Peaceful Gulf Solution," *Washington Post*, 16 November 1990, A24.
28. Author interview with Powell.
29. Author interview with Sununu.
30. Bush and Scowcroft, *A World Transformed*, 381.
31. Author interview with Fitzwater. According to another account, Cheney obtained the idea from a civilian official in the Pentagon named Henry Rowen, who served as Assistant Defense Secretary for International Security Affairs. Gordon and Trainor, *The General's War,* 143.
32. *The Road to War.*
33. *Frontline* interview with Colin Powell.
34. President's Opening Remarks at Cabinet meeting, 9 January 1991 (GBPL).

35. Memo from Bush to Shultz (GBPL).

36. Press briefing by Marlin Fitzwater (GBPL).

37. For instance, see memo from Haass to Scowcroft (GBPL).

38. Bush and Scowcroft, *A World Transformed*, 332.

39. Author interviews with Scowcroft and Fitzwater.

40. Author interview with Gates.

41. Author interview with Scowcroft.

42. Ibid.

43. Author interview with Webster.

44. Author interview with Haass.

45. Ibid.

46. Author interview with Pickering.

47. Bush and Scowcroft, *A World Transformed*, 353.

48. Ibid., 386–87.

49. Memo from Bush to Fitzwater (GBPL).

50. Diary entry in Bush, *All the Best, George Bush*, 489.

51. Drew, "Letter from Washington," 4 February 1991, 83.

52. Author interview with Pickering.

53. Smith, *George Bush's War*, 222; author interview with Scowcroft.

54. Woodward, *The Commanders*, 336.

55. On Saddam's perceptions, see text of interview with Saddam, *Mexico City XEW Television Network*, FBIS: NESA, 26 December 1990, 20.

56. Letter from Bush to Congress (GBPL).

57. Dan Balz, "Letter Requests Endorsement of U.N. Deadline," *Washington Post*, 9 January 1991, A1.

58. The President's News Conference, 12 January 1991, 32.

59. Quoted in "Baker and Aziz Arrive in Geneva; France May Push Plan if Talks Fail," *Washington Post*, 9 January 1991, A1.

60. Author interview with Charles.

61. Author interview with Freeman.

62. "Speech to the Islamic Conference," FBIS: NESA, 91–009, 20–24.

63. Quoted in "Will He Blink?" *Newsweek*, 19 November 1990, 23.

64. Bush and Scowcroft, *A World Transformed*, 377.

65. Author interview with Pickering.

66. *Frontline* interview with Tariq Aziz.

67. See text of interview with Saddam, *Mexico City XEW Television Network*, FBIS: NESA, 26 December 1990, 18.

69. Nisbett and Ross, *Human Inference*, 235.

69. Jervis, *Perception and Misperception*, 69.

70. For instance, see interviews with these officials on ABC News, "This Week With David Brinkley, 12 and 19 August 1990. Also, see Saddam Hussein's speech in Amman, Jordan, 24 February 1990, in Bengio, *Saddam Speaks*, 37–49.

71. On such thinking, see Baram, "The Iraqi Invasion of Kuwait," 21–25.

72. *Frontline* interview with Tariq Aziz.

73. Ann Devroy, "Bush Denies Preparing U.S. for War," *Washington Post*, 2 November 1990, A1.

74. Scowcroft interview with Kenneth Walsh, *US News and World Report*, 24 December 1990.

75. Memo from Haass to Mitsler and Popadiuk; Memo from Fred McClure to assistant secretaries (both GBPL).

76. Draft of talking points with key members of Congress. Memo from Haass to Scowcroft, 14 December 1990 (GBPL).

77. *Frontline* interview with Tariq Aziz.

78. Author interview with Freeman.

79. Freedman and Karsh, *The Gulf Conflict*, 221.

80. Remarks at a Fundraising Dinner for Gubernatorial Candidate John Rowland in Stamford, Connecticut, 23 October 1990 in Bush, *PPP*, 1990, 1455.

81. Memo from Stephen Rademaker and Ron Vonlembke to C. Boyden Gray (GBPL).

82. Text appears in Bengio, *Saddam Speaks*, 148.

83. *Frontline* interview with Mikhail Gorbachev. See Aziz interview in *London Al-Tadamun*, FBIS: NESA, 26 September 1990, 29–32.

84. Ibid. For an insider's account, see also Palazchenko, *My Years with Gorbachev and Shevardnadze*, 212–16.

85. Bush and Scowcroft, *A World Transformed*, 377–78.

86. Yevgenni Primakov, "The Inside Story of Moscow's Quest for a Deal," *Time*, 4 March 1991, 42.

87. Palazchenko, *My Years with Gorbachev and Shevardnadze*, 223.

88. For a good analysis of Saddam's personality, see Post, "Saddam Hussein of Iraq," 279–89.

89. "Saddam Husayn's Message to President Bush," 16 January 1991 in Bengio, *Saddam Speaks*.

90. See, for instance, *Baghdad INA*, in FBIS: NESA, 17 September 1990, 24.

91. For the speech, see *Baghdad Domestic Service*, FBIS: NESA, 10 January 1991, 1–4.

92. Text of Saddam Husayn's Reply to Soviet Leader, 20 January 1991, in ibid.

93. Quoted in Sciolino, *The Outlaw State*, 31.

94. Author joint interview with Kimmitt, Baker, and Charles.

95. *Frontline* interview with James Baker. The president's actual letter is different from the one widely published (OA/ID CF01361, Virginia Lampley Files, NSC, GBPL).

96. *Frontline* interview with Tariq Aziz.

97. Ibid.

98. Author interview with Pickering.

99. For the text, see *Baghdad Voice of the PLO* in FBIS: NESA, 10 January 1991, 5.

100. See Aziz news conference, in *Amman Jordan Television*, 10 January 1991, 27.

101. Author interview with Charles.

102. See Aziz news conference, in *Amman Jordan Television*, 10 January 1991, 27.

103. Author interview with Baker.

104. Bush interview with Bernard Shaw, CNN, 2 March 1996.

105. Author interview with Sununu.

106. Sorensen, *Decision-Making In The White House*, 26.

107. *Frontline* interview with James Baker.

108. Author interviews with Gates, Haass, and Charles.

109. *The Road to War*.

110. President Reagan referred to this lack of military readiness for Gulf contingencies as a "shame" in *Middle East Economic Digest*, 7 November 1980.

111. These two paragraphs are based on Yetiv, *America and the Persian Gulf.*

112. See Memorandum from J. H. Binford Peay III, Lieutenant General (Powell Papers).

113. For details on this infrastructure, see *Conduct of the Persian Gulf War*, Appendix F.

114. We can represent this range by an interval and model mathematically how various phenomena can narrow it. See Fearon, "Rationalist Explanations for War," esp. 403.

115. Smith, *George Bush's War*, 89–90.

116. Freedman and Karsh, *The Gulf Conflict*, 265–66.

117. Ibid., 267–68.

118. "Rafsanjani makes bid for diplomatic solution," *Middle East Economic Digest* (15 February 1991), 12–13.

119. For a good discussion of Soviet motivations in this time period, and Iraq's position, see Freedman and Karsh, *The Gulf Conflict*, 374–378.

120. Ibid., 378.

121. For the Soviet peace proposal, see Sifry and Cerf, *The Gulf War Reader*, 345.

122. Palazchenko, *My Years with Gorbachev and Shevardnadze*, 262–63.

123. Baghdad Radio, "Acts of Treachery Against Iraq's Struggling Forces," translated by Reuters.

124. On the political elements of the plan, see *Financial Times*, 23–24 February 1991. See also Yevgeny Primakov, "The Inside Story of Moscow's Quest for a Deal," *Time*, 4 March 1991.

125. Author interviews with off-the-record sources.

126. Discussion with Joseph Nye (Cambridge, Mass., September 1993).

127. On this broad literature, see Whicker, "The Case AGAINST the War," 114–16.

CHAPTER NINE: Tackling Puzzles and Developing Theory

1. Fuller and Adlag, "Organizational Tonypandy," 169.

2. McCauley, "The Nature of Social Influence," 251; Janis, *Groupthink*, 11.

3. Such as an explanation, for instance, that decision makers stumbled upon a positive outcome fortuitously or by chance, despite groupthink. That argument explains the positive outcome but not how groupthink could be paired with it. It also does not account for the real causes demonstrated herein of both groupthink and a positive outcome, real causes that make it hard to make the case for randomness or chance.

4. See Adlag and Fuller, "Beyond Fiasco," 543.

5. For instance, George, *Presidential Decisionmaking*, 145–49; Preston, "Following the Leader," 193, 197, 206.

6. On how leadership style can affect other antecedent conditions, see Neck and Moorhead, "Groupthink Remodeled," esp. 550–51.

7. See Preston, "Following the Leader," esp. 205–7; Hermann, ed., *A Psychological Examination of Political Leaders*; and Falkowski, ed., *Psychological Models in International Politics*. For a good synopsis of case studies of individual leaders, see Winter, "Personality and Foreign Policy," 85–86.

8. Hart, *Groupthink In Government*, 31.

9. Ibid., 36.

10. See Vertzberger, *Risk Taking and Decisionmaking*, 74–77.

11. Janis, *Groupthink*, 250.

12. Author interview with Baker.

13. Author interviews with Fitzwater and Gates.

14. Author interview with Gates.

15. Ibid. On this estimate, see U.S. Department of Defense, *Report on the Gulf War* (Washington, D.C.: GPO, 1991).

16. Memo from Bush to Fitzwater (GBPL).

17. See FBIS: USSR, 23 August 1990, 18–19.

18. Author interviews with Baker, Haass, Scowcroft, and Sununu. *Frontline* interview with Baker. See also Hiro, *Desert Shield to Desert Storm*, 165–73.

19. Author interviews with Haass and Scowcroft.

20. For instance, see Haney, *Organizing for Foreign Policy Crises*, esp. chap. 5. Burke, *The Institutional Presidency*, 132.

21. Author interviews with Scowcroft and Haass.

22. Janis, *Groupthink*. Also, George and George, *Presidential Personality & Performance*, 200–202.

23. George, *Presidential Decisionmaking*, 86.

24. On such a style, see Haney, *Organizing for Foreign Policy Crises*, 83–84.

25. Author interview with Scowcroft.

26. George, *Presidential Decisionmaking*, 145–49. Preston, "Following the Leader," 193, 197, 206.

27. Ibid., 198.

28. *Frontline* interview with Brent Scowcroft.

29. Author interview with Powell.

30. All interviewees I asked about this confirmed it.

31. Draft of President's Opening remarks at a cabinet meeting, (GBPL). Letter from Bush to Drew Lewis (GBPL).

32. Author interview with Pickering.

33. Author interview with Gates.

34. See Bendor and Hammond, "Rethinking Allison's Models," 315. This assumption can also be gleaned from the revised edition of *Essence of Decision*.

35. Author interview with Gates.

36. Ibid.

37. William Webster, for instance, acknowledged the impact of the analogy on Bush's behavior as well as on his own. Author interview with Webster.

38. See DiMaggio and Powell, "The Iron Cage Revisited," 71–72.

39. See Munch and Smelser, eds., *Theory of Culture*, esp. chaps. 4 and 7.

40. Under conditions of higher camaraderie, we would then expect less serious conflict over decisions. See Janis, *Groupthink*.

41. Author interview with Kimmitt.

42. Author interviews with Scowcroft, Powell, Baker, Cheney, and Sununu.

43. See, for instance, George, *Presidential Decisionmaking*, 83. One exception is suggested by the fairly large size of President Kennedy's EXCOM during the Cuban missile crisis.

44. Author interview with Webster.

45. Author interview with Fitzwater.

46. Author interview with Gates.

47. Author interview with Jeremiah.

48. On such expectations, see Halperin, *Bureaucratic Politics and Foreign Policy*, 58. On the antipathy towards Baker's approach, see Bush and Scowcroft, *A World Transformed*, 460–61. Gates also describes this gaffe as a mistake, as Baker "getting carried away." Author interview with Gates.

49. On military doctrine and behavior, see the research findings presented in Betts, *Soldiers, Statesmen, and Cold War Crises*, esp. 4–5. See also the Weinberger Doctrine and subsequent official statements. Caspar W. Weinberger, speech to the National Press Club, 28 November 1994.

50. Author interview with Sununu, Scowcroft, and Fitzwater.

51. Janis, *Groupthink*, 143.

52. Blight and Welch, *On The Brink*, 305. Paterson, "John F. Kennedy's Quest for Victory and Global Crises," esp. 6.

53. Allison and Zelikow, *Essence of Decision*, 329–30.

54. Ibid., esp. chap. 6.

55. Janis, *Groupthink*.

56. Author interview with Gates.

57. For a good analysis of such procedures, see George and Stern, "Harnessing Conflict."

CHAPTER TEN: Understanding Government Behavior

1. On the literature on this subject, see Hudson, "Foreign Policy Analysis," 209–38.

2. For a different definition that treats preferences as less transient, see Moravcsik, "Taking Preferences Seriously," 519.

3. Ruggie, "What Makes the World Hang Together?
" 876, 879; Moravcsik, "Taking Preferences Seriously," esp. 522.

4. For an explication of this theory, see Moravcsik, "Taking Preferences Seriously."

5. Most rational choice theorists, in particular, accept that individuals are not usually utility maximizers, certainly not in the form of economic man, but view such an assumption as useful for building theory, predicting outcomes, and/or capturing certain behaviors.

6. McDermott, *Risk-Taking in International Politics*, 21.

7. Moravcsik recognizes the challenge but leaves the question open. Moravcsik, "Taking Preferences Seriously," 542.

8. For other work related to this, see Milner, "Rationalizing Politics," esp. 784–85. Kahler, "Rationality in International Relations," 933–38.

9. For a good, brief discussion, see Knopf, *Domestic Society and International Cooperation*, 14–22.

10. Mintz and Geva, "The Poliheuristic Theory of Foreign Policy Decisionmaking," 84–85.

11. For another explanation based on noncompensatory behavior, see Mintz, "The Decision to Attack Iraq," 604–605.

12. Milner, "Rationalizing Politics," 784–85. Kahler, "Rationality in International Relations," 933–38. Lake and Powell, eds., *Strategic Choice*.

13. Elster, *Ulysses Unbound*, 5.

14. See Fearon, "Domestic Political Audiences," 577–92.

15. Using a theoretical vehicle such as social choice theory might be useful in making Fearon's model more determinate by dealing with this question.

16. One key exception is the interesting work by Mintz and Geva on the poliheuristic model which does allow for us to explain an event by assuming that decision makers use more than one decision strategy to reach decisions. See their *Decisionmaking on War and Peace*.

17. Khong, *Analogies at War.*

Postscript: From War to War

1. Hilsman, *George Bush vs. Saddam Hussein.* Record, *Hollow Victory.* U.S. News and World Report, *Triumph Without Victory.*

2. Author interview with off-the-record source.

3. Author interview with off-the-record source.

4. Author interviews with Powell and Baker.

5. Author interviews with Powell and Scowcroft.

6. Quoted in Freedman and Karsh, *The Gulf Conflict,* 404.

7. Author interview with off-the-record source.

8. *Frontline* interview with Robert Gates.

9. Author interview with Freeman.

10. Author interview with Eagleburger.

11. This section is based on several Osama bin Laden videos shown on CNN in the period from 15 September to 15 October 2001. On such opposition during the Gulf crisis, see Baghdad INA, in FBIS: 10 October 1990, 27. On the Saudi context's effect on bin Laden's views, see Fandy, *Saudi Arabia and the Politics of Dissent.*

12. For the texts of major U.N. resolutions adopted in 1991, see *U.N. Security Resolutions on Iraq: Compliance and Implementation,* Report to the Committee on Foreign Affairs by the CRS (Washington, D.C.: GPO, March 1992).

13. This doctrine is encapsulated in chapter 5 of *The National Security Strategy of the United States of America* (Washington: The White House, September 2002).

14. For the text of U.N. Resolution 1441, see *Arms Control Today* 32 (December 2002), 28–32.

15. Quoted in Woodward, *Bush At War,* 341.

16. For details, see http://money.cnn.com/2003/02/25/news/economy/consumer/index.htm.

17. On the Iraq War, see Woodward, *Bush At War,* 344 49.

18. Interviewed by Tom Brokaw, "Inside the White House at War," aired on 25 April 2003.

19. For classic analyses, see Sidney Hook, *The Hero In History*; Thomas Carlyle, *Sartor Resartus: On Heroes and Hero Worship* (1838; New York: E.P. Dutton, 1959); and Fred I. Greenstein, *Personality and Politics: Problems of Evidence, Inference and Conceptualization* (Princeton: Princeton University Press, 1969). For a bibliography on individual factors in decision-making, see Hudson, "Foreign Policy Analysis," 217, 218, 226.

Bibliography

BOOKS AND ARTICLES

Algosaibi, Ghazi A. *The Gulf Crisis: An Attempt to Understand*. London: Kegan Paul International, 1993.

Allison, Graham and Philip Zelikow. *Essence of Decision: Explaining the Cuban Missile Crisis*. 2nd ed. New York: Longman, 1999.

Baker, James A., III. *The Politics of Diplomacy: Revolution, War and Peace, 1989–1992*. New York: G.P. Putnam, 1995.

Baram, Amatzia. "The Iraqi Invasion of Kuwait: Decision-Making in Baghdad." In *Iraq's Road to War*, edited by Amatzia Baram and Barry Rubin. New York: St. Martin's Press, 1993.

———. "U.S. Input into Iraqi Decisionmaking, 1988–1990." In *The Middle East and the United States: A Historical and Political Assessment*, edited by David W. Lesch. Boulder: Westview Press, 1999.

Barnett, Michael N. *Dialogues in Arab Politics: Negotiations in Regional Order*. New York: Columbia University Press, 1998.

Bendor, Jonathan and Thomas H. Hammond. "Rethinking Allison's Models." *American Political Science Review* 86 (June 1992).

Bengio, Ofra. *Saddam's Word: Political Discourse in Iraq*. New York: Oxford University Press, 1998.

———, ed. *Saddam Speaks on the Gulf Crisis: A Collection of Documents*. Tel Aviv: Tel Aviv University, 1992.

Bennett, D. Scott and Allan C. Stam. "A Universal Test of an Expected Utility Theory of War." *International Studies Quarterly* (September 2000).

Berlin, Isaiah. *The Hedgehog and the Fox: An Essay on Tolstoy's View of History*. New York: Simon & Schuster, 1953.

Berman, Larry and Bruce W. Jentleson. "Bush and the Post-Cold-War World." In *The Bush Presidency: First Appraisals*, edited by Colin Campbell and Bert A. Rockman. New Jersey: Chatham House, 1991.

Bernstein, Barton J. "Understanding Decisionmaking, U.S. Foreign Policy, and the Cuban Missile Crisis" (review essay). *International Security* 25 (Summer 2000).

Betts, Richard K. *Soldiers, Statesmen, and Cold War Crises*. Cambridge: Harvard University Press, 1977.

Blight, James G. and David A. Welch. *On The Brink: Americans and Soviets Reexamine the Cuban Missile Crisis*. New York: Hill and Wang, 1989.

Bostdorff, Denise M. *The Presidency and the Rhetoric of Foreign Crisis*. Columbia, S.C.: University of South Carolina Press, 1994.

Bowie, Robert R. and Richard H. Immerman. *Waging Peace: How Eisenhower Shaped an Enduring Cold War Strategy.* New York: Oxford University Press, 1988.

Brace, Paul and Barbara Hinckley. *Follow the leader: opinion polls and the modern presidents.* New York: Basic Books, 1992.

Brecher, Michael. "International Studies in the Twentieth Century and Beyond: Flawed Dichotomies, Synthesis, Cumulation." *International Studies Quarterly* 43 (June 1999).

Bueno de Mesquita, Bruce. *The War Trap.* New Haven: Yale University Press, 1981.

—— and David Lalman. *War and Reason.* New Haven: Yale University Press, 1992.

Burke, John P. *The Institutional Presidency.* Baltimore: The Johns Hopkins University Press, 1992.

Bush, George. *All the Best, George Bush: My Life In Letters And Other Writings.* New York: Scribner, 1999.

—— (with Victor Gold). *Looking Forward.* New York: Doubleday, 1987.

—— and Brent Scowcroft. *A World Transformed.* New York: Simon & Schuster, 1999.

Byman, Daniel L. and Kenneth M. Pollack. "Let Us Now Praise Great Men: Bringing the Statesman Back In." *International Security* 25 (Spring 2001).

Camerer, Colin F. *Behavioral Game Theory: Experiments in Strategic Interaction.* Princeton: Princeton University Press, 2003.

Campbell, Colin S. "The 'Let's Deal' President." In *The Bush Presidency: First Appraisals,* edited by Colin Campbell and Bert A. Rockman. Chatham, N.J.: Chatham House, 1991.

Carlsnaes, Walter. "The Agency-Structure Problem in Foreign Policy Analysis." *International Studies Quarterly* 36 (1992).

Cheney, Richard B. In *From Cold War to New World Order: The Foreign Policy of George W. Bush,* edited by Meena Bose and Rosanna Perotti. Westport: Greenwood Press, 2002.

Clark, David H. "A United Model of War Onset and Outcome." *Journal of Politics* 65 (February 2003).

Clark, Ramsey. *The Fire This Time: U.S. War Crimes in the Gulf.* New York: Thunder's Mouth Press, 1992.

Cooper, Chester L. *The Lost Crusade: America in Vietnam.* New York: Dodd, Mead, 1970.

Crabb, Cecil V. and Kevin V. Mulcahy. *American National Security: A Presidential Perspective.* Pacific Grove, Calif.: Brooks/Cole, 1991.

Dannreuther, Roland. *The Gulf Conflict: A Political and Strategic Analysis.* Adelphi Paper No. 264. London: International Institute for Strategic Studies, Winter 1991–92.

DeRouen Jr., Karl. "Presidents and the Diversionary Use of Force: A Research Note." *International Studies Quarterly* 44 (June 2000).

DiMaggio, Paul J. and Walter W. Powell. "The Iron Cage Revisited: Institutional Isomorphism and Collective Rationality in Organizational Fields." In *The New Institutionalism In Organizational Analysis,* edited by Powell and DiMaggio. Chicago: The University of Chicago Press, 1991.

Dorman, William A. and Steven Livingston. "News and Historical Content." In *Taken by Storm: The Media, Public Opinion, and U.S. Foreign Policy in the Gulf War,* edited by W. Lance Bennett and David L. Paletz. Chicago: University of Chicago Press, 1994.

Drew, Elizabeth. "Letter from Washington." *The New Yorker,* 4 and 21 February 1991; 11 March 1991.

Drezner, Daniel W. "Ideas, Bureaucratic Politics, and the Crafting of Foreign Policy." *American Journal of Political Science* 44 (October 2000).

Duffy, Michael and Dan Goodgame. *Marching in Place: The Status Quo Presidency of George Bush.* New York: Simon & Schuster, 1992.

Ebert, Barbara Gregory. "The Gulf War and Its Aftermath: An Assessment of Evolving Arab Responses." *Middle East Policy* 1 (1992).

Edelman, Murray. *Constructing the Political Spectacle*. Chicago: University of Chicago Press, 1988.

Elman, Colin. "Horses For Courses: Why Not Neorealist Theories Of Foreign Policy?" *Security Studies* 6 (Autumn 1996).

Elster, Jon. *Ulysses Unbound: Studies in Rationality, Precommitment, and Constraints*. Cambridge: Cambridge University Press, 2000.

Falkowski, Lawrence S., ed. *Psychological Models in International Politics*. Boulder: Westview Press, 1979.

Fandy, Mamoun. *Saudi Arabia and the Politics of Dissent*. New York: St. Martin's Press, 1999.

Farkas, Andrew. "Evolutionary Models in Foreign Policy Analysis." *International Studies Quarterly* 40 (September 1996).

Farnham, Barbara Rearden. *Roosevelt And The Munich Crisis: A Study Of Political Decision-Making*. Princeton: Princeton University Press, 1997.

Fearon, James D. "Bargaining, Enforcement, and International Cooperation." *International Organization* 52 (Spring 1998).

——— . "Domestic Political Audiences and the Escalation of International Disputes." *American Political Science Review* 88 (1994).

——— . "Domestic Politics, Foreign Policy, and Theories of International Relations." *Annual Review of Political Science* 1 (1998).

——— . "Rationalist Explanations for War." *International Organization* 49 (Summer 1995).

Freedman, Lawrence and Efraim Karsh. *The Gulf Conflict 1990–1991: Diplomacy and War in the New World Order*. Princeton: Princeton University Press, 1993.

Freedman, Robert O. "Moscow And The Iraqi Invasion Of Kuwait." In *The Middle East after Iraq's Invasion of Kuwait*, edited by Robert O. Freedman. Gainesville: University Press of Florida, 1993.

Friedman, Milton. *Essays in Positive Economics*. Chicago: University of Chicago Press, 1953.

Fuller, Sally Riggs and Ramon J. Adlag. "Organizational Tonypandy: Lessons from a Quarter Century of the Groupthink Phenomenon." *Organizational Behavior And Human Processes* 73 (February/March 1998).

Gaenslen, Fritz. "Decision-Making Groups." In *Political Psychology and Foreign Policy*, edited by Eric Singer and Valerie Hudson. Boulder: Westview Press, 1992.

Garrett, Geoffrey. "Global Markets and National Politics: Collision Course or Virtuous Circle?" *International Organization* 52 (Autumn 1998).

Gates, Robert M. *From the Shadows: The Ultimate Insider's Story of Five Presidents and How They Won the Cold War*. New York: Simon & Schuster, 1996.

George, Alexander L. "From Groupthink to Contextual Analysis of Policy-making Groups." In *Beyond Groupthink: Political Dynamics and Foreign Policy-making*, edited by Paul 't Hart, Eric K. Stern, and Bengt Sundelius. Ann Arbor: University of Michigan Press, 1997.

——— . *Presidential Decisionmaking in Foreign Policy: The Effective Use of Information and Advice*. Boulder: Westview Press, 1980.

——— and Juliette L. George. *Presidential Personality & Performance*. Boulder: Westview Press, 1998.

——— and Eric K. Storm. "Harnessing Conflict in Foreign Policy Making: From Devil's to Multiple Advocacy." *Presidential Studies Quarterly* 32 (September 2002).

Glad, Betty, "Figuring Out Saddam Hussein." In *The Presidency and the Persian Gulf War*, edited by Marcia Lynn Whicker, James P. Pfiffner, and Raymond A. Moore. Westport, Conn.: Praeger, 1993.

Goldberg, Jacob. "Saudi Arabia: The Bank Vault Next Door." In *Iraq's Road To War*, edited by Amatzia Baram and Barry Rubin. New York: St. Martin's Press, 1993.

Gordon, Michael R. and General Bernard E. Trainor. *The General's War: The Inside Story of the Conflict in the Gulf*. Boston: Little, Brown, and Co., 1995.

Grafstein, Robert. *Choice-Free Rationality: A Positive Theory of Political Behavior*. Ann Arbor: University of Michigan Press, 1999.

Graubard, Stephen R. *Mr. Bush's War: Adventures in the Politics of Illusion*. New York: Hill & Wang, 1992.

Green, Donald P. and Ian Shapiro. *Pathologies of Rational Choice Theory: A Critique of Applications in Political Science*. New Haven: Yale University Press, 1994.

Greitemeyer, Tobias and Stefan Schulz-Hardt. "Preference-Consistent Evaluation of Information in the Hidden Profile Paradigm: Beyond Group-Level Explanations for the Dominance of Shared Information in Group Decisions." *Journal of Personality and Social Psychology* 84 (February 2003).

Halperin, Morton H. *National Security Policy-Making: Analyses, Cases, and Proposals*. Lexington, Mass.: D.C. Heath, 1975.

———. *Bureaucratic Politics and Foreign Policy*. Washington, D.C.: The Brookings Institution, 1974.

Haney, Patrick J. *Organizing for Foreign Policy Crises: Presidents, Advisers, and the Management of Decision Making*. Ann Arbor: University of Michigan Press, 1997.

Hart, Paul 't. *Groupthink In Government: A Study Of Small Groups And Policy Failure*. Amsterdam: Swets and Zeitlinger, 1990.

———, Eric K. Stern, and Bengt Sundelius, eds. *Beyond Groupthink: Political Dynamics and Foreign Policy-making*. Ann Arbor: University of Michigan Press, 1997.

Hays, Peter L., Brenda J. Vallance, and Alan R. Van Tassel, eds. *American Defense Policy*. 7th ed. Baltimore: The Johns Hopkins University Press, 1997.

Heikal, Mohamed. *Illusions of Triumph: An Arab View of the Gulf War*. New York: HarperCollins, 1993.

Hensley, Thomas R. and Glen W. Griffin. "Victims of Groupthink: The Kent State University Board of Trustees and the 1977 Gymnasium Controversy." *Journal of Conflict Resolution* 30 (September 1986).

Hermann, Margaret G., ed. *A Psychological Examination of Political Leaders*. New York: The Free Press, 1977.

——— and Thomas Preston. "Presidents, Advisors, and Foreign Policy: The Effect of Leadership Style on Executive Arrangements." *Political Psychology* 15 (1994).

Herrmann, Richard K., James F. Voss, Tonya Y. E. Schooler, and Joseph Ciarrochi. "Images in International Relations: An Experimental Test of Cognitive Schemata." *International Studies Quarterly* 41 (September 1997).

Hiebert, Ray Eldon. "Public Relations as a Weapon of Modern Warfare." In *Desert Storm and the Mass Media*, edited by Bradley S. Greenberg and Walter Gantz. Cresskill, N.J.: Hampton Press, 1993.

Hilsman, Roger. *George Bush vs. Saddam Hussein: Military Success! Political Failure?* Novato, Calif.: Lyford Books, 1992.

Hiro, Dilip. *Desert Shield to Desert Storm: The Second Gulf War*. New York: Routledge, 1992.

Hirschbein, Ron. *What if They Gave a Crisis and Nobody Came?: Interpreting International Crisis*. Westport, Conn.: Praeger, 1997.

Hook, Sidney. *The Hero In History*. New York: The Humanities Press, 1943.

Hoyt, Paul D. and Jean Garrison. "Political Manipulation within the Small Group: Foreign Policy Advisers in the Carter Administration." In *Beyond Groupthink: Political Dynamics and Foreign Policy-making*, edited by Paul 't Hart, Eric K. Stern, and Bengt Sundelius. Ann Arbor: University of Michigan Press, 1997.

Hudson, Valerie M. (with Christopher S. Vore). "Foreign Policy Analysis Yesterday, Today, and Tomorrow." *Mershon International Studies Review* 39 (1995).

Humphrey, David C. "Tuesday Lunch at the Johnson White House: A Preliminary Assessment." *Diplomatic History* 8 (Winter 1984).

Hybel, Alex Roberto. *Power Over Rationality: The Bush Administration and the Gulf Crisis*. New York: State University of New York Press, 1993.

Jaber, Kamel S. Abu. "Jordan and the Gulf War." In *The Gulf War and the New World Order*, edited by Tareq Y. Ismael and Jacqueline S. Ismael. Gainesville: University Press of Florida, 1994.

Janis, Irving L. *Groupthink: Psychological Studies of Policy Decisions and Fiascoes*. 2nd ed. Boston: Houghton Mifflin, 1983.

——— and Leon Mann. *Decision Making: A Psychological Analysis of Conflict, Choice, and Commitment*. New York: The Free Press, 1977.

Jensen, Robert. "Fighting Objectivity: The Illusion of Journalistic Neutrality in Coverage of the Persian Gulf War." *Journal of Communication Inquiry* 16 (Winter 1992).

Jervis, Robert. *Perception and Misperception in International Politics*. Princeton: Princeton University Press, 1976.

Jowett, Garth S. "Toward a Propaganda Analysis of the Gulf War." In *Desert Storm and the Mass Media*, edited by Bradley S. Greenberg and Walter Gantz. Cresskill, N.J.: Hampton Press, 1993.

Kahler, Miles. "Rationality in International Relations." *International Organization* 52 (Autumn 1998).

Karabell, Zachary. "Backfire: US Policy Toward Iraq, 1988–2 August 1990." *Middle East Journal* 49 (Winter 1995).

Karsh, Efraim and Inari Rautsi. *Saddam Hussein: A Political Biography*. New York: The Free Press, 1991.

Kelman, Herbert C. "The Reaction of Mass Publics to the Gulf War." In *The Political Psychology of the Gulf War: leaders, publics, and the process of conflict*, edited by Stanley A. Renshon. Pittsburgh: University of Pittsburgh Press, 1993.

Khadduri, Majid and Edmund Ghareeb. *War in the Gulf, 1990–91: The Iraq-Kuwait Conflict and its Implications*. Oxford: Oxford University Press, 1997.

al-Khalidi, Walid. "The Gulf Crisis: Origins and Consequences." *Journal of Palestine Studies* 20 (Winter 1991).

al-Khalil, Samir. *The Republic of Fear: Saddam's Iraq*. Berkeley: University of California Press, 1989.

Khong, Yuen Foong. *Analogies at War: Korea, Munich, Dien Bien Phu, and the Vietnam decisions of 1965*. Princeton: Princeton University Press, 1992.

Kiewe, Amos. *The Modern Presidency and Crisis Rhetoric*. Westport, Conn.: Praeger, 1994.

Kissinger, Henry. *Years of Renewal*. New York: Simon & Schuster, 1999.

Knopf, Jeffrey W. *Domestic Society and International Cooperation: The Impact of Protest on US Arms Control Policy*. Cambridge: Cambridge University Press, 1998.

Kozak, David C. and James M. Keagle, eds. *Bureaucratic Politics And National Security: Theory and Practice*. Boulder: Lynne Rienner, 1988.

Krasner, Stephen D. "Are Bureaucracies Important? (Or Allison Wonderland)." *Foreign Policy* 7 (Summer 1972).

Krosnick, Jon A. and Laura A. Brannon. "The Media and the Foundations of Presidential Support: George Bush and the Persian Gulf Conflict." *Journal of Social Issues* 49 (Winter 1993).

Lake, David A. and Robert Powell, eds. *Strategic Choice and International Relations.* Princeton: Princeton University Press, 1999.

Lesch, Ann M. "Contrasting Reactions to the Persian Gulf Crisis: Egypt, Syria, Jordan and the Palestinians." *Middle East Journal* 50 (Winter 1991).

Levy, Jack S. "Prospect Theory and the Cognitive-Rational Debate." In *Decisionmaking on War and Peace: The Cognitive-Rational Debate*, edited by Nehemia Geva and Alex Mintz. Boulder: Lynne-Rienner, 1997.

Manheim, Jarol B. "Strategic Public Diplomacy." In *Taken by Storm*, edited by W. Lance Bennett and David L. Paletz. Chicago: University of Chicago Press, 1994.

May, Ernest R. *Lessons of the Past: the use and misuse of history in American foreign policy.* New York: Oxford University Press, 1973.

——— and Philip D. Zelikow, eds. *The Kennedy Tapes: Inside the White House During the Cuban Missile Crisis.* New York: W.W. Norton & Co., 2002.

McCauley, Clark. "The Nature of Social Influence in Groupthink: Compliance and Internalization." *Journal of Personality and Social Psychology* 57 (1989).

McDermott, Rose. *Risk-Taking in International Politics: Prospect Theory in American Foreign Policy.* Michigan: University of Michigan Press, 2001.

——— and Jacek Kugler. "Comparing Rational Choice and Prospect Theory Analyses: Operation 'Desert Storm', January 1991." *The Journal of Strategic Studies* 24 (September 2001).

Medvedev, Roy. *Post-Soviet Russia: A Journey Through the Yeltsin Era.* New York: Columbia University Press, 2000.

Miller, Eric A., and Steve A. Yetiv. "The New World Order in Theory and Practice: The Bush Administration's Worldview in Transition." *Presidential Studies Quarterly* (March 2001).

Miller, Judith and Laurie Mylroie. *Saddam Hussein and the Crisis in the Gulf.* New York: Times Books, 1990.

Milner, Helen V. "Rationalizing Politics: The Emerging Synthesis of International, American, and Comparative Politics." *International Organization* 52 (Autumn 1998).

Mintz, Alex. "The Decision to Attack Iraq: A Noncompensatory Theory of Decision Making." *Journal of Conflict Resolution* 37 (December 1993).

———. "Foreign Policy Decisionmaking: Bridging the Gap Between the Cognitive Psychology and Rational Actor 'Schools.' " In *Decisionmaking on War and Peace: The Cognitive-Rational Debate*, edited by Nehemia Geva and Alex Mintz. Boulder: Lynne-Rienner, 1997.

———, ed. *Integrating Cognitive and Rational Theories of Foreign Policy.* New York: Palgrave, 2003.

——— and Bruce Russett. "The dual economy and Arab-Israeli use of force: A transnational system?" In *Defense, welfare and growth*, edited by Steve Chan and Alex Mintz. London: Routledge, 1992.

——— and Nehemia Geva. "The Poliheuristic Theory of Foreign Policy Decisionmaking." In *Decisionmaking on War and Peace*. Boulder: Lynne-Rienner, 1997.

Mohamed, A. Amin and Frank A. Wiebe. "Toward A Process Theory Of Groupthink." *Small Group Research* 27 (August 1996).

Moore, Will H. and David J. Lanoue. "Domestic Politics and U.S. Foreign Policy: A Study of Cold War Conflict Behavior." *Journal of Politics* 85 (May 2003).

Moorhead, Gregory, Christopher P. Neck, and Mindy S. West. "The Tendency toward Defective Decision Making within Self-Managing Teams: The Relevance of Groupthink for the 21st Century." *Organizational Behavior and Human Decision Processes* 73 (February-March 1998).

Moravcsik, Andrew. "Taking Preferences Seriously: A Liberal Theory of International Politics." *International Organization* 51 (Autumn 1997).

Morgan, T. Clifton and Kenneth N. Bickers. "Domestic Discontent and the External Use of Force." *Journal of Conflict Resolution* 36 (March 1992).

Mueller, John. *Policy and Opinion in the Gulf War.* Chicago: University of Chicago Press, 1994.

Munch, Richard and Neil J. Smelser, eds. *Theory of Culture.* Berkeley: University of California Press, 1992.

Nash, John. "The Bargaining Problem." *Econometrica* 18.

Neck, Christopher P. and Gregory Moorhead. "Groupthink Remodeled: The Importance of Leadership, Time Pressure, and Methodical Decision-Making Procedures." *Human Relations* 48 (1995).

Neustadt, Richard E. *Presidential Power and the Modern Presidents: The Politics of Leadership from Roosevelt to Reagan.* 5th ed. New York: Free Press, 1990.

—— and Ernst R. May. *Thinking in time: The use of history for decision making.* New York: Free Press, 1986.

Nisbett, Richard and Lee Ross. *Human Inference: Strategies and Shortcomings of Social Judgment.* Englewood Cliffs, N.J.: Prentice-Hall, 1980.

Palazchenko, Pavel. *My Years with Gorbachev and Shevardnadze: The Memoir of a Soviet Interpreter.* University Park, Penn.: Pennsylvania State University Press, 1997.

Palmer, Michael A. *Guardians of the Gulf: A History of America's Expanding Role in the Persian Gulf, 1833–1992.* New York: The Free Press, 1992.

Park, Won-Woo. "A Review of Research on Groupthink." *Journal of Behavioral Decision Making* 3 (1990).

Parmet, Herbert S. *George Bush: The Life of a Lone Star Yankee.* New York: Scribner, 1997.

Paterson, Thomas G. "John F. Kennedy's Quest for Victory and Global Crises." In *Kennedy's Quest For Victory: American Foreign Policy, 1961–1963,* edited by Thomas G. Paterson. Oxford: Oxford University Press, 1989.

Patomaki, Heikki and Colin Wight. "After Postpositivism? The Promises of Critical Realism." *International Studies Quarterly* 44 (June 2000).

Paulus, Paul B. "Developing Consensus about Groupthink after All These Years." *Organizational Behavior and Human Decision Processes* 73 (February-March 1998).

Peled, Mattityahu. "The Gulf Crisis: An Israeli View." *Journal of Palestine Studies* 20 (Winter 1991).

Pffifner, James P. "Presidential Policy-Making and the Gulf War." In *The Presidency And The Persian Gulf War,* edited by Marcia Lynn Whicker, James P. Pfiffner, and Raymond A. Moore. Westport, Conn.: Praeger, 1993.

Pollack, Kenneth M. *The Threatening Storm: The Case for Invading Iraq.* New York: Random House, 2002.

Post, Jerrold M. "Saddam Hussein of Iraq: A Political Psychology Profile." *Political Psychology* 12 (Spring 1991).

Powell, Colin. *My American Journey*. New York: Random House, 1995.

Preston, Thomas. "Following the Leader." In *Beyond Groupthink: Political Dynamics and Foreign Policy-making*, edited by Paul 't Hart, Eric K. Stern, and Bengt Sundelius. Ann Arbor: University of Michigan Press, 1997.

Putnam, Robert. "Diplomacy and Domestic Politics: The Logic of Two-Level Games." *International Organization* 42 (1988).

Quayle, Dan. *Standing Firm: A Vice-Presidential Memoir*. New York: HarperCollins, 1994.

Record, Jeffrey. *Hollow Victory: A Contrary View of the Gulf War*. Washington, D.C.: Brassey's, 1993.

Redd, Steven B. "The Influence of Advisers on Foreign Policy Decision Making." *Journal of Conflict Resolution* 46 (June 2002).

Rhodes, Edward. "Do Bureaucratic Politics Matter?: Some Disconfirming Findings from the Case of the U.S. Navy." *World Politics* 47 (October 1994).

Rosati, Jerel A. "Developing A Systematic Decision-Making Framework: Bureaucratic Politics in Perspective" (research note). *World Politics* 32 (January 1981).

Rozell, Mark J. *The Press and the Bush Presidency*. Westport, Conn.: Praeger, 1996.

Ruggie, John Gerard. "What Makes the World Hang Together? Neo-utilitarianism and the Social Constructivist Challenge." *International Organization* 52 (Autumn 1998).

Schafer, Mark and Scott Crichlow. "The Process-Outcome Connection in Foreign Policy Decision Making: A Quantitative Study Building on Groupthink." *International Studies Quarterly* 46 (March 2002).

Schofield, Richard. *Kuwait and Iraq: Historical Claims and Territorial Disputes*. London: The Royal Institute of International Affairs, 1991.

Schwarzkopf, General H. Norman. *It Doesn't Take A Hero*. New York: Bantam Books, 1992.

Sciolino, Elaine. *The Outlaw State: Saddam's Quest for Power and the Gulf Crisis*. New York: John Wiley & Sons, 1991.

Sifry, Micah L. and Christopher Cerf, eds. *The Gulf War Reader: History, Documents, Opinions*. New York: Random House, 1991.

Simon, Herbert. *Models of Bounded Rationality*. Cambridge: MIT Press, 1982.

Skidmore, David and Valerie Hudson, eds. *The Limits of State Autonomy: Societal Groups and Foreign Policy Formation*. Boulder: Westview Press, 1993.

Smith, Jean Edward. *George Bush's War*. New York: Henry Holt, 1992.

Smith, Steve. "Allison and the Cuban Missile Crisis: A Review of the Bureaucratic Politics Model of Foreign Policy Decision-Making." *Millennium: Journal of International Studies* 9 (Spring 1980).

Snyder, Jack. *Myths of Empire: Domestic Politics and International Ambition*. Ithaca: Cornell University Press, 1991.

Sorensen, Theodore C. *Decision-Making In The White House: The Olive Branch or the Arrows*. New York: Columbia University Press, 1963.

Spellman, Barbara A., Jodie A. Ullman, and Keith J. Holyoak. "A Coherence Model of Cognitive Consistency: Dynamics of Attitude Change During the Persian Gulf War." *Journal of Social Issues* 49 (Winter 1993).

Stern, Eric and Bengt Sundelius. "The Essence of Groupthink" (review article). *Mershon International Studies Review* 38 (1994).

Suedfeld, Peter, Michael D. Wallace, and Kimberly L. Thachuk. "Changes in Integrative Complexity Among Middle East Leaders During the Persian Gulf Crisis." *Journal of Social Issues* 49 (Winter 1993).

Sultan, HRH General Khaled Bin (with Patrick Seale). *Desert Warrior: A Personal View of the Gulf War by the Joint Forces Commander.* New York: HarperCollins, 1995.

Sylvan, Donald A. and James F. Voss, eds. *Problem Representation in Foreign Policy Decision Making.* Cambridge: Cambridge University Press, 1998.

Tarrow, Sidney. *Power in Movement: Social Movements and Contentious Politics.* New York: Cambridge University Press, 1998.

Telhami, Shibley. "Middle East Politics in the Post Cold War Era." In *Beyond the Cold War,* edited by George Breslauer, Harry Kreisler, and Benjamin Ward. Berkeley: Institute for International Studies, 1991.

Thatcher, Margaret. *Downing Street Years.* New York: HarperCollins, 1993.

———. *The Path to Power.* London: HarperCollins, 1995.

Tetlock, Philip E. and Aaron Belkin. *Counterfactual Thought Experiments In World Politics: Logical, Methodological, And Psychological Perspectives.* Princeton: Princeton University Press.

Tucker, Robert W. and David C. Hendrickson. *The Imperial Temptation: The New World Order and America's Purpose.* New York: Council on Foreign Relations press, 1992.

U.S. News and World Report. *Triumph Without Victory: The Unreported History of the Persian Gulf War.* New York: Random House, 1992.

Vance, Cyrus R. *Hard Choices: Critical Years in America's Foreign Policy.* New York: Simon & Schuster, 1983.

Vertzberger, Yaacov Y. I. *The World in Their Minds: Information Processing, Cognition, and Perception in Foreign Policy Decisionmaking.* Stanford: Stanford University Press, 1990.

Voss, James F., Jennifer Wiley, Joel Kennet, Tonya E. Schooler, and Laurie Ney Silfies. "Representations of the Gulf Crisis as Derived from the U.S. Senate Debate." In *Problem Representation in Foreign Policy Decision Making,* edited by Donald A. Sylvan and James F. Voss. Cambridge: Cambridge University Press, 1998.

Wallace, Michael D., Peter Suedfeld, and Kimberley Thachuk. "Political Rhetoric of Leaders Under Stress in the Gulf Crisis." *Journal of Conflict Resolution* 37 (March 1993).

Waltz, Kenneth N. *Theory of International Politics.* Reading: Addison-Wesley, 1979.

———. "International Politics Is Not Foreign Policy." *Security Studies* 6 (Autumn 1996).

Welch, David A. "The Organizational Process and Bureaucratic Politics Paradigms: Retrospect and Prospect." *International Security* 17 (Fall 1992).

Whicker, Marcia Lynn. "The Case AGAINST the War." In *The Presidency and the Persian Gulf War,* edited by Marcia Lynn Whicker, James P. Pfiffner, and Raymond A. Moore. Westport, Conn.: Praeger, 1993.

Winter, David C. "Personality and Foreign Policy: Historical Overview of Research." In *Political Psychology and Foreign Policy,* edited by Eric Singer and Valerie Hudson. Boulder: Westview Press, 1992.

Woodward, Bob. *The Commanders.* New York: Simon & Schuster, 1991.

———. *The Shadow.* New York: Simon & Schuster, 1999.

———. *Bush At War.* New York: Simon & Schuster, 2002.

Yetiv, Steve A. *America and the Persian Gulf: The Third Party Dimension in World Politics.* Westport: Praeger, 1995.

———. "Testing the Government Politics Model: U.S. Decision Making in the 1990–91 Persian Gulf Crisis." *Security Studies* 11 (Winter 2001/2).

———. "Groupthink and the Gulf Crisis." *British Journal of Political Science* (forthcoming, July 2003).

Zey, Mary. *Rational Choice Theory And Organizational Theory: A Critique*. London: Sage Publications, 1998.

DOCUMENTS, GEORGE BUSH PRESIDENTIAL LIBRARY (GBPL), TEXAS A&M UNIVERSITY, COLLEGE STATION, TEXAS.

National Security File (NSC): Files of:
   Nancy Berg Dyke
   David Gomport
   John Gordon
   Richard Haass
   Jane E. Holl
   Walter Kansteiner
   Virginia Lampley
   Daniel Poneman
   Roman Popadiuk
   Bruce O. Riedel
   Peter Rodman
   Nicholas Rostow
Communications Office (Files of Paul McNeill)
Chief of Staff (File of John Sununu)
Counsels Office: Files of:
   C. Boyden Gray
   Nelson Lund
   John Smitz
Media Affairs: Files of:
   John Undeland
   Katherine Holt
   Miscellaneous Files
Public Liaison: Files of:
   William Caldwell
   Bobbie Kilberg
   Leigh Ann Metzger
   James Shaefer
   Jeff Vogt

SPECIFIC DOCUMENTS (GBPL)

"Excerpt From Remarks To Republican National Committee." 25 January 1991. OA/ID 03922, Cabinet Affairs, Will Gunn Files.

"Letter from Bush to Congress." 8 January 1991. OA/ID 03194–011, Persian Gulf Working Group, Congress.

"Letter from Bush to Drew Lewis." 10 January 1991. OA/ID 210212 ND016.

"Letter from Bush to Fereydoun." 12 September 1990. OA/ID CF1478, Working Files-Iraq, Richard Haass Files, NSC.

"Letter from Bush to Foley." 9 August 1990. OA/ID CFO1362, Virginia Lampley Files, NSC.

"Letter from Bush to Foley." 16 November 1990. OA/ID CFo1361, Jane E. Holl Files, NSC.

"Letter from Bush to House Speaker, Tom Foley." 16 January 1991. OA/ID 208544, WHORM File, Office of the President.

"Letter from Bush to the Emir of Kuwait." 17 October 1990. Declassified by author's request under the Freedom of Information Act.

"Letter from David Demarest to John Sununu." 2 January 1991. OA/ID 03195, Notebooks of David Demarest.

"Letter from Dole to Bush." 13 November 1990. OA/ID 205464, NDo16.

"Letter from Webster to Les Aspin." 10 January 1991. OA/ID CFo1361, Virginia Lampley Files, NSC.

"Letter from Wellstone to Bush." 28 November 1990. OA/ID CFoo472, Chief of Staff, John Sununu Files.

"Memo from Baker to Bush." 7 December 1990. Includes attachment. OA/ID 205441, Whorm-Subject File.

"Memo from Bruce Gelb, Director of the United States Information Agency, to James Baker." 7 August 1990. OA/ID CFO1447, Kuwait Crisis, Richard Haass Files, NSC.

"Memo from Bush to Marlin Fitzwater." 25 September 1991. Includes attachment of Bush's proposed answers to an interview by Kenneth Walsh. OA/ID PRo10 202278, Philip Brady Files.

"Memo from Bush to Shultz." 14 December 1990. OA/ID 207563 NDo16, Whorm General File.

"Memo from Fred McClure to Assistant Secretaries for Legislative Affairs." 10 January 1991. (OA/ID 03922, Cabinet Affairs, William Gunn Files.

"Memo from Haass to Mitsler and Popadiuk." 14 December 1990. OA/ID CFO1584, Working Files-Iraq, Richard Haass Files, NSC.

"Memo from Haass to Scowcroft. 14 December 1990." OA/ID CFO1361, Virginia Lampley Files, NSC.

"Memo from Stephen Rademaker and Ron Vonlembke to C. Boyden Gray." 4 February 1991. OA/ID CFoo537, Counsel's Office, Nelson Lund Files.

"Memo from Stephen Rademaker to Scowcroft." 11 December 1990. OA/ID CFo1361, Virginia Lampley Files, NSC.

"Memo from Sununu and Scowcroft." 28 November 1990. OA/ID 03195, Persian Gulf Working Group: Notebooks of David Demarest, Communications, Files of Paul McNeill.

"Note from Bush to Dan Rostenkowski." 17 January 1991. OA/ID CFoo472, Chief of Staff, John Sununu Files.

"Presidential Statement To Be Broadcast on Voice of America radio in Arabic, with written revisions." OA/ID CFO1933, Nancy Dyke Files, NSC.

"President's Opening Remarks at Cabinet meeting." 9 January 1991. OA/ID CFO1584, Richard Haass Files, NSC.

"Press briefing by Marlin Fitzwater at the White House." 4 January 1991. OA/ID CFo1361, Virginia Lampley Files, NSC.

"Press Conference By The President, The White House." 30 November 1990. OA/ID CF)1361, Virginia Lampley Files, NSC.

"Press Conference by the President." 8 August 1990. OA/ID, CF0703, Roman Popadiuk Files, Office of the Press Secretary.

"Remarks by the President Upon Departure to Camp David." 3 August 1990. OA/ID CF0703, Roman Popadiuk Files, Office of the Press Secretary.

"Remarks for the Republican National Committee." 25 January 1991. OA/ID 03922, Cabinet Affairs, Will Gunn Files.

"Report, Meetings on the Persian Gulf." OA/ID CF 01361, Virginia Lampley Files, NSC.

"Statement by Secretary of State James A. Baker, III To The UN Security Council." United Nations, New York City. 29 November 1990. OA/ID 03195, Notebooks of David Demarest, Communications, Files of Paul McNeil.

"Statement by the Honorable Richard Cheney, Secretary of Defense, Concerning Operation Desert Shield Before the Committee on Armed Services, US Senate." 30 December 1990. OA/ID CF01361, Virginia Lampley Files, NSC.

"Text of Bush's Radio Address." 4 October 1990. OA/ID 03195, Persian Gulf Working Group: Notebooks of David Demarest, Communications, Paul McNeil Files.

"Webster document." OA/ID CF01361, Virginia Lampley Files, NSC.

SELECTED PUBLIC AND GOVERNMENT DOCUMENTS

ABC News. "A Line in the Sand: What Did America Win?" 50 minutes. 1991.

ABC News. Schwarzkopf. "How the War Was Won." 70 minutes. 1991.

BBC Summary of World Broadcasts/Middle East. 27 August 1990.

Bush interview with Sir David Frost. PBS. 16 January 1996.

Bush interview with Bernard Shaw. CNN. 2 March 1996.

Book TV. Schwarzkopf interview with Brian Lamb. C-SPAN 2. 1 October 1990.

Chemical Weapons Use in Kurdistan: Iraq's Final Offensive. Washington, D.C.: GPO, October 1988.

Conduct of the Persian Gulf War: Final Report to Congress. Department of Defense. Washington, D.C.: GPO, April 1992.

Council of Economic Advisers. *Economic Report of the President.* Washington, D.C.: GPO, 1992.

Foreign Broadcast Information Service (various reports on and transcripts of Iraqi speeches, proposals, and statements, and those of officials from other states).

Frontline. Interviews with key players in the crisis. Broadcast 9 and 10 January 1996.

Frontline interview with Tariq Aziz. "Voices in the Storm: the brink of war." http://www.pbs.org/wgbh/pages/frontline/gulf/voices/1.html.

Give Sanctions a Chance. Hearings Before the Senate Armed Services Committee. Washington, D.C.: 10 November 1990, GPO.

Iraqgate: Saddam Hussein, US Policy, and the Prelude to the Persian Gulf war. Washington, D.C.: The National Security Archive and Chadwyck-Healey.

Kelly, John H. *U.S. Relations with Iraq: Statement of Assistant Secretary Kelly Before the Senate Foreign Relations Committee.* 23 May 1990.

Kurdistan in the Time of Saddam Hussein. Washington, D.C.: GPO, November 1991.

Memorandum from J. H. Binford Peay III, Lieutenant General, USA, to the Director and Joint Staff of the Army. *2nd Draft of the Final Report to Congress.* 26 November 1991. Colin Powell Papers, National Defense University, SJS 2571/604–10.

The Middle East. 7th ed. Washington, D.C.: Congressional Quarterly, 1991.

The Road to War: American Decision Making During the Gulf Crisis. Princeton: Films for the Humanities & Sciences, 1993.

Public Papers of the Presidents of the United States (PPP). Various volumes regarding Presidents Bush and Reagan. Washington, D.C.: Government Printing Office (GPO).

U.S. Senate, General H. Norman Schwarzkopf, Commander of U.S. Central Command, *Witness Statement Before the Senate Armed Services Committee.* 8 February 1990.

U.S. Department of Defense. *Report on the Gulf War.* Washington, D.C.: GPO, 1991.

Various issues. *US Department of State Dispatch.*

Index